India-China Dialogues Beyond Borders

Swati Mishra · Ranjana Sheel
Editors

India-China Dialogues Beyond Borders

Cultural, Social Economic and Political Perspectives

Springer

Editors
Swati Mishra
Faculty of Arts
Banaras Hindu University
Varanasi, India

Ranjana Sheel
Faculty of Social Sciences
Banaras Hindu University
Varanasi, India

ISBN 978-981-99-4325-8 ISBN 978-981-99-4326-5 (eBook)
https://doi.org/10.1007/978-981-99-4326-5

This Springer imprint is published by the registered company Springer Nature Singapore Pte Ltd.
The registered company address is: 152 Beach Road, #21-01/04 Gateway East, Singapore 189721, Singapore

Paper in this product is recyclable.

Dedicated

To

Banaras Hindu University

Foreword

India–China engagement is an absorbing theme, not only for the policy-makers but also for scholars and analysts. It has several dimensions—civilizational and cultural, economic, political and strategic—and contrasting flavours of conflict and cooperation/creative coexistence. The Banaras Hindu University has been intellectually resourceful to undertake an impressive initiative to explore some of the important aspects of this engagement in the present Volume.

The trajectory of India–China relationship has not been straight, nor its narrative very smooth. There was a creative coexistence between the two for a long period, from first to the eighteenth century when both of them together dominated world economy, accounting for more than 50% of its wealth. While India was ahead of China with more than 25% share until fifteenth century, China took over subsequently. This was also the period when Buddhism helped them to bond together. Up to seventh century, Buddhism flowed from India to China, but afterwards, with its decline in India against the reassertion of Hinduism, China itself emerged as the hub and source of spreading Buddhism in Southeast and Central Asian region. Both countries interacted with each other in these regions, learning cultural and social norms, economic and political practices, and governance styles in many direct and discreet ways. Chinese pilgrims and scholars have for long acknowledged India as their *Dharmguru*, religious teacher and source of spiritual inspiration, for providing Buddhism. The Chola empire in southern India carried its foreign trade through Southeast Asia to China.

The rise of the British empire in India and the declining Chinese empire brought the two countries into friction and competition, particularly in the Himalayas. The British, in their search for buffers in the Himalayas to keep the Russian/Soviet advance towards south during nineteenth and early twentieth centuries, contested as well as collaborated with the Chinese. The British attempts to draw the boundaries of influence and territorial possessions inserted fault lines for the post-British relationship between India and China. The British in India were calculatedly not meticulous in drawing their lines of division with China, like the McMahon Line, which left their territorial status vague and undefined. They were only focussed on the immediate strategic gains and losses to suit their requirements. China has disowned these divisions and reasserted its territorial claims of the imperial era. Independent

India took the British inheritance seriously and is still struggling to secure Chinese acceptance of the British defined territorial divisions in the Himalayas.

Two strategically significant developments on the Chinese side sharpened the fault lines of influence and possession with India. The first was the establishment of a communist state in China with the success of the Maoist revolution in 1949 and the second was China's military takeover of Tibet in 1951. The first development pushed China away from its Buddhist heritage that was responsible for forging creative bonds with India, and the second development changed China's status vis-a-vis India from a *distant* neighbour to an *immediate* one. The immediate and long-term implications of both these developments proved heavy for India. In its efforts to carry forward its vision of Asian resurgence and its battle against the Cold War, India grudgingly accepted the strategic costs of these two Chinese developments. Perhaps it had no other option as it was neither militarily strong nor politically willing to protect Tibet and confront China. It withdrew its stakes from Tibet and Xinjiang in the Himalayas in return for Chinese assurances to respect Tibet's religious and cultural autonomy and sought peaceful coexistence with China. The Chinese response was partial and strategically calculated. It accepted Tibetan autonomy only until its political and military control in the land of the Lamas could be consolidated. It kept studied silence on its imperial territorial claims in the Himalayas in return for India's efforts to get China's communist regime integrated with the international community, including the United Nations.

The phenomenal rise of China in its economy and military capabilities for the past three decades has made it more defiant and assertive, not only against the US but also against other Asian neighbours, including India. More so under the ambitious and powerful leadership of President Xi Jinping. The conflict and competition for territorial claims in the Himalayas and influence in Asia between India and China is a result of this. China has deviated from a number of mutual confidence building measures worked out with India between mid-90s and the first decade of this century. It is worried that India's strategic tilt towards the US may frustrate its ambitions in Asia, though by itself, China would not like to treat India as a major player in building Asian futures. India has worked hard, even though informal summits between Prime Minister Modi and President Xi, to restore the spirit of coexistence and reduce the enhanced trust deficit but to no avail. It seems as if China's assertive and aggressive stance towards India and other Asian neighbours has got intertwined with its internal dynamics of power struggle related to President Xi's rise. China and its President Xi must know that their dream of building a robust "Asian Century" can never be realized without working out an amicable engagement with its Asian neighbours like India, Japan and Vietnam.

In the prevailing stressful context of India–China relationship, the BHU volume is a bold contribution to revisit the depth and spread of this multi-dimensional engagement. The thrust of this Volume is on civilizational and cultural dimensions that underline the creative and constructive aspects of traditional coexistence between two major Asian powers. In-depth analyses of the role of Buddhism, of language and culture and of the significance of trade, through and beyond the old Silk Road, have been presented in various chapters. There are also chapters on contemporary themes of the extensive but lop-sided economic interdependence between the two countries and their competition in the emerging strategic dynamics of the Indo-Pacific region. BHU may consider undertaking yet another similar exercise to explore the strategic and security aspects of this relationship that are vitiating their respective basic and long-term interests and threatening peace in the whole of Asia.

S. D. Muni
Professor Emeritus, JNU
Former Ambassador and Special
Envoy, GOI

Preface

The volume is based on the web-based international conference "India China Dialogues beyond Borders: Cultural, Social, Political/Diplomatic Perspectives" organized by the Department of Foreign Languages, Faculty of Arts, Banaras Hindu University. The impetus for organizing this conference came during a departmental meeting held in January 2020. We planned to organize it sometime at the end of the year, but the COVID-19 outbreak put things on hold. Finally, it shaped up as an e-conference which was organized in October 2020. It brought together many distinguished scholars working on India–China studies. The volume is an exclusive and eclectic compilation of the contributions by eminent participants. Each contribution is an attempt to understand and strengthen the relationship between India and China.

It is evident that India–China relations is of global significance and interest. Their rich history of interactions is often invoked to offset the current tensions and interplay of complex economic and strategic factors. Significant contacts started with Buddhism, but the exchange between the two countries is much older. Ancient linguistic records show some common words and concepts used in Sanskrit and Chinese, indicating the linguistic influences on each other. During the modern period, academic and other exchanges significantly decreased. Colonial India and semi-colonial China became separately entwined with the Imperial world that placed more emphasis on income-generation for their industrialization and capitalist growth. The British East India Company's interest in importing Chinese tea, porcelain and silk to make enough profit to expand their occupation and control over China increasingly brought in Indian opium to make purchases in China market. The triangular trade redefined and politicized the traditional trade pattern keeping in view national interests. Increasing consumption of opium and the outflow of resources created serious crises leading finally to wars and the entry of foreign imperialist powers in China. Imperialists' aspirations forced conversion of both India and China from harmonious civilizational states to rival nation-states competing for defined boundaries as per their respective national interests. Demarcation and re-demarcation of territories through treaties and conferences played a major role in defining India–China relations, legacies of which continued to impact their historical "connectedness" even after both countries achieved freedom after a long and protracted struggle.

On the other hand, some intellectuals of both India and China kept visiting each other in search for the cultural-political solutions for overcoming the civilizational or national crisis. Kang Youwei, Hunag Mocai, Hu Shi from China and Benoy Kumar Sarkar, Rabindranath Tagore and S. Radhakrishnan were among the early visitors who talked about issues other than borders and left meaningful records. They prepared ground for the continuation of friendly Sino-Indian contacts.

However, legacies of the imperialist-inspired nation-state and nationalism brought forth the border issues once again and led to the Sino-India war of 1962 which terribly soured the relationship between the two countries. After resuming diplomatic contact in the 1990s, while relationship between two countries improved on various fronts and the process of globalization even entwined their economies, lingering border issues keep popping up and dragging behind a fully trustworthy relationship (we saw a bitter standoff even in 2020). Yet, it cannot be denied that these two populous neighbouring countries with historically long civilizations are now among the fastest growing economies of the world and are expected to shape the future of the current century both in Asia and the world.

The present volume is therefore an attempt to revisit India and China relations not in the context of modern boundaries but more in terms of their long historical interactions. It may enhance our knowledge and comprehension about each other as had been in the ancient times. Contributions to this volume thus primarily focus on the spread of Buddhism, various facets of China–India relationship in ancient, modern and contemporary times, and linguistic and literary commonalities and connections. We hope that students and researchers in the field would get some comprehensive perspective on India–China studies and take it forward to pursue further researches enriching scholarship on India and China.

Varanasi, India

Swati Mishra
Ranjana Sheel

Acknowledgements

The journey from organizing a conference to bringing it to print is a long continuum that necessarily results in many debts. This volume is no different. We first acknowledge our appreciation and thanks to all colleagues, students and staff of Department of Foreign Languages, Faculty of Arts, BHU, especially Prof. Vinodanand Tiwari, Head of the Department for organizing the conference in October 2020 and for constant support in innumerable ways.

In the making of this volume, our thanks to all our contributors who somehow persevered through our reminders and deadlines. We would also like to thank the editorial committee members, Professors Anita Sharma, Vinodanand Tiwari and Sanjay Kumar for their editorial guidance and constant support. We express our sincere gratitude to Prof. S. D. Muni for agreeing to write the foreword and for his constant encouragement. Of course, as with every activity related to Chinese Studies in BHU, Prof. Kamal Sheel was a pillar of support in this venture too. Professor Keshav Mishra and Dr. Dhrub Kumar Singh from Department of History, BHU provided steady support.

Our sincere thanks to all the reviewers for their exceptional cooperation throughout this period. Our gratitude to Springer Nature for undertaking the publication of this volume. Our families have supported us with their patience, words of thanks cannot suffice.

Contents

Editors and Contributors

About the Editors

Swati Mishra teaches Chinese at Banaras Hindu University. Swati obtained her bachelor's and master's degree in Chinese studies at the Centre for Chinese and East Asian Studies, Jawaharlal Nehru University, New Delhi. She then joined the University of Peking on a Government of India scholarship where she studied Chinese language and Chinese history. Her research interest includes socio-political developments in contemporary China and India-China relationship in general. Her doctoral thesis was entitled "State and Society in Contemporary China".

Ranjana Sheel is Professor in the Department of History at Banaras Hindu University, Varanasi, India. Her research interests are in social history and women's studies with a focus on India and East Asia. She has been recipient of Japan Foundation and Shastri Indo-Canadian Faculty Fellowships and was Visiting Fellow at Asia Research Institute in Singapore. Her works such as *The Political Economy of Dowry* (Manohar, 1999), *Thirteen Months in China* (OUP, 2017) with Anand Yang and Kamal Sheel, research papers on marriage and migration, are some of the outcomes of her research interests.

Contributors

Hemant Adlakha Jawaharlal Nehru University, New Delhi, India

Avijit Banerjee Cheena Bhavan, Visva-Bharati, Santiniketan, India

Rathijit Chakraborty Department of Foreign Languages, Tezpur University, Tezpur, India

Mao Shi Chang Lanzhou University, Lanzhou, China

Dayawanti Jawaharlal Nehru University, New Delhi, India

Prashant Kaushik Central University of Gujarat, Gandhinagar, Gujarat, India

Mahendra P. Lama School of International Studies, Jawaharlal Nehru University, New Delhi, India

Xinru Liu College of New Jersey, Ewing, NJ, USA

Yuet Keung Lo National University of Singapore, Singapore, Singapore

Yu Longyu Shenzhen University, Shenzhen, China

Keshav Mishra Department of History, Faculty of Social Sciences, Banaras Hindu University, Varanasi, India

Rakesh Kumar Mishra Banaras Hidnu University, Varanasi, India

Gadde Omprasad Centre for South Asian Studies, Jawaharlal Nehru University, New Delhi, India

Saumya Pandey Jawaharlal Nehru University, New Delhi, India

Arpana Raj Dept. of Far East Languages-Chinese, Central University of Jharkhand, Cheri-Manatu, Ranchi, Jharkhand, India

Devendra Singh Rawat Jawaharlal Nehru University, New Delhi, India

Lalji 'Shravak' Banaras Hindu University, Varanasi, India

Kamal Sheel Banaras Hindu University, Varanasi, India

R. S. Vasan Chennai Center for China Studies, Chennai, India

Wangbang Wei Peking University, Beijing, China

Part I
Keynote Addresses

Chapter 1
Knowing China: Sinomania to Sinophobia

Hemant Adlakha

With a focus on China's growing cultural influence and the connections between China's domestic politics and its attempts to brand itself internationally, Michael Barr, in his book Who's Afraid of China a decade ago had asked: If China suddenly democratized, would it cease being labeled as a threat? In his reply, the author argued that the rising Asian power touches a nerve in the Western psyche—a psyche that originates from the West's past, hopes, and fears of China. In other words, the phenomenon is called Sinophobia. Earlier in mid-February this year, a BBC news report, entitled "Sinophobia: How a virus reveals many ways in which China is feared," stated that discrimination against China and Chinese people is not new—Sinophobia is a well-documented phenomenon that has existed for centuries. In recent months, we have witnessed our own Indian brand of the phenomenon, thanks to the ongoing border standoff with China. Unsurprisingly, the expression Sinophobia, a noun, is described in any English dictionary as "a fear or dislike of China, Chinese people, their language or culture." It is in this backdrop. I am going to use the opportunity offered to me by the organizers of this international conference which couldn't have been held at a more opportune time and which carries an extremely thoughtful theme, to examine over the next half an hour or so why and how of what the CPC leadership has been advocating for some years now. I am, of course, referring to President Xi's favorite and oft-repeated theme: "Tell China Story well."

In November 2012, the CPC 18th Party Congress anointed Xi Jinping as its general secretary to lead the party's current ruling regime. A few months later, in March 2013, Xi Jinping was elected as the president of the People's Republic of China at the country's parliament—the National Peoples' Congress. Since then, "improve ways to tell well the China story to the world" has remained Xi's favorite, an oft-repeated theme. First announced at the national propaganda and ideology meet in August 2013, the new Chinese leader urged the party and state organs to find newer and better ways to "tell China's story well, and properly disseminate China's voice."

H. Adlakha (✉)
Jawaharlal Nehru University, New Delhi, India

S. Mishra and R. Sheel (eds.), *India-China Dialogues Beyond Borders*,
https://doi.org/10.1007/978-981-99-4326-5_1

The recurring theme was most recently heard when President Xi, extolling China's "coronavirus warriors," said, "We must improve and better disseminate to the world the story of China's fight against the pandemic."

1.1 What is the China Story?

Not well-versed with the intricate world of the phonetics—especially the four tones—of a Chinese character and still lost in trying to demystify the self-woven myth of ideographic nature of the written Chinese character, the outside world or, to be more precise, the Western world, has been found wanting in decoding what Xi Jinping has been reiterating for the past 7 years, i.e., "讲好中国故事" Jiǎnghǎozhōngguógùshì or as it is meant in English "tell well China story." In fact, as many participants here today are well-versed with Mandarin, let me spend a couple of minutes on how non-Chinese, non-native Mandarin speakers have often misinterpreted or misunderstood and therefore wrongly communicated the actual meaning of what Xi Jinping means when he advocates "讲好中国故事"?

Curiously enough, Jiǎnghǎozhōngguógùshì has been often wrongly translated as "tell good China story to the world." I say curious because the wrong translation is more a "Freudian slip" than a translation error. Let me try and explain.

According to available recent Western writings on the theme of "China story," as China's top leader and chief messenger, Xi Jinping is being described as the custodian of "China story." That is an authorized version of how China and the CPC leadership ought to be perceived in the world outside of China. President Xi went on to earn the title of "Master Storyteller." Unlike his two predecessors—Hu Jintao and Jiang Zemin—Xi has been credited with writing five books, the latest one was released in June 2017 and is available on Amazon under the title Xi Jinping Tells A Story《习近平讲故事》. However, Western scholarship or the international media conveniently do not reveal to us why under Xi Jinping, the CPC and the PRC have vigorously launched the "propaganda" to tell China's story to the world better and become internationally influential. Essentially, to combat the negative images of China spread for centuries by the West. But why China or its leaders are suddenly in this combative mood? According to Josep Borrell, the European Union's Foreign Policy Chief, the idea of "China story" is a result of the ongoing "battle of narratives" between the Beijing Consensus and the Washington Consensus, originating in the early part of the current millennium with China's unprecedented economic prowess.

In fact, "tell China story well" propaganda precedes Xi's ascent to power. In his recent blog post, David Bandurski, the Director of the China Media Project and also the Editor of the project's website—chinamediaproject.org—explains the idea of "China story" as a coherent narrative reflecting the Party-state agenda, as a product of centrally conceived "soft power." According to Bandurski, "The phrase appeared in the Party's official People's Daily as early as 2004 and a 2010 commentary in the newspaper under the pen name 'Guo Jiping' (国记评), adamantly stressing that 'China's story must become a world story."

So, why tell China's story now? Why has the CPC leadership been in a combative mood since the early twenty-first century? What is the "battle of narratives"? Last but not least, what is the Freudian slip here?

To seek an answer to all these questions, we must turn to the topic of my presentation today: Sinomania to Sinophobia.

As most of you may be aware, both "Sinomania" and "Sinophobia" have originated in the West. In fact, both conceptual terms were preceded by "tales of wonder" about China in the accounts of Marco Polo. It is, therefore, historically not incorrect to divide the modern Western or European understanding of and knowledge on China into four equal periods of two centuries each. That is, fourteenth and fifteenth centuries based on Marco Polo's reports; sixteenth and seventeenth centuries knowledge on China largely supplied by the Jesuit missionaries and merchants; eighteenth and nineteenth centuries when more authentic information started pouring into the public domain in the West on imperial China; and finally the twentieth and twenty-first centuries when the previous awe and admiration gave way to and was quickly replaced with an attitude filled with contempt mingled with racist alarm. It was during the past two centuries during which Sinomania quickly capsized into Sinophobia—the transformation was essentially premised on the knowledge that China or the Qing Dynasty regime was militarily weak, economically backwards, and socially-culturally in a state of fragmenting.

To see things in a proper perspective, let me luxuriously cite here a long passage from Perry Anderson's insightful review essay from the London Review of Books (LRB, 2010): "Marco Polo's reports of China, now judged mostly hearsay, fixed fabulous images that lasted down to Columbus setting sail for the marvels of Cathay. But when real information about the country arrived in the seventeenth and eighteenth centuries, European attitudes towards China tended to remain an awed admiration, rather than fear or condescension. From Bayle and Leibniz to Voltaire and Quesnay, philosophers hailed it as an empire more civilized than Europe itself: not only richer and more populous, but more tolerant and peaceful, a land where there were no priests to practice persecution and offices of the state were filled according to merit, not birth. Even those skeptical of the more extravagant claims for the Middle Kingdom—Montesquieu or Adam Smith—remained puzzled and impressed by its wealth and order."

It is pertinent to point out a long-held notion that China provided observers in the West with a host of extremes and paradoxes—for example, the Great Leap Forward and the Great Proletarian Cultural Revolution in the early Mao period and now Socialism with Chinese Characteristics, i.e., Red Capitalism—too more often than not has its roots in the extreme ways in which the West or the outside world itself perceives the Middle Kingdom. Viewed thus, both the approaches—Sinomania and Sinophobia—are problem-ridden. As Hung Ho-Fung emphatically observed in his seminal essay entitled "Sinomania: Global crisis, China's crisis?" in the Socialist Register (2011). "At a time when the global economic status quo seems to be crashing down, the seemingly endless hyper-capitalist growth of China has spurred such admiration and even euphoria from a wide circle of observers as may indeed justify the use of the term Sinomania," Hung wrote.

In other words, Hung was indignant and reacting to the celebration of the Chinese miracle, which Hung believes has been informed by inadequate understanding of China's political economy and is just as superfluous and superficial as eighteenth-century Sinomania among Enlightenment intellectuals which were based on cursory, exotic, and sometimes deliberately distorted information about China compiled by Jesuit missionaries. In fact, both Perry Anderson and Hung Ho-Fung were reacting to the ensuing debate at the time in the mainstream media and in the academia, which best reflected the two extremes prevailing a decade ago among the China observers in the West. The two extremes are a book by Martin Jacques in 2009 called When China Rules the World: The Rise of the Middle Kingdom and the End of the Western World on the one hand, and another book refuting Jacques claims by Hung Ho-fung The China Boom: Why China will not Rule the World.

The reason why I am invoking the two extremes in the West, i.e., eighteenth-century adulation for China among the Enlightenment intellectuals and the drastic turnaround in attitudes among the nineteenth-century Western predators toward a declining Qing Empire, explains in a way why President Xi took up the CPC mantle to start asserting with unprecedented enthusiasm the Tell China Story Well propaganda. Armed with never experienced before the confidence of saying goodbye to centuries of victimhood at the hands of foreign imperialist forces, the source of which lay in China's rise to the world's second-largest economy status, the CPC-led China had evolved onto the world stage. It was gearing up for the foreseeable impending confrontation the US was threatening to impose with the launch of "pivot to Asia" strategy.

Furthermore, Tell China Story Well now increasingly seemed embedded in China's One Belt One Road strategy. Unlike under Mao, the imperial past was a burden to be shaken off. Selectively invoking history became the most efficient way for the current CPC regime to back up its unchallengeable "mandate" to rule. It will be a historic error in judgment to view Xi Jinping's Tell China Story Well as aimed at China's push for achieving a superpower status or "ultra-nationalism." Instead, as most Chinese would interpret it, Tell China Story Well entails the success story of "New" China's trajectory to claim its rightful place and status in the world. Or perhaps, Tell China Story Well embodies socialist China's newly attained confidence to realize the "Chinese Dream" and finally put an end to "China's uneasy relationship with the history" of the past 200 years which is plagued with accounts of savage violence and still haunts China's 1.4 billion people.

By looking at the conference's theme, India China Dialogues beyond Borders: Cultural, Social and Political/Diplomatic Perspectives, you may be wondering whether my talk today is out of step with the deliberations over the coming 3 days. No, I am not talking Greek or French. Because however strange it may sound, the truth is the contemporary Indian discourse on China too is a product of the Western knowledge system on China. The early Indian thinking on China—be it beginning from the two world wars in Europe in the first half of the past century or even if we take our starting point as post-Independence—it is hard not to accept the influence and imprint of Nehru's thinking on China as the dominant trend. In fact, in China itself, most strategic affair experts and India specialists believe that India's China policy has remained unchanged throughout the past seven decades and irrespective of whichever political combination has been ruling in New Delhi, including the present dispensation. It cannot be denied that the Indian political elite's world outlook has been influenced and even determined by the Anglo-American perspectives on and perceptions of China. Be it Sinomania or Sinophobia.

Time and space limitations do not allow me to dwell upon China's Indian knowledge system and know-how. We are faced with a similar dilemma today in the current ongoing border standoff along the LAC that we had faced in 1962: a huge knowledge deficit on our northern neighbor? What could be more ironical than the fact that in the face of escalating tensions and threat of military confrontation with our number one enemy, instead of quickly expanding the magnitude of our national resources, both human and material, being utilized in consolidating our institutional knowledge infrastructure with a focus on China, the country's policy orientation as reported, is threatening to go in the reverse direction?

Let me finally conclude and leave you with these and other issues to be taken up in the coming 3 days for deliberations. I do not wish to sign off the keynote address on a pessimistic note but going by the geopolitical changes in recent years. In recent months, both globally and in our neighborhood, respectively, and not to forget the impact of the COVID-19 pandemic, as well as the outcome on the world economy of the ensuing Sino-US "decoupling"—consequences of both phenomena are impossible to gauge—China studies in India, as perhaps also in the world at large, is staring at grim prospects as the days of constructive engagement with China it seems are gone…!

Chapter 2
The Indic Words with Cīna: A Story of Peach and Pear Told by Xuanzang

Wangbang Wei

Peach and pear are two fruits seen everywhere today, both in China and India. We believe people have planted them as cultivated fruit trees for over two thousand years. However, for a long time, no one mentioned whence and where they were planted excepting Xuanzang, a well-known Chinese Buddhist monk who went to India in searching the Dharma in the early seventh century. In the fourth scroll of his *Great Tang Dynasty Records on the Western Regions*, a book written according to his travel to India, he talked on a country called "*Cīnabhukti*" in India:

> The country of *Cīnabhukti* has a circumference of more than two thousand *li*, and its capital city has a circumference of fourteen or fifteen *li*. It is abundant in grains, but fruit trees are scarce. The inhabitants are enrolled in household registration and live in peace and contentment. The state treasury has rich and profuse resources. The climate is temperate and warm, and the people are timid and weak by custom. They study the theories of both the transcendental and the conventional truth in a comprehensive way and believe in heterodoxy and orthodoxy. There are ten Buddhist monasteries and eight *tīrthaka* temples.

The exact location of *Cīnabhukti* is not very clear today. According to *The Great Tang Dynasty Record on the Western Regions* and Xuanzang's biography, *The Life of Tripiṭaka Master Xuanzang of the Great Ci'en Monastery*, very possibly, *Cīnabhukti* might be in today's Punjab in north-western India. However, here, the concern is not its geographical location but its name. The front part of the name "*Cīnabhukti*" is *Cīna*, a Sanskrit word referring to China since very early in India.

It is striking that the name of a small country in ancient India contained the word "*Cīna*," meaning "China". Did it have anything to do with China? In his book, Xuanzang provided an explanation:

> When King Kaniṣka ruled an enormously great area, his fame reached neighbouring countries, and his prestige radiated to distant lands with different customs. Fearing his power and prestige, a vassal state west of the Yellow River sent him a prince as a hostage. King

W. Wei (✉)
Peking University, Beijing, China
e-mail: bwmitra@pku.edu.cn

S. Mishra and R. Sheel (eds.), *India-China Dialogues Beyond Borders*,
https://doi.org/10.1007/978-981-99-4326-5_2

> Kaniṣka received the prince with generous hospitality, provided him three residences for the three seasons of the year and appointed four divisions of soldiers to serve as his guards. This country was where the prince lived, thus called *Cīnabhukti* or *Hanfeng*, the Fief of Han or China. Because the hostage prince lived here, the country got this name.

Xuanzang mentioned this story previously in the first scroll of *The Great Tang Dynasty Record on the Western Regions*: "Upon receiving the hostage prince, King Kaniṣka treated him with special kindness and courtesy, providing him with different lodgings according to the seasons. In the winter, he stayed in various countries in India, in the summer he returned to the country of Kāpiśī, and in the spring and autumn he stayed in the country of Gandhāra". *Cīnabhukti* was likely the primary place the hostage lived in India during winter.

Xuanzang explained that "*Cīnabhukti*" means "*Hanfeng*" (Fief of Han or China in Chinese). The word "*Cīnabhukti*" is comprised of "*Cīna*," "China" in Sanskrit, and "*bhukti*," meaning "fief". Together, "*Cīnabhukti*" means "China's fief" in Sanskrit. Though it is unlikely that the hostage prince came from central China, where the Han ethnic people lived, he very possibly was from somewhere in today's Xinjiang area of China. In the eyes of local people of *Cīnabhukti*, that area was part of *Cīna* or part of *Mahācīna*, i.e., Great China, so they called him a Han or Chinese prince. Anyhow, the name of *Cīnabhukti* is derived from China, and some other things in India were related. Xuanzang continued:

> This country, and beyond it in other parts of India, previously no pear and peach were planted, and the hostage prince first grew them. Thus, peach are called *cīnanī* ("being brought from China"), and pear are called *cīnarājaputra* ("Chinese prince"). Therefore, the people of this country have a deep respect for the person from East Land, i.e. China, they said to one another: "This is a man from the land of our former king."

The Sanskrit word "*cīnanī*" consists of two parts: *cīna* (meaning "China") and *nī* (meaning "brought from" or "coming from"). When the two parts are put together, the word means "being brought from China." The Sanskrit word "*cīnarājaputra*" consists of three segments: (representing "China"), *rāja* (meaning "king"), and *putra* (meaning "son"), so the entire word means "Chinese prince," just the same as Xuanzang translated.

Modern botanists agree that peach and pear are endemic to China. Although the story says that the hostage prince from China was the first person to plant peach and pear in India may require further discussion, the two fruit species are indeed considered to have been introduced to India from China. Xuanzang was the only person to record this story throughout history, and he had little reason to fabricate information in this regard. Not only peach and pear, but a number of other things in India are also related to China, and silk is the most prominent example.

Sericulture and silk were great inventions by Chinese people thousands of years ago. In ancient times, China had already become a renowned producer of silk. In ancient Rome, silk was even considered synonymous with China. Since the early days, the Sanskrit word "*cīnapaṭṭa*" refers to silk from China in Indian texts. A paragraph in *Arthaśāstra*, a Sanskrit book on statecraft in ancient India, reads: "*kauśeyaṃcīnapaṭṭaś ca cīnabhumijāḥ*" ("*kauśeya* and bunches of silk from China").

As Xuanzang explained in the second scroll of *The Great Tang Dynasty Record on the Western Regions, kauśeya* refers to silk spun by wild silkworms. *Cīnapaṭṭa* is a different kind of silk from *kauśeya*. What is it different? In Sanskrit, *cīnapaṭṭa* means silk spun by homegrown silkworms. The line in *Arthaśāstra* clearly states that this kind of silk came from China ("*cīnabhumijā*" in Sanskrit). Another related Sanskrit word, *cīnasicaya*, means "silk clothes."

Although it is debatable when exactly *Arthaśāstra* was written, no one disputes the book's long history. The mainstream consensus among scholars is that the text dates to the fourth century B.C., equivalent to the Spring and Autumn Period (770–476 B.C.) and the Warring States Period (475–221 B.C.) in China. This indicates that Chinese silk was introduced to India before ancient Rome. The description of "bunches of silk" implies that Chinese silk was exported to India through international trade by today's Silk Road.

With the word *cīna*, we can see some other examples:

Sanskrit word *cīnajā* refers to "steel." *Cīnajā* means "things from China," including steel. Why did ancient Indians call steel *cīnajā*? Did India import steel from China or introduce China's steel-making technology in ancient times? The word *cīnajā* implies that such conjectures are possible at first thought.

Another Sanskrit word, "*cīnakaṭikā*," refers to a kind of gourd melon. Its English translation is "Chinese melon." As its name implies, this plant species was likely introduced to India from China. Camphor and the camphor tree are called *cīnakarpūra* in Sanskrit, and this means their origin in India might also be related to China.

Those Sanskrit words indicate the foreign origins of those things, just like some foreign loanwords in Chinese, such as "*hu luobo* 胡萝卜" (carrot), "*fan qie* 番茄" (tomato), and "*fan shiliu* 番石榴" (guava).

Miniumite, also called "red lead," is a mineral that has been long used as a standard medicinal ingredient in traditional Chinese medicine, especially in surgical treatment, since ancient times. In Sanskrit, it is called *cīnapiṣṭa* or *cīnavaṅga*. It isn't clear how this mineral was introduced to India from China, and some scholars suggest it may be related to the practice of alchemy of Chinese Taoism. However, it remains debatable whether Taoism had much influence in India historically because little evidence shows it did. But it is undisputed that the Sanskrit word for miniumite contains the prefix "*cīna*."

These are examples of Sanskrit words beginning with the prefix "*cīna*." That means they had something to do with China or were popularly believed to be related.

Sanskrit is an ancient language in India. Today, Indians don't speak Sanskrit anymore in daily life, but various regional languages. However, the regional languages still preserve many Sanskrit words. Presently, Hindi and Bengali are among India's most widely used languages. Some words in those two languages also have connections to China. The most notable example is "*Cīnī*." From the etymological perspective, *Cīnī* and the Sanskrit word *Cīna* both refer to China despite a different ending sound.

In Hindi and Bengali, *Cīnī* means "sugar" as well. It is understandable how *Cīnī* could refer to China. But sugar originated in India, not China. Historically, ancient

Indians were the first to plant sugarcane and invent making sugar by boiling it in water. The method eventually spread to other countries around the world. The words evidence this for "sugar" in languages of various countries. In Sanskrit, sugar is called śarkarā, which was converted into "sugar" in English, "sucre" in French, "Zucker" in German, "azúcar" in Spanish, "Zucchero" in Italian, and "caxap" in Russian. In ancient China, śarkarā was transliterated into "煞割令" (pronounced "shageling").

Before the Tang Dynasty, Chinese people did not plant sugarcane, let alone make sugar from sugarcane. The change happened while the technique of making sugar was introduced into China in the early years of the Tang period. According to Chinese historical records, Emperor Taizong of the Tang sent people to Magadha, an ancient kingdom of India, to learn how to press, boil, and dry sugar from sugarcane. After returning to China, they began to use sugarcane from Yangzhou to produce sugar. The sugar produced in China even had better quality than that in India. From then on, China had its granulated sugar.

This event was associated with Xuanzang. Buddhist monk Daoxuan, a contemporary of Xuanzang, wrote in his *Biography of Xuanzang* in the fourth scroll of *Sequel to Biographies of Eminent Monks*: "Xuanzang earned fame across the five parts in India. He talked and praised much of the prominent people and things of China. For a long time, King Śīlāditya and monks of Mahābodhi Temple wanted to know more about China, but the kingdom did not receive envoys from China, so they are not sure of what they heard."

Śīlāditya was the most powerful King in India when Xuanzang visited, and he once called himself the King of Magadha. After meeting with Xuanzang, "King Śīlāditya sent envoys carrying precious gifts to China, as well as the monks of Mahābodhi Temple carrying the Buddhist texts. Thus, after Xuanzang's arrival, the diplomatic relations established between India and China."

The earliest diplomatic delegation sent by King Śīlāditya to the Tang Empire arrived in Chang'an, then the capital, in 641, the 15th year of the Zhenguan Reign. The event was recorded in *The New Tang History, The Old Tang Histor*y, and *The Cefu Yuangui* ("*The Original Archives Kept in the Burea*u"). Afterward, Emperor Taizong of the Tang dispatched envoys to India, and King Śīlāditya sent envoys for a return visit. From then on, China and India frequently sent envoys to each other, as Monk Daoxuan described:

> After the Indian envoy returned, (the emperor) sent a delegation of more than 20, headed by Wang Xuance, on a diplomatic mission to *Daxia (*here means India) with more than 1,000 rolls of silk as gifts for the King and monks in different numbers accordingly. The delegates recruited sugar-making artisans at the Mahābodhi Temple, then two artisans and eight monks were dispatched to China. After they arrived in China, under the order of the Tang emperor, they went to Yuezhou to make sugar with sugarcane, all with successful results.

Mahābodhi Temple, known as the place where Buddha Śākyamuni attained enlightenment, has been one of Buddhism's holiest sites since ancient times. The temple was located in the kingdom of Magadha in India. Wang Xuance was the most famous Chinese envoy to India during the early Tang Dynasty. From the reign of Emperor Taizong to Emperor Gaozong, he visited India three times. What Monk Daoxuan described in his book roughly matches the relevant records in *The New*

Tang History. According to historical records, India sent sugar artisans to China. Those artisans and Indian monks then went to Yuezhou (today's Shaoxing and neighboring areas in Zhejiang Province) to make high-quality granulated sugar with local sugarcane.

Many records indicate that China's boiled sugar-making technique was imported from India. So how could the word for sugar in ancient India, where the boiled sugar-making technique was invented, be associated with China? This question continues perplexing and still lacks any convincing answers. The question drew the attention of Ji Xianlin, a renowned scholar at Peking University. After lengthy and thorough research, Ji concluded that India—at least some certain regions or in some specific periods—once imported granulated sugar and its production techniques from China. For this reason, Indian people could have started calling sugar "*cīnī*."

To sum up, though these names of things I mentioned above look not unusual, it reflects some subtle but important angles of historical China–India cultural exchange. Behind each of those Indic words consisted of *Cīna*, there must have a number of stories related to cultural exchanges between China and India. The cultural exchanges between these two great nations have always involved the spiritual realms and the material matters. The story of peach and pear told by Xuanzang in his *Great Tang Dynasty Records on the Western Regions* is just one example, together with more of the other Indic words.

Part II
Features of India China Connections

Chapter 3
Buddhist Art Broke Language Barriers to Spread to Central Asia and China

Xinru Liu

It took almost a thousand years for Buddhism from its origin in Magadha in Lower Ganges Plain to reach and flourished in the Central Plain of China. The propagation passed through Gandhara on upper Indus Valley, Bactria in Afghanistan, Sogdiana and Tarim Basin in Central Asia. The disciples of the Buddha encountered numerous languages and passed through many cultural domains when preaching in the land outside of their homeland. To make people understand the teachings of the Buddha, they had to teach their language and writing to their audiences, or they had to learn the languages of their audience. As translation is a long and arduous process, Buddhists from early time used artistic images to illustrate the stories and doctrines to get their messages cross.

Shakya Muni Buddha cultivated his ideas and organized his sangha while roaming around the "Great Magadha" area, i.e., the lower Ganges plain that touching the foothills of the Himalayas to the north and forests of Deccan Plateau to the south. Although we cannot be sure what exact language Buddha spoke, the assumption could be that the language was the vernacular Prakrit of the Magadha region, i.e., Magadhi. The compiler of Pali Buddhist canon Buddhagosha in the fifth century claims that the Magadhi, equals Pali, was the authentic language of the Buddha thus Pali text is the most authentic canon. The written Pali Buddhist texts survived in Buddhist institutions in Sri Lanka and Southeast Asia. Whether Pali Buddhist text was the most and the only authentic text of the voice of the Buddha is a matter of discussion. Vocabulary and syntax of Pali in Buddhist texts, however, correspond roughly to Magadhi inscriptions of Ashoka's time and Buddhist inscriptions after Ashoka in Magadha region, i.e., on Sanchi and Bharhut stupas. Those inscriptions were carved in Brahmi script of Magadhi or Pali language. In other words, Pali was probably the language most close to that spoken in Magadha at the time of the Buddha. The geographical and ecological contexts and economic conditions shown

X. Liu (✉)
College of New Jersey, Ewing, NJ, USA
e-mail: liux@tcnj.edu

S. Mishra and R. Sheel (eds.), *India-China Dialogues Beyond Borders*,
https://doi.org/10.1007/978-981-99-4326-5_3

in Pali Buddhist texts reflect Magadha region of the middle first millennium BCE. With archaeological data as background, Pali texts look much more like the real scene than any other Buddhist texts. In short, the language of early Buddhist sangha should be the Pali without later hybrid, i.e., the Madadhi.

Buddhism as a faith and an institution started to spread out of the Great Magadha after the passing of the Buddha. That is to say, followers of the Buddha had to overcome language barriers to recruit new followers and to spread their messages. Buddha spoke a local vernacular of Sanskrit, thus he could directly communicate with the common people of the region to reveal the Noble Truths. In his lifetime, Buddha gained many followers in various social circles, but mostly in the Magadha region where his teaching could be understood. As Buddhist sangha opened to individuals and communities at the edge of the developing urban–agricultural society, Buddha had to address to those who were not in the Indo-European language domain and thus could not perfectly understand even the vernacular in Magadha. Those non-Magadhi speakers who joined the sangha surely had learned the language of the Buddha before their induction ceremony. The religious practice of monks and nuns begging for daily food from lay followers was important channel of communication. Once they accepted the promise that the reward of feeding the sangha would be a better afterlife, those who wanted to join the community of lay followers could express their devotion by the action of supplying food, even if they could not express it by words. After the passing of Buddha, the sangha elders gathered to collect the teachings of the Buddha and codified them into the canon, first by reciting, then sometime later the memorized words were canonized in written form. Without the charismatic Buddha in person looming behind them, Buddhist sangha had to communicate with its supporting society via languages as well as imagery expressions comprehensible to new audiences to sustain and expand the sangha.

During the life time of the Buddha, Buddhists in Magadha already had contacts with other language speakers. In one of the early Pali texts *Vinaya* (Disciplinary Rules), the name of the city Takshashila (Taxila in Greek) in Gandhara appeared as the center of intellects and education. Gandhara at that time was one of the satrapies of the Achaemenid Persian Empire. The famous physician Jivaka went to Takshashila to study medicine and returned to the city of Rajagaha in Magadha to serve the kings, householders, and Buddhist Sangha. In the *Jatakas*, a collection of didactic stories in the name of the Buddha's life and former lives, Takshashila was the place for education of Vedas, Sanskrit, and all kinds of Brahmanical and non-religious learning. Panini the first Sanskrit grammarian, a late contemporary of the Buddha, hailed from Gandhara. In short, Buddhists as residents of the great Magadha region had information or even direct contacts with speakers of Gandharan Prakrit and various Persian languages, including Persian or Aryan, Elamite, Aramaic. Meanwhile, in Gandhara Panini compiled his Sanskrit grammar *Ashtadhyyi* and therefore started the codifying of classical Sanskrit. Young people from Magadha traveled to Takshashila to study Vedas and Sanskrit including the Panini-style Sanskrit, and returned to the Lower and Middle Ganges to pursue their Brahman missions. Though Buddha never taught in Sanskrit, a number of his outstanding disciples were born as Brahmans and thus could be well versed in Vedic Sanskrit and probably were also familiar with the Sanskrit of Panini. That is to say, Sanskrit was the language that Brahmanically educated could communicate verbally even if their native languages varied. However, Gandhara and Magadha were far apart, thus communication needed to be in written form. It was the time when scribes appeared in cities of North India as a new profession. Aramaic language and script were introduced by Persian administration and traders to Gandhara. Meanwhile, Brahmi and Kharoshthi were created on the base of Aramaic, probably was also influenced by Greek script. When the elders of the sangha compiling the teachings of the Buddha after his passing, they should have used the coded Magadhi language, and sometimes later written in Brahmi script. After Buddhist messages reached Gandhara, probably soon after Buddha's passing, and flourished under the Mauryan King Ashoka (r. 268–231), the earliest known written form of Buddhist texts—Gandhari in Kharoshthi script—appeared in the beginning of the Common Era.

Even under their greatest royal patron Ashoka, Sanskrit was neither the official language of the empire nor that of the Buddhist sangha. Inspired by the trilingual edicts inscribed on monuments by Persian kings, and for the purpose of communication with Persian- and Greek-speaking population in Kandahar, Ashoka issued edicts in the regions in bilingual inscriptions. One was inscribed with Greek and Aramaic, another was in Aramaic transliteration of Ashoka Magadhi, along with Aramaic translation of an edict. In addition of carving his edicts on rocks and pillars, another way that Ashoka implemented his policy to the vast as well as diverse empire was to have stupas built to set up the stations that Buddhist sangha could gather for their *uposatha* meetings to review Buddha's teachings and discussing theological questions and disciplinary issues. At that time, the Ashoka edicts in Great Magadha, e.g., edict at the Sanchi Stupa, were using language similar to the Pali language in Buddhist texts. Sanchi was located at the border of settled communities of residents obedient to the king and the forest region where tribes were often restless. The forest people supplied the agricultural societies with forest products such as trained elephants and timber, but were not in the cultural domain. Therefore, they were not fluent in Magadhi vernacular. With all his intention to bring peace all over his territory, Ashoka faced the untamed population of forest people.

To address the faithful who came from the margins of the main stream, mainly women, one of the latest appeared Pali texts provided a narrative telling life stories of the many beautiful musicians and dancers in the heaven and what merits they earned in the world uplifted them to the heaven. Many of the women did not have known family background, thus most likely they came from forests and marshland community but migrated to the cities. Some were born in decent households but suffering for infertility after marriage. Some gained fame as artists or courtesans, some suffered as domestic servants. They diligently provided alms to monks and nuns to wish a better life after death. This book *Vimānavatthu*, or *Stories of the Mansions*, was one of the collection called "minor text" (Khuddaka-nikāya), which could be handbooks for monks to carry about for teaching by telling stories. Maha-Moggallana, one of the most dedicated disciples of the Buddha, traveled to the sphere of devas or gods, a heaven called the "Realm of Thirty-Three," to see how the residents in there doing. The Realm of Thirty-Three is one of the destinations that human beings will end up after death, according to the scheme of rebirth of Buddhist cosmology. When the realm of nirvana is the ultimate relief of suffering, reborn to the Realm of Thirty-Three is the next best path, above all other paths including the realms of human, *asura*, animals, and the hell. In the deva heaven that Maha-Moggallana visited, women who gave alms to Buddha and sangha when living in the world of human now reside in big mansions in the heaven. Many of the women reached there were downtrodden maids and mistreated daughters-in-law, and several of them were famous dancers and singers when they lived in the world. Here in the heaven they gained the status of *devata* or secondary deva.

The scene of musicians and dancers playing on the stage of the heaven appeared vividly on the Bharhut Stupa, another monument using visual arts and writing to convey the messages of Buddhist teachings thus enacting dialogs between the sangha and lay followers. Bharhut stupa was erected after the Mauryan Dynasty transitioned to the Sunga Dynasty, which shift the capital of the empire from the Mauryan Pataliputra to Vedisa, a former frontier town into the Deccan forests, not far from Sanchi Stupa. Many donors to Sanchi stupa lived in Vedisa according to their inscriptions of donations, which were inscribed besides artistic reliefs carved on pillars and beams of the railings surrounding the stupa. A group of finely executed relief panels displaying Ashoka's pilgrimage to a stupa were donations from a guild of ivory artisans. Ivory carving was a profession using resources from forest to supply the new urban elite. A reassessment of the site of Bharhur Stupa reveals that it was not an isolated monument either, but were associated with residential caves for Buddhist sangha. Stone reliefs on the railing surrounding the stupa show even more deities and symbols of folk religions.

In a heavenly scene carved on Bharhut stupa, there was an orchestra of musicians playing for a dancing troupe of four women and a little child. The performance was not purely entertaining, but also didactic. Of the four female dancers, the one on the lower left is wearing a man's headgear. A little child is jumping between the dancers. There is obviously a theme of the performance, which could be related to the story of Buddha as an infant. The theme is not clear to us as modern viewers, but could have been obvious to the brothers and sisters who were there to tell the stories to those who were faithful but could not read. Names of the musicians and dancers are inscribed around the stage. At least three of them were listed in the *Stories of the Mansions* (Fig. 3.1):

Alambusā Accharā,
Misakesi Accharā,
Sabhādā Accharā.

Accharā here stands for *apsaras*, the Sanskrit form of nymph, or goddess in water. In Chap. 18, "Slave-women's Mansion," (Dāsīvimāna) of *the Stories of the Mansions*, there was a slave woman of a householder in the city of Savatthi. The householder was devoted to the Buddha and dedicated four meals for the sangha every day. He ordered the slave women to prepare food for the sangha. She got up early every morning, diligently cooked the food, spread perfume on the floor to waiting for the brothers to come, and requested them to teach her after eating. This woman worked

Fig. 3.1 Orchestra and dancing in the heaven, Indian Museum catalog 273, American Institute of Indian Studies photo negative no. 484.58, courtesy of the Library of the University of Pennsylvania

on behalf of her master and was not even given a name but arrived at the heaven after death. As an attendant of Sakka, or Indra in Brahmanism, the woman enjoyed performances of numerous musicians and dancers. The three *āccharās* are named among the long list of players in the orchestra and dancing troop, but here they are called devatās. The similar list of musicians and dancers appeared in the story of another mansion where Rajjumala a former slave girl of a Brahman household now dwelled. Rajjumala was a slave girl in a small village near Gaya, the very place Buddha attained enlightenment. In that household, the daughter-in-law, a daughter of a Brahman, tortured her by pulling her hair to drag her around. She had her hair cut to avoid the torture, but only made her mistress even angrier thus tying a rope on her neck to drag her. She was thus called Rajjumala, meaning a rope garland, as she wore the rope on her neck all the time. When Rajjumala could not bear this torture she went out the house carrying a jar telling she was getting water for the household. She tried to hang herself in a woods where Buddha happened to meditate. After enlightened by the Buddha she went back to the household in high spirit. Surprised by her new state her master asked her what happened. Rajjumala told the master about her encounter with the Buddha. The householder realized the bad karma of torturing Rajjumala and thus disciplined his daughter-in-law and became a follower of the Buddha himself. Rajjumala ascended to the heaven after death enjoying the heavenly mansion named after her, wearing a true garland befitting a devata, dancing along with many of the heavenly musicians and dancers.

Being a dancer in Sakka's palace was a great achievement that only those who gained merits in human world were qualified for it. The following relief panel on Bharhut stupa shows a scene of devas celebrating the enlightenment of the Buddha in the heavenly palace. A dancing troop and an orchestra perform in front of devas led by Sakka. Four of the seven musicians are men, but all the four dancers are women. The inscriptions on the stone panel do not provide the names of the artists, but the *Stories of the Mansions* tells life stories of the women who became the celebrated artists in the Sakka's palace. A young woman Lata from Savatthi was a good daughter of a household and an obedient daughter-in-law and good wife after marriage. She died young, probably did not give birth of children. Her merits in life as a good daughter and daughter-in-law were sufficient to provide the best skill of dancing among five dancers in the heavenly troop (Fig. 3.2).

After the Mauryan power receded from the northwest of the Indian subcontinent, Hellenistic polities in Bactria and Gandhara survived till the coming of the nomads from Central Asia, including the Kushans who came from the steppe and established a sedentary regime across Central Asia and South Asia. The crossroad of Central Asia and South Asia was a region of many languages. Since the Achaemenid Persia included Bactria and Gandhara into its empire in the sixth-century BCE, several languages and writings used in Persian Empire entered the region. The Aramaic and Greek writing could be the inspiration of earliest Indian scripts, the Kharoshthi and Brahmi. As rulers from the steppe who had not created their own written language, the Kushans had to rely on scholars among their subjects to help them inscribing their messages on monuments and coins. Like the Greeks, Sakas and Parthians who

Fig. 3.2 Celebration of the enlightenment of the Buddha in Deva Sabha, Bharhut Stupa. Calcutta, Indian Museum no. 182, American Institute of Indian Studies photo, neg. No. 484.76. Courtesy of the Library of the University of Pennsylvania

came to India through Bactria before them, the Kushan kings in Bactria used bilingual legends, Greek and a local Prakrit to mark the coins issued under their name. Discovered coins of Kushan kings Kujula Kadaphises (c. 40–95 or 40–90 CE) and Vima Kadphises (c. 100–127 or 105 -127) show Greek language written in Greek letters, and local Prakrit in Kharoshthi script. King Kanishka (c. 127–150 CE) left coins inscribed in Greek letters of Prakrit language. On the edict inscribed on the Robataka inscription, Kanishka stated that the edict was originally issued in Greek, then translated into Aryan language, i.e., the Bactrain dialect of Persian. Communities of various languages under the Kushan Empire were integrated into a special cultural domain where several languages and writing systems co-existed and mingled.

Buddhist scholars arrived and flourished in the multicultural environment of Kushan Empire. Monasteries in the great Gandhara used Kharoshthi script to write local Gandharian Prakrit language to copy Buddhist texts on birch bark. A number of them were preserved in jars, dated to the first-century CE. The effort of copying Buddhist texts and preserving the copies meant copying texts was an action of meritorious for Buddhist followers. The manuscripts contain many texts known in Pali Buddhist texts, but also some compositions unknown in large corps of Buddhist canon but including some local stories. Meanwhile, Sanskrit was the vehicle of communication for newly developed Mahayana Buddhism which could reach a large geographic scope. The major themes of the Mahayana Sanskrit texts were to divinize the Buddha and introduce the many bodhisattvas who delayed their own nirvana by staying in the world to help all the creatures. *Saddharmapundarika* introduces the Bodhisattva Avalokiteshvara who vowed to stay in the world to help all the creatures to cross the ocean of suffering before he crosses the threshold into nirvana. *Sukhavativyuha* tells the Bodhisattva Amitabha created a heaven for those who were not ready to go to nirvana when dying to take a sojourn in this land of bliss before reborn into the world. The *Jatakamala* is a collection of 36 stories in Sanskrit selected from the large corpus of Pali *Jataka* stories. The *Ashokavadana is* a legendary account of the Mauryan king of Ashoka in Sanskrit. This Sanskrit text derived information from Ashoka's edicts, but also added many new details of his deeds as karma in the Buddhist context. The *Ashokavadana* thus makes it a hagiography of the Buddhist king. The *Lalitavistara* created magic details of Buddha's life since his birth, such as the infant jumping out from his mother's right side to strike seven steps. This version of Buddha's life stories promoted the Buddha as god and could had been developed from lore of earlier Buddhist community.

Buddhist scholar Ashvaghosha was the first Sanskrit writer who pinned his name on literary works he wrote for the cause of Buddhism. The author of Sanskrit dramas and stories in Kushan India, where many different languages were spoken, reinvented the life story of Buddha in *Budhacarita.* This biography of Buddha added many magical details and extravagant exaggerations of urban life enriched by the Silk Road trade passing through the Kushan Empire into the life stories of the Buddha. From his birth to enlightenment and departure from home to his preaching, the stories were the source materials for propagation of Mahayana to Central Asia and China. The *Mahavastu,* or the Great Event, further divinizing the Buddha into an eternal existence forever transcendental. All his actions in the human world were

Fig. 3.3 Buddha on the stage marked by Corinthian columns (en.wikipedia.org/wiki/Greco-Buddhist_art#/media/File:BuddhistTriad.JPG)

performances of the divine being for the purpose of teaching. Divinization of the Buddha got rid of the social context of Buddha's enlightenment of the Noble Truths. The *devas*, instead of his own life experience, revealed the eternal suffering of all creatures.

The Sanskrit literature of Buddhist themes thus provided the scripts for the artistic expressions of Gandharan Buddhist art. Here the images of Buddha appeared, which was a total break from the taboo of showing the human form of Buddha in earlier Buddhist art. The iconography of the Buddha as the supreme divine being emerged as a center figure, sitting or standing with either two disciples or two bodhisattvas on his sides. The events in his life have been displayed on panels of reliefs like snapshots of actions in drama (Fig. 3.3). Dionysian legacy including dramatic performance propelled viniculture and theater in Hellenistic Bactria to the Kushan domain. Even though no theater had been discovered in Gandhara, the relief panels showing the stage of performance on Buddhist stupas in Monastic settings suggest the courtyards of the monasteries could be the locations where the drama was staged. The sculpture on a stupa in Gandharan region shows Dionysian performances on stages. Actors and actresses in steppe dresses and Creek styles play music, dance, drink, or serve grape wine. Those relieve sculptures likely present the prelude of a drama (Fig. 3.4). Stories from *Lalitavistra* and *Buddhacarita* displayed on relief sculptures like snapshots of drama or illustrations of texts for guides to explain the stories to an audience.

Focusing on Buddha's life stories and the role of bodhisattvas, the musicians and dancers recorded in Pali texts and portrayed on early Buddhist art were almost lost in Buddhist Gandharan art. The newly composed Sanskrit texts, though, did not eliminate those *apsarases*, or the *accharas* in Magadhi. In Ashvaghosha's *Buddhacarita*, at the birth of the Shakya Prince, the festive scene in the city of Kapilavastu mimics the

ıl from Chakhil-i-Ghoundi stupa, Hadda, 1st–2nd century AD).

Fig. 3.4 Sculpture of Dionysian scene on a stupa in Gandhara (https://en.wikipedia.org/wiki/Greco-Buddhist_art#/media/File:Indo-GreekBanquet.JPG)

heaven of Kuvera celebrating the birth of the son of the god of wealth that apsarases danced around.

Buddhism spread to China through Central Asia following the trade on the Silk Road. Sogdiana, the land between the Syr and Amu Rivers, bred many traders who reached India, Persia, the steppe, and China. Though Zoroastrianism was the dominant religion in Sogdiana, the Sogdians were among the first batch of Buddhist missionaries-cum-merchants brought Buddhist rituals and texts to China. However, Buddhist practices remained mostly within diaspora of foreign traders in China till the fourth century when nomads on the steppe flooded north China forcing structural changes of Chinese Society. Meanwhile, the collapse of the Kushan Empire in the third century sent refugees including Buddhist followers to Central Asia east to the Pamir Plateau, i.e., oases surrounding the Takla Makan Desert. Kucha, the first oasis state east to the Pamir, developed into a Buddhist center. By the mid-fourth century, when Kumarajiva the first scholar and translator who brought Mahayana Sanskrit literature to China was born in Kucha, Buddhism there was a well-established institution and enjoyed patronage from the strong and stable royal family. Buddhist institution in Kucha developed its unique form, fitting the oasis environment, that is, pastoralism and agriculture created wealth to provide sufficient livelihood for cultural pursuits. Communities continued to perform rituals to their local cults; immigrants came to Kucha from the other side of the Pamir Plateau were not only Buddhist of various sects, but also Zoroastrians, Brahmans, etc. Various religious and ethnic groups brought several languages into the community. Buddhist missionaries were particularly active in creating artworks—sculptures, wall painting, stucco figurines, silk paintings—in and around stupas and temple caves. The themes of the art works were stories of the lives of the Buddha and Buddhist saints, and the deified Buddha. Learned scholars mastered Indic languages including Gandhari and Iranian language such as Bactrian, and Sanskrit of Mahayana Buddhism and Vedas. Sanskrit Buddhist texts such as *Buddhacarita*, *Saddharmapundarika*, and *Jatakamala* should have been the scripts for the artists in Kucha.

Kumarajiva immersed in the intellectual and cultural environment of Kucha, and learned from the Buddhist teachers and scholars of other religions along the Central Asian Silk Road, and participated studying, discussing, and debating of various fields of knowledge. In Kashgar, Kumarajiva studied the *Four Vedas* with their commentaries, and other knowledge such as astrology. The study of Brahmanical literature should have taught him Sanskrit, which is quite different in grammar and pronunciation from earlier Buddhist texts he had studied so far. Around that time, two princes, namely, Shache Prince and Canjun Prince, appeared in the scene as outstanding Buddhist teachers. There is no indication where the princes were from. Kumarajiva, probably already fluent in Sanskrit, learned Mahayana Buddhism from them and since geared his study to Mahayana. It is likely that the two princely Buddhist teachers came from the former Kushan territory where Mahayana theology in Sanskrit matured and Mahayana institution took shape and prospered. Kumarajiva made a successful career of translating Sanskrit Mahayana text in China. His mastering of Sanskrit made his translations succeed earlier translators.

Kumarajiva was among a handful of Buddhist scholars who mastered Sanskrit language in their study of Buddhism and Indian culture at that time in Central Asia. Kucha was then a center of Buddhist studies attracting novices from all over the Tarim Basin. Royal women from oases east to the Pamir thronged to the three major nunneries in Kucha. The oasis states around the Takla Makan shared ecological features but not necessarily the same language. Buddhist arts, especially mural paintings, in cave monasteries around oasis cities were the platforms of displaying the stories of the Buddha and the sangha. On the murals in Kezil Cave Monasteries outside the Kucha City, the characteristic Central Asian apsarases filled many spaces of the outliers of main didactic scenes (Fig. 3.5). Those musical playing apsarases were musicians flying in the sky to celebrate certain events, as described in *Buddhacarita, Sukhavativyuha*, and *Jatakamala*. The main themes of the Buddhist arts now were the divinized Buddha, the heavens created by the bodhisattvas such as Amitabha, illustrations of stories of Buddha in his life and former lives based on the Mahayana texts. Musicians and dancers were playing a side show to the major event, there their own stories of life and paths to the heaven became oblivious to the viewers. This composition of Buddhist cave arts started from Kucha spread to the Tarim oases and all the way to the Hexi Corridor, notably the murals of the Dunhuang grottoes art (Fig. 3.6). The flying apsarases fill the space of mural painting without providing messages of Buddha's teachings.

Divinized Buddha and semi-divinized bodhisattvas arrived China as the iconography of Buddhist art. The apsarases, more musicians than dancers, followed the main

Fig. 3.5 Apsaras in a Kezil Cave, Kucha (Politics.people.com.cn/n1/2016/0921/c366035-28,731,058–6.html)

icons on the edge of the composition of sculptures and murals. A rare discovery of a horde of more than four hundred sculptures buried in an underground storage of Longxingsi monastery, Qingzhou, Shandong Province, in 1996, provides examples of the early Buddhist iconography in China. The sculptures were made during the sixth century when the Northern Dynasties built by the Toba Clan of nomads transferred themselves into Chinese rulers claiming their legitimacy from Buddhism. Most of the sculptures were free-standing figures of Buddha and bodhisattvas, and a number of them were reliefs on a water drop-shaped panels. Analyses of the style of the sculptures show strong affinity with those of Mathura, Gandhara, and Kucha. The Buddha with bodhisattvas on his sides was the major motif of the scene. Apsaras musicians are flying above carrying their instruments escorting a stupa (Fig. 3.7). Here the theme is the divine power of the Buddha and the helpful bodhisattvas. The musicians are beautiful but do not convey important messages.

Buddhist iconography in China developed by and large under the guide of Buddhist art of Central Asian caves and sculptural works from Gandhara and Mathura. Chinese translations of Buddhist texts before the fourth-century CE were from Gandhari or other Prakrit. However, the translators in the early stage did not master Chinese, and Chinese Buddhist scholars were not mature enough to master Buddhist ideas, thus the influence on Chinese audience was limited. Kumarajiva was the most influential translator of Mahayana Sanskrit texts, who made Sanskrit the major language vehicle transmitting Buddhism to China. Since then, Chinese translations of Buddhist knowledge mostly based on Sanskrit Mahayana texts were the most influential, the themes of the presentations were prescribed by Sanskrit Buddhist texts, mostly Mahayana cosmology. Chinese Buddhist pilgrims traveled to Central Asian sites and India to obtain statues and copies of paintings of Buddha

Fig. 3.6 Flying apsaras in Dunhuang (Collection.sina.com.cn/cqyw/2016–03-09/doc-ifxqaffy3778530.shtml)

Fig. 3.7 Flying apsarases above the Buddha Longxingsi Monastery (Kknews.cc/zh-hk/culture/xovr28.himl)

and bodhisattvas, and Buddhist preachers also brought models from Central Asia and India to China. By the time of the Tang the pilgrimage became an industry, all pilgrims carried statues or paintings in addition to texts. The list of statues brought by Xuanzang to the Tang court includes one from Mathura, one from Sarnath, one from the Eagle Peak near Rajagaha in Magadha, etc. The sacred images from India were all about the Buddha and bodhisattvas as described in Mahayana texts.

From the time of Ashoka, the king of Mauryan, who tried to spread the teachings of Buddha to his empire and beyond, Buddhist teachers broke through language barriers to enlighten people outside the mainstream by adding artworks illustrating stories of salvation of downtrodden people especially women. Pali texts and the stories expressed on the early stupas provided a parallel channel to get the teachings to the people who could not comprehend the language and the script. The messages brought from the great Magadha region westward to the entire Ganges plain and Gandhara, and southward to Sri Lanka, inevitably encountered language barriers. The Pali tradition was established and flourished in Sri Lanka Buddhist monasteries and from there to Southeast Asian Buddhist Institutions. In Gandhara, Buddhist teachers rendered the messages in both local Prakrit dialect and Sanskrit. The Hellenistic cultural residue and steppe culture under the Kushan Empire provided the environment to dramatize stories embodying the wisdom of Buddha. The development in Gandhara created the iconography of Buddha, whose image till then was absent in early Buddhist art. This transition to Sanskrit language and artistic expressions facilitated Buddhism spreading out from India. When basic doctrine of the Buddhism, the Four Noble Truths and the Eight Right Paths, transcended all the different languages to the faithful, certain messages from early Buddhist communities could not reach the new audience. The stories of salvation of the women who suffered miserably in human world but ascended to the heaven to play music and dance by their own efforts are lost much, though not totally, in the transitions. Sanskrit and Chinese Buddhist texts shifted the focus on the Buddha the god and numerous bodhisattvas who could help all the creatures who are willing to cross the ocean of suffering. The beautiful apsaras musicians retreated to the edge of the stage. The loss of information was due to many factors. Changes of languages that carrying the messages of the Buddha, theological developments that changed the theme of narrative and artistic expression, are apparent reasons for the loss and gain of information throughout the transmission. Fundamentally, however, all the texts and arts did not and could not transplant the social context of the early Buddhist sangha, therefore some of the stories were destined to get lost.

References

Corpus Inscriptionum Indicarum, vol II, Part II. *Bharhut Inscriptions* (H Lüders, Ed., and E Waldsehmidt, MA Mehendale, Revised). Archaeological Survey of India, New Delhi (1963)

Falk H (2006) Asokan sites and artefacts. Verlag Philippe Von Zabern, Mainz am Rhein

Huili, Yanzong (1983) Da Ciensi Sanzang Fashi Zhuan《大慈恩寺三藏法师传》(S Yutang, Ed.). Zhonghua Shuju, Beijing
Hultzsch E (1969) Corpus Inscriptionum Indicarum, vol 1. Inscriptions of Ashoka, New ed., Ph.D. first published in 1924, reprint by Delhi, Indological Book House
Marshall J, Foucher A (1982) The monument of Sanchi. Swati Publications, Delhi
Vimānavatthu: Stories of the Mansions (IB Horner, Transl and Annotated). Published by the Pali Text Society, London, distributed by Routledge & Kegan Paul Ltd.
僧祐:《出三藏記集》序卷第11,《续修四库全书》1288卷

Chapter 4
India–China Connectedness: Some Observations

Kamal Sheel

Under the contemporary scenario, such India–China dialogues on the border and struggle overwhelm and overshadow the age-old historical linkages. However, it must be noted that any discussion of the borders without getting into the long history of the frontier does not make any sense. The political border of the nation-state must be seen in the longer perspective of cultural frontiers that intersected empire and civilization and formed with the shift from the civilizational-state to the nation-state. In the morning sessions, there were excellent and meaningful discussions about "Sinophobia", which has emerged as an important factor in shaping the foreign policy of India and other countries vis a vis China. This, however, skipped an exploration of the long tradition of "Sinophilia", which characterized India–China cultural interaction. In this context, In the following paragraphs, I present some observations on salient features of historical connectedness between India and China to comprehend the varying nature of their dialogues.

India and China are unique examples of historically longest continuing civilization and culture, they share similarities as large agrarian societies, they together constitute almost one-third of the world population belonging to different races, temperaments, and even languages, occupy a major share of the world economy throughout their long histories, they both suffered under foreign domination in modern time, and they responded with the protracted struggle for emancipation. Foundations of China and India as modern nation-states were laid during the first half of the twentieth century when both societies waged perhaps the longest political struggle in world history for national sovereignty and negotiating the demands of nationalism and modernity. Their phenomenal growth in the era of globalization beckons the present century as the Asian century. Yet, both followed different paths in evolving a modern nation-state and in embracing modernity following a shift from a civilizational state to a nation-state and the beginning of a process to configure a nation-state with trappings of a civilizational state. This impacted the nature of dialogues between the two modern

K. Sheel (✉)
Banaras Hindu University, Varanasi, India

S. Mishra and R. Sheel (eds.), *India-China Dialogues Beyond Borders*,
https://doi.org/10.1007/978-981-99-4326-5_4

nation-states. Civilizational bonhomie that had characterized the genealogy of this dialogue began to have succumbed to national anxieties and concerns.

In this context, I propose to highlight some of the basic features of Their civilizations that contributed to the development of an "organic dialogue" between them.[1] Tagore emphasizes the organic connection between India and China. Writing on the connection between India and China, he asks what is it in China for those who come from another land to feel at home in this land of an ancient civilization. This is neither materialism nor brute physical strength. He says, "I cannot bring myself to believe that any nation in this world can be great and yet be materialistic. I believe that no people in Asia can be wholly given to materialism. There is something that somehow gives us an understanding of the inner music of existence to which none of us is deaf." These are beautiful words about how organically related India and China are. They indicate that both share a common genealogy in passion for morality and spirituality. Their moral strength acts as a normative principle to sustain civilization and leads to perfection.

Further, geographical proximity between India and China provided myriad meaningful interactions through Buddhists and various other connections, extending a natural affinity among people of both the countries from high to subaltern levels. The question is, how to negotiate these underlying features of India–China civilizational connectedness? The task is tall and hazardous. The long historical course of encounters has led to the total absorption of outside elements in their respective cultures or has faded their original alien nature. Scholarly debates on the issue of cultural borrowing have been contentious due to the difficulty in separating the wheat from the chaff after the lapse of considerable historical time. For example, was the Chinese monkey sage god "Sun Wukong", an imagination based on similar Indian tales based on the monkey sage god "Hanuman" of the Ramakathas, or did he originate from the indigenous Chinese legends or tales?[2] The nationalist-inspired narrative further distracts our attention from the fact that both cultures could have shared a common belief and faith in a monkey sage king or god. Civilizational sensibility thus often gets distorted under nationalist anxieties and concerns.

In this context, some favorable processes in Indian and Chinese history need to be accounted for rooting the civilizational affinities between the two. This may be seen in two broad characteristics that highlight the process of a state formation during almost the same time in India and China, respectively, in the Mauryan and Han dynasty periods. These characteristics are credited to have significantly contributed to developing certain basic contours of their respective cultures.

First, both the countries lacked a unified religious orthodoxy and promoted syncretism. Han syncretism enthusiastically engaged with a variety of divergent philosophical ideas and thoughts ranging from Legalism, Daoism to Buddhism in

---

[1] For a comprehensive and illuminating discussion of India-China historical interactions see Sen (2018). Also useful are Lin (1993), Tan (1998), Tan et al. (2013), Sheel (2006).

[2] See Mair (1989).

many versions to synchronize with Confucianism to elevate latter to the state orthodoxy. This produced rationalization and justification for three distinct religious-ethical traditions with the same essence. Similarly, the Mauryan state formation in India is credited with cultural diffusion and religious syncretism. Emperor Ashok Maurya's formulation of moral, social codes in the form of the policy of dhamma was based on the principles of tolerance and peaceful co-existence. His exaltations for how people in a multicultural society should live with each other and how the state should act in such a rainbow society promoted the incorporation and patronage of Buddhism, Jainism, and Hinduism in the state ideological system and a dynamic flourishing of diverse ideas. In this context, it is also difficult to discount certain similarities in the pristine religion in both India and China in developing seemingly common rituals and customs that appear to reinforce their civilizational affinity. For example, unlike the Abrahamic religion, religion in both countries lacked a founder-prophet. There is no one divinely authorized book for initiation or conversion, and it is also very difficult to point to a historical specific time of their origin. Instead, both emphasized the primacy of the texts and their divine characteristics in binding human beings with the cosmos. Texts were more important than the god or person. Powered by texts, rituals, as characterized by Li in China and Dharma in India, acquired significance. These were invoked to stress "the ultimate unity of subject and object, meaning and reference, self and deity, individual and cosmos and thus the identification of heaven with ultimate order of things."[3]

Second, not unlike syncretism of thought, politico-cultural syncretism bringing together the native and the others (earlier often translated as barbarians) prevailed in both countries. The inter-continental silk route connected people and cultures of different regions to international trade. This trade route carried not only silk but a variety of goods and exotica. It promoted a distinct hybrid form of knowledge and ideas not limited to the vehicles of Buddhism only.

Such interaction and circulation of ideas, knowledge, and goods brought different cultural zones and regions together. As part of the basic features of polity and society, internationalism and cosmopolitism emerged and took shape as the process of state formation in India and China began. This promoted the thirst to know about others, to embellish and elevate the status of their respective state in all respects. Lack of religious orthodoxy, the zeal for preserving, flourishing profitable trade with the others, and the emergence of intersecting "universals" kept strands of pluralism active in both civilizations. Harmony against conflict characterized this early era. This remained so until the great age of cosmopolitism got over due to the onset of various other historical forces.

Such representations of India at the Tang court after its first encounter with Zhang Qian of the Han dynasty at Bactria promoted and advanced Buddhism as a compatible complement to secular Confucian ideology. More than that, this also convinced the

[3] See special issue on *Dharama* and *Li* in *Philosophy: East and West* (1972, 22:2) and especially articles by Gimmelo, and Macdermott; also Theodore and Yao (2014) which highlights various points of similarities and connectedness in Indian and Chinese philosophical discourses. Mohanty (2000) emphasizes the significance of texts in Indian and Chinese philosophical and religious order.

Tang court to open diplomatic channels through the exchange of embassies between the imperial Tang court of China and the kingdom of Kannauj in India. This recognized that China, the land of men, excels in political ethics and India, the land of elephants, is the authority on spiritual matters. They are two centres of the world, equal in authority in separate moral realms. Xuan Zang thus can be credited with bringing India on par with China in the Chinese worldview. India was the only country on the globe to receive such an exalted position. The Indian knowledge system was not treated as heterodox but was accepted, circulated, and absorbed. Hu Shi, one of the most recognized philosophers and intellectuals of modern China, refers to this as the "Indianization of China" without any war or coercion.[4] Appropriation, absorption, and sinification or Indianization of aspects of their culture through a variety of exchanges during a long period of interaction kept discourses and connections between the two countries alive, even though with varied intensity in different historical periods. This produced a kind of discourse inherently based on civilizational affectations or bonhomie between them.

Even in the early twentieth century, Chinese and Indian intellectuals and travellers kept invoking the civilizational similarities and bonding despite differences over ideologies and models of emerging nationalism. For example, Kang Youwei, often recognized as the first Chinese intellectual-modernizer, while traveling in India in 1901, was so wary of his disciple Liang Qichao's support for the West-inspired nationalism that he wrote a strong rebuttal. In the long public letter to Liang, he rhetorically asks, "Which country is so similar to our country" and answers, "this is India."[5] It has been the source of civilization that impacts most world civilizations in the east and west. Its linkages with China are now more than 2000 years old, and India introduced China's bamboo products and medicinal herbs like betel nuts and leaves.

Further, after the arrival of Buddhist scriptures in China on the "white horses" (as per the Chinese mythological account) and its translation in Chinese, the Bodhi dharma [Buddhism], along with its religious and cultural relics like bells, drums, and symbols has abundantly enriched the spiritual life and culture of the people. "The mind, soul, precept and temple are the treasures that entered China."[6]Kang considered his trip to India significant. His enchantment with the country owed much to the civilizational affinity that both India and China shared over a long period of history.

Indian and Chinese civilizations, Kang writes, are so much intimately entwined that making any comparison between India and China is difficult and finding differences is more challenging. So, using a Confucian location, he writes that India and China are like two famous ancient Chinese brothers, Lu and Wei; how can they be compared?[7] Another modern Chinese intellectual, Zhang Taiyuan, similarly veers towards "Weishi" Buddhism in his attempt to save China from the onslaught of

---

[4] See Sheel (2014) on Hu Shih and "The Indianisation of China".

[5] Kang (2007a: 509). See also his (2007a, b) for the detailed discussion on India–China comparison.

[6] Kang (2007a: 509).

[7] Kang (2007b: 343).

the West-inspired nationalism and the global capitalist modernity. Hu Shi's views supported contemporary modernist Chinese intellectuals labeling India under the British as a ruined civilization, failed state, or incapable role model for the agenda of modernity.[8] Yet, these did not overlook affinity, mutual respect, and admiration for those in India searching for indigenous roots to modernity. His famous observation that "India conquered and dominated China culturally for twentieth century without ever having to send a single soldier across her borders" is one of the most quoted sentences in any study of Sino-Indian encounters and connections. Similarly, while in cultural and brotherly affinity, voluntaristic expression dominated modern suburban Indian perception of China and overrides colonial states' agenda and Westerners' derisive and contemptuous descriptions of people and region.

The author of the first modern Indian travelogue to China, Thakur Gadhara Singh, wrote in 1900 also writes rhetorically who does not know that India and China are the two largest and most fertile countries in the Asian region. Civilizationally, both are the best. His compatriot Mahendra Lal Garg in another travelogue, Cheen Darpan, enthusiastically confirmed this. His book begins with the statement, "the difference between India and China is only the Himalayan Mountain which shields one from another. If there had been no Himalayas, both countries would probably have been the subject of one king, their religion and cultures would have been absolutely the same as today many of the Chinese customs are like Hindus."[9]

The 1911 revolution and the establishment of a republican China created intense nationalistic euphoria in intellectual circles in India. This was seen as the first victory in the east for a republican movement and the end of the monarchy. It also marked the beginning of Asia's resurgence in response to the Western hegemony. Writing about the 1911 revolution, Madan Mohan Malviya, one of the most eminent early Indian nationalists and the chief editor of the newspaper "Abhyuday", emphasized that if an unchanging old and autocratic country, China could take a bold step toward progress and modernity, how could India remain behind. Binay Sarkar, another Indian who was probably the first Indian visiting fellow at the Chinese Academy of Social Sciences in 1915, visited China soon after the 1911 Revolution and about a decade earlier than Tagore. Like Kang Youwei, he promoted conservative nationalism and sought to confront the predicament arising out of Western-inspired nationalism and the virtue of civilizational states. His variety of nationalism has then been more supported as it resonated with the conservative nationalist Indian modernizers like Madan Mohan Malviya and others. He formulated his idea by highlighting cultural and spiritual unity between Indian and Chinese civilizations. He finds that the socio-religious world into which Shakya Buddha was born was identical to that of Confucius. These two great sages found in their respective compatriots the same mental biases and spiritual attitudes and preached to their disciples the self-same gospel. "The celestial [Chinese] and the Hindu of the twentieth century BCE lived in the same world of morals, manners and sentiments. If the Chinese happen to be in India, they would not feel any distance from the natives except only in language. If the Hindus happened

[8] See Sheel (2014) for a discussion on Hu Shi's "Indianization of China" discussion.

[9] Garg (1901: 11).

to be in China, they would enter into the spirit of the Chinese people despite the language barrier".[10] It thus emphasizes the unity of Asian minds and culture. This, as we have earlier noted, was also endorsed by Tagore.

However, the civilizational bonhomie in the India-China discourse began to fade with the rise of West-inspired nationalism and the subsequent inventions or reinventions of a nationalist ideology and spirit. This necessitated the incorporation of an agenda of modernization mirroring the Western enlightenment vision of nationalism, modernity, and progress. A rising group of Indian and Chinese intellectuals-modernizers thus began to engage with the issue of "western" modernity to save their respective country. To be sure, the process of shift from the civilizational-state to the "modern/western" nation-state produced dilemmas and predicaments when placed in a liminal space of eroding culture and tradition on the one hand and evolving concepts of nationalism and modernity on the other. Nationalist modernizers sought to make political and cultural authority congruent by legitimizing territorialized nation-states and resolving identity crises. Such a balancing act generated more and more dilemmas leading to rising national anxieties.

China's recent effective and dynamic pursuit for 'wealth and power' has been at the cost of disrupting socialist aspirations and denying capitalist outcomes. This is opening up new fissures within society. The Chinese state's louder and louder exaltation for building a society with Chinese characteristics, erecting a harmonious society and pursuit of the Chinese dream and many other such slogans and guidelines carry potent ideas. These can mean anything, but the strong drive to go back to the roots and configure and assert a Chinese identity is common in all. To peruse the goal of projecting a strong nation-state with Chinese characteristics, a concerted pursuit for re-enlivening or redeeming historically available modes of network, identities and linkages is being more and more made to compare with challenges from the West. They are being justified through such ideological constructs as new Confucianism, new nationalism, new humanism and many such new campaigns and mobilization.

Thus, the selective projection of voices that reject the West's mimicry and support Confucian or traditional civilizational moral basis for preserving Harmony and peace is evident. Ideals and visions characterized by the Enlightenment-inspired narratives of modernity and nationalism become self-contradictory. These voices are being revived, promoted, and carefully adapted to project the powerful appeal of the success story of Chinese characteristics and allay fears and anxieties produced by contemporary development.

Many representative intellectuals of the May 4th generation and later would tackle the question of modernity and nationalism in their way based on the comprehension of Chinese history and culture. They now recall and present alternative voices which were earlier misunderstood and rejected. For example, works of Zeng Guofan, Kang Youwei, and even Chiang Kaishek are all being republished, recalled, and rediscussed by the Chinese. So, the alternative voices are likely to be resourced further and further by the state in its quest to construct a hybrid nationalism or modernity with Chinese characteristics. In doing so, it is doubtful that their original intent and

[10] Sarkar (1916 rpt 1988: 72).

meaning may remain the same. It is hazardous to predict whether these alternative voices may assuage the tension arising from the mounting irreconcilable difference between the state and society. It is, however, certain that the dilemma and predicament of Enlightenment-inspired modernity and nationalism may inaugurate a new form of modernity, sourced less from the West and based more on Chinese historical experiences.

India–China connectedness seen from a historical perspective has thus been shifting from bonhomie, which was the product of peace and Harmony of the civilizational state, to competitive rivalry, conflict, and anxieties inherent in the West-inspired territorial nationalism and its accompaniments. The contemporary Chinese quest to hybridize their ideas and visions for nationalism and modernity propelled by rising national anxieties has variously colored India–China discourses making them more complex and contradictory. Nevertheless, many of the riddles present in contemporary India–China discourses may become more comprehensible and manageable if we delve into the history of connectedness beyond the immediate past. Tracing the historical journey from Sinophilia to Sinophobia may unveil myriad ways to do that.

References

Dharma and Li: Special Issue, 1972, Philosophy East and West, vol 22, no 2, April 1972

Garg M (1901) Cheen Darpan. Sukhsanchaarak Press, Mathura

Lin C (1993) Zhongyin Renmin you hao guanxi shi:1851–1949. Beijing daxue chuban she, Beijing

Literature (1991) Taipei: Academia Sinica, 1989; also rpt. Indian J Asian Stud 3(1–2)

Kang Y (2007a) Yinduyouji. In: Yihua J, Zhang R (eds) Kang Youweiquanji, vol V. Beijing renminchuban she, Beijing, pp 509–550

Kang Y (2007b) Yu tongxue zhuzi LiangQichao deng lun guo yindu wangguo youyu gesheng zhili shu. In: Yihua J, Zhang R (eds) *Kang Youwei quanji*, vol VI. Beijing renmin chuban she, Beijing, pp 334–349

Mair V (1989) Suen Wu-Kung = Hanumat? The progress of a scholarly debate. In: *Proceedings of the Second International Conference on Sinology*, Taipei. pp.659-752

Mohanty JN (2000) Classical Indian philosophy. Rowman and Littlefield, Lanham, PA

Sarkar BK (1916) (rpt. 1988). Chinese religion through Hindu Eyes: a study in the Tendencies of Asiatic Mentality. Asian Educational Services, New Delhi

Sen T (2018) India, China, and the world: a connected history. Oxford University Press, New Delhi

Sheel K (2006) Some observations on Chinese discourses on India. Indian History Congress Presidential Address (Countries other than India) at the 66th Session held in Visva Bharati, Sntiniketan

Sheel K (2014) Hu Shih and 'The Indianisation of China. China Report 50(3 August 2014):177–188

Tan C (ed) (1998) Across the Himalayan gap: an Indian quest for understanding China. Indira Gandhi National Centre for Arts. Gyan Publishing House, New Delhi

Tan C, Zhang M, Thakur R (eds) (2013) Across the Himalayan gap: a Chinese quest for understanding India. Konark Publishers, New Delhi

Theodor I, Yao Z (eds) (2014) Brahman and Dao: comparative studies of Indian and Chinese philosophy and religion. Lexington Books, New York

Yang A, Sheel K, Sheel R (2017) Thirteen months in China: aSubaltern Indian and the Colonial world. Oxford University Press, New Delhi

Chapter 5
How to Make Your Debt Count: Repaying Your Parents in Buddhist China

Yuet Keung Lo

It is perhaps well known that filial devotion is considered a cardinal virtue unique to Chinese culture in pre-modern China. Understood as such, it had been often translated into various personal, cultural, and even political practices. In early China, parents were generally glorified for giving birth and raising the children, as demonstrated in the *Odes* (*Shi* 詩), which around the second century BCE became canonized as one of the *Five Confucian Classics*. Typically, no concrete details about parental hardship or sacrifice were given in the glorification while filial children were expected to take good care of their living parents. Nothing much is known about the specifics of the good care in those times. Presumably, it was essentially about material sustenance. With regard to filial offspring, no later than the end of the third century BCE, they were anticipated to make a name for themselves often in a political career and bring honor to the family, as this particular aspiration was then documented in the *Classic of Filial Devotion* (*Xiaojing* 孝經). Filial sons were obliged to carry on the bloodline of the family; inability to produce male offspring was deemed the gravest violation of filiality. When their parents died, children observed rigorous mourning rituals and continued to pay regular sacrifices to them thereafter.

All this changed when Buddhism was introduced to China around the first century CE. As the foreign religion gradually gained acceptance, Buddhist converts began to serve their living parents in different ways and novel ideals of filiality gradually overrode indigenous norms of filial conduct. Filial devotion was also given new expression, as karmic reincarnation was believed to affect the post-mortem destiny of deceased parents. How one fully repaid filial debts became a critical concern. In time, the Buddhist influence even inspired religious Daoist conceptions of filial devotion that would work in tandem with the erstwhile foreign religion to change Chinese filial practices for good. This paper will outline the evolution of filial practices as a

Y. K. Lo (✉)
National University of Singapore, Singapore, Singapore
e-mail: yklo@nus.edu.sg

S. Mishra and R. Sheel (eds.), *India-China Dialogues Beyond Borders*,
https://doi.org/10.1007/978-981-99-4326-5_5

case study of cross-fertilization and mutual accommodation between Chinese culture and Buddhist religion in early medieval China.[1]

5.1 Lost in Translation

Ideas are merely ideas, and they remain unchanged unless they are prompted to be translated either linguistically or conceptually, or into actual behavior. Only then will they become embodied, different, operative, and relevant in real life. Such translation is never done in the vacuum; ideas are always rendered in particular sociohistorical contexts, whether between two different cultures or into cultural practices. A good case in point is the idea of *xiao* (孝) in Chinese culture, which is typically translated as filial piety in English. Seemingly innocuous, this time-hallowed and widespread interpretation is in fact problematic. For reasons to be explained below, it is better to render *xiao* as filial devotion.

It is actually a dubious if not erroneous claim that filial devotion was a cardinal virtue unique to Chinese culture in pre-modern China. The problem lies in the word "unique." Inasmuch as filial devotion concerns filial affection and dutiful conduct toward one's parents, it is simply not true that it is unique to Chinese culture even though it might well be the most fundamental virtue to the Chinese people—at least after Confucius (551–479 BCE) [*Analects* 1.2., Lau 1979: 59]. Yet if we compare how a Chinese person and, say, a Caucasian American, would show their filial affection and interact with their parents, how they would treat and care for them, especially when the latter get old and pass away, significant differences will very likely reveal themselves. This means that *practices* of filial devotion differ but the practitioners would be considered filial in their respective cultures. In this case, *xiao* and filial devotion are equivalent to cultural praxis. Filial affection is universal, while filial practices vary with cultures; indeed, filial practices, while informed by prevailing conceptions of filiality, could shape and help to reconceptualize what constitutes filiality over the long course of history. What makes filial devotion unique in Chinese culture is the way it was enshrined as a cardinal virtue. Thus, it is easy to understand that filial devotion is not given nearly as much importance in the white American context, and in fact, what constitutes filial devotion in pre-modern China would not at all be what is filial devotion in modern America.

Conceptually, *xiao* and filial devotion, or filial piety, as it is typically translated in English, are not exactly the same. In modern Chinese, *xiao* is normally expressed in a binome called *xiaoshun* (孝顺), which literally means filial (孝) *and* obedient (顺), or filial obedience as one may be tempted to render. Yet, it is obvious that the modern binome effectively reconceptualizes the dual notion of *xiao* and *shun*

[1] This paper does not attempt to compare the Chinese and the Buddhist notions of filiality on a full scale, though it must be noted that the changing conception of Chinese filiality did reflect the incorporation of Buddhist practices. For a comprehensive and ahistorical comparison with different findings, see Guang (2013).

and reduces them to a singular virtue called obedience, which plainly concerns the offspring; without specifying what constitutes *filial* obedience, *xiao* becomes a purely descriptive term. The binome, however, is by no means a modern invention because *xiao* and *shun* were paired up and used together as early as the sixth century BCE. It appears for the first time and only once in the *Sayings of the States* (*Guoyu* 國語), but its meaning is neither self-evident nor contextually precise to us today. Yet, as far as textual evidence is concerned, this relatively late accretion of "obedience" to filial conduct suggests that the notion of filiality was different in much earlier times. On *xiaoshun* in the *Guoyu* passage, the commentator Wei Zhao's 韋昭(201–273) said, "being respectful and restrained (*gongjian* 恭儉) is the way to serve one's parents" (*Guoyu* 1978: 529–530). No doubt, *shun* took on the peculiar meaning of "respectful and restrained" rather than the ordinary sense of "orderly" or "going along." Since the first century BCE during the Han dynasty until its end in the early third century, emperors were often commended for being *xiaoshun* when they were praised for following the political legacy of their predecessors (Ban 1964: 1.10.328). Meanwhile, at least one empress was criticized for not observing proper rituals and etiquettes in serving her mother-in-law (Fan 1973: 8.72.2324). Evidently, *xiaoshun* was then not understood as "obedience" in an ordinary sense. Similarly, commoners might be considered *xiaoshun* as well, though their pertinent conduct was not specified (Fan 1973: 1.5.211). It seems that Wei Zhao's understanding of *xiaoshun* was informed by the consensus of his time, which might or might not be identical with that in the sixth century BCE. In this connection, it is worth pointing out that in late imperial times (thirteenth century onward) *xiaoshun* could mean offering gifts in an attempt to curry favor with anybody except one's parents.[2] Clearly, the exact meaning of filial devotion needs to be contextualized and historicized.

A historical perspective must be kept in mind when unpacking the evolving meanings of *xiao*. While obedience is certainly not incompatible with filial conduct, the two notions are not identical. One can be obedient to one's superiors without being filial. Thus, there must be something unique to filial obedience. On the other hand, while piety means "fidelity to natural obligations (as to parents)," it also denotes "dutifulness in religion" but the connotation of obedience, if any, is tenuous. In contrast, devotion has a weaker religious connotation but it refers to "the fact or state of being ardently dedicated and loyal" (in Merriam-Webster.com. Retrieved 22 Dec, 2021, from https://www.merriam-webster.com/dictionary/devotion), thus its emphasis on dedication and loyalty is not quite the same as obedience. Recently, Henry Rosemont Jr. and Roger Ames render *xiao* as "family reverence" as it appears in the classic called *Xiaojing* 孝經 (which they translate as *Classic of Family Reverence*) (Rosemont and Ames 2009). The advantage of "reverence" lies in the fact that it is relatively free of religious connotations and denotes honor or respect—the reason why the translators opt for it. Ironically, as will be seen later, *xiao* in the *Classic* did have the explicit religious sense of dedication. While the meanings of honor and respect are captured in reverence, the crucial sense of obedience is missing. Thus, the translation of *xiao* into reverence is inadequate, if not inaccurate.

---

[2] For example, see *Xiyou ji* (n.d.), Chap. 42: 482.

It is now clear that when an idea travels through time and between languages, it is very easy to morph, often without anyone noticing it rather than just having a face-lift. The example I will show actually concerns a diachronic travel of *xiao* across two cultures of different origins in India and China, but even within the same culture of the same origin, ideas under the same name can differ tremendously from one period to the next. Thus, it is dangerous to assume that the idea represented by the same Sinitic graph always remains unchanged over time. *Xiao* is a good case in point.[3]

5.2 Early Conceptions of *Xiao* 孝 (Filiality)

The earliest Sinitic graph for *xiao* might have come from the oracle bone inscriptions from the Shang dynasty over 3,000 years ago, which apparently depicts an elderly person in a proper standing posture. To date, there is so far only one such sample available and it was used in a place name. The graph also appears in the inscription on a bronze vessel from around the same time where it signified the name of a person. Thus, it is not clear what the graph really meant on its own then as a semantic symbol.

Later in the Zhou dynasty (1046–256 BCE), the construction of the graph had changed; in bronze inscriptions, *xiao* now depicts a young person carrying an elderly one on his back. This suggests a human relationship where the elderly person needs physical care and is no longer independent. The composite graph might well be suggestive of the children's natural obligations to their living parents but more importantly, *xiao* had become at this time synonymous with another graph *xiang* (享), which means to make sacrificial offerings to one's deceased parents (Chen 2002: 247–268). Clearly, *xiang* was a religious ritual, and the construction of the graph indicates that it was performed in an ancestral shrine of some kind. As such, *xiao* clearly involved religious dedication and devoutness. It would seem that the filial care for living parents, which was natural in a family setting, gradually evolved into sacrificial offerings to *deceased* parents. The fact that *xiao* became synonymous with *xiang* provides the evidence. The distinctive nature of *xiao* had changed from mundane physical care to perhaps non-utilitarian reverential feelings of religiosity and the focus on the parent–child relation might have also shifted from this-worldly service to other-worldly benediction. Unlike care for living parents on a daily basis, sacrificial offerings require the bereaved offspring particular effort such as remembering the death anniversaries of their deceased parents and the dates of pertinent ritual services as well as the sustained determination to perform the sacrifices appropriately. All this presumes and necessitates the survivor's genuine affection for the departed. It characterizes the essence of filial devotion and even transforms itself into religious piety. However, it should be noted that such new practice of *xiao* was in all likelihood restricted to the male members of the royal family and the aristocratic

[3] This is indeed one of the major failings in Guang Xing's ahistorical survey (see note 1) of Chinese filiality vis-à-vis Buddhist notions of filial piety.

class. We do not have any evidence about the filial practices of the commoners of this time. Chronologically, the Shang and the Zhou were continuous, but they represented different cultures from the East and the West of early China. It is not clear if the difference in the conceptions and practices of *xiao* was a result of gradual evolution from one dynasty to another, or simply the unique expressions of two separate contemporaneous cultures from different regions. In any event, this new sense of religiosity integral to *xiao* was well preserved in the *Xiaojing* even 1,000 years later. Viewed in such light, the translation of *xiao* as family reverence loses its religious character.

As the *Xiaojing* explains it, the principle of *xiao*, allegedly in the voice of Confucius, runs as follows:

> Your physical person with its hair and skin are received from your parents. Vigilance in not allowing anything to do injury to your person is where *xiao* begins; distinguishing yourself and walking the proper way (*dao*) in the world; raising your name high for posterity and thereby bringing esteem to your father and mother- it is in these things that *xiao* finds its consummation. This *xiao*, then, begins in service to your parents, continues in service to your lord, and culminates in distinguishing yourself in the world (Rosemont and Ames 2009: 105).

The principle appears to be egalitarian and cuts across all social classes. Ironically, the practices of *xiao* are differentiated by social stratification, from the emperor to the hereditary lords, the ministers and high officials, the lower officials, and finally to the common people (Rosemont and Ames 2009: 106–108). Filiality now is constituted of physical care, obedience, and moral vigilance; most importantly, it can be and should be extended to political loyalty. This in fact might well have inspired the virtue of *xiaoshun* of the Han emperors about a century later. For the common people, the realization of *xiao* is totally down-to-earth and it requires only taking good care of the livelihood and material well-being of the parents.

Notably, the consummation of *xiao* does not concern the offspring's obligations to their deceased parents; it is all about this-worldly achievement. Yet, in the Chapter on "Sagely Governance" intended for the ruler, we are told that.

> Of old, the Duke of Zhou performed the *jiao* sacrifice on the outskirts of the capital to the first ancestor of Zhou, Hou Ji, to place him on a par with *tian*, and in the Hall of Brilliance he performed the ancestral sacrifice to is father, King Wen, to place him on a par with *shangdi*.[4] It was for this reason that all of the nobility within the four seas came each according to his office to assist in the sacrifices. How then could there be something in the excellence of the sages that surpasses *xiao*? (Rosemont and Ames 2009: 110).

No doubt only the emperor, Son of Heaven, was entitled to provide "sagely governance" to all under Heaven. It is clear that the emperor was mandated to perform ancestral sacrifice to his deceased father and put him on par with Lord on High (*shangdi* 上帝), in contrast to the practices of *xiao* pertaining to all other social classes. In this differentiated praxis, the religious and other-worldly nature of *xiao* persisted, at least as an ideology. It was an ideology because in third-century China

---

[4] As Rosemont and Ames explain in a footnote, "*Shangdi* is the ancestral and cultural deity of the Shang dynasty that was appropriated and used interchangeably with their own ancestral deity, *tian*, by the conquering Zhou dynasty." See Rosemont and Ames (2009: 117), note 14.

BCE, the feudal system of the Zhou dynasty had long collapsed and the aristocratic class had virtually become obsolete. The strict class stratification described in the *Xiaojing* was history long gone. In other words, this ideal picture of differentiated filiality was not grounded in historical reality.

If ideology could be considered the mirror image of reality, it is plausible that *xiao* had lost its religiosity by the time China was to be unified by the First Emperor of Qin in 221 BCE. In the *Xiaojing*, physical care, obedience, and moral vigilance were emphasized in the service of the living parents. By conviction as well as by extension, such personal cultivation would be translated into respect and loyalty (*zhong* 忠) to political superiors. This was a new dimension of *xiao* as China entered into the imperial age of a unified empire under the rulership of a single emperor.

Xiao thus evolved in response to this newfound political landscape.[5] When political allegiance was pledged by virtue of kinship as it was in the hereditary vassal system in Zhou feudalism, loyalty typically referred to an aristocrat's dedication to the public good and responsibility to his superiors as well as the common people under his charge. Under the imperial administration, however, unfailing commitment to the emperor even at the expense of one's life was promoted. The translation of *xiao* filiality into political loyalty, natural and innocuous as it might now seem, represented an innovative and practical shift toward a new system of governance. It was no coincidence that the term *zhongchen* (loyal official 忠臣) appeared for the first time around the third century BCE when the *Xiaojing* was composed. Beginning with the Han dynasty (205 BCE–220 CE), young children routinely would study the *Xiaojing* as one of their gateways to education. As a political career was exclusive to men, the practice of filiality was certainly differentiated between the sexes (Lo 2014: 293–330). And one of the criteria to recruit local officials was the filial character of the candidate.

5.3 Intrinsic Merit and Non-Transactional *Xiao*

So far, we have analyzed what is stated or implied about filial devotion in the *Xiaojing*. But what is not mentioned of it is perhaps even more important in light of how it would be advocated later in Chinese Buddhism. This, indeed, is a point that has been overlooked in the abundant studies on filial piety in Chinese Buddhism. Despite the fact that material support and quotidian care for one's parents are customary for filial conduct in pre-imperial times, owing to the hardship they had suffered for giving birth and raising their offspring, the effort to provide for them was always expressed within this philosophy as *voluntary*. Put bluntly, the desire to express gratitude was framed

[5] It should be noted that there were other views on filiality around the time of the composition of the *Xiaojing* in the third century BCE or earlier such as those found in the Daoist work *Zhuangzi* and the Legalist work *Hanfei Zi*, however, as emphasized in this paper, they could not respond and address the growing concerns and needs when the socio-political world evolved and underwent historic transformations when formerly feudalistic states gave way to a centralized bureaucratic empire.

and taught as self-motivated rather than by the need to conform to the prevailing social mores. The literal sense of indebtedness was missing. In other words, the genuine exercise of filial gratitude was commensurate with the unconditional kindness of one's parents; repaying one's parents was not a transaction or deemed as such.

From this, one can see the origin of the proverbial expression (*yu bao zhi de, haotian wangji* 欲報之德，昊天罔極), which was first recorded in the *Odes* and asserted that no filial gratitude was sufficient to requite parental kindness which was as boundless as heaven. The *Xiaojing* quotes Confucius as saying, "Of all the creatures in the world human being is the most noble. In human conduct, there is nothing more important than filial devotion" (*tiandi zhi xing, ren wei gui, ren zhi xing, mo dayu xiao* 天地之性, 人為貴。人之行, 莫大於孝) (Rosemont and Ames 2009: 110). It is perhaps precisely the self-motivated and non-utilitarian wish to repay one's parents that undergirded the Master's affirmation of human nobility. In fact, when a disciple asked about being filial, Confucius replied, "Nowadays for a man to be filial means no more than that he is able to provide his parents with food. Even hounds and horses are, in some way, provided with food. If a man shows no reverence, where is the difference?" (*Analects* 2.7, Lau 1979: 64).

It is therefore the genuine affection in the offspring's heart that really matters when they serve their parents; material support in itself does not count for filial devotion. The reason, as Confucius explained, is that one must "feel at ease" (*an* 安) in interacting with one's parents even when they are dead (*Analects* 17.21, Lau 1979: 147). Indeed, it is the genuine feeling itself that truly matters as an expression of gratitude, which is usually manifested in bodily gesture, physical behavior, and most challenging of all, facial countenance.[6] It is clear that Confucius was contrasting outward expressions with genuine reverence in the heart that seeks fulfillment in expressing itself.

Nearly two centuries later, Mencius echoed the same sentiment, saying:

> What is the most important duty? One's duty toward one's parents. What is the most important thing to watch over? One's own character. I have heard of a man who, not having allowed his character to be morally lost, is able to discharge his duties towards his parents; but I have not heard of one morally lost who is able to do so. There are many duties one should discharge, but the fulfillment of one's duty towards one's parents is the most basic. There are many things one should watch over, but watching over one's character is the most basic.
>
> Zeng Zi, in looking after Zeng Xi, saw to it that he always had meat and drink, and, on clearing away the food, always asked to whom it should be given. When asked whether there was any food left, he always replied in the affirmative. After Zeng Xi's death, when Zeng Yuan looked after Zeng Zi, he, too, saw to it that he always had meat and drink, but, on clearing away the food, never asked to whom it should be given. When asked whether there was any food left, he always replied in the negative. He did this so that the left-over food could be served up again. This can only be described as looking after the mouth and belly. Someone like Zeng Zi can truly be said to be solicitous of the wishes of his parent. One

[6] When his disciple Zixia asked about being filial, Confucius replied, "What is difficult to manage is the expression on the face. As for the young taking on the burden when there is work to be done or letting the old enjoy the wine and the food when these are available, that hardly deserves to be called filial" (*Analects* 2.8). See Lau, *The Analects*, p. 64.

does well if one can emulate the way Zeng Zi treated his parent (*Mencius* 4A19, Lau 1984: 125–126).

According to Mencius, serving one's parents is thus tantamount to preserving one's own personal integrity. It is not so much about conforming to customary filial obligations as fulfilling one's own life. Being filial is self-fulfilling in itself; it humanizes a person and makes him noble. Mencius glorified the son who yearns for his parents all his life and ascribed "Supreme Filiality" (*daxiao* 大孝) to him (*Mencius* 5A1, Lau 1984: 138–139). This undying yearning for the affective union with one's parents is in effect a continuous striving for self-fulfillment in filial capacity. Sage-king Shun yearned for his parents at the age of 50 and was venerated as the paragon of filiality, however, even he, in a strict sense, had yet to live up to the Mencian ideal because Supreme Filiality had to persist till one's demise. If the discharge of one's filial duty is reduced to a quotidian transaction, Mencius would certainly decry that one has lost one's moral character.

As indicated previously in the *Xiaojing*, the practice of filiality begins with the protection of the physical body with its hair and skin because it is received from the parents. Filial offspring would stay vigilant throughout their lives to make sure it is free from injury, particularly as a result of penal punishment for crimes. It is a lifelong commitment as much as is Supreme Filiality. The physical body is a "gift" from the parents; offspring are literally custodians entrusted to safeguard it and they are obliged to return it intact to their parents when they breathe their last.[7] This is entirely different from the idea of a debtor who seeks to pay back his creditor. Indebtedness is repaid when the beneficiary honors the benefactor by living an honorable life of moral integrity. In fact, the possible benefits of the parents are hardly mentioned in the performance of the offspring's filial conduct. In this sense, gratitude itself, albeit materialized in physical care, affection for the parents, and bringing honor to the family and clan, is ultimately personified in the offspring's humanity.

5.4 The Buddhist Transformation of *Xiao*

Given its rejection of the householder's life and advocacy of celibacy, Buddhism was often perceived to be against family when it came to China. For a long time in modern scholarship, the Buddhist promotion of filial devotion in China was considered only as an expedient strategy of cooptation in order to seek acceptance on Chinese soil; Buddhism was assumed to be against filiality. This is in fact a myth that has since been debunked. Filiality was a fundamental value in Buddhism; indeed, filial obligations were highly regarded and practiced by Indian Buddhists (Schopen 1984; Strong 1983). As Guang Xing has observed, "Filial piety was practiced by the early Indian Buddhists (1) as a way of requiting the debt to one's parents; (2) as a chief ethical

[7] Confucius' disciple Zeng Can asked his own students to check if his hands and feet were in good shape as he was about to die. When affirmed, he was relieved to say that he had ultimately avoided having his limbs injured (*Analects* 8.3). See Lau (1979: 92).

good action; and (3) as Dharma, the social order" (Guang Xing 2005). Nevertheless, as mentioned earlier, ideas do not exist in a cultural vacuum. Similar ideas of filiality reveal their differences when put into practice and may in fact turn out to be compatible. In the *Sutra in Forty-two Sections* 四十二章經,—possibly the earliest sutra translated into Chinese known to us today though later revisions and additions are evident,[8]—parts of one section say:

> It is better to feed one solitary buddha (*pratyekabuddha*) than to feed one billion saints. It is better to help to liberate one's parents with the teaching of the Honored Ones [namely, the Buddha, Dharma, and Sangha] in this lifetime than to feed ten billion solitary buddha. It is better to feed one Buddha, aspire to become a Buddha and save all sentient beings than to educate one hundred billion parents. To feed good-natured people will bring the most bountiful blessings. It is better to be filial to one's parents than to serve heaven and earth and the spirits; the parents are the most miraculous (CBETA T17n784_p0722c5-6).

While parents are put on the lofty pedestal just below the Buddha and filial devotion is vigorously promoted, its practice is decidedly different from that in China prior to Buddhism's arrival. Filial offspring should instruct their parents on the Buddhist teaching thereby helping them to liberate from the cycle of birth and death. To be sure, Confucius also instructed his disciples to give counsel to their parents but he was concerned about how it was done rather than preach about the benefits of such attempts. Filial offspring should be persistent yet considerate enough to negotiate with their parents, patient enough to find the most opportune moment to get their advice heard. Success would be the reward itself. Furthermore, success is not the end of counseling, which would continue until the death of either party. This is similar to the Mencian Supreme Filiality manifested in lifelong yearning for the parents. In contrast, the Buddhist attempt to help to instruct one's parents to attain deliverance from the cycle of rebirth, if successful, can be a one-off endeavor. It concerns the spiritual welfare of the parents; the benefits of the offspring are not mentioned. Nevertheless, the idea of earning filial merits for some sort of ultimate reward was novel to the Chinese, yet its transactional nature would prove to have a widespread and long-lasting impact on Chinese practices of filiality.[9]

In a scripture entitled *Sutra on the Difficulty to Repay Parental Kindness Spoken by the Buddha* (佛說父母恩難報經), translated by An Shigao 安世高 in the mid-second century, soon after he arrived in the capital of the Han regime in 168, the Chinese were introduced to the Buddhist idea of filiality. The scripture says,

> At that time the World-honored One said to the monks, "The father and mother do what is greatly beneficial to their son, giving him milk and food and rearing him up appropriately so that he can grow up. Even if he carries his father on his right shoulder and his mother on his left shoulder for one thousand years and let them defecate on him without resentment,

[8] Because of later revisions and additions, multiple versions of the scripture are now extant. I use the earliest one included in the critical edition in Chinese Buddhist Electronic Tripitaka Association (CBETA). For the dating and nature of the *Sutra in Forty-two Sections*, see Sharf in (Lopez 1996: 360–364) (a translation of the scripture is provided in 364–371).

[9] Robert Sharf claims that "the phrasing and context of the references to filial piety in this passage marks it as a Chinese insertion." He does not elaborate the reason but his claim cannot be substantiated. See Lopez (1996: 363).

> it is still not sufficient for him to requite their kindness. If the parents do not have faith in Buddhism, help them to cultivate it so that they can be free of vexation. If they do not follow the Buddhist precepts, teach them so that they can free of vexation. If they have not heard the Buddhist teaching, instruct them so that they can free of vexation ...." (CBETA T16n0684_778c28-779a19).[10]

In the original Indic scripture, the thrust of the Buddha's sermon is about how the offspring could and should requite parental kindness. No doubt that its translation provided Chinese converts a new avenue to achieve meaningful success in this endeavor. However, the truly radical lesson in this Buddhist scripture is that filiality can be *transactional*. The hyperbolic description of the hardship of the parents is precisely meant to throw into relief the extraordinary efficacy of the Buddhist teaching. Needless to say, this efficacy hinges on the truth of the Buddhist teaching itself on the ultimate meaning of life in order to make the filial attempt worthwhile in the first place.

An Shigao's translated message did not go unheeded. Although the hardship of the parents was emphasized, details in this short scripture of fewer than 400 words were brief with few specifics. Later, Chinese converts were so persuaded that some of them decided to embellish the details to propagate the Buddhist lesson for the benefit of the Chinese population. In the *Sutra on the Deep Kindness of the Parents* (父母恩重經), an apocryphal scripture written in China[11]—so apocryphal, in fact, that the author did not even bother to pretend it was an authentic scripture from India, it explains why the kindness of the parents is so deep: The Buddha said,

> When a person is born, he has mother and father as his parents. Without father, he would not be born; without mother, he would not be reared. Thus, he stays in the mother's womb for ten months and when the time is ripe, he will come out and be born with his mother on the grass. In nurturing him, mother and father put him in a cart filled with orchids and they hold him in their chests. They talk to him in a gentle voice but he just smiles without being able to speak. When hungry, he needs food but he would have no food without his mother; he needs to drink when thirsty but he would have no milk without his mother. ... If we try to measure the kindness of his mother, it is as boundless as heaven. Alas! How can we repay the kind mother? (CBETA T85n2887_1403b23-1403c06).[12]

It should be noted that the graphic details of parental kindness are now compared to the boundless heaven, the classic trope for the hardship and love of the parents in

---

[10] The same message in virtually identical description can be found in the *Kataññu Sutta* of the *Anguttaranikāya* in the Pāli Canon. See https://www.accesstoinsight.org/tipitaka/an/an02/an02.031.than.html. Chinese equivalent is found in the *Ekottarāgama*, see CBETA T02n0125_p0600c03-28.

[11] It is not clear when the scripture was composed but no later than the eighth century Buddhist monastics already lectured on it. A copy of the lecture (父母恩重經疏) by the monk Tiqing 體清 was brought back to Japan in 847 by the Japanese monk Ennin 圓仁 (794–864). See CBETA T55n2167_p1083b22.

[12] The apocryphal scripture in manuscript form was recovered from the Dunhuang Cave at the end of the nineteenth century. For a full translation, see by Arai (2005: 117–126). For a recent study, see Xing (2008). The author explains why the indigenous scripture was produced and compares it with An Shigao's *Sutra on the Difficulty to Repay Parental Kindness Spoken by the Buddha*, which he, too, considers authentic. His argument, however, is unconvincing.

the *Odes* dating back to the Zhou dynasty. Still, there is another important message in the scripture as follows:

> Any sentient beings who can cultivate merits for their parents by copying this scripture, burning incense, and paying homage to the Buddha, making offering to the Three Jewels and feeding the sangha; this person, rest assured, can requite the kindness of his parents (CBETA T85n2887_p1404a18-19).

Instead of instructing the parents on Buddhist teaching, the offspring now could requite their boundless kindness by transferring salvific merits to their parents and spreading it to the wider public and by performing religious rituals—perhaps precisely the same pious altruism that motivated the composition of the forgery. According to An Shigao's message, parents, with the repaying service of their filial offspring, still need to practice Buddhist teaching in order to attain liberation. But with the apocryphal teaching, they can now enjoy the payback without even embracing Buddhism themselves. The transactional nature of filiality is prominent. Furthermore, the religious dimension of filiality, which was stripped for all but the emperor in the *Xiaojing*, was reintroduced but for an entirely different purpose. Whereas the emperor performed ritual sacrifices for his deceased ancestors who were revered as if they were Heaven, Buddhist converts themselves participated in a religious realm where they repaid in Buddhist currency of salvific merits the profound kindness of their parents, deceased and living alike, as well as any other sentient beings with their blessings. Ultimately, the Buddhist religion itself would benefit in spreading its influence in China.

Still, the embellished details of the hardship of the parents in the *Sutra on the Deep Kindness of the Parents* were not deemed sufficient for the enlightenment of the general public. In the *Sutra about the Difficulty of Requiting the Deep Kindness of Parents* (佛說父母恩重難報經), an apocryphon attributed to the translation by Kumārajīva (344–413), a long month-by-month elaboration of the hardships and dangers of pregnancy is given, followed by a detailed explanation of the ten types of kindness bestowed by the mother on the child.[13] The intent, evidently, was to underscore the enormous debt the offspring owes his parents for his birth and for their unfailing love and care. Furthermore, this forgery goes on to point out all the ungrateful and heartless behaviors of the offspring and condemn them with the doom of grotesque sufferings in hell. To redeem himself, the offspring must, for the benefits of his parents, copy the forged scripture and recite it, repent and make offerings to the Three Jewels, as well as observe the precepts and a vegetarian diet. Only then can he be considered a filial offspring. Otherwise, he is merely a hell being.[14] With the *Sutra about the Difficulty of Requiting the Deep Kindness of Parents*, not only

---

[13] In an authentic Indic Buddhist scripture translated by the *Tripiṭaka* master Prajña from Kapisa in the Tang period (618–907), the suffering of the 10-month-long pregnancy was alluded to without the excruciating details. See *Dacheng bensheng xindi guan jing* (大乘本生心地觀經), in CBETA T03n0159_p0297a24-0297b19.

[14] The *Sutra about the Difficulty of Repaying the Deep Kindness of Parents* is not included in the Buddhist *Tripiṭaka*, or even CBETA. It is available at http://book.bfnn.org/books/0022.htm. A similar message about filial redemption can also be found in yet another indigenous scripture called the *Sutra on Requiting Parental Kindness Spoken by the Buddha* (佛說報父母恩德經). This has

did filial debt gain enormity and magnitude but also now destined to be settled even if the due date was deferred to the offspring's afterlife, with horrific consequences in hell. Naturally, the way to repay it would be vastly different from what it used to be in pre-Buddhist times while filiality as a cardinal virtue remained the same to Buddhist converts and non-believers alike.

5.5 Concluding Remarks

With the gradual yet steady success in reinterpretations of the practice of filial devotion, Buddhism continued to be assimilated into Chinese thinking and human interactions of every sort over time. Its increasing influence certainly became a threat to many scholar-literati and drew severe attacks from this sphere, particularly from the eighth century onwards. Yet, the contention should not be overemphasized as civil and earnest intellectual exchange on filial practices, among other concerns, between scholar-literati and the monastics was common. After all, intellectual or even ideological debates were usually spun out on rather circumscribed occasions, or merely on paper as it were, their impact on filial praxis among sons and daughters with genuine devotion or calculative motives were too insignificant to matter. The fact that such debates continued unabated, ironically, suggests that they had little to do with the common people who felt the practical need to follow the Buddhist advice on filial practices rather than seek a scholastic clarification on filiality. On the other hand, the new praxis of Buddhist filiality did not replace indigenous ones; this only goes to show that Buddhist proselytization and apologetics failed to achieve full if significant success. On another front, however, it inspired emulation from the religious Daoists who composed scriptures of their own that mimicked the Buddhist apocrypha. By the eleventh century, Chinese Buddhist monks such as Qi Song 契嵩 (1007–1072) argued that Buddhist praxis of filiality was indeed superior to native practices even as they attempted to reconcile them.[15] The outcome of the polemics, however, did not change the reality that the Buddhist praxis of filiality continued to thrive until the end of imperial times and in some significant way still prospers today in Chinese-speaking communities.

References

Anon (1978) *Guoyu*. Shanghai Guji Chubanshe, Shanghai

escaped the attention of all scholars working on the Sinification of Buddhist filiality. The scripture probably dated from the Tang period but was lost after the twelfth century. Fragments of it were quoted in a Buddhist work on rituals on repaying parental kindness. See CBETA ZW08n0068_p0215a08-216a12.

[15] For a study of Qi Song, see Morrison (2010)

Anon. *Kataññu Sutta* of the *Anguttaranikāya* (Pāli Canon). https://www.accesstoinsight.org/tipitaka/an/an02/an02.031.than.html. Accessed 22 Dec 2021

Arai K (2005) *Apocryphal scriptures*. Numata Center for Buddhist Translation and Research, Berkeley

Ban G (1964) 班固: *Han shu* 漢書 (History of the former Han). Zhonghua Shuju, Beijing

CBETA (Chinese Buddhist Electronic Tripitaka Association). https://www.cbeta.org. Accessed 22 Dec 2021

Chen Z (2002) 陳致: "Yuan xiao" 原孝 "On the Origin of Filiality" (in Chinese). 中國哲學與文化 Chin Philos Cult 8:247–268

Fan Y (1973) 范曄. *Hou Han shu* 後漢書 (History of the Latter Han). Zhonghua Shuju, Beijing

Guang X (2005) Filial Piety in Early Buddhism. *J Buddhist Ethics* 12(1):82–106

Guang X (2008) A Study of the Apocryphal Sutra *Fumu Enzhong Jing*. *Int J Buddhist Thought Cult* 11:105–146

Guang X (2013) Early buddhist and confucian concepts of filial piety: a comparative study. *J Oxf Cent Buddhist Stud* 4:8–46

Kumārajīva (attributed): *Sutra on Requiting Parental Kindness Spoken by the Buddha* (佛說報父母恩德經). http://book.bfnn.org/books/0022.htm. Accessed 22 Dec 2021

Lau DC (tr) (1979) The *Analects*. Penguin Classics, Harmondsworth, Middlesex, England

Lau DC (tr) (1984) *Mencius*. Penguin Classics, Harmondsworth, Middlesex, England

Lo YK (2014) On the dearth of filial daughters in Pre-Tang China (in Chinese). *Bull Inst Chin Philos Literat* 24:293–330

Lopez D (ed) (1996) *Religion of China in practice*. Princeton University Press, Princeton

Morrison EA (2010) The power of patriarchs: Qisong and Lineage in Chinese Buddhism. Volume 94 of Sinica Leidensia, Brill Academic Publishers, Leiden

Rosemont H Jr, Ames R (2009) *The Chinese Classic of Family Reverence: a philosophical translation of the Xiaojing*. University of Hawai'i Press, Honolulu

Schopen G (1984) Filial piety and the monk in the practice of Indian buddhism: A Question of 'Sinification' Viewed from the Other Side. *T'oung Pao* LXX: 110–126

Sharf R (1996) The scripture in forty-two sections. In: Lopez Jr. DS (ed) *Religion of China in Practice*. Princeton University Press, Princeton, pp 360–371

Slater P, Wiebe D (eds) *Traditions in Contact and Change: Selected Proceedings of the XIVth Congress of the International Association for the History of Religions*, vol 3. Wilfred Laurier University Press, Waterloo

Strong J (1983) Filial piety and buddhism: The Indian Antecedents to a 'Chinese' Problem. In: Slater P, Wiebe D (eds) *Traditions in Contact and Change: Selected Proceedings of the XIVth Congress of the International Association for the History of Religions*, vol 3. Wilfrid Laurier University Press, Waterloo, pp 171–186

Wu C (n.d.) *Xiyou ji* (Journey to the West 西遊記). Xingzhou Shijie Shuju, Singapore

Chapter 6
Paramārtha, the Predecessor of Xuanzang and His Contribution to Chinese Buddhism

Lalji 'Shravak'

6.1 Introduction

In the history of Buddhism in China as well as in the history of Chinese translation of Buddhist texts, Paramārtha has played a significant role and has an important place. He is considered one of the greatest translators of Buddhist scriptures in Chinese. His translated texts brought about fresh waves of ideas on the scene of Chinese Buddhism. It is very important to note that before traveling to India Xuanzang studied some important texts translated by Paramārtha and after returning to China he also translated those texts again.

6.2 Biography of Paramārtha[1]

Paramārtha (499–569 CE) was an Indian monk from Ujjainī or Ujjaina (優禪尼 You-chan-ni) of Central India. It is said that his personal name was Kulanātha (拘那羅陀 Ju-na-luo-tuo) which means "Refuge of the Family or Clan".[2] His name is translated as Qinyi 親依". His religious name was Paramārtha (波羅末陀 Bo-luo-mo-tuo), which means "Ultimate Goal" and it is translated as Zhendi (眞諦).[3] He

[1] Paramartha's biography is included in *Xu Gaoseng chuan* (續高僧傳, T. 50. 2060, pp 429/c/6–432/a/9, *Continued Biographies of Eminent Monks*), which was compiled by Daoxuan (道宣596–667) of the Tang Dynasty in A.D. 645. It is in continuation of *Gaoseng chuan* (高僧傳, T. 50. 2059, *Biographies of Eminent Monks*). Daoxuan has recorded approximately 340 eminent monks and 60 of their assistants, from A.D. 520 to 641.

[2] Huikai 慧愷 (T. 50. 2059, p 161/b/2) has referred the name as Ju-luo-na-ta 俱羅那他.

[3] T. 50. 2060, pp. 429/c/6-7; Paul 1982: 47.

L. 'Shravak' (✉)
Banaras Hindu University, Varanasi, India
e-mail: laljis@gmail.com

S. Mishra and R. Sheel (eds.), *India-China Dialogues Beyond Borders*,
https://doi.org/10.1007/978-981-99-4326-5_6

is known in China by his translated religious name as Zhēndì (真諦 Paramaartha). Paramārtha belonged to the lineage of Guṇamati and Sthiramati of the Vijñānavāda School of Valabhī Mahāvihāra.[4]

Paramārtha was born in A.D. 499.[5] In the propagation of Buddhism, the first destination of Paramārtha was Funan,[6] modern Cambodia. Emperor Wu (梁武帝) of the Southern Liang Dynasty (南梁, 502–57)[7] sent his ambassador to Funan (扶南) to bring Paramārtha to the Liang imperial court. Paramārtha arrived at Guangdong (廣東 the then called Nanhaijun 南海郡) in 546 CE at the age of 48.[8]

Paramārtha was welcomed by Emperor Wu in 548 CE. At the time of the arrival of Paramārtha, Emperor Wu showed an extremely rare reverence to him and had an audience with him in the Baoyun temple (寶雲寺). At the time of their meeting, Paramārtha was 50 years old and Emperor Wu was 85 years old. Only 2 months after the arrival of Paramārtha at Jianye (建業)[9] (Nanjing), the rebellion had started by Hou Jing (侯景). Rebellious general Hou Jing captured the capital Jianye in 549 and held both Emperor Wu and Crown Prince Xiao Gang (蕭綱)[10] under his power. In 549 CE, Emperor Wu died of starvation while he was under house arrest. It made the Paramārtha unsettled (Paul 1982: 50). After the death of Emperor Wu, Crown Prince Xiao Gang took the throne as Emperor Jianwen of Liang (梁簡文帝), but he

---

[4] Takakusu (1956: 84) considers the three lines (lineages) of the transmission of Yogācāra idealism after Vasubandhu. The first was the line of Dignāga, Asvabhāva, Dharmapāla, Śīlabhadra, etc. The transmission center of this lineage was Nālandā Mahāvihāra. The second was the line of Guṇamati, Sthiramati. Center of the transmission of this line was Valabhī Mahāvihāra. Paramārtha belonged to this lineage. The third was line of Nanda, whose tenet was followed by Jayasena and Paramārtha also.

[5] Paul (1982: 39; 1984: 14) stated that approximately 150 years after the Yogācarin philosopher Vasubandhu, Paramārtha was born, which needs more clarification.

[6] At the time of Paramārtha, Funan was an ancient Indianised state from the first to sixth century CE. It was a centre of international trade. This region was very prosperous through maritime trade and agriculture. It incorporates modern Cambodia, parts of Thailand, and the lower part of the Mekong delta in Vietnam.

[7] Emperor Wu had originally been the follower of Daoism. In 504 CE, he converted as Buddhist and became ardent follower of Buddhism. He constructed many Buddhist temples. The most famous one was the Tongtai temple (同泰寺), constructed in 521–527 CE, which drained the state treasury. In 527 CE, at the age of 63, Emperor Wu became a Buddhist monk for some time. He used to be engaged with Buddhist practices. He used to participate in the Dharma Assemblies. In order to raise donations from wealthy aristocratic families for the temple fund, in 546 and 547, he followed unusual practices of surrendering himself as a temple servant for a day and performed the acts of a temple servant. Because of these zealous practices, Emperor Wu was praised as *Pu-sa tianzi* (菩萨天子, The Bodhisattva, Son of Heaven). Emperor Wu made a sincere effort to seek out Buddhist missionaries and donated large sums of money to make Buddhism prosperous (Paul 1982: 42–43; 1984: 16–17).

[8] Paul, 1982: 41-42; 1984 : 24; JIABS, 31, 2008 (10): 144; *Zhongguo Fojiao* (中國佛教) (协会编), 二, p 86[6]. According to the information of *Zhongguo Fojiao* 中國佛教(二, p 86[6-7]), Paramārtha arrived at Guangdong (廣東) in 546 CE at the age of 50.

[9] It is also known as Jiankang (建康). It was the capital city of the Eastern Wu (229–265 and 266–280 CE), the Jin dynasty (317–420 CE), the Southern Dynasties (420–552), and the Chen dynasty (557–589 CE). In modern time, it is known as Nanjing.

[10] Xiao Gang (蕭綱) was known as Emperor Jianwen of Liang (梁簡文帝).

was completely under the control of Hou Jing. In 551, Hou Jing overthrew Emperor Jianwen and put him under house arrest. Finally, Emperor Jianwen was suffocated by Peng Jun (彭雋) and Wang Xiuzuan (王修纂). Hou Jing made Xiao Dong (蕭棟), the Prince of Yuzhang, emperor. Xiao Dong was also entirely under the control of Hou Jing. In 551, Hou Jing overthrew Emperor Xiao Dong and declared himself the Emperor of Han.

After the unfortunate death of Emperor Wu, the patronage of Paramārtha was disrupted and the forthcoming political crisis upset him. Paramārtha fled to Fuchun (富春), in Zhejiang (浙江). Liu Yuanzhe (陸元哲), the regional governor of Fuchun and a recent convert to Buddhism patronized Paramārtha. At this time, there was continuous warfare and famine, which caused to decline of the *Dharma* (Buddhism). But, under the patronage of Governor Liu Yuanzhe, Paramārtha got the opportunity to resume his translation activities there with the assistance of Śramaṇa Baoqiong (寶瓊 504–584) and other 20 accomplished monks. He initiated the translation of the *Shiqi di lun* (十七地論 *Saptadaśabhūmiśāstra, Treatise on the Seventeen Bodhisattva Stages*) during the fourth year of Taiqing 太清 (550 CE).[11] He completed only five chuan, his work was interrupted again by the same political trouble.[12] Rebel Chief Hou Jing (侯景) came to know the activities of Paramārtha at Fuchun, he summoned him to court at Jianye. On the invitation of Hou Jing Paramārtha returned to the capital city again in 552 CE (Paul 1982: 51; 1984: 26).

Hou Jing also executed Xiao Fangzhu, a son of Xiao Yi (蕭繹).[13] Forces of Xiao Yi attacked Jianye (Jiankang) under the command of General Wang Sengbian (王僧辯) and General Chen Baxian (陳霸先). Hou Jing was defeated by Chen Baxian and fled from Jiankang.[14] In 552, Xiao Yi declared himself emperor as Emperor Yuan of Liang (梁元帝 Liang Yuandi), but he was still staying at Jiangling (江陵, in modern Jingzhou, Hubei). During the reign of Emperor Yuan, Paramārtha settled at Jianye (Nanjing) in Zhengguan temple (正觀寺) and with the assistance of the 20 monks translated the *Suvarṇaprabhāsa-sūtra* (金光明經 *Jin guangming jing*).[15]

In 554, forces of the Emperor Gong of Western Wei (西魏恭帝 537–557) attacked Jiangling and imprisoned Emperor Yuan. In the beginning of the year 555, Emperor Yuan was put to death. Emperor Gong of Western Wei declared Xiao Cha (蕭詧), a nephew of Emperor Yuan, the Emperor of Liang (Emperor Xuan 宣帝)[16] to be a vassal to Western Wei. Both the Generals of Emperor Yuan, Wang Sengbian, and

[11] The text is now lost (Paul 1982: 50).

[12] Paul 1982: 50; 1984: 26; T. 2060: 429/c/20–25; *Zhongguo Fojiao* (中國佛教) (二), p. 86 [10-11].

[13] Xiao Yi was the seventh son of the Emperor Wu, founder of Liang dynasty. He was made the Prince of Xiang dong. By 547, he was made the governor of the Jing Province (荊州, modern Central and Western Hubei).

[14] Hou Jing was killed by his guard Yang Kun (羊鵾).

[15] Paul, 1982: 52; 1984: 27; T. 2060: 429/c/25–29; *Zhongguo Fojiao* (中國佛教) (二), p. 86[14]. For detailed discussion regarding the translation of *Suvarṇaprabhāsa-sūtra* (金光明經 *Jin guangming jing*), see Paul 1982: 52—53; 1984: 27.

[16] Since Xiao Cha (蕭詧) took the Liang throne with the support of Emperor Gong of Western Wei, his regime is known as the Western Liang dynasty and he is known as Emperor Xuan of (Western) Liang (西)梁宣帝).

Chen Baxian did not recognize Xiao Cha as emperor. They invited Xiao Fangzhi (蕭方智), 12 years old son of Emperor Yuan and the Prince of Jin'an, to Jiankang, and formally declared him as the successor of Emperor Yuan to take imperial powers with the title Prince of Liang.

Emperor Wenxuan of Northern Qi (北齊文宣帝 526–559), forced Wang Sengbian to accept Xiao Yuanming (蕭淵明), cousin of Emperor Yuan and Duke of Jian'an (建安公), as Emperor of Liang. On the promise that Xiao Fangzhi will be declared as crown prince, finally Wang Sengbian accepted Xiao Yuanming as emperor, but Chen Baxian, another General of Emperor Yuan was not agreed with this settlement. He launched a surprise attack on Wang and forced him to surrender. On that night Chen Baxian put Wang Sengbian and his son Wang Wei (王頠) to death. He overthrew Xiao Yuanming and declared Xiao Fangzhi emperor, as Emperor Jing of Liang (梁敬帝; 543–558), and took the regency over Xiao Fangzhi. In 557, He seized the throne from Emperor Jing and declared himself as Emperor Wu. Chen Baxian (陳霸先) brought peace, law, and order to the region.[17]

Paramārtha also had to bear the tensions of such a politically sensitive situation for very long. Psychological as well as scholarly difficulties affected his work of rendering the original Sanskrit text into Chinese. From 554 to 557 CE, Paramārtha resided in three different places. In 554 CE, he stayed at Baotian temple (寶田寺) in Yuzhang (豫章), and with the help of Huixian (慧顯) and ten other monks completed the translations of the *Mi-le xiasheng jing* (彌勒下生經 *Sūtra of Maitreya's Descent* [*from Heaven*]) and the *Ren wang pan-ruo jing* (仁王般若經 *Sūtra of the Perfection of Wisdom of the Benevolent King*). He moved to Xinwu (新吳) from Yuzhang, where he resided at the Meiye temple (美業寺) and translated the *Jiu shiyi zhi* (九識義記 *Commentary on the Theory of Nine Consciousnesses*) in two *chuan*. From there, he moved to Shixing (始興), where he stayed at Jianxing temple (建興寺) and translated the *Ta-Cheng qi xin lun* (大乘起信論 *Awakening of Faith in Mahāyāna*).[18] It is also said that at Shixing (始興), Paramārtha translated the *Suixiang lunzhong shiliu di shu* (隨相論中十六諦疏 *A Commentary on the Theory of Sixteen Truths found in the Lakṣaṇānusāra Śāstra*).[19] In the year 557, Paramārtha completed the translation of the *Wushangyi jingshu* (無上依經疏 *Anuttarāśraya-sūtra, Supreme Foundation Sūtra*). (Paul 1982: 55–56; 1984: 30).

In the year 558, Paramārtha returned to Yuzhang for a third time[20] again and resided at Qiyin temple (栖隐寺), then proceeded toward Linchuan (臨川), Jin'an (晋安). At Linchuan, he translated two treatises, *Zhongbian fenbie lun* (中邊分别論, *Madhyāntavibhāgaśāstra, Discernment of the Middle and Extremes*) and the

---

[17] Chen Baxian (陳霸先) founded Chen Dynasty (陳, 557–589) and declared himself as Emperor Wu of Chen (陳武帝; Chen Wudi; 503–559). He was the first emperor of this dynasty.

[18] Paul, 1982: 54; 1984: 29;*Zhongguo Fojiao* (中國佛教) (二), p. 86[15-17].

[19] This text is extant as the *Suixiang lun* 隨相論, T. 1641 (13). It is a commentary on the *Abhidharmakośa* attributed to Guṇamati (Funayama 2008 (10): 149; Ui, 1965: 96–97).

[20] Paul (1982: 56) has mentioned "third time", but in her other work (Paul 1984: 30) she has mentioned "'Second Time".

Weishi lun (Treatise on Consciousness-Only) of Vasubandhu.[21] From Linchuan, Paramārtha moved to the port city Jin'an (晋安) and resided at Foli temple (佛力寺).[22] There he translated *Zhenglun shiyi* (正論釋義 *An Explanation of Correct Doctrines*).[23]

In 561, he traveled by small boat from Jin'an to Liang'an (梁安).[24] He resided at Jianzao temple (建造寺) and translated *Jiejie jing* (解节經) and other texts.[25]

Paramārtha became upset with the political circumstances. In 562, he decided to leave China. From Liang'an (梁安), he went to the West in order to return to his country. Unexpectedly, wind direction changed and he returned to Guangzhou (廣州) in 563CE.[26] There Prefectural Governor Ou Yangwei (欧阳頠) invited him to reside at Zhizhi temple (制旨寺). On the request of Huikai, OuYangwei, and others he agreed and residing there produced some of his most important and best-known works, the translation of *Saṃgrahaśāstra* (*She Dacheng lun* 摄大乘論), *MahāyānaVijñaptimātraśāstra* (大乘唯識論) and *Viṃśatikā* (唯識二十論).[27] At Guangzhou Fatai (法泰), Sengzong (僧宗), Huikai (慧愷), and others went to the Zhizhi temple to take the instruction from Paramārtha's teachings.[28] In 564, he translated and explained [*Abhidharma*] *Kośaśāstra* (*Ju-she lun* 俱舍論). In 566 at Jinming temple (晋明寺), he explained *Ju-she lun* to Huikai (慧愷), Sengren 僧忍, and others. In 567 again explained *She dacheng lun* (摄大乘論) to Sengzong (僧宗), Fazhun (法准), and others. In 568 at Nan Hai (南海), on the request of Fatai (法泰), he translated *Lü ershier mingliao lun* (律二十二明了論).[29]

By the year 563 CE, Paramārtha became very famous throughout southern China. Many eminent monks, traveled from long distances, and reached out to him to hear his teachings on the *Saṃgrahaśāstra*. There developed an ardent group of disciples, including Huikai (慧愷), Sengzong (僧宗), Jingshao (警韶), Fakan (法侃), and Fatai (法泰).[30]

After 5 years of rigorous translation work, an unfortunate event occurred in the life of Paramārtha. In 568 CE, Paramārtha felt extremely tired and hopeless with his life. He went into the mountains north of Nanhai [Canton] and intended to commit suicide. He was retrieved with the effort of Huikai [Zhikai 智愷] and the governor

---

[21] Paul 1982: 56; 1984: 30–31.

[22] Paul 1982: 56; 1984: 31; *Zhongguo Fojiao* (中國佛教) (二), p. 86[18-19] has not mentioned Linchuan (臨川).

[23] Paul 1982: 57; 1984: 31.

[24] Paul (1982: 56; 1984: 31) has mentioned that Ui Hakuju, (*Indo tetsugakukenkyu*, VI, pp 24–25) identified Liang'an with Jin'an.

[25] *Zhongguo Fojiao* (中國佛教)(二), p 86[21–22.]

[26] *Zhongguo Fojiao* (中國佛教) (二), p 86[23]–87[1].

[27] *Zhongguo Fojiao* (中國佛教) (二), p 87[1–3].

[28] Paul 1982: 56; 1984: 31.

[29] *Zhongguo Fojiao* (中國佛教) (二), p. 87[3–7].

[30] Paul 1982: 58; 1984: 32–33.

OuYanghe and was persuaded to stay at Wangyuan temple (王園寺) with his closest disciples Sengzong and Huikai.[31]

Two months later, in 568 CE, Huikai, the favorite disciple of Paramārtha, died. Paramārtha grieved deeply for him. He continued the translation of the *Abhidharmakośa,* without the assistance of Huikai. Soon he himself became very sick. On February 12, 569, at noon, 5 months after the death of Huikai, Paramārtha died at the age of 71.[32] The next day his body was cremated and a *stupa was* erected at Chaoting (潮亭 near Canton). After the death of Paramārtha, his disciples carried out the work and lineage of Paramārtha.

6.3 Translation Works of Paramārtha and Their Impact on Chinese Buddhism

It is very interesting to note from the biography of Paramārtha that because of the political disturbances, Paramārtha moved from province to province and from one place to another. Wherever he stayed, he continued his translation work from Sanskrit into Chinese. From his arrival in China in 546 during the Southern Liang Dynasty till his death in 569 during the Southern Chen Dynasty (南陳, 557–89), in these 23 years, Paramārtha translated 64 texts in 278 fascicles into Chinese. Of these 64 translated texts, only 30 are extant in Chinese. I would like to mention some of the most important translated texts, which are as follows:

In 550 CE, 如實論 *Rushi lun, Tarkaśāstra*; T. 1633, Nj. 1252.

In 553 CE, 大乘起信論 *Dacheng qixin lun* (*Mahāyānaśraddhotpādaśāstra*, Treatise on Awakening the Faith in the Mahāyāna, written by Aśvaghoṣa 馬鳴); T. 1666, Nj. 1250.

In 557 CE, 無上依經 *Wushangyijing* (*Anuttarāśrayasūtra*, Sūtra of the Unsurpassed Reliance, in 2 fascicles; T. 0669, Nj. 259.

In 557–559 CE, 佛性義 *Foxingyi* (*Buddha svabhāvārtha, Treatise on Buddha Nature*) in 4 fascicles, Written by Vasubandhu; T. 1610, Nj.1220.

In 557–569 CE, 三無性論 *San wuxing lun, Tryasvabhāvaśāstra*?; T. 1617, Nj. 1219.

In 557–569 CE, 中邊分別論 *Zhongbian fenbie lun, Madhyāntavibhāgaśāstra*; T. 1599, Nj. 1248.

In 557–569 CE, 佛阿毗曇經 *Fo A-pi-tan jing, Buddhābhidharmasūtra*; T. 1482, Nj. 1107.

In 557–569 CE, 十八空論 *Shiba konglun, Aṣṭādaśaśūnyatāśāstra*; T. 1616, Nj. 1187.

In 557–569 CE, 十八部論 *Shiba bulun, AṣṭādaśaNikāyaśāstra*; T. 2032, Nj. 1284. Etc.

In 557–569 CE, 四諦論 *Sidi lun, Catursatyaśāstra*; T. 1647, Nj. 1261.

---

[31] T 2060: 430a27-b3.; *Zhongguo Fojiao* (中國佛教) (二), p 87[8-10]; Paul 1982: 59–60; 1984: 34.

[32] *Zhongguo Fojiao* (中國佛教)(二), p. 87 [8–14]; Paul 1982: 60; 1984: 35.

In 557–569 CE, 大乘唯識論, *Dacheng Weishi lun; Mahāyāna Vijñaptimātraśāstra*; T. 1589, Nj. 1239.

In 557–569 CE, 大宗地玄文本論, *Dazong dixuanwen benlun Mahāyānabhūmiguhyavācāśāstra*; T. 1669, Nj. 1299.

In 557–569 CE, 寶行王正論 *Baoxing wangzheng lun*; T. 1656, Nj. 1253.

In 557–569 CE, 決定藏論 *Jueding zanglun, Piṭakaviniścayaśāstra*(?), T. 1584, Nj. 1235.

In 557–569 CE, 解拳論 *Jiequan lun*; T. 1620 Nj. 1255.

In 557–569 CE, 轉識論 *Zhuanshi lun* (*Pravṛttivijñānaśāstra*?);T. 1587, Nj. 1214.

In 557–569 CE, 遺教經論 *Yijiao jinglun* (*Śāsanasūtraśāstra*?);T. 1529, Nj. 1209.

In 557–569 CE, 隨相論 *Suixianglun, Lakṣaṇānusāraśāstra*; T. 1641, Nj. 1280

In 557–569 CE, 顯識論 *Xianshi lun, Vijñānanirdeśaśāstra*?;T. 1618, Nj. 1217.

In 557–569 CE, 無相思塵論 *Wuxiang sichen lun, Ālambanaparikṣāśāstra* of Diṅnāga; T. 1619, Nj. 1172

In 558 (559) CE, 立世阿毗曇論 *Li shi A-pi-tan lun, Lokasthiti Abhidharmaśāstra*; T. 1644, Nj. 1297.

In 558–559 CE, 解節經 *Jiejie jing, Sandhinirmocanasūtra*;T. 0677, Nj. 156.

In 562 CE, 金剛般若波羅蜜經 *Jingang ban-ruo bo-luo-mi jing Vajracchedikā Prajnāpāramitā Sūtra, Diamond Sūtra*); T. 0237, Nj. 12.

In 563 CE, 攝大乘論 *Shedacheng lun* (*Mahāyānasaṃgrahaśāstra* of Asaṅga's (無著), *Treatise on Adopting the Mahāyāna*; in 3 fascicles; T. 1593, Nj. 1183.

In 563 CE, 攝大乘論釋 *She dacheng lunshi* (*Mahāyānasaṃgrahaśāstravyākhyā*) in 18 fascicles, Chinese version of Vasubandhu's *Commentary on Mahāyānasaṃgrahaśāstra*; T. 1595, Nj. 1171.2.

In 563 CE, 廣義法门經 *Guangyi famen jing* (*Arthavistara Dharmadvārasūtra*, Sūtra of the Dharma Door with a Broad Meaning; T. 0097, Nj. 587.

In 564–567 CE, 阿毗達磨俱舍釋論 *A-pi-da-mo ju-she shilun* (Commentary on the Treasury of the Abhidharma (*Abhidharma-kośa-bhāṣya*) in 22 fascicles; T. 1559, Nj. 1269.

In 568 CE, 律二十二明了論 *Lü ershier mingliao lun;* T. 1461, Nj. 1139, (*Vinaya dvāviṃśatisphuṭārthaśāstra*?[33] of Buddhatrāta).

On the basis of the deep studies of some texts, there developed Schools in the history of Chinese Buddhism.

6.3.1 *A: Translation of* Abhidharmakośabhāṣya *and Foundation of Kośa School*

Though, by the beginning of the fifth century CE, many *Abhidharma* texts of Sarvāstivāda namely *Abhidharmāṣṭagranthaśāstra, Abhidharmāmṛtaśāstra, Vibhāṣāśāstra, Ārya Vasumitra Bodhisattva Saṅgītiśāstra, Satyasiddhiśāstra,*

---

[33] (?) Question mark, put after the title of the text, indicates that this Sanskrit title is not available to me and it is reconstructed by me on the basis of its Chinese title.

Abhidharmahṛdayaśāstra, Sāriputrābhidharmaśāstra were translated into Chinese in North China, but the teaching of *Abhidharma* could not become popular. After the translation of *Miśrakābhidharmahṛdayaśāstra* of Dharmatrāta[34] by Saṅghavarman in 434 CE in South China, *Abhidharma* studies became popular and spread widely. This very text became so popular and was studied so deeply and extensively that a new "Abhidharma School (毗曇宗)" came into existence in South China.[35] It represents the Gandhara branch of Sarvāstivādins.[36] We can consider this as the first phase of the translation and studies of *Abhidharma* texts.

The second phase of the translation of *Abhidharma* texts started with the arrival of Paramārtha in South China. He introduced the *Abhidharmakośabhāṣya-śāstra* (T. 1559) of Vasubandhu for the first time in China. He and his disciples popularized the studies of this important text. *Abhidharmakośa* was studied so extensively and seriously that this led to the foundation of the realistic Kośa School in China (Takakusu 1956: 82). In the course of time, this newly developed school replaced the Abhidharma School. It was also known as Realistic School (Takakusu 1956: 63). It is interesting to note that the Abhidharma texts were initially translated in North China, but its deep studies were done in South China and there developed Abhidharma and Kośa Schools. He also translated *Catursatyaśāstra, Lakṣaṇānusāraśāstra. Aṣṭādaśa-nikāyaśāstra, Abhidharmakośavyākhyāśāstra, Lokasthityabhidharmaśāstra* into Chinese.

6.3.2 B: Translation of **Mahāyānasaṃgrahaśāstra** *and Foundation of Saṃgrahaśāstra School*

Among the translations by Paramārtha, the translation of *Mahāyāna-saṃgraha-śāstra* (T. 1593) of Asaṅga (無著 Wu-zhe) and *Mahāyānasaṃgrahaśāstrabhāṣya* (T. 1595) of Vasubandhu, a commentary on Asaṅga's treatise, were very important. These are the key Buddhist texts belonging to the Yogācāra School, in which a systematic exposition of the Yogācāra system is explained.

Yogācāra text was introduced for the first time in North China by Dharmakṣema (曇無讖 Tan-wu-chen) in 414–421, and it was followed by Guṇavarman (求那

---

[34] The name of the work of Dharmatrāta in Chinese translation is *Za a-pi-tan xinlun* (雜阿毗曇心論), which is not available in Sanskrit original. This work is based upon the work of Dharmaśreṣṭhin named as in Chinese translation *A-pi-tan xin lun*. For detail on this '*Miśrakābhidharmahṛdayaśāstra*' nomenclature Cf. Lalji 'Shravak'; 1995, "Za a-pi-tan xin lun: An Introduction (in Hindi), *The Indian Journal of Buddhist Studies*; Vol. 7, No. 1 & 2,Varanasi, pp.52-82; and Lalji 'Shravak'; 2001, "*Miśrakābhidharmahṛdayaśāstra* : Fusion of Bahirdeśaka and Kāśmīra Abhidharma Traditions", in *The Indian International Journal of Buddhist Studies*; No. 2, Varanasi; pp.71-84; Lalji 'Shravak', 2006, *Miśrakābhidharmahṛdayaśāstra (Za A-pi-tan xin lun 雜阿毗曇心論),* Critical study and its translation from Chinese into Hindi.

[35] Cf. Lalji 'Shravak', 2019, "Contribution of *Miśrakābhidharma-hṛdaya-śāstra* (Za a-pi-tan xin lun 雜阿毗曇心論) in the Development of the Abhidharma School in China" published in the *Journal of Buddhist Studies,* Vol. XVI, pp 129–140, ed. Bhikkhu KL Dhammajoti, Centre for Buddhist Studies, Colombo, Sri Lanka and Buddha-Dharma Centre of Hong Kong. (ISSN: 1391-8443).

[36] Takakusu 1956:14&63; Willemen, Dessein, Cox, 1998: 266.

跋摩 Qiu-na-ba-mo, 431 CE), Guṇabhadra (求那跋陀羅 Qiu-na-ba-tuo-luo, 435–443 CE), Bodhiruci (菩提流支 Pu-ti-liu-zhi, 513–14 CE) who translated different Yogācāra texts in which the *Ālayavijñāna* was introduced and explained.

Buddhaśānta (佛陀扇多 Fo-tuo-shan-duo) introduced the developed Yogācāra philosophy in North China in 520 CE. He translated *Mahāyāna-saṃgrahaśāstra* (T. 1592) of Asaṅga for the first time, in which the Yogācāra ideaology was greatly developed. Theories of *Ālayavijñāna, Vijñaptimātra* were also elaborated in this text.

In spite of the translations of these Yogācāra texts in North China, the study of Yogācāra philosophy could not develop. Paramārtha (眞諦 Zhen di) translated *Mahāyānasaṃgrahaśāstra* (T. 1593)[37] of Asaṅga and *Mahāyānasaṃgrahaśāstrabhāṣya* (T. 1595)[38] of Vasubandhu, for the first time in south China. After this translation, the Yogācāra ideology received firm grounds to develop on Chinese soil. He also translated *Vijñaptimātratāśastra* (T. 1589)[39] of Vasubandhu, which also became very popular.

Paramārtha, in his translation and interpretation, established the taintless consciousness (*amalavijñāna*) as the ninth consciousness (*vijñāna*) and regarded it to be a separate function of *vijñāna* different from the *Ālaya-vijñāna*. (Takasaki 1983: 46). Paramārtha wrote an independent work *Jiu shiyi ji* (*A Note on the Meaning of the Nine Vijñānas*). This work is now lost (Takasaki 1983: p 44). Diana Paul (2003:489) has stated that Paramārtha developed some new idea that departs from the tenets of Sthiramati and Vasubandhu's school of thought.

As mentioned above, it was a chaotic time of the Liang and Chen dynasties when Paramārtha reached China. In spite of his difficult wandering life, he translated many texts and popularized them. Paramārtha had many able disciples, among them Huikai, Zhijiao, Daoni, Fatai, Caobi, Sengzong, and Huikuang were very famous.[40] The lineage of Paramārtha and his disciples extended the studies of Yogācāra texts and succeeded in popularizing the doctrines of Yogācāra School. *Mahāyānasaṃgrahaśāstra* (T. 1593) of Asaṅga and *Mahāyānasaṃgrahaśāstrabhāṣya* (T. 1595) of Vasubandhu became so popular and were being studied so deeply and extensively that a new school called "She lun zong (攝論宗 Saṃgrahaśāstra School)" developed in China. Takakusu (1956: 81) states that these two texts are the first and the foremost comprehensive work which set forth the doctrine of Mere Ideation and are the representative compendium of the Idealistic School.

---

37 *She dachenglun* (攝大乘論, T. 1593; Nj. 1183).

38 *She dacheng lunshi* (攝大乘論釋, T. 1595; Nj. 1171(2)).

39 *Dacheng weishi lun* (大乘唯識論, T. 1589).

40 *Zhongguo Fojiao* (中國佛教), 1980. Vol. I, p 256[11-12].

6.4 Study of Xuanzang in China Before Journey to the West and in India

6.4.1 A. Mahāyānasaṃgrahaśāstra (攝大乘論)

Before undertaking the journey to the West Land, Xuanzang studied some important texts which were translated by Paramārtha. He studied *Saṃgrahaśāstra* (攝論 *She lun*) for the first time when he was only 13 years old, with Dharmācārya Yan (嚴法師) at Luoyang (洛阳). He became so well-versed in this text that he frequently delivered lectures on the philosophy of this text. Before going to India, Xuanzang studied this *Saṃgrahaśāstra* under seven different teachers at different places at different times. Among these teachers, Huixiu[41] and Zhining[42] were of the lineage of Paramārtha.

Xuanzang found discrepancies in the opinion of his teachers regarding the theory of this school. He could not decide which one was correct and followed the original. So he resolved to go to India to learn this doctrine directly from an able Indian teacher. By that time *Yogācāraśāstra* was not translated into Chinese. Xuanzang was very much interested to study the *Yogācāraśāstra*. Giving his introduction to Śīlabhadra at Nālandā, he expressed his main purpose to come to India to study the *Yogācāraśāstra*.[43]

Xuanzang travelled and stayed in India for 17 years. At Nālandā he stayed for five years and studied under Śīlabhadra, an eminent scholar of Yogācāra, the Chief Priest of Nālandā Mahāvihāra and the pupil of Great Śāstra Master Dharmapāla. At Yaṣṭivana hill, Xuanzang stayed for two years with a householder named Jayasena and enquired about some doubtful points of the *Yogācāraśāstra* and other *Śāstra*s. Thus, Xuanzang studied the doctrine of Yogācāra from the viewpoint of all the three lineages of this theory that is Guṇamati–Sthiramati lineage from the translation by Paramārtha and his lineage in China, and Dignāga lineage from Śīlabhadra and the lineage of Nanda from Jayasena in India.

6.4.2 B. Study of Abhidharmakośa

Abhidharmakośa is a very famous text compiled by Vasubandhu, a great teacher of Sarvāstivāda School in India. Paramārtha with his favorite disciple Huikai translated *Abhidharmakośa* (阿毗達磨俱舍釋論 *A-pi-da-mo ju-she shi lun*, T. 1559; Nj. 1269)

---

[41] Huixiu (慧休548–645) studied *Saṃgrahaśāstra* with Daoni, the disciple of Paramārtha. Lineage is as: Paramārtha 眞諦→ Daoni 道尼→ Huixiu慧休→ Xuanzang 玄奘. Cf. *Zhongguo Fojiao* (中國佛教), Vol. I, p. 256^{21} –257^{8}.

[42] Zhining (智凝 562?–609?) was the disciple of Jingsong who studied this text with Fatai, the disciple of Paramārtha. Lineage is as: Paramārtha 眞諦→ Fatai 法泰→Jingsong 靖嵩→ Zhining 智凝→Xuanzang 玄奘. Cf. *Zhongguo Fojiao* (中國佛教), Vol. I, p $257^{20–23}$.

[43] T.2053a, b, p 236/c/19–20; Beal, 1914:107.

in the year 564–569 CE at the time of Chen Dynasty (557–589).[44] After the death of Parmārtha, his disciples carried out the work and lineage of Parmārtha. Daoyue, a self-styled disciple of Huikai, studied *Zaxin* first, later on, he switched over to the study of *Abhidharmakośa*.[45] Hui Li has informed that before going to India Xuanzang studied *Abhidharmakośa* with Dharma Master Yue (Daoyue) at Chang'an.[46] Xuanzang studied this text with Xuanhui (玄會, 582–640) also, who was the disciple of Daoyue (道岳568–636 CE). Daoyue was the disciple of Daoni (道尼), who studied under Paramārtha.[47] Thus, Xuanzang studied *Abhidharmakośa* also from the lineage of Paramārtha.

6.4.3 C. Study of Vijñaptimātratāśāstra

It is not mentioned that before undertaking his journey to the West land, whether Xuanzang studied *Vijñaptimātratāśāstra* or not, but it is well-known fact that this text was already translated in 538–41 CE by Bodhiruci (菩提流支 Pu-ti-liu-zhi (T. 1588)) and in 558–560 CE by Paramārtha (T. 1589). Xuanzang recognized the importance of this text, and in India, he studied this text at Nālandā and other places.

6.5 Translation Works of Xuanzang and Its Significance

After returning to China, Xuanzang translated 74 texts. He considered the importance of the study of the work of Asaṅga and Vasubandhu and paid more attention to Paramārtha. Though Paramārtha already translated *Abhidharmakośabhāṣya* and *Mahāyānasaṃgrahaśāstra* earlier, Xuanzang, before going on his journey to the West, studied both the *Śāstra*s thoroughly from many teachers of Paramārtha's lineage, he again translated them. He translated *Mahāyānasaṃgrahaśāstra* of Asaṅga (T.1594) and its two commentaries—one by Vasubandhu (T. 1597) and the other by Asvabhāva (T. 1598). Later on, he worked on *Yogācāra* (*Yogācārya*) *bhūmiśāstra* (T. 1579) of Asaṅga/Maitreya Bodhisattva, and its commentary by Jinaputra and others (T. 1580).

Xuanzang also translated *Abhidharmakośa* (T. 1558). He and his disciples Puguang, Fabao, and others further encouraged the study of this text so much so that the Kośa School (Ju-she zong俱舍宗) popularized and developed by Paramārtha and his disciples, flourished in China, and Far-East countries Korea and Japan.

Xuanzang translated *Vijñaptimātratāśāstra* (*Viṃśatikā* T. 1590 and *Triṃśikā* T. 1586) of Vasubandhu. The commentary by Dharmapāla and nine other teachers on

---

[44] *Zhongguo Fojiao* (中國佛教) Vol. II, p. 87 $^{8-14}$; Paul 1982: 60; 1984: 35.

[45] *Zhongguo Fojiao* (中國佛教) Vol. I, p 261$^{3-5}$;

[46] Beal, 1914: 9; T. 2053a, b, p 222/b/ 20; *Zhongguo Fojiao* (中國佛教) Vol. I, p 263$^{1-2}$.

[47] *Zhongguo Fojiao* (中國佛教) Vol. I, p. 257$^{1-5}$.

Vijñaptimātratāśāstra of Vasubandhu is an important work of Idealistic school, which explains the subject of YogācāraVijñānavāda more distinctly. Xuanzang translated it also (T. 1585) and transmitted this idealistic doctrine to his able disciple Kuiji. Both, Xuanzang and Kuiji, popularized the doctrine of *Vijñaptimātratāśāstra*, and thus a new school called "Weishi lun zong (Vijñaptimātratāśāstra School)"[48] came into existence.

During the middle of the Tang Dynasty Weishi lun School (Weishilun zong, Vijñaptimātratāśāstra School) flourished in China. On account of widespread studies of this very text, this school became so popular that the existing She lun zong (Saṃgrahaśāstra School 摄論宗), the representative of Idealistic school (Yogācāra Ideology) founded by Paramārtha in China, merged with this new school.

6.6 Conclusion

The popularity of *Abhidharma* and the theory of *Ālayavijñāna* and *Vijñaptimātratā* of Yogācāra attracted much attention and created much interest among the people. The studies of *Abhidharmakośa, Mahāyānasaṃgrahaśāstra, Vijñaptimātratāśāstra* etc popularized by Paramārtha and his disciples were developed as Ju-she zong (Kośa School 俱舍宗) and Shelun zong (Saṃgrahaśāstra School). Xuanzang and his disciples further encouraged the studies of these texts so much so that Ju-she zong (Kośa School 俱舍宗) flourished by its previous name and She lun zong (Saṃgrahaśāstra School 摄論宗) merged with Wei shi lun zong (Vijñaptimātra School). These schools had influenced not only the Chinese mind and thoughts but also the Japanese and Korean mind for centuries.

The extensive translations and exegeses of Paramārtha are highly valued by all Buddhist Schools in China. According to Diana Y. Paul (1982: 38), "Not only Ch'an (Chan) and Hua Yan Buddhists but also the later neo-Confucians owed a considerable debt to Paramārtha's systematic thought." Thus, it is a great contribution of Paramārtha to East Asian countries China, Japan, Korea, etc. In this very sense, Paramārtha proved to be the predecessor of Xuanzang and has made a great contribution to Chinese Buddhism.

[48] The central idea of this school is derived from the very first stanza of *Viṃśatikākārikā* of Vasubandhu–"*Vijñaptimātramevaitadasadarthāvabhāsanāt*", which emphasizes the theory of existence of Ideation only. The world is ideation only. It does not exist. It is an illusion. It is only the fabrication of our consciousness. In China Wei shi Lun School was popular also with its name as Faxiang School. In Japan this school is known as Hossō School. Since staying in the Ci en temple (慈恩寺) at Changan (長安), Xuanzang and Kuiji developed this school, and thus it is also called Ci en School (Ci en zong 慈恩宗) (Takakusu, 1956:80).

References

Funayama, Toru 2008 (2010) The work of Paramārtha: An example of Sino-Indian cross-cultural exchange, JIABS, 31(1–2)

JIABS = *Journal of the International Association of Buddhist Studies*

JBS = *Journal of Buddhist Studies,* ed. Bhikkhu KL Dhammajoti, Centre for Buddhist Studies, Colombo, Sri Lanka and Buddha-Dharma Centre of Hong Kong

Lalji 'Shravak' (2003) Contribution of Xuanzang to the Abhidharma studies in China. In *Buddhism —In Global Perspective*, Eds Shankarnarayan K, Panth R, Ogawa I. Mumbai. II, pp 237–253

Lalji 'Shravak' (2006) Weishilunzong (VijñaptimātraŚāstra School): Its Rise and development. In *Contrib Buddhism World Cult,* Eds. Shankarnarayan K, Panth R, Ogawa I, Mumbai. II, pp 247–260

Lalji 'Shravak' (2010) On Xuanzang's contribution as translator to the development of Buddhism in China. In *India on Silk Road*, eds Kamal Sheel- C. Willemen- Lalji 'Shravak'. Buddhist World Press, Delhi, pp 95–121

Lalji 'Shravak' (2019) Contribution of *Miśrakābhidharma-hṛdaya-śāstra* (Za a-pi-tan xinlun雜阿毗曇心論) in the development of the Abhidharma school in China, published in the *JBS*, XVI, pp 129–140, ed. Bhikkhu KL Dhammajoti, Centre for Buddhist Studies, Colombo, Sri Lanka and Buddha-Dharma Centre of Hong Kong

Paul D (1982) The life and time of Paramārtha (499–569). *JIABS,* 5(1):37–69

Paul D (1984) *Philosophy of mind in Sixth-Century China: Paramartha's 'evolution of consciousness'* Stanford University Press. California, Stanford

T. = Taisho Edition of the Buddhist Tripiṭaka in Chinese, (大藏經 *Dazangjing*), Ed. Takakusu, J. and Watanabe, K., 1924–35. The Taishō Issaikyō Kankōkai, Tokyo

T. 1593, *She dacheng lun* (摄大乘論)

T.1641 (13), *Suixiang lun* (隨相論)

T. 1595, *She dacheng lunshi* (摄大乘論釋)

T. 2053a (Vol. 50), *Da Tang Daciensi Sanzang Fashi Zhuan* (大唐大慈恩寺三藏法師傳). (Nj. 1494) by Huili

T. 2053b (Vol. 50),*Gaoseng chuan* (高僧傳, *Biographies of Eminent Monks*)

T. 2060 (Vol. 50), *Xu Gaoseng chuan* (續高僧傳) (*Continued Biographies of Eminent Monks*), compiled by Daoxuan (道宣596–667)

Takakusu J (1904–1905) On the Abhidharma Literature of the Sarvāstivāda, *J.P.T.S.*, London

Takakusu J (1905) A study of Paramartha's life of Vasubandhu and the date of Vasubandhu. J.R.A.S, London

Takakusu J (1956) (IIIrd ed.). *The Essentials of Buddhist Philosophy*, Honolulu

IIJBS = *The Indian International Journal of Buddhist Studies*, B.J.K. Institute of Buddhist and Asian Studies, Varanasi, India.

IJBS = *The Indian Journal of Buddhist Studies*, B.J.K. Institute of Buddhist and Asian Studies, Varanasi, India

Willemen C (1999–2000) The Indian Background of Buddhism in China: Some Facts and Remarks. In *IIJBS*, 1, Varanasi, India

Willemen C (2001) Sarvāstivāda development in North western India and in China. In *IIJBS* 2, Varanasi, India

Willemen (1975) (Trans.). *The Essence of Metaphysics Abhidharmahṛdaya.*, Publications de l'Institut, Belge des Hautees Études Bouddhiques, Série Études et Textes 4, Brussel. Republished with new introduction Willemen C 2006 *The Essence of Scholasticism, Abhidharmahṛdaya.* Motilal Banarasidass Publishers Pvt. Ltd., Delhi

Willemen Ch, Dessein B, Cox C (1998) *Sarvāstivāda Buddhist Scholasticism*, Brill, Leiden

Zhongguo Fojiao (中国佛教史), 1980–89. Vols. I–IV. Zhishi chubanshe, Beijing

Chapter 7
Discovering "Cotton Route"

Yu Longyu

7.1 Introduction

Our world is about the "destiny". From the year 1960, I started writing a novel titled "Huang Dao Fo" based on my old lectures given in Hindi. After 50 years, I delivered a lecture at Varanasi, the famous cultural city of India, webinar was organized by Banaras Hindu University. The main character of the novel "Huang Dao Fo" has also a long relationship with India. If we talk about the history of cotton production in China, cotton came more in practice in China since around the Han era.

It is interesting to note that, although China is one of the leading producers in the world, cotton is not native to China.[1] As mentioned by Mallory and Mair, based on some archeological research on the mummies found in Tarim Basin, there is evidence of cotton textiles in China in the first millennium BCE. The research suggests that its origin may be traced to India.[2]

In the context of India, spinning and making cotton has always been very significant. Its produced and used since very ancient days. Its origin can be traced back to 4000 BCE. Cotton production and spinning and producing cotton cloth were normal practices since ancient India. In the modern world, it has become one of the major producers and exporters of cotton today. It plays a very important role in the country's industrial and agricultural economy. When the Britishers came to India, they started shipping raw cotton from India to England. Though it benefited their interest, the finished material coming from England to India brought more harm to local farmers. The Swadeshi movement initiated by Mahatma Gandhi encouraged

[1] Kuo, 1922.

[2] Mallory and Mair, 2000.

Y. Longyu (✉)
Shenzhen University, Shenzhen, China
e-mail: szucis@szu.edu.cn

S. Mishra and R. Sheel (eds.), *India-China Dialogues Beyond Borders*,
https://doi.org/10.1007/978-981-99-4326-5_7

Indians to come out of poverty and spin and produce more and more cotton products at home (in India). It spread a message of self-reliance. Khadi (cloth woven from spinning wheel) became more popular through his Swadeshi movement, and it became a symbol of resistance.

The novel Huang Dao discusses the Chinese cotton textile industry and its connections with India.

7.2 Huang Dao Fo and the Chinese Cotton Textile Industry

There are three women who are the most famous in Chinese history: Hua Mu Lan, Mu Gui Ying, and Huang Dao Fo. Hua Mu Lan has a famous story that she joined the army to protect her country to fulfill her father's dream. Huang Dao Fo, as a technology user, her contribution to the cotton textile industry made her hometown Shanghai the center of China's cotton textile industry, and she also gained a reputation as a woman "making cotton textile available to the common public". Although, invention of cotton spinning technique is a great contribution to human civilization by the Indian people. Through the "cotton route", the cotton spinning technology reached China, Southeast Asia, Japan, Europe, Africa, and the American continent from India.

It is well known that Shanghai was the biggest center of the Chinese cotton textile industry. Later on, the cotton spinning of Shanghai gradually developed into cotton-producing areas like Wu Xi, Chengzhou, Xi'an, and Xinjiang. Thus, China and India, in the area of the world cotton textile industry got an important place. Huang Dao Fo's contribution to the great achievement that China has achieved in the world cotton textile industry is incomparable, which cannot be separated from the Chinese cotton textile industry.

The period of Huang Dao Fo was the end of the Song Dynasty of China and the beginning of the Yuan Dynasty (about the thirteenth century). At that time, there was a situation of war in China, Jiangnan city was very prosperous at one time but due to the ravages of war, the city was no longer suitable for common people to survive, and the general public began to flee. Huang Dao Fo, who was married as a child, became more and more miserable, having died every day after her young husband died of illness. She could not bear the persecution and one day she escaped in the night and reached the island of Hainan by boat. Huang Dao Fo not only survived but also learned a magnificent weaving craft with the help of relatives of the Li tribe. But she always thought of her village and her relatives there; she wanted to teach her hometown residents the skills of knitting clothes she learned from the Li tribe to help them live a good life.

Eventually, after 20 years, Huang Dao Fo returned to the city of Wu Ni Jing in Shanghai. Huang Dao Fo brought back the textile weaving craft with her and greatly improved the work capacity and living conditions of the villagers. Jiangnan people began to learn the art of weaving from Huang Dao Fo. After a few years, many famous textile cities settled on both sides of the Huangfu River, Huang Dao Fo's textile weaving skills spread all over the Jiangnan region after some years of hard struggle. Many temples were built in memory of Huang Dao Fo in Shanghai and Jiangnan area after her death, folk songs were sung praising her. After the founding of New China in 1949, because of Huang Dao Fo's contributions, the government put her great works into the school curriculum, the "Huang Dao Fo Memorial Hall" was built in the village of Wu Ni Jiang, where thousands of people come to pay tribute to her every year.

I and Huang Dao Fo are from the same place. I have properly studied the culture, history, and customs of both sides of the Huang Fo River, so I started writing <Huang Dao Fo> as my first novel. In 1949, I came to Shenzhen University after 19 years of study and teaching at Peking University, while leaving Peking University, I gave all my valuable things to others, brought with me only one vessel and a box of 24 books. I had brought that gift from the Hindi Department's teacher of Peking University given to me on the occasion of my marriage, two boxes of the 24 boxes of books containing the manuscripts of the novel <Huang Dao Fo>. I had a pot and some books. Both of these were enough for my teaching and life. It was a big change for me to join as a Chinese teacher from a Hindi teacher; I did not have enough time to revise the manuscript of the novel <Huang Dao Fo> .

So far, Huang Dao Po is still in the process of publication. It includes literary critics, historians, university vice-chancellor, and economists. Zhou Siming, a famous literary and art critic in Shenzhen, has written a book review entitled "Writing the Legend of Life beyond Suffering", published in the famous magazine "Book House".

All this suggests that Huang Dao Po is a historical novel, and it also has some narrations of India and the Cotton Road.

7.3 The Cotton Route and Silk Route Are Enhancing Each other's Beauty

Eastern civilization has made a great contribution to the development and progress of world civilization. This contribution was mainly achieved through the "cotton route" and the "silk route". It is well known that not only cotton and silk goods were exchanged through cotton routes and silk routes but also led to cultural–ideological exchanges. Besides, these two ways have been increasing the beauty of each other, "I am in you, you are in me", both are incomplete without each other.

"One Belt One Road" International Cooperation Summit was held in Beijing on 14–15 May 2017, which was very successful, but India did not join it although " One Belt One Road " is the modern version of the ancient silk route and sea silk route, that has a very close relationship with India. For example, we take the logo of the conference; "One Belt One Road" have many Indian elements, besides the English word silk's "S", the "Pagoda" of the famous city of Xi'an has also come from India which is the Chinese version of the Indian Stupa. The English word silk has evolved from Sanskrit, both the form and the pronunciation of "Pagoda" has come from India. After the conclusion of the International Cooperation Summit, the world-famous song <Mo Li Hua> was sung. It is a folk song of Jiangsu Province of China. Li Hong Chang (1823–1901), a minister of the Chinese King, went to attend a conference in Europe during the Qing Dynasty of China (1644–1912). At the beginning of the conference, all the delegates sang the national songs of their respective countries. At that time in China, there was no national song, Minister Li Hong Chang sang the folk song < Moli Hua > of his region, after that the song became world-famous. The word "Moli" comes from India, the word "Moli" is derived from the Sanskrit word "Mali or Mallika". It is a flower, which is known as the jasmine flower in the local language.

Cotton came from India, the discovery and production of cotton have proved to be the most beneficial for mankind, it is the biggest contribution to human civilization by the Indian people. So far, cotton clothing is still the most important, environment-friendly, and is the most practical textile material.

In the Medieval era, cotton and cotton spinning techniques reached the whole world through the "cotton route". Due to the geographical proximity of China's Hainan Island, the people of the Li Tsu tribe continued to update and change the spinning technique with a continuous process of learning. Cotton sowing, spinning, weaving, and dyeing were the most common after Huang Dao Fo reached Hainan Island. Huang Dao Fo After learning these techniques, brought them to her hometown of Shanghai and inspired them to make new advances in cotton weaving skills by combining them with local weaving skills.

China's cotton technology has come from India; varieties of cotton have also come from India. The ancient name of cotton is "Siba, Pentandra", came from the Malaysian word "Kapok". It is Kapok's cotton, but the people of the Tang and Song period of China did not differentiate between Kapok's cotton and ordinary cotton. There are two main routes of entry of cotton, the first entered the Yunnan province via Southeast Asian countries during the time of the Eastern Han Dynasty, another type of cotton was in vogue in Yunnan's minority groups, and the second was during the Southern–Northern Dynasty; it entered in Xinjiang province by way of the northern route. Large-scale cultivation of cotton and large-scale production of cotton cloth began at the end of the Song Dynasty and the beginning of the Yuan Dynasty. ("Chinese Traditional Culture Dictionary" p. 69), Huang Dao Fo was born at the right time and made her immortal contribution to the promotion and development of cotton in the Jiang Nan region.

American historian Sven Beckert said in his book *Cotton Empire: A Global History of Capitalism*, "For a long time, Europe has no place to stand in this colorful, dynamic and economically important cotton world. Europeans have always been marginalized in cotton cultivation, production, and consumption. Even after Europeans began importing small amounts of cotton cloth in The Greek and Roman periods, Europe remained insignificant to the global cotton industry. In Europe, Linen and wool have been worn since the Bronze Age.[3] Sven, in his book, quotes Mahatma Gandhi on this issue, "while India was supplying cotton to Europe, the Europeans themselves were still immersed in savagery, ignorance and rudeness".

[3] Sven, 2015: 28.

Gandhi's pledge to wear khadi (cotton) and to hard spinning were the inseparable part of his philosophy. He chose to wear Khadi to promote Swadeshi Movement and to boycott British goods and culture. It was also aimed to create economic independence for India's poor population. With this movement, Gandhi urged Indian people to spin their own traditional Indian clothing.

"The boycott of foreign cloth will succeed only when the twenty-two crores of our peasants begin to use khadi. And to convert them to the use of khadi means to explain to them the science of khadi, to show them the advantages of self-help and to teach them the entire process of khadi production. For this we need volunteers, mobile schools and preparation and distribution of booklets describing the processes of spinning, carding, etc."[4] Mahatma Gandhi.

Cotton is the softest thing in the world, but in the hands of cotton imperialism, it has become a sharp and ruthless weapon. Sven Beckett says: "Initially, the expansion in South Asia was the most important event in which European businessmen and politicians got involved in the global cotton industry network. As a result, Europeans began to gain a foothold in the trans-oceanic trade of Indian textiles." "As early as 1621, the British East India Company is estimated to have imported about 50,000 pieces of cotton textiles into England. Forty years later, that number has quintupled. In fact, cotton textiles became the East India Company's most important trade goods; by 1766, cotton textiles accounted for 75 percent of the company's total exports."

India's cotton technology has contributed greatly to the development of Britain's modern economy. Britain was originally an unnamed island country in the Atlantic Ocean and relied on coal mining and cotton spinning. Coal provides energy and mechanical strength, and this made the cotton textile industry prosper in the UK international market. The cotton textile industry proved to be the first gold for Britain. The raw material of the cotton textile industry mainly comes from India, and cotton textile technology was also mechanized based on the basic technology of India. Therefore, India was called the jewel inlaid in the crown of the Queen of England.

7.4 Conclusion

Spinning wheel and making traditional clothing were once a symbol of poverty and backwardness in India. Later, it was turned into a representation of self-reliance and nonviolence by Mahatma Gandhi. Spinning wheel and producing Kadi helped him to establish contact with people and to carry his message of Swadeshi and Swaraj to them.

For historical reasons, the historical contribution of the cotton route has not been carefully studied, and the achievements of the Indian people to mankind have not been properly demonstrated. One should know the past and learn from the present, only by knowing where we have come from, we can adequately move toward the future. A lot of effort is required to study the cotton route. We can produce films

[4] Joshi 2002: 7.

and TV series based on the Cotton Route and "Huang Dao Fo", and we can also organize a "Cotton Route Seminar" under the aegis of the BOYA Asia Forum on Hainan Island where Huang Dao Fo has lived for 20 years.

References

Beckert, Sven (2015) Empire of cotton: a new history of global capitalism, Allen Lane, Random House Digit

Gandhi MK (1955) Khadi: Why and How, ed Bharatan Kumarappa, Ahmedabad: Navajivan Publ House

Goldstone, Jack A (1996) Gender, work, and culture: Why the industrial revolution came early to england but late to China, Sociol Perspect, Sage J, 39:1, pp-1–21

Hoh Jae Sung, Ko Sung-jie (1966) Styles of industrial development in asia, a comparative history of cotton industry in Japan, China and Korea, Michigan, Univ Pa Press

Joshi, Divya, (2002) Gandhiji on khadi: Selected and compiled with an introduction, Mumbai: Mani Bhavan Gandhi Sangrahalaya

Kuo L-C (1972) The technical transformation of agriculture in communist China, the university of Michigan. Praeger

Malory JP, Mair Victor H (2002) The tarim mummies: ancient China and mystery of the earliest peoples of the west. Thomas and Hudson, London

Part III
India and China in Contemporary Contexts

Chapter 8
Understanding India's China Dependence Syndrome

Mahendra P. Lama

8.1 Backdrop[1]

The first meeting of the leaders of the Non-aligned Movement (NAM) in Belgrade, Yugoslavia in 1961 was a landmark global gathering. This event guided and determined the foreign policy discourse and directions of international relations of a majority of the developing countries for at least the next four decades. As against the now much vilified concept of non-alignment, Pandit Jawaharlal Nehru had delineated and stated that, "We call ourselves the conference of non-aligned countries. Now the word non-aligned may be differently interpreted but basically it was used and coined, almost with the meaning: non-aligned with the great power blocks of the world. Non-aligned has a negative meaning but if you give it a positive connotation it means nations which object to this lining up for war purposes, military blocs, military alliances and the like. Therefore, we keep away from this and we want to throw our weight, such as it is, in favour of peace" (Appadorai and Rajan 1985; Chand 1983).

It was to a large extent the NAM that highlighted the critical wedge between the developed countries in the North and developing countries in the South. Developed countries were the Centre as they played dominant, active roles in world trade, debt and development finance. International movement of capital occurred from them and global technology development and flow was fully controlled by them. On the other hand, developing countries in the periphery that had just come out of the yolk of colonialism played a passive role in world trade and remained import dependent and borrowers of capital and technology (Mehta 1986).

[1] This article has its first framework published as a fortnightly column by this author in Kathmandu Post. https://kathmandupost.com/art-entertainment/2018/05/23/make-in-india.

M. P. Lama (✉)
School of International Studies, Jawaharlal Nehru University, New Delhi, India
e-mail: mahendra_lama1961@yahoo.co.in

S. Mishra and R. Sheel (eds.), *India-China Dialogues Beyond Borders*,
https://doi.org/10.1007/978-981-99-4326-5_9

8.2 Rise of a New World Order

India's foreign policy narratives and discourse were largely dominated by this non-aligned thinking, design and practices. In fact, India with Egypt, Indonesia and Yugoslavia became the flag bearers of this idea of non-alignment, which by the end of the twentieth century had more than 120 member countries. Developing and newly decolonized countries looked for India's global leadership. This movement became a widely accepted forum for the developing countries, mainly because of the common cause these countries together propounded. This led to many powerful conglomerations like the Group of 77 (G 77) and also the setting up of United Nations Conference on Trade and Development (UNCTAD) in 1964 (ECDC 1983; MEA 1983; RIS 1987a).

These institutions later became the vanguard of negotiations with the North on critical issues like stability of commodity prices, transfer of technology, development assistance to developing countries and also opening of markets and several other politico-strategic issues. The North was literally forced to agree to the appointment of two global commissions, viz., the Pearson Commission in 1968[2] and Brandt Commission[3] in 1977, both of which strongly supported the cause of the Global South. Both of these reports highlighted how the developing countries were deprived of the entire space of interdependence. They delved into invasive technology, camouflaged participation of investors and halted trickle down of technologies. Both these Commissions solidly advocated that at least 1% of the Gross National Product of the developed countries be transferred to the countries in the South as Official Development Assistance (ODA). India's role in generating enlivening global debates on terms of trade, technology transfer, development finance, global debt and disarmament in forum like NAM, UNCTAD and G 77 actually shaped the UN General Assembly Resolution on New International Economic Order (NIEO) in 1974.[4]

---

[2] Pearson and Lester (1969). Pearson Commission (under the leadership of Lester Pearson (former Prime Minister of Canada) was the first global commission appointed in 1968 to examine the issues between North and the South and to recommend ways to durably tackle them. Popularly known as the Pearson Report on "A New Strategy of Global Development" (1969), this report for the first time highlighted the kaleidoscope of the Third World, vistas of inequalities and under development and its tragic consequences, debt relief and volume of aid, population control to technical assistance, foreign investment and trade to crisis of confidence.

[3] The Brandt Commission (1983). In the aftermath of wide spread disappointments on the ways and instruments and lack of implementations of the Pearson Report by the North (for example, 1 percent of GNP of the wealthier nations in the North to devolve to the South as Official Development Assistance by 1975 was not even remotely achieved), a new Independent Commission on International Development Issues (ICIDI) was appointed in 1977 under the Chairmanship of Willy Brandt, former Chancellor of Germany which submitted its Report entitled "North-South: A Programme for Survival" (1980). Brandt Commission Report made some significant recommendations including on Hunger and Food, Population, Disarmament and Development, Commodity Trade, Energy, Transnational Corporation Investment and Technology, World Monetary Order, Development Finance and International Organizations and Negotiations.

[4] Resolution adopted by the General Assembly, 3201 (S-VI). Declaration on the Establishment of a New International Economic Order, 1 May 1974.

8.3 Unfair Practices

In all these North–South negotiations, a crucial issue had been the secular decline in primary commodity prices thereby very deeply and adversely affecting the terms of trade (price of export/price of import) and balance of trade (value of export minus value of import) of developing countries. Raul Prebisch and Hans Singer (Raffer and Singer 2001) empirically demonstrated how developing countries were made to export primary commodities—basically raw materials like bauxite, iron ore, cotton, copper, wool, etc.—and how these commodities were converted into the final products and re-exported back to developing countries at a price many times higher than the cost of raw materials. (RIS 1987b; Lama 1986). Therefore, the terms of trade of the developing countries recorded a secular decline leading to staggering balance of trade dificits.

In the process, the cream of development that could have otherwise gone to developing countries with rich natural resources endowments, were usurped by the developed countries. These developed countries in Europe, United States and later even Japan had the distinct advantage of having technology, capital, industrial ventures, human resources and control over the policies that govern the world trading and investment system. Besides the political regimes, India's international negotiators and intellectual leaders like Sukhomoy Chakravarty, G Prathasarathy, LK Jha, KB Lall, Nikhil Chakravarty, Muchkund Dubey and many others vehemently fought against such discriminatory practices.

Unlike today's geo-strategic impetus to align with the United States (Smith 2018), India had been a fierce fighter for getting better deal in the global market for its primary commodities and other exports. The Africans, South East Asians and Latin Americans were all partners with India to fight against the developed countries on its unfair trade practices. However, the organisation like NAM has gone into oblivion. The World Trade Organization (WTO) has however injected relatively much freer regimes with liberal market provisions. India for at least last three decades no longer remained the voice of developing countries as most of these countries started deeply aligning themeselves with metropolitan and super powers. However, the G20 Presidency of India has once again brought it to the centre stage of global South. "Many developing countries are struggling with unsustainable debt, while trying to ensure food and energy security for their people. They are also the ones most affected by global warming caused by richer countries. This is why India's G20 Presidency has tried to give a voice to the Global South. No group can claim global leadership without listening to those most affected by its decisions." (Video Message by Prime Minister Shri Narendra Modi at G20 Foreign Ministers' Meeting, March 02, 2023; https://mea.gov.in/Speeches-Statements.htm?dtl/36314/Video_Message_by_Prime_Minister_Shri_Narendra_Modi_at_G20_Foreign_Ministers_Meeting). However, India has once again become the victim of the same trend and practice that prevailed at the global level during 1950–1980s. The differrence this time has been that the theatre of operation is not global. It is

http://www.un-documents.net/s6r3201.htm.

now regional and the critical actor and the market is not United States or Europe. It is its own neighbour China. Also, the situation is not like that of the immediate post-colonial era of the1950s, it is now a post-cold war continuum of the twenty-first century where China has emerged as the second largest economy in the world and a critical player and competitor in the global market.

8.4 Dependency Syndrome: Domain of Exports

We find that in the North–South discourse, China despite a "century of humiliation" inflicted on it after the tumultuous Opium Wars, very diligently, consistently and consciously kept it out of the entire debate for full four crucial decades of 1950s–1980s. However, today the countries in the global South including India once again witness the same phenomenon of making them the core bastion of raw material supplies by China. This has been so visibly inbuilt in case of Chinese foreign policy, economic strategy and commercial interactions with these countries from Africa to Asia and Latin America. Today also the means, market, instrumentalities and even the comparative advantages are strikingly similar to what occurred during the colonial regimes and for the subsequent decades of 1950–1980s. The victims remain the same, i.e. essentially the nations in the global South. However China has emerged as the key actor in importing the raw materials from countries in the global South and exporting the final products back to these countries. It is in this context; this article discusses India–China trade relations.

India–China trade that stood at US$ 3.40 million in 1970 slowly reached $ 49 million in 1990. However, it jumped to $ 2.95 billion by 2000, $ 57.65 billion in 2010 and 86.39 billion in 2020 (Table 8.1). This is just the officially recorded formal trade figures provided by the Government of India that could be largely underestimated. There could be a significant volume of import from China which fall into the precincts of unauthorized, illegal and unrecorded transborder trade. These happen through various sea routes, borderlands and other means like deflection, under invoicing and over invoicing. The deflection of imports from China by landlocked countries like Bhutan and Nepal to India, as most of these imports come through Indian ports including Vishakhapatnam and Calcutta to pass through their various land border-based customs stations (LCS) and Integrated Check Posts (ICPs) has also been found to be pretty high. In addition, noticeable reimports of and reexports of significant quantity of items with or without value addition by Bangladeshi, Sri Lankan and Myanmarese traders/merchants/agencies to their Indian counterparts occur informally through their respective ICPs/LCSs and sea ports with India. The complex nature of LCSs and ICPs located in various border regimes in terms of geography, history, culture, political systems and cross-border informal institutions also make this unrecorded trade immensely possible. Studies carried out at various institutions in India including at ICRIER, JNU, ORF, CUTS and RIS (Taneja 2004; Pohit and Taneja 2000; CUTS 2017; Bhattacharjee 2019; Lama 2005; RIS 2011; Das 2016) do show these trends rather clearly (Table 8.2). Besides, there would be some major imports with strong Chinese contents from countries like that of ASEAN with which India has entered into free trade agreement or countries with which India is negotiating free trade regime (like Australia). This would, if not sceintfically and accurately measured in terms of rules of origin criteria could enhance the actual volume of India-China trade significantly.

As a result, China's share in India's total global trade that was recorded at merely 0.08% in 1970 and 0.12% in 1990, steadily increased to 3.10% in 2000, 9.30% in 2010 and 12.59% in 2020. This shows how from an insignificantly low-ranking partner in India's globally dispersed trade, China steadily consolidated its ranking particularly since 2010 to acquire the position of the top trading partner in 2015 and maintaining more or less the same status till today. This is the first indicator of deepening trade relations with China and also indicates how two economies of India and China steadily integrated in areas of trade cooperation particularly in the last two decades (Table 8.3). The core issue of enquiry revolves around whether this integration is driven by the matrices of dependency or interdependency.

Amidst this bourgeoning India–China trade relations what merges conspicuously is the steady increase in balance of trade deficit vis-à-vis India. During the entire 30-year period from 1990 to 2020, India's imports from China have been hugely bigger than its exports thereby, injecting a massive increase in trade deficit of India. From a mere $ 13 million deficit in 1990, it reached $ 671 million in

Table 8.1 India's Exports to and Imports from China and World (US $ Million)

Year	India's global exports	India's exports to China	(b) as % of (a)	India's global imports	India's imports from China	(e) as % of (d)
	(a)	(b)	(c)	(d)	(e)	(f)
1970	2024.04	3.00	0.15	2094.60	0.40	0.02
1975	4364.10	5.10	0.12	6197.80	2.10	0.03
1980	7995.00	7.00	0.09	13,181.00	81.00	0.61
1985	8265.00	21.00	0.25	16,329.00	104.00	0.64
1990	17,813.00	18.00	0.10	23,990.00	31.00	0.13
1995	30,537.00	283.00	0.93	34,484.00	811.00	2.35
2000	44,298.00	1230.00	2.78	49,724.00	1717.00	3.45
2005	103,090.52	6,759.10	6.55	129,691.77	10,868.05	8.39
2010	249,815.53	14,168.86	5.67	369,769.12	43,479.76	11.75
2015	262,291.07	9,011.36	3.43	381,007.47	61,707.95	16.19
2019	313,361.04	16,612.75	5.30	474,709.28	65,260.75	13.75
2020	291,808.47	21,187.15	7.26	394,435.85	65,212.25	16.53
2021–22	305,026.13	17,122.55	5.61	440,923.52	67,629.12	15.34

Source Up to 2000, Estimated from IMF, *Direction of Trade Statistics Yearbook,* Various Issues. https://data.imf.org/regular.aspx?key=61013712
Ministry of Commerce, Government of India, https://tradestat.commerce.gov.in/eidb/iecnttopn.asp

Table 8.2 India's Integrated Check Posts (ICPs)[5] and Land Custom Stations[6] (LCSs) with Bangladesh, Bhutan, Myanmar and Nepal

Land customs stations/state in NER	Route and Cargo vehicle movement
With Bangladesh at:	
Golakganj (Assam)	Sonahat to Golakganj
Karimganj Steamerghat (Assam)	Kusiyara, Longai and Surma river
Sutarkandi (Assam)—ICP	Sylhet-Karimganj Trunk Road
Dawki Dry Port (Meghalaya)	Piyan River, Shillong-Sylhet Road, and Rangpani River Dhaka-Guwhati Bus (2015) passes through Dawki—Tamabil
Ghasuapara (Meghalaya)	Gandhibor to Karaitoli—Haluaghat (Bangladesh) and Minssingitta to Haluaghat (Bangladesh);
Shella Bazaar (Meghalaya)	Ichamati River, Land route from Pyrkan through Phrankaruh to Dastola in Bangladesh, Shella River
Agartala (Tripura)	Agartala—Akhaura (Bangladesh
Manu (Tripura)	Kailasahar to Murtichera leading to Samshernagar Kailasahar to Samshernagar and River Manu-Fatikrai to Manughat
Srimantapur (Tripura)—ICP	Gumti river Udaipur-Comilla road
Petrapol (West Bengal)—ICP	Links Benapole, largest land port of Bangladesh located in Jessore district
With Bhutan at:	
Hatisar, Chirang district (Assam)	Motorable Road from Samthiabari to Gaylegphug (Bhutan) via Runikhata and Deosiri in the District of Kokrajhar of Assam
Darranga, Darranga Melabazar, Baksa district (Assam): Upgraded to Border Trade Centre	Rangia-Tamulpur (Kamrup district, Assam) Motorable road from Darranga to Samdrup Jhonkhar (in Bhutan)

(continued)

[5] There are nine operational ICPs with one-stop solution that provide regulatory agencies/ facilitations such as immigration, customs and border security. Another set of 12 ICPs are under development at Dawki (Meghalaya), Panitanki, Birthamode, Fulbari, Jaigaon, Gojadhanga and Mahadipur (West Bengal), Rupaidiha, Sonauli (Uttar Pradesh), Banbasa (Uttarakhand), Kawrpuichhuah (Mizoram), Sabroom (Tripura). In 2020–21, ICPs in India facilitated trade worth Rs 95,488 crores and passenger movement of 2,62,396 persons.

https://lpai.gov.in/en.

[6] Land Custom Stations provide facilities like transit, customs and immigration and cargo handling services for goods and passengers travel between two countries. Many of the LCSs are being developed as ICPs.

Table 8.2 (continued)

Land customs stations/state in NER	Route and Cargo vehicle movement
Jaigaon (West Bengal)	Highway through Jaigaon (West Bengal) and Phunsoling (Bhutan) to capital Bhutan
With Myanmar at:	
Moreh (Manipur)—ICP	Manipur Imphal-Pallel-Tamu Road (N.H. 39)
Zorinpui, Lawngtlai (Mizoram)	Authorized immigration check post to and from Myanmar. Zorinpui is 287 km away from Sittwe Port in Myanmar
Zokhawthar, Rih sector (Mizoram)	Champai to Zokhawthar. A double-lane highway linking Zokhawthar LCS from Champhai is under construction
With Nepal at:	
Raxaul (Bihar)—ICP	Link to Birgunj, Nepal
Jogbani (Bihar)—ICP	Link to Biratnagar, Nepal
Nautanwa (Bihar)	Link to Bhairahawa, Nepal
Panitanki (West Bengal)	Link to Kakarbhitta (Nepal) and Phulbari (India border with Bangladesh)
Nepalganj (border with Rupaidiha in Uttar Pradesh)	Link to Nepalgunj Road Nepalgunj, Nepal

Sources (i) NEDFI (2021)
(ii) *Study and Assess the Infrastructure based on the Act East Policy*, NEDFi Report, Mott MacDonald, Gauhati (2018)

Table 8.3 China's share and ranking in India's total global trade 1990–2022

	Total global trade of India	Total trade with China	China's share in India's global trade	China's rank in India's total global trade
1990–91	41,803.0	49	0.12	Very low
1995–96	65,021.0	3644	0.99	Very low
2000–01	95,016.43	2947	3.10	12th[a]
2005–06	232,739.35	17,627.15	7.57	3rd
2010–11	619,581.79	57,648.62	9.30	2nd
2015–16	642,096.63	70,719.31	11.01	1st
2019–20	788,070.32	81,873.5	10.39	2nd
2020–21	686,242.51	86,399.40	12.59	1st
2021–22	1035055.9.1	115830.367	11.196	2nd

[a] Its rank in India's total trade steadily improves from 13th during 1997–98 to 4th by 2003–04

2000 and a significant level of $ 29.31 billion in 2010 and a hopping $ 44 billion in 2020. In fact, the trade deficit hit a hefty $ 73.31 billion by 2021–2022 and $ 83.199 billion 2022–2023 (https://tradestat.commerce.gov.in/eidb/iecnttopn.asp). This exponential increase in trade deficit has serious geo-strategic slant in terms of setting in dependency syndrome and dominance phenomenon.

It is quite discernible that increase in India's trade deficit vis-à-vis China in total global trade balance (deficit) of India has far outplaced China's share in India's global trade. China's share in India's global trade balance (deficit) increased from a mere 0.21% in 1990 to 11.23% in 2000 and reached a staggering figure of 42.89% in 2020. (came down to 31.62% by 2022–23)This is something quite awkward against the fact that China's share in India's global trade stood at 12.59% in 2020 whereas the share in India's global trade balance (deficit) stood at almost 43% (Table 8.4). This share of China in India's global trade went down to 9.76% by 2022–23 and trade deficit vis-a-vis China as a percentage of India's global trade deficit improved to 31.62% by 2022–23. (https://tradestat.commerce.gov.in/eidb/iecnttopn.asp)

This huge distortion in the volume of trade and bourgeoning quantum of protracted deficit very clearly reveal that there exists low level of trade complementarity between India and China. This also indicates that India's export basket does not suit Chinese import preferences and does not meet import requirements. On the other hand, this also demonstrates that China's export basket very well match with India's import preferences. Within this broadly sweeping narrative what remains as an underplayed theme has been the severe restrictions and unfair trade practices that China actually resorts to vis-a-vis its imports from India. This is acutely so in potential exports of India like pharmaceuticals (Karackattu 2013).This is well corroborated by the Indian Embassy in Beijing too where it states "The growth of trade deficit with China could be attributed to two factors: narrow basket of commodities, mostly primary, that we export to China and second, market access impediments for most of our agricultural

Table 8.4 China's share in India's global balance of trade 1990–2022 (US Million $)

Year	Global trade balance of India (deficit)	India's trade balance with China (deficit)	China's share in India's global trade balance
1990	−6177.00	−13.00	0.21
1995	−3947.00	−528.0	13.37
2000	−5,976.17	−670.89	11.23
2005	−26,601.25	−4,108.95	15.45
2010	−119,953.58	−29,310.90	24.43
2015	−118,716.40	−52,696.60	44.39
2019	−161,348.24	−48,648.00	30.15
2020	−102,627.38	−44,025.10	42.89
2021–22	−191047.13	−73310.78	38.37

Source Up to 2000, Estimated from IMF, *Direction of Trade Statistics Yearbook,* Various Issues. https://data.imf.org/regular.aspx?key=61013712
Ministry of Commerce, Government of India, https://tradestat.commerce.gov.in/eidb/iecnttopn.asp

products and the sectors where we are competitive in, such as pharmaceuticals, IT/ IteS, etc".[7]

8.5 Post-Galwan Valley Conflict

However, this in a way reveals that India has deepened its dependence on China made goods. Whereas China's dependence on India made goods are mostly of peripheral nature that could be done away within a specific time frame. On the other hand, India has to make a long-term plan to source these products either from its own domestic production facilities and/or access from other trading partners in the world. So, given the intensity of dependence on China, getting decoupled from it, carries in it the intense and efficient management of three crucial variables of time space, domestic production capabilities and alternative sources of imports. How deeply India is entangled on dependence syndrome on China is demonstrated rather eloquently during the post-Galwan Valley conflict[8] and other border imbroglios between these two countries since May–June 2020. India as a retaliatory measure resorted to banning Chinese apps,[9] reviewed the foreign direct investment (FDI) policy for curbing opportunistic takeover/acquisitions of Indian companies due to the COVID-19 pandemic[10]; and also announced a new regime of *Aatmanirbhar Bharat* (to both enhance production capability and reduce import and to deal with the adverse impact of COVID-19 pandemic).[11] India's Power Minister announced that India "will not allow any

---

[7] https://www.eoibeijing.gov.in/eoibejing_pages/Mjg and https://www.eoibeijing.gov.in/eoibejing_pages/MjQ.

[8] https://www.bbc.com/news/world-asia-india-53076781.

[9] Government of India banned 59 apps in June 2020, 117 in Sept 2020, 43 in November and 54 in January 2022. These banned apps range from TikTok to PUBG and WeChat to AliExpress. https://indianexpress.com/article/technology/tech-news-technology/garena-free-fire-and-53-other-chinese-apps-banned-full-list-7772673/, https://www.reuters.com/world/india/sea-owned-game-free-fire-unavailable-india-after-ban-chinese-apps-2022-02-15/.

[10] Amendments in Para 3.1.1 of extant FDI Policy as contained in Consolidated FDI Policy, 2017 were made as follows.

3.1.1(a) A non-resident entity can invest in India, subject to the FDI Policy except in those sectors/activities which are prohibited. However, an entity of a country, which shares land border with India or where the beneficial owner of an investment into India is situated in or is a citizen of any such country, can invest only under the Government route. Further, a citizen of Pakistan or an entity incorporated in Pakistan can invest, only under the Government route, in sectors/activities other than defence, space, atomic energy and sectors/activities prohibited for foreign investment.

3.1.1(b) In the event of the transfer of ownership of any existing or future FDI in an entity in India, directly or indirectly, resulting in the beneficial ownership falling within the restriction/ purview of the para 3.1.1(a), such subsequent change in beneficial ownership will also require Government approval.

https://pib.gov.in/PressReleasePage.aspx?PRID=1615711.

[11] https://www.investindia.gov.in/atmanirbhar-bharat-abhiyaan.

https://prsindia.org/policy/report-summaries/summary-announcements-aatma-nirbhar-bharat-abhiyaan.

imports from Prior Reference countries China and Pakistan. There could be malware or Trojan horse in those (including imports from China) which they can activate remotely (to cripple our power systems) … We will not allow you (states) to import anything from China and Pakistan"[12] In the same vein, India's Minister of Road Transport and Highways said India "will not give permission to joint ventures that have Chinese partners for road construction. We have taken a firm stand that if they (Chinese companies) come via joint venture in our country, we will not allow it."[13]

It was against this backdrop, amidst devastating Covid-19 and series of lock downs, Prime Minister announced a package of Rs 20 lakh crore - equivalent to almost 10% of India's GDP- to achieve 'Atmanirbhar Bharat' (self reliant India). He stated that atmanirbhar bharat (12 May 2020) will stand on five pillars viz. Economy, which brings in quantum jump and not incremental change; Infrastructure, which should become the identity of India; System, based on 21st century technology driven arrangements; Vibrant Demography, a source of energy; and Demand, whereby the strength of demand and supply chain should be utilized to full capacity. It underlined the importance of strengthening all stakeholders in the supply chain to increase, as well as fulfill, the demand and emphasised on 'vocal for our local products and make them global' (https://pib.gov.in/PressReleasePage.aspx?PRID=1623391). Since the "advancement of ties … was clearly predicated on ensuring that peace and tranquillity were not disturbed"[14] the public mood in general widely supported decoupling with China on any kind of exchanges and keeping China away from any major bilateral economic, social, cultural and other exchanges including boycott of "Made in China" goods. Naturally, people at large expected that India's policies of decoupling with China could show instant result and one of the critical indicators would be the volume and composition of trade.

However, when the bilateral trade figures started emerging for the year 2020–2021 and 2021–2022, it suddenly donned in public and the government that it is a very intricate and cumbersome process to decouple and disengage with China. In fact, though during the peak COVID-19 onslaught of mid-2020, the trade figures slightly went down, the 2021 – 2022 figure showed that the India-China trade engagement increased in an unprecedented manner to $ 115.83 billion against the pre-Galwan valley bilateral trade figure of $ 81.87 billion (2019–2020). Nowhere in the past 50 years, such a record year to year jump ($ 33.96 billion) taken place in just one

[12] https://www.ndtv.com/india-news/union-minister-rk-singh-says-we-wont-allow-power-equipment-imports-from-china-pakistan-2256416.

[13] https://www.ndtv.com/india-news/wont-allow-chinese-partners-in-road-and-highway-projects-says-nitin-gadkari-2255255.

[14] Remarks of India's Foreign Secretary at the seminar on "Leveraging China's economy", Pune, October 21, 2021 https://mea.gov.in/Speeches-Statements.htm?dtl/34407/foreign+secretarys+remarks+at+the+seminar+on+leveraging+chinas+economy.

fiscal year 2020–21 to 2021–2022.[15] In fact in normal course, the trade volume was expected to reach over $ 100 billion by 2025.

It did, nevertheless, show the existence of apparent contradiction between domestic political announcements and postures of India and actual actions that get into the process of reducing trade engagements with China. How does one explain this? Does one call it a policy mismatch, action dilemma and absence of coherent harmonization and coordination among various domestic and transborder actors and institutions in India? Was it a misplaced understating of how India had been consistently induced and later forced to reach this critical threshold of dependence by China? Could it be the case that onslaught of COVID-19 pandemic in two virulent phases (March 2020 and June 2021) actually dislocated the operationalization of India's plan of actions on disengagements with China in bilateral exchanges? Did the people unreasonably expect instant result of *aatamanirbhar* paradigm? How long will it actually take in terms of realizing actions on critical variables of time space, enhancing domestic production capabilities and identifying alternative sources of imports. This involves result oriented actions on multiple critical and inter-connected fronts including massive investment on R&D, varieties of technological innovations, generating trained and skilled human capital, massive market expansion, liberal finance, far reaching reforms and liberalisation, induction of foreign capital, and effective governance process.

8.5.1 Aatmanirbhar *(self reliance) Paradigm*

The very evolution, nature and composition of India–China trade actually demand a pretty long gestation period for the delivery outcomes of *aatmanirbhar* paradigm to come into effect and fully realize its objectives. As building domestic production capabilities and finding alternative sources of imports are arduous process largely dependent on so many domestic policy criss-crosses, foreign policy matrices and confidence building actions among the industrial players of all varieties and also orientations of the political parties and their leadership in India. This decoupling even in the long run involves rounds of all round reforms sometimes hurting and destabilising the orthodox institutions and actors, several technological innovations with colossal increase in R&D, substantial building of human capitals, setting up chain of multi-modal infrastructures and institutions, deeper de-bureaucratization, linking with global players and of course, political stability and forward-looking leadership.

---

[15] In fact US $ 125.66 billion of trade volume in 2021 was quoted by Global Times , Shanghai as sourced from General Administration of Customs (GAC), Government of PRC. Sutirtho Patranobis in *Hindustan Times*, 14 January 2022. https://www.hindustantimes.com/world-news/sinoindia-trade-at-record-125bn-for-2021-amid-border-tension-deficit-widens-101642166288374.html.

If not planned scientifically and with extraordinary conviction, even the incremental decoupling could inject destabilising external shocks and exact a disproportionate cost on India rather than affecting China. Such efforts of decoupling to be meaningful should be well harmonized with what Japan through its relocations of its corporates and ventures from China to other countries and the United States through its rounds of popular "trade war" have been undertaking vis-à-vis China. And more so, the decoupling must align with the global governance principles of supra institutions like World Trade Organization to put China more intensely and durably in the basket of globally accepted norms and regulatory framework and exert pressures on its domestic constituencies to appreciate and advocate inter-dependence.

Dependence on China has evolved over the decades under particular domestic and global policy regimes and various political party-based foreign policy orientations. Therefore, unless there are some sort of drastic unilateral restrictions or even sanctions, in normal course, it is unreasonable to expect any meaningful cut down in Chinese imports and expansion in Indian exports to China in course of just few years. An indication towards this is now available Since August 2023, the import of laptops, tablets, all-in-one personal computers, and 'ultra small form factor' computers and servers falling under HSN 8741 are now restricted and brought under valid licence for restricted imports (https://indianexpress.com/article/explained/explained-economics/new-restriction-personal-computers-laptop-imports-explained-8874853/). At the same time, if *atmanirbhar bharat* is used to promote "economic autarky," thereby putting severe restrictions on India's intermediate inputs, technology, ancillary parts, etc. from China, there could be a situation where its partnership in the global supply chain would be deftly affected.

Why variables of time space, domestic production capabilities and alternative sources of imports remain so very critical for India to decouple vis-à-vis China, could be partly explained by the composition and nature of ingredients of India–China bilateral trade.

Despite being a manufacturing hub, Indian exports to China are overwhelmingly primary commodities, i.e., raw or semi-raw materials. The foremost of these are cotton, copper, iron ore, organic chemicals, aluminium, diamonds/natural gems and other minerals. And its imports are a plethora of finished products like telecom equipment, electrical machinery, computer and mobile hardware and fertilizer. Many of these goods that have high demand and public consumption are low priced and widely accessible in any corners of India (Tables 8.6 and 8.7).

Available data show that at the HS code 2-digit level too, ores, slag and ash constituted number 1 export of India ($ 155.32 million) in 2000–01 constituting over 12% of total exports to China, $ 4767.11 in 2010–2011 (33.4%), $ 2356.97 million in 2019–20 (14.18%),[16] $ 4382.42 million in 2020–21 (20.68%) and $ 1,972.78 million in 2021–22 (11.51%). Besides, other primary commodities like copper, cotton, salt, animal or vegetable fats have mostly figured as some of the top items of exports from India. (Table 8.5). A study (PHDCCI 2018) found that India's top 10 export

[16] Iron ore constituted the second major export item, the first being organic chemicals with $ 2702.44 (16.26%).

items constituted 73% of the overall exports to China and share of raw materials have however, recorded a decline from 60% in 2006 to 25% in 2016 and the share of intermediate goods increased from 34.5 to 50% respectively.

8.6 Core Competence: Operation Flood in the Export Basket[17]

The core competence of India based on community mobilization and participation has some rare comparisons in China. Yet in the macro narrative of dependency syndrome, all these comparative advantages are swept under the carpet. The governments tend to protractedly negotiate on IT and related services yet side-lining traditionally built product and community services. For example, in the non-farm sector, India's proven core competence in dairying and dairy products is one area which could inject a community-based sustained demand in China and could act as a major constituent in its export basket of India. Given the changing pattern of food consumption and demand particularly among the new generation, crave for healthy-organic food, and a staggering demand—supply gaps in liquid milk and dairy products, China could be a major destination of India's milk products essentially driven by the farmers and the non-farming communities. When India provides a stable and bourgeoning market to China and in lieu, it can always press China to open market for product and services where it has no core competence vis-a-vis India.

The story of India's Operation Flood Programme (OFP) led White Revolution itself could be its major soft power instrument in making forays into the Chinese provinces, towns and villages. This story has strong ingredients of struggle against poverty and deprivation, community mobilization, getting rid of dominance from the giant wheels of milk production in Europe and the United States, innovation made in layers of appropriate technological insertions and most seriously availability of affordable fresh liquid milk both in bulk easily accessible and friendly bulk vending machines and as grocery item too.

India's successful White (Milk) Revolution, making it the largest producer of milk in the world could be a major arena of India-China cooperation. Developed under Anand Milk Union Limited (AMUL) Model, initially to thwart the adverse dependency on food aid from the western countries, a new strategy with three tiers of milk procurement and distribution was designed. Layers of modern technologies were inducted at each stage of milk production, processing and marketing. Milk farmers receive remunerative procurement prices with a range of production services. The

[17] This section draws from my own professional engagements as a young Executive in early 1990s with the National Dairy Development Board led by Father of White Revolution in India ebullient Verghese Kurien at Anand, Gujarat. NDDB spearheaded the cooperative movement to organize the farmers all over the country and evolved a globally celebrated brand widely known as AMUL (Anand Milk Union Limited) model.

Table 8.5 Composition of Major Exports of India to China 2000–2022

HS code (2 digit level)	Commodity	US million $
2000–2001		
26	Ores, slag and ash	155.32
3	Fish and crustaceans, molluscs and other aquatic invertebrates	115.78
29	Organic chemicals	108.09
39	Plastic and articles thereof	80.97
25	Salt; sulphur; earth and stone; plastering materials, lime and cement	47.95
72	Iron and steel	27.39
84	Nuclear reactors, boilers, machinery and mechanical appliances; parts thereof	17.55
74	Copper and articles thereof	15.54
15	Animal or vegetable fats and oils and their cleavage products; pre. Edible fats; animal or vegetable waxes	13.85
2010–2011		
26	Ores, slag and ash	4767.11 (33.4)
52	Cotton	1891.46
27	Mineral fuels, mineral oils and products of their distillation; bituminous substances; mineral waxes	825.14
72	Iron and steel	748.61
29	Organic chemicals	701.81
39	Plastic and articles thereof	399.75
25	Salt; sulphur; earth and stone; plastering materials, lime and cement	371.74
84	Nuclear reactors, boilers, machinery and mechanical appliances; parts thereof	318.25
3	Fish and crustaceans, molluscs and other aquatic invertebrates	273.72
23	Residues and waste from the food industries; prepared animal fodder	244.4
	Animal or vegetable fats and oils and their cleavage products; pre. Edible fats; animal or vegetable waxes	234.57
68	Articles of stone, plaster, cement, asbestos, mica or similar materials	127.48
67	Prepared feathers and down and articles made of feathers or of down; artificial flowers; articles of human hair	100.67
2019–2020		
29	Organic chemical	2702.44
26	Ores, slag and ash	2356.97 (14.18)

(continued)

Table 8.5 (continued)

HS code (2 digit level)	Commodity	US million $
27	Mineral fuels, mineral oils and products of their distillation; bituminous substances; mineral waxes	2128.57
3	Fish and crustaceans, molluscs and other aquatic invertebrates	1336.57
85	Electrical machinery and equipment and parts thereof; sound recorders and reproducers, television image and sound recorders and reproducers and parts	862.33
39	Plastic and articles thereof	843.06
84	Nuclear reactors, boilers, machinery and mechanical appliances; parts thereof	804.31
52	Cotton	777.96
25	Salt; sulphur; earth and stone; plastering materials, lime and cement	614.13
72	Iron and steel	513.91
15	Animal or vegetable fats and oils and their cleavage products; pre. Edible fats; animal or vegetable waxes	394.56
74	Copper and articles thereof	265.91
2020–2021		
26	Ores, slag and ash	4382.42 (20.68)
72	Iron and steel	2,512.55
29	Organic chemical	2,416.35
52	Cotton	1,277.24
27	Mineral fuels, mineral oils and products of their distillation; bituminous substances; mineral waxes	1,046.55
39	Plastic and articles thereof	949.2
15	Animal or vegetable fats and oils and their cleavage products; pre. Edible fats; animal or vegetable waxes	875.91
3	Fish and crustaceans, molluscs and other aquatic invertebrates	860.74
74	Copper and articles thereof	779.26
84	Nuclear reactors, boilers, machinery and mechanical appliances; parts thereof	750.73
85	Electrical machinery and equipment and parts thereof; sound recorders and reproducers, television image and sound recorders and reproducers and parts	717.37
9	Coffee, tea, mate and spices	674.49
25	Salt; sulphur; earth and stone; plastering materials, lime and cement	628.72
2021–2022		
26	Ores, slag and ash	1,972.78 (11.51)

(continued)

Table 8.5 (continued)

HS code (2 digit level)	Commodity	US million $
29	Organic chemical	1,928.24
27	Mineral fuels, mineral oils and products of their distillation; bituminous substances; mineral waxes	1,478.52
72	Iron and steel	1,268.42
52	Cotton	1,162.39
76	Aluminium and articles thereof	1,112.16
74	Copper and articles thereof	988.72
3	Fish and crustaceans, molluscs and other aquatic invertebrates	891.4
84	Nuclear reactors, boilers, machinery and mechanical appliances; parts thereof	824.75
25	Salt; sulphur; earth and stone; plastering materials, lime and cement	627.86
9	Coffee, tea, mate and spices	476.02
67	Prepared feathers and down and articles made of feathers or of down; artificial flowers; articles of human hair	407.39

Source Data deduced from the Ministry of Commerce, Government of India, https://tradestat.commerce.gov.in/eidb/iecnttopn.asp

hygienic liquid milk and products have been made available to the consumers across the country in affordable prices through Mother Dairies and bulk vending.

Most impressive aspects have been the governance pattern and injection of appropriate, friendly and cost-effective technologies which had a chain of socio-economic gains as over 70% of the milk producers are small, marginal and landless households. Besides the gainful employment, it could also reduce diabolical practices like caste and class barriers, economic inhibitions and communal biases. In the aftermath of reforms in 1991, the delicensing of the dairy sector opened the floodgates to the private sectors. The milk cooperative societies are vehemently opposing imports from highly mechanized producing countries like Australia and New Zealand.

How relevant is the entire AMUL model so engrossingly and inclusively designed by visionaries like Tribhuvan Das Patel and Verghese Kurien in the Kheda district of Gujarat? How exchange of technologies and management techniques could enhance China's milk production and improve living standards of the farmers? And what are the scope and avenues of cooperation including in people-centric Governance patterns? The Father of White Revolution in India, Varghese Kurien, set out with three dreams while he chose Anand in Gujarat as his take off bastion in 1960s. First, India should be the highest milk-producing country with its cascading impact on landless and marginal farmers. Second, quality and affordably priced milk and milk products should be a grocery item reaching the remotest of consumers. This could facilitate tackling both malnutrition and poverty. And third, making milk as a major item in India's export basket and its zero dependence on milk imports.

Table 8.6 Composition of Major Imports from China 2000–2022

HS code (2 digit level)	Commodity	US million $
2000–2001		
27	Mineral fuels, mineral oils and products of their distillation; bituminous substances; mineral waxes	263.27
29	Organic chemicals	249.26
84	Nuclear reactors, boilers, machinery and mechanical appliances; parts thereof	188.65
85	Electrical machinery and equipment and parts thereof; sound recorders and reproducers, television image and sound recorders and reproducers and parts	161.43
50	Silk	113.34
25	Salt; sulphur; earth and stone; plastering materials, lime and cement	82.42
28	Inorganic chemicals; organic or inorganic compounds of precious metals, of rare-earth metals, or radi. elem. or of isotopes	50.67
30	Pharmaceutical products	1.4
2010–2011		
85	Electrical machinery and equipment and parts thereof; sound recorders and reproducers, television image and sound recorders and reproducers and parts	11,857.72
84	Nuclear reactors, boilers, machinery and mechanical appliances; parts thereof	7,699.90
29	Organic chemicals	3,853.42
98	Project goods; some special uses	3,181.56
72	Iron and steel	1,986.38
31	Fertilizers	1,517.44
89	Ships, boats and floating structures	1,213.39
73	Articles of iron or steel	1,178.18
39	Plastic and articles thereof	855.71
87	Vehicles other than railway or tramway rolling stock, and parts and accessories thereof	733.65
71	Natural or cultured pearls, precious or semiprecious stones, pre.metals, clad with pre.metal and artcls thereof; imit.jewlry; coin	685.02
90	Optical, photographic cinematographic measuring, checking precision, medical or surgical inst. And apparatus parts and accessories thereof	655.4
38	Miscellaneous chemical products	541.19
28	Inorganic chemicals; organic or inorganic compounds of precious metals, of rare-earth metals, or radi. Elem. Or of isotopes	533.45

(continued)

Table 8.6 (continued)

HS code (2 digit level)	Commodity	US million $
94	Furniture; bedding, mattresses, mattress supports, cushions and similar stuffed furnishing; lamps and lighting fittings not elsewhere specified or inc	401.3
69	Ceramic products	366.94
50	Silk	358.36
59	Impregnated, coated, covered or laminated textile fabrics; textile articles of a kind suitable for industrial use	329.77
40	Rubber and articles thereof	356.8
54	Man-made filaments	305.19
76	Aluminium and articles thereof	258.25
32	Tanning or dyeing extracts; tannins and their deri. Dyes, pigments and other colouring matter; paints and ver; putty and other mastics; inks	245.97
70	Glass and glassware	256.46
	Toys, games and sports requisites; parts and accessories thereof	238.4
48	Paper and paperboard; articles of paper pulp, of paper or of paperboard	237.5
30	Pharmaceutical products	85.76
2019–2020		
85	Electrical machinery and equipment and parts thereof; sound recorders and reproducers, television image and sound recorders and reproducers, and parts	19,104.15
84	Nuclear reactors, boilers, machinery and mechanical appliances; parts thereof	13,322.13
29	Organic chemicals	7,970.43
39	Plastic and articles thereof	2,714.82
31	Fertilizers	1,820.88
73	Articles of iron or steel	1,588.76
90	Optical, photographic cinematographic measuring, checking precision, medical or surgical inst. And apparatus parts and accessories thereof	1,340.39
87	Vehicles other than railway or tramway rolling stock, and parts and accessories thereof	1,273.88
38	Miscellaneous chemical products	1,205.06
72	Iron and steel	1,121.33
76	Aluminium and articles thereof	957.33
94	Furniture; bedding, mattresses, mattress supports, cushions and similar stuffed furnishing; lamps and lighting fittings not elsewhere specified or inc	899.44
28	Inorganic chemicals; organic or inorganic compounds of precious metals, of rare-earth metals, or radi. Elem. Or of isotopes	746.71

(continued)

Table 8.6 (continued)

HS code (2 digit level)	Commodity	US million $
70	Glass and glassware	604.51
32	Tanning or dyeing extracts; tannins and their deri. Dyes, pigments and other colouring matter; paints and ver; putty and other mastics; inks	567.62
54	Man-made filaments	561.20
27	Mineral fuels, mineral oils and products of their distillation; bituminous substances; mineral waxes	506.60
48	Paper and paperboard; articles of paper pulp, of paper or of paperboard	488.42
68	Articles of stone, plaster, cement, asbestos, mica or similar materials	470.65
59	Impregnated, coated, covered or laminated textile fabrics; textile articles of a kind suitable for industrial use	455.39
83	Miscellaneous articles of base metal	402.51
60	Knitted or crocheted fabrics	389.34
64	Footwear, gaiters and the like; parts of such articles	371.12
55	Man-made staple fibres	359.54
96	Miscellaneous manufactured articles	354.49
69	Ceramic products	345.29
82	Tools implement, cutlery, spoons and forks, of base metal; parts thereof of base metal	325.00
42	Articles of leather, saddlery and harness; travel goods, handbags and similar cont. articles of animal gut (other than silk-warm) gut	318.45
40	Rubber and articles thereof	283.30
81	Other base metals; cermets; articles thereof	219.14
86	Railway or tramway locomotives, rolling-stock and parts thereof; railway or tramway track fixtures and fittings and parts thereof; mechanical	204.67
61	Articles of apparel and clothing accessories, knitted or crocheted	201.46
2020–2021		
85	Electrical machinery and equipment and parts thereof; sound recorders and reproducers, television image and sound recorders and reproducers, and parts	20,328.53
84	Nuclear reactors, boilers, machinery and mechanical appliances; parts thereof	13,987.55
29	Organic chemicals	8,974.24
39	Plastic and articles thereof	2,530.53
90	Optical, photographic cinematographic measuring, checking precision, medical or surgical inst. And apparatus parts and accessories thereof	1,732.52
31	Fertilizers	1,551.23
38	Miscellaneous chemical products	1,386.24

(continued)

Table 8.6 (continued)

HS code (2 digit level)	Commodity	US million $
	Vehicles other than railway or tramway rolling stock, and parts and accessories thereof	1,375.68
73	Articles of iron or steel	1,317.92
72	Iron and steel	895.38
28	Inorganic chemicals; organic or inorganic compounds of precious metals, of rare-earth metals, or radi. Elem. Or of isotopes	662.25
94	Furniture; bedding, mattresses, mattress supports, cushions and similar stuffed furnishing; lamps and lighting fittings not elsewhere specified or inc	589.94
32	Tanning or dyeing extracts; tannins and their deri. Dyes, pigments and other colouring matter; paints and ver; putty and other mastics; inks	578.63
54	Man-made filaments	588.47
70	Glass and glassware	470.94
55	Man-made staple fibres	380.77
68	Articles of stone, plaster, cement, asbestos, mica or similar materials	377
60	Knitted or crocheted fabrics	361.39
98	Project goods; some special uses	350.06
48	Paper and paperboard; articles of paper pulp, of paper or of paperboard	339.41
83	Miscellaneous articles of base metal	326.76
96	Miscellaneous manufactured articles	311.14
59	Impregnated, coated, covered or laminated textile fabrics; textile articles of a kind suitable for industrial use	306.95
95	Toys, games and sports requisites; parts and accessories thereof	289.72
69	Ceramic products	286.54
63	Other made-up textile articles; sets; worn clothing and worn textile articles; rags	228.27
27	Mineral fuels, mineral oils and products of their distillation; bituminous substances; mineral waxes	209.15
30	Pharmaceutical products	207.56
2021–2022 (April–December)		
85	Electrical machinery and equipment and parts thereof; sound recorders and reproducers, television image and sound recorders and reproducers, and parts	20,163.94
84	Nuclear reactors, boilers, machinery and mechanical appliances; parts thereof	14,302.97
29	Organic chemicals	9,314.44
39	Plastic and articles thereof	3,222.42

(continued)

Table 8.6 (continued)

HS code (2 digit level)	Commodity	US million $
31	Fertilizers	2,615.55
38	Miscellaneous chemical products	1,333.94
73	Articles of iron or steel	1,230.31
87	Vehicles other than railway or tramway rolling stock, and parts and accessories thereof	1,225.91
72	Iron and steel	929.47
54	Man-made filaments	718.78
27	Mineral fuels, mineral oils and products of their distillation; bituminous substances; mineral waxes	712.39
28	Inorganic chemicals; organic or inorganic compounds of precious metals, of rare-earth metals, or radi. Elem. Or of isotopes	692.73
32	Tanning or dyeing extracts; tannins and their deri. Dyes, pigments and other colouring matter; paints and ver; putty and other mastics; inks	690.92
94	Furniture; bedding, mattresses, mattress supports, cushions and similar stuffed furnishing; lamps and lighting fittings not elsewhere specified or inc	510.83
70	Glass and glassware	475.59
82	Tools implement, cutlery, spoons and forks, of base metal; parts thereof of base metal	359.16
59	Impregnated, coated, covered or laminated textile fabrics; textile articles of a kind suitable for industrial use	390.32
60	Knitted or crocheted fabrics	351.67
68	Articles of stone, plaster, cement, asbestos, mica or similar materials	350.82
48	Paper and paperboard; articles of paper pulp, of paper or of paperboard	336.22
55	Man-made staple fibres	300.63
69	Ceramic products	277.89
96	Miscellaneous manufactured articles	265.57
74	Copper and articles thereof	237.77
40	Rubber and articles thereof	214.46

Source Data deduced from the Ministry of Commerce, Government of India, https://tradestat.commerce.gov.in/eidb/Icntcom.asp

With 208.98 million tons and 22.76% out of the Global 918.16 million tonnes, India is today the largest milk producer in the world (https://amul.com/m/gcmmf). In a highly populous country, the per capita availability of milk has steadily increased from 132 gms in 1951, 180 gms in 1997, to 351 gms in 2018 and 444 gms in 2022. For this advent of self-sufficiency, Kurien's team made seven critical policy interventions. Firstly, given the long-term adverse dependency impact of food aid

Table 8.7 A glimpse of items covered under Import Category of Nuclear Reactors, Boilers, Machinery and Mechanical Appliances; parts thereof (8-digit HS Code 84)

HS code	Commodity description	HS code	Commodity description
84,011,000	Nuclear reactors	843,351	Combine harvester-threshers
840,220	Super-heated water boilers	84,341,000	Milking machines
840,310	Heating boilers	843,420	Dairy machinery
84,031,000	Central heating boilers	84,381,001	Bakery machinery
840,420	Condensers	84,383,001	Sugar cane crushers
840,610	Turbines for marine propulsion	843,840	Brewery machinery
840,710	Air-craft engines	843,850	Machinery for prepration of meat/poultry
840,729	Marine propulsion engines	84,386,001	Fruit ets. drying or dehydrating machinery
84,079,001	Petrol engines	84,393,010	Laminating machine
84,079,002	Kerosene engines	84,425,004	Printing machines
841,410	Pumps, fans, compressors	84,433,210	Printers
8415	Air conditioning machines	84,451,210	Cotton combing machines
841,610	Furnace burners refrigerators, freezers	84,451,902	Jute fibre processing machines
84,186,910	Ice-making machinery	84,451,904	Silk processing machines
84,186,920	Water cooler	84,451,905	Wool processing knitting machines
84,192,090	Sterilizers, dryers	84,472,019	Knitting machines, n.e.s
84,198,101	Solar cooker	845,110	Dry-cleaning machines
84,198,903	Water treatment plant	845,229	Sewing machines
84,198,950	Pasteurizers	845,410	Converters
84,211,100	Cream separators	845,430	Casting machines
842,112	Cloth dryers	84,569,001	Electro-chemical machines
8422	Dish washing machines	84,690,010	Word processing machines
84,223,001	Capsule filling machine	84,690,030	Electric braille typewriters
84,223,002	Gas filling machine/plant or equipment	847,040	Accounting machines
84,238,110	Beam scale	84,712,001	Large/mainframe computer
84,239,010	Weighing machine	84,712,002	Microcomputer/processor
842,410	Fire extinguishers	84,713,010	Personal computer (laptop, palmtop, etc.)
84,248,100	Appliances for horticultural/ agricultural work	84,716,003	Data-entry terminal
84,248,910	Painting equipment	84,717,010	Floppy disc drives
842,620	Cranes	84,717,060	CD-ROM drive
84,269,910	Ropeway and telphers	84,719,007	VGA/CGA monitors

(continued)

Table 8.7 (continued)

HS code	Commodity description	HS code	Commodity description
84,281,011	Lifts of a kind used in buildings	84,721,000	Duplicating machines
84,282,020	Elevators	84,729,010	Stapling machines (staplers)
842,840	Escalators and moving walkways	847,420	Crushing/grinding machines
84,285,010	Wagon marshalling equipment	84,748,001	Brick and tile-making machinery
84,304,101	Tube well drilling machinery	84,748,002	Ceramic and clay-making machinery
84,304,102	Petroleum and gas well drilling equipment	84,768,910	Money changing machines
84,304,109	Other self-propounded boring/ sinking machinery	84,768,920	Postage stamps vending machines
84,304,110	Tube well drilling and core drilling machinery	84,792,001	Oil seed crushing/grinding machinery (including purifying tanks)
84,304,120	Petroleum and gas well drilling equipment	84,794,000	Rope/cable-making machines
84,304,130	Rock drilling machinery (including diamond drilling), scrapers	847,950	Industrial robots
843,210	Ploughs	84,798,904	Soap-manufacturing machinery
843,241	Manure spreaders	84,798,905	Tea-leaf cutting/rolling machinery
		84,798,906	Air humidifire and de-humidifier equipments/plant
843,242	Fertilizer distributors	84,821,090	Ball bearings
84,328,010	Lawn and sports ground rollers		

extended under PL-480 of the United States and World Food Programme in 1950s–1970s, the imported butter oil and schemed milk powder were judiciously recombined with the indigenous milk production and sold to the consumers. This inspired the farmers to participate in dairy activities. As a result, the imports of milk products as percentage of the total throughput steadily came down from 67% (1950–51) and 36% (1960–61), 10.2% (1989–90) to nil in 1990–91 onwards.

Secondly, an apex institution known as National Dairy Development Board was established in 1965 (https://www.nddb.coop) primarily to undertake Operation Flood Programme (OFP) launched in 1970. Third, a new model with three tiers of milk procurement and distribution was designed. The village cooperatives at the grass root producers' level have been the nucleus. These village-level cooperatives together constitute milk unions at the district and dairy cooperatives federation at the state level like Gujarat Cooperative Milk Marketing Federation (GCMMF) with very clear functions and responsibilities. It started with Anand Milk Union Limited (AMUL) in

Kheda district of Gujarat and steadily spread over to other districts and the states. It involves intensive and extensive participation of the farmers in the decision-making process. By 2021, 0.22 million village cooperatives had 18 million members (NDDB, Annual Report 2021–22, https://www.nddb.coop/about/report). This has come a long way from 1588 village cooperatives and 0.28 million members in 1970.

Fourth, layers of modern technologies were inducted at each stage of milk production. Fifth, milk farmers were provided remunerative procurement prices with a range of production services. Sixth, hygienic liquid milk and products were made available to the consumers in affordable prices. Mother Dairies in the metropolitan cities as bulk vendors of milk and pouched and other packages in smaller towns and suburbs gave easy daily access to fresh and hygienic milk. And seventh, the new generation interventions like Internet-based Dairy Information System that connects co-operative organizations in the dairy sector across the country on various information sharing has been initiated. Centres of methane measurement from ruminants are now widely available. This potent greenhouse gas emitter rooted at enteric fermentation of feed by ruminants has been a major global concern.

Most impressive aspects of the OFP have been the injection of appropriate, friendly and cost-effective technologies. These innovative technologies at the village level related to changing the herd composition and bovine culture to raise productivity. To induce structural change in the bovine pattern, induction of newer strains having genetic superiority and means like artificial insemination, cross-bred techniques, and embryo transfer were made. This was needed as the indigenous varieties of cow-like Sahiwal, Gir, Red Sindhi and Kankrej had much lower yield than Jersey and Holstein Friesian.

In order to make the feed-fodder and milk conversion ratio more efficient, technologies like special feed and licking of urea molasses block were introduced. Teak vaccination and foot and mouth disease treatment, prophylactic inoculations and other new generation preventive cures were innovated by its bio-technology wing. The fat testing machine and adulteration detection kit were made available, which could be used even by an illiterate farmer. Milk was then priced on its fat and solid non-fat and organoliptic quality basis under the two-axis formula. In 2018 the per kg fat price stood at US$ 12. This brought common pricing policy for both cow and buffalo.

A farmer is given the cash on a daily and weekly basis at the village cooperative society. Many of the societies are run by women members only. At the district level, these procured milk would see another layer of interventions. Once milk is procured, it is brought to the district union and put through chilling plants. It then undergoes the process of pasteurization, ultra-heating and conversion into various products like cheese, ghee, curd, butter and ice cream. At the federation level, the milk is then marketed both as liquid and products in all the *Mother Dairy* booths.

India for long confronted with two serious problems of seasonality and geographical scarcity in milk production and availability. The former was caused by the herd composition wherein areas having overwhelming cow population had milk scarcity in summer. In cities like Delhi and Bombay, the sale of sweet meats was banned in summer. This was soon overcome. The later was triggered by inadequate production like in Calcutta in winter. This was overcome through bulk supplies by refrigerated trains under national milk grid. The winter glut supplies of the west were dispatched to the scarcity-prone eastern region.

The celebrated AMUL has emerged as the largest Indian milk and dairy products manufacturer. Its dairy producer's cooperative supplies 27 million litres of milk daily. In 2018 alone its apex body GCMMF produced 24,939 MT of butter, 19,119 MT skimmed milk powder, 15,897 MT spray, 5441 MT ghee, 1429 MT curd and 5 million litres of flavoured milk. Its exports market varies from United States, to New Zealand, Japan to Singapore, Bangladesh to Nepal, Vietnam to Dubai and Maldives to Mauritius. By 2022–2023 its turnover reached $ 7.2 billion.

The OF Programme had a chain of socio-economic gains as over 70% of the milk producers are small, marginal and landless households. Besides the gainful employment, it could also reduce diabolical practices like caste and class barriers, economic inhibitions and communal biases. A village milk cooperative society is a symbol of democratically constituted institutional force. Its income is even used towards creating durable social and economic assets like schools, roads, water ponds, tree plantings, etc.

In the aftermath of reforms in 1991, the delicensing of the dairy sector opened the floodgates to the private sectors including General Foods, Nestle and Glaxo. This also led to a plethora of milk-producing and marketing ventures outside the AMUL model. The cooperative societies are vehemently opposing imports from highly mechanized producing countries like Australia and New Zealand.

China imports huge quantity of milk as there has been a marked increase in the demand of milk and milk products. It brings milk and products all the way from western countries—Australia, New Zealand, Germany and others. Can India seriously bid for sending Amul model to China and see what it can do to improve the ever-negative terms of trade. Amul model will engage communities in China as it has engaged in India. And also, durably bring forth Indian technologies, practices, institutions in China.

8.7 Silent Repeat of Recent History

Given the plethora of high-value imports from China, India has been facing a serious issue of unfavourable terms of trade as reflected in the colossal balance of trade deficit. It was the same issue of unfavourable and distorted terms of trade that galvanized the entire newly decolonized and other developing countries to come to a common platform against the developed market economies at the global level. This along with technology transfer, debt burdens and rescheduling, share of official development assistance in their GNP had in fact triggered a protracted and fierce North–South negotiations. India did play a pivotal role in fora like NAM, G-77 and UNCTAD to highlight all these serious issues of conscious undercutting and undermining of export bases of developing countries by confining themselves to trading in primary commodities mainly raw materials.

However, unlike during the four decades of the 1950s to the 1980s, India has displayed literally no stand on this very ominous trend and practice of deteriorating terms of trade as injected by China. Except few studies (Mohanty 2014; Yuan 2016; PHDCCI 2018; Boothalingam 2020), and references[18] raising this concern, no consistent and collective voice has been raised and no conscious and effective measures are taken to correct the situation. On the other hand, China has adopted exactly the same pathways, what countries in the North followed or very doggedly pursued in 1950s, 60 s, 70 s till 1980s, i.e., the countries in the North tried to very consciously keep the countries in the south dependent and far away from the discourse of interdependence. China's stand has been typically endorsed by *Global Times* published from Shanghai when it states "India has long hoped to reduce its trade deficit with China, but making bilateral trade more balanced cannot be done by curbing Chinese exports to India, which would only hurt the Indian economy. Further boosting China's imports from India is the right way to go, and there is room for coordination between the two sides in this regard, and it should be a joint effort."[19]

This has already happened for more than 20 years now. China has done this to other developing countries and regions including Africa and South East, Central and South and Middle East Asia. This is a quiet intrusion into the prolific natural endowments of neighbouring and other countries. The increasing demonstration of "resource nationalism" among the countries that continue to export raw materials partly explains a new genre of partnership within the fraternity of developing countries to protest against China's increasing attempt to propagate dependency. This was essentially carried out by the developed market economies during 1950–1980s.

This is where Prime Minister Narendra Modi's initiative of "Make in India" stands to be critical, where the country's raw materials are used by its own manufacturing and other production bases. It is in this context Production Linked Incentive (PLI) Schemes for 14 key sectors have been announced (2020–2023) with an outlay Rs. 1.97 lakh crore (over US$26 billion) to enhance India's Manufacturing capabilities and Exports. These sectors include: (i) Mobile Manufacturing and Specified Electronic Components, (ii) Critical Key Starting Materials/Drug Intermediaries & Active Pharmaceutical Ingredients, (iii) Manufacturing of Medical Devices (iv) Automobiles and Auto Components, (v) Pharmaceuticals Drugs, (vi) Specialty Steel, (vii) Telecom & Networking Products, (viii) Electronic/Technology Products, (ix) White Goods (ACs and LEDs), (x) Food Products, (xi) Textile Products: MMF segment and technical textiles, (xii) High efficiency solar PV modules, (xiii) Advanced Chemistry

[18] Last time India raised this issue was in Modi-Jinping informal summit in Chennai in 2019. Two leaders stated in their statement "in pursuit of their efforts to further deepen economic cooperation and to enhance their closer development partnership, the two leaders have decided to establish a high-level economic and trade dialogue mechanism with the objective of achieving enhanced trade and commercial relations, as well as to better balance the trade between the two countries. They have also agreed to encourage mutual investments in identified sectors through the development of a manufacturing partnership and tasked their officials to develop this idea at the first meeting of the high-level economic and trade dialogue." https://www.mea.gov.in/press-releases.htm?dtl/31938/2nd_IndiaChina_Informal_Summit.

[19] https://www.globaltimes.cn/page/202112/1243425.shtml.

Cell (ACC) Battery, and (xiv) Drones and Drone Components. These sectors under this Scheme will attract investments in key sectors and cutting-edge technology; ensure efficiency and bring economies of size and scale in the manufacturing sector and make Indian companies and manufacturers globally competitive. These sectors are likely to significantly boost production, employment and economic growth over the next five years or so and will have a cascading effect on the country's MSME ecosystem (https://pib.gov.in/PressReleaseIframePage.aspx?PRID=1945155). This allows India to enjoy the huge value-added benefits that emanate from the regional and global markets. This would also restrict literally unbridled exports of raw materials and inspire research and development activities within the country. Therefore, PM Modi's government has a formidable challenge—to go back to history, check why India historically fought against such a trend and how it mobilized the global South for this purpose and to correct these distortionary and discriminatory trade practices. Can the "Make in India" campaign be globalized and fit into the perspectives of other developing countries? Can India lead from the front? Could India float a newer global platform to do so? These are the important questions too. Some of these issues did figure in the G20 New Delhi Leaders Declaration made in Delhi in September 2023 and also in the Outcome Document & Chair's Summary of trade and investment ministerial meeting (Jaipur, August 2023) (https://www.g20.org/en/media-resources/documents/doc-outcomes/).

8.8 Import Dependence

On the other hand, the top items of imports from China have gradually changed since 1990s. Even in 2000–01, mineral fuels, mineral oils and products of their distillation; bituminous substances; mineral waxes constituted 15.33% of India's total imports from China followed by organic chemicals (14.51%), nuclear reactors, boilers, machinery and mechanical appliances (10.98%) and electrical machinery and equipment; sound recorders and reproducers, television image and sound recorders and reproducers (9.40%).

By 2010–11 electrical machinery and equipment; sound recorders and reproducers, television image and sound recorders and reproducers became the top import item constituting 27.27%, followed by nuclear reactors, boilers, machinery and mechanical appliances (17.7%) and organic chemicals (8.8%). In 2019–20 electrical machinery and equipment and parts thereof; sound recorders and reproducers, television image and sound recorders and reproducers, and parts constituted 29.27% of total imports from China followed by nuclear reactors, boilers, machinery and mechanical appliances; parts thereof (20.41%) and organic chemicals (12.21%).

In fact, the share of electrical machinery and equipment; sound recorders and reproducers, television image and sound recorders and reproducers increased to over 31% in 2020–21 along with nuclear reactors, boilers, machinery and mechanical appliances (21.44%); organic chemicals (13.76%). The predominance of these three sets of products remained more or less same during 2021–22. This means even the

COVID-19 pandemic did not usher in any fundamental change in the composition of imports from China (Table 8.6).

A study by PHDCCI (2018) revealed that the share of capital goods grew from 22.4% in 2001 to 56.4% in 2016. And import penetration[20] increased from 1.9% in 2007 to 2.6% in 2016. Similarly, China's trade intensity index (TII)[21] in India grew from 0.88 in 2012 to 1.24 in 2016 whereas India's TII in China reached consistently fell to 0.34 in 2016 from 0.94 in 2007. It also found many of the Chinese products do not meet the technical standards set by Bureau of Indian Standards yet this low quality and one time use products get easy passage to India as most of the laid down 18,000 standards are voluntary as far as their compliance are concerned. Despite anti-dumping (90 Chinese products are under this ambit) and countervailing duties, these products are still competitive in Indian markets as their costs are so low.

8.9 Decoupling Constraints

These import figures do show that decoupling from China as a source of import is going to be a formidable challenge and would not be possible in very near future. The variety and complexity of imports have been such that it would be very cumbersome task for India firstly, to develop own production capabilities in diverse areas as revealed by the composition of imported item or/and also locate alternative sources of such imports. In both cases, the issues of cost, accessibility and quality would come up imminently. Further, the steady innovations in China to make these products further attractive in terms of efficiency, cost competitiveness and quality enhancement would be another serious challenge to India. These quicker and substantive innovations could blunt any comparative advantages that remain with India.

Why disengagements in terms of steady reduction of imports in overwhelming majority of the imports from China particularly in the three sets of top import items, viz., electrical machinery and equipment; sound recorders and reproducers, television

[20] Import penetration ratios are defined here as the ratio between the value of imports as a percentage of total domestic demand. The import penetration rate shows to what degree domestic demand D is satisfied by imports M. It is calculated as M/D, where the domestic demand is the GDP minus exports plus imports, i.e., [D = GDP-X + M)]. https://stats.oecd.org/oecdstat_metadata/ShowMetadata.ashx?Dataset=CSP6&Coords=%5BSUB%5D.%5BIMPPENET%5D&Lang=en.

[21] Trade intensity index is the ratio of a trading partner's share to a country/region's total trade and the share of world trade with the same trading partner. It is calculated as:

$$TII_{ij} = \frac{t_{ij}/T_{iw}}{t_{wj}/T_{ww}}$$

where t_{ij} is the dollar value of total trade of country/region i with country/region j, T_{iw} is the dollar value of the total trade of country/region i with the world, t_{wj} is the dollar value of world trade with country/region j, and T_{ww} is the dollar value of world trade. An index of more than one indicates that trade flow between countries/regions is larger than expected given their importance in world trade.

https://aric.adb.org/integrationindicators/technotes.

image and sound recorders and reproducers (HS Code 85); nuclear reactors, boilers, machinery and mechanical appliances (HS Code 84) and organic chemicals (HS Code 29) do not seem to be both viable and feasible in near future is reflected in the diversity, depth and variety of items imported by India. These have penetrated into the markets of all geographies in India. Table 8.7 provides a glimpse of these wide varieties of imports (at 8 digit HS code) in very essential areas of production, and their critical utilities in diverse areas of economic operations and household level consumption. A simple decomposition of second top import category of nuclear reactors, boilers, machinery and mechanical appliances; parts thereof (HS code 84) as done below could display the length and breadth of imports from China. However, India already has a substantive production base in most of the products that figure in Table 8.7.

However, why the traders and consumers still prefer the Chinese goods are largely explained by cost, quality and other efficiency parameters. For example, many of the ceiling fan producers have abandoned their production factories in India and directly entered into production contracts with their Chinese counterparts focusing on their brands in India and market they command. This is done to solicit quick and attractive innovations in both designs and output in fans produced in China and also to avoid increasing labour cost and unrest in India. In a way, the comparative advantages that China have in terms of relatively lower wage rates, restricted labour law regimes, better scale of production and prolific institutions of innovations have been internalized by Indian manufacturers and traders through regular imports.

These deepening dependence on Chinese imports is further demonstrated by India's import dependence on pharmaceutical inputs and electronic particularly mobile phones and computers and parts thereof. When COVID-19 started setting in India in an alarming manner in March 2020, Confederation of Indian Industry[22] published a glimpse of the impact analysis of the coronavirus - Covid-19 on shipping, pharmaceuticals, automobiles, IT and mobiles, electronics, textiles, chemicals, solar power and tourism and aviation.

It found that China accounted for 45% of India's total electronics imports, 33% of machinery, 40% of organic chemicals, 25% of automotive parts and fertilizers, almost 90% of certain mobile phone parts, and close to 100% for many critical antibiotics and antipyretics. That meant, almost 70% of India's active pharmaceuticals ingredients (APIs) actually come from China and if there are any restrictions on the movement of raw materials related to pharmaceuticals and its ingredients, there is a huge possibility in India for the prices of pharmaceuticals products to go up and , also some of the industries to collapse.[23]

Another study (Kumar and James 2021) made three significant revelations in India–China global trajectories in pharmaceutical trade. It found that India's price competitiveness existed in 1996 and continued till 2009 in most of the pharmaceutical

[22] https://www.cii.in/publications.aspx.

[23] However, Government has identified 53 active pharmaceutical raw materials imported from China that are used for treatment of diseases like tuberculosis, cancer, steroids and vitamins that cater to 85–90 percent of local demands and also used for exports to other countries by India. Two production-linked incentive schemes have been rolled out to supporting local manufacturing of these APIs and intermediaries. *Times of India*, Delhi 23 April 2022.

products. However, it lost this competitiveness with almost all major exporters more significantly vis-à-vis China in last 10 years. Secondly, India as a "Pharmacy of the World," its huge dependence on China for API for both manufacturing of formulation or finished pharmaceutical products, makes it pretty tough to maintain the price competitiveness and profit line with China. This is because China has already been a cheap producer and supplier of API and its manufacturing cost would be relatively low. And thirdly, it mentioned that Indian manufacturing companies of bulk drugs have lower cost efficiency in comparison to China despite enjoying a lower labour cost and hence face serious competition.

The other aspect of dependency syndrome is, when India' Power Minister went on to say that "the total import in the power sector in 2018–19 was ₹ 71,000 crore of which ₹ 21,000 crore was from China. We cannot tolerate this. A country which tries to transgress into our territory, kills our soldiers and we create jobs in that country?" He further stated that this may have crippling effects on Indian energy sector-power systems, precisely because some of these instruments must have got inserted into malwares and trojan.[24]

Dependence extends to other huge market segments. As of July 2021, in the $ 38 billion India's smartphone market, Chinese company Xiaomi had the highest shipment share of 28%, Vivo (15%) and Oppo (10%). The only other dominant partners have been South Korea's Samsung (18%) and India's Realme (15%).[25] These products dominate the communities and geographies of mountains, coastal areas, desert ecology and mofussil towns and cities in India along with the gods and goddesses made for various Indian festivals and especially produced in production and export centres like in Guangzhou in China.

This shows that there is cabbage-like layers of this dependency syndrome of India vis-a-vis China. This has steadily crept into the bilateral relations in the last two decades or so. Even after the heavy crackdown on the popular Chinese apps and also effectively banning over 320 of these apps, the Chinese apps have made visible re-entries into the Indian market in a sophisticatedly camouflaged manner. A news report mentioned that "A *Rest of World* audit of the Google Play store indicated that at least eight of the 100 most-downloaded free apps in India may be owned by large Chinese parent companies, such as ByteDance, Xiaomi, Alibaba, and Joyy. These apps include short-form video apps Tiki and Zili, the video-streaming app PlayIt, music video-makers Noizz, Mast, and Mivo, and the ByteDance-owned streaming app Resso. Several of these apps are registered under one-off developer names, with front-end holding companies in Singapore and the British Virgin Islands—a common practice among Chinese tech firms as a means of sidestepping taxation and domestic regulations."[26]

Besides the terms of trade and related balance of trade deficit concerns, these dominance and dependence relationship have its own cascading effects that spill

---

[24] https://www.ndtv.com/india-news/union-minister-rk-singh-says-we-wont-allow-power-equipment-imports-from-china-pakistan-2256416.

[25] https://www.counterpointresearch.com/india-smartphone-share/.

[26] Andrew Deck in https://restofworld.org/2022/india-chinese-apps/, 5 October 2022.

Table 8.8 Chinese mobile handset brands: under scanner for possible tax evasion (Rs. Crore)

	Year	Total income	Total expenditure[a]	Profit/loss EBIDTA[b]	Performance reward from head quarters[c]	Profit/ Loss before Tax	Net Worth
Xiaomi	2016–17	8379	8144	235	–	230	119
	2017–18	23,061	22,606	454	–	449	412
	2018–19	35,427	37,853	−2426	2227	−220	3783
	2019–20	38,197	41,324	−3127	3865	588	4182
Oppo	2016–17	8239	8276	−37	N/A	−63	(−299)
	2017–18	12,023	12,498	−475	N/A	−534	(−657)
	2018–19	21,724	22,624	−900	N/A	−1043	(−1345)
	2019–20	38,757	41,721	−2965	N/A	−3283	(−3552)
Vivo	2016–17	6239	6393	−100	N/A	−116	(−286)
	2017–18	11,179	11,261	−82	N/A	−125	(−410)
	2018–19	17,377	17,329	48	N/A	−21	(−429)
	2019–20	25,124	25,472	−348	N/A	−495	(−778)

Note [a] Except financial charges and depreciation
[b] Profit/loss Before interest, depreciation and tax
[c] Received from Xiaomi; Reward for market performance; financial numbers of Fiscal Year 2021 were still to be filed at the end of Dec 31, 2021. All minus signs indicate losses/deficits
Source Doval (2022)

over to other segments of finance and management in India. For instance, a report published in *Times of India* (January 10, 2022, Delhi)[27] mentioned about a multi-agency (Directorate of Revenue Intelligence, Income Tax, Registrar of Companies, Competition Commission of India and others) probe initiated by the Government of India against the Indian operations of top Chinese phone companies Xiaomi, Oppo and Vivo, amid allegations of "lapses and discrepancies" in their statutory financial filings and other reporting over the last few years. The other cause of this probe would be their business practices including alleged non-transparent methods in sourcing components, distribution of these products, abuse of dominant position, restrictive trade practices, possible tax evasion, concealment of earnings and manipulation of books. How despite strong sales these companies are showing operational losses is an intriguing question (Table 8.8).

Another newspaper reported that Xiaomi was slapped with three show cause notices for demand and recovery amounting to Rs 653 crore under the Customs Act, 1962.[28]

---

[27] https://timesofindia.indiatimes.com/business/india-business/multiple-agencies-to-probe-chinese-phone-companies/articleshow/88797980.cms.

[28] https://economictimes.indiatimes.com/industry/cons-products/electronics/multiagency-probe-ordered-against-indian-operations-of-chinese-smartphone-makers/articleshow/88804032.cms.

In fact a full fortnight before (December 26, 2021) *Global Times* newspaper in China published a related news item which stated that:

> Two Chinese chambers of commerce in India have urged New Delhi to change its irregular tax probe practice and treat foreign investors equally, and to actively create an open, fair, and non-discriminatory business environment for Chinese enterprises operating in India. The confidence of a business group that invested $3 billion and created 500,000 local jobs in recent years is shaken, as India launched a broad investigation into Chinese companies. The Chinese Chamber of Commerce in India and the India China Mobile Phone Enterprise Association, in a statement sent to the Global Times on Sunday, said that Chinese mobile phone companies in India are facing unprecedented difficulties, and as a result of sudden inspections and fines by the Indian authorities, the companies are unable to carry out normal production and operations.

As a sequel, in April 2022 the Enforcement Directorate (ED) seized Rs. 5,551.27 crore from the bank accounts of Xiaomi India, a wholly owned subsidiary of China-based Xiaomi group. This was done on account of the alleged "illegal remittances" in foreign currency equivalent to Rs. 5,551.27 crore to three foreign-based entities which included one Xiaomi group entity, in the guise of royalty. Xiaomi which started its operations in India in 2014 also remitted funds to other two US-based unrelated entities for the ultimate benefit of the Xiaomi group entities whereas it "procured completely manufactured mobile sets and other products from the manufacturers in India and has not availed any service from these three foreign based entities to whom such amounts have been transferred."[29] Later in September 2022, an Indian appellate authority confirmed this seizure by the ED of India amidst the Company denying any wrongdoing.[30]

A new variety of intangible grassroot dependence of India on China is demonstrated in how surreptitious venture of the China-based companies has been in the loan business, which has now been often considered as within the spectrum of China's "financial invasion." There have been several complaints and arrests on issues of easy loan extension to Indian loan seekers followed by inhumanly harsh conditions and actions of recovery by these companies and finally victims committing suicides.[31] The bank accounts belonging to Chinese apps running online betting have been frozen.[32] The ED raided the premises of widely known Indian companies like Razorpay Pvt Ltd, Cashfree Payments, Paytm Payment Services Ltd and entities controlled/operated by Chinese nationals in September 2022. These Indian companies are alleged to have acted as payment gateways and carried out money laundering and involved in illegal betting. According to ED, some Chinese nationals floated multiple companies in India with the help of Indian chartered accountants,

---

[29] https://thewire.in/business/ed-seizes-rs-5551-crore-from-xiaomi-india-for-fema-violation.

[30] https://thewire.in/law/ed-order-to-seize-rs-5551-crore-from-xiaomi-upheld.

[31] https://www.indiatoday.in/india/story/the-making-of-A-chinese-betting-shark-1759330-2021-01-15.

[32] https://www.hindustantimes.com/india-news/ed-freezes-accounts-of-four-chinese-firms/story-gK7O0YktgQs4UUJJhSqeQN.html/.

using Indian directors to incorporate them and after some time Chinese nationals travelled to India and took directorship in these companies.[33] After the bank accounts were opened, the internet access credentials were couriered by the Indian employees to China, and payment instructions came from the owners there. The accused companies floated a number of similar looking websites that were hosted through Cloudfare. These non-banking financial companies (NBFCs) misused personal data and resorted to predatory lending practices and high-handed methods to extort high interest rates from those who took loans."[34]

8.10 The AIIB Dimension[35]

There has been another facet of India's China dependence syndrome. Even in India's partnership, as the second highest shareholder (8.36%), in the China (the highest shareholder 29.78%) dominated Asian Infrastructure Investment Bank (AIIB), there are visible contradictions between former's conspicuous opposition to the Belt and Road Initiative (BRI) and inclusion of regionalism venture like Bangladesh, China, India and Myanmar (BCIM) in the BRI (Lama 2021a; Uberoi 2014, 2016) while at the same time joining and borrowing from the AIIB, which is supposedly designed to finance the BRI projects. Though the Articles of Agreement of the AIIB[36] do not mention about its relations with the BRI, the Office of the Leading Group for Promoting the Belt and Road Initiative clearly mentions that "in fulfilling its own purposes and missions, the bank (AIIB) has become one of the key multilateral platforms for building the Belt and Road, along with other multilateral development banks."[37] Two other official publications stated that AIIB could "invest more efficiently in the vitality and growth of Asia and better serve the Belt and Road Initiative" (Liu). While highlighting the fact that "to drive the execution of the Belt and Road

[33] https://www.timesnownews.com/business-economy/industry/chinas-financial-invasion-hundreds-of-chinese-controlled-apps-siphon-off-thousands-of-crores-from-india-article-94109567.

[34] https://indianexpress.com/article/india/chinese-loan-apps-case-ed-raids-razorpay-paytm-cashfree-8128703/.

[35] This section draws ideas and data from the author's earlier published ICS Occasional Paper entitled "Fledgling Sub-Regionalism in Eastern South Asia: Reasons for China's Shift towards Bilateralism in BCIM", No. 65, January 2021. https://www.icsin.org/publications/fledgling-sub-regionalism-in-eastern-south-asia-reasons-for-chinas-shift-towards-bilateralism-in-bcim.

[36] It states that "The purpose of the Bank shall be to: (i) foster sustainable economic development, create wealth and improve infrastructure connectivity in Asia by investing in infrastructure and other productive sectors; and (ii) promote regional cooperation and partnership in addressing development challenges by working in close collaboration with other multilateral and bilateral development institutions."

file:///C:/Users/hp/Desktop/AIIB%20Articles_of_agreement%20Feb%202,020.pdf accessed on 16 February 2020 and https://www.aiib.org/cms/en/search/index.html?category=documents&mudium=all&query=share%20holders%20in%20AIIB.

[37] With the authorized capital stock of US $ 100 billion, AIIB membership grew from 50 countries in June 2015 to 103 countries spread across five continents by mid-2020.

Table 8.9 AIIB: approved projects for India 2016–February 2022

Country	Number of projects	States/provinces covered	Sector	Loan supported by AIIB (US million $)
India	32[a]	Andhra Pradesh, Assam, Gujarat, Madhya Pradesh, Karnataka, Kerala, Maharashtra, Rajasthan, West Bengal, Tamil Nadu, Government of India	Water/Water Supply and Sanitation; Energy (Power); Transport/Urban Rail; Transport and Roads; Financial Institution; Irrigation and Flood Protection; India Infrastructure Fund; National Investment and Infrastructure Fund; Social/ Public Health Infrastructure; COVID-19 management, education, others/exceptions	7863
Total projects approved as of February 2022	159		Total amount approved as of end February 2022	33,164.8

[a] Many of these projects have Indian and State Governments, ADB, World Bank and other private investors as co-investors/financers

Source Calculated and deduced from various approved project documents of Bangladesh, India and Myanmar[38] https://www.aiib.org/en/projects/approved/index.html

Initiative, China has taken the initiative to establish AIIB, BRICS Development Bank, SCO Development Bank and Silk Road Fund" another document delved into more serious issue of political risk hedging with an example from Myanmar:

AIIB and China's Belt and Road Initiative supplement each other. In fact, the financial risks associated with the execution of the Belt and Road cannot be completely solved by simply depending on bilateral relations. Instead, AIIB, as a multilateral arrangement, may provide more solutions to political issues. For instance, the President of Burma, ….. Thein Sein suddenly announced in September 2011 to unilaterally suspend the cooperation with China in building Myistsone dam for the reasons of "respecting the will of the people," causing heavy losses to the investment by China. Had the project been invested by AIIB, the environmental evaluation would have been strict and transparent, and would have given more thought to the interests of the local people.' (Jin)

India has also shown steady rise in dependency on AIIB and has borrowed heavily from it for both federal and province level projects in various sectors. Even for the COVID-19 management, India borrowed funds (US $ 1250 million in May and June 2020) from the AIIB (Table 8.9).

Within the course of 6 years (2016–2022), India borrowed over US$ 7.863 billion for 32 projects. And by 28 February 2022, India alone constituted over 20% of the

[38] https://www.aiib.org/en/projects/approved/index.html; accessed on 5 March 2022.

total 159 projects and over 23% of the total approved loans of US$ 33.164 billion by AIIB. This means financial dependency on China has steadily shown an upward trend along with other deepening dependence on trade, investment and technology. This deft dependency on China squarely exposes and highlights the dilemma, inhibitions and engagement fatigue of India. The *Atamanirbhar* mission of India has to deal with this newer facet of dependency deftly and sustainably.

8.11 New Regionalism: Blunting Chinese Influence in the Neighbourhood

What would be a kind of possible pathway for India to really adopt interdependence matrix ? This is a critical question. Even if India is able to decouple, in the next decade or so, there is a huge question of ways and means to deal with how China has engaged with India's neighbours. Decoupling with China by India but other politico-economic situations in the neighbourhood remaining intact with increasing influence of China would make this venture meaningless. This is because India has been the pivot in the region historically, has huge and multiple connectivity projetx amidst a variety of border regimes from open to porous and barbesd wire fenced to natural. More than this most of the neighbouring countries are well integrated with India in terms of cultural exchanges, politico-historical linkages and development dynamics.On the other hand, Chinese penetration into South Asia with a vibrant strategy called *Trishul* († -trident) approach has been both amazing and far reaching. Under this, it has been using three pronged instruments of local,[39] national[40] and regional[41] engagements. All these three prongs (Table 8.9) of Trishul are intricately interconnected, sophisticatedly interwoven and solidly integrated (Lama 2021b). China started consciously designing a clear regional policy based on *wending zbhoubian*

[39] Entry through Khunjerab pass in Karakoram to Pakistan, Tatopani and Kerung-Rasuwagadhi in Nepal, Wakhan corridor in Afghanistan, Nathula (Sikkim), Shipki La (Himachal Pradesh) and Lipulekh (Uttarakhand) passes in India. All these local integration instruments are likely to be mainstreamed and transformed, interconnected with national and cross-regional connectivity of China.

[40] China has used bilateralism in a much conscious and a strident manner in South Asia. Trade (Mobile brands like Huawei, Oneplus and Oppo), investment (Payra Power Plant in Bangladesh), economic assistance (airports in Nepal), technology, BRI-related infrastructure projects (China–Pakistan Economic Corridor), credit-driven projects (Hambantota port in Sri Lanka) and elements of soft power (food, language, cinema) are used by China to consolidate bilateral relations at the national level. For example, in the last 30 years, China and South Asia had trade of just 1.18 billion dollars in 1990 increased to 5.57 billion dollars in 2000 and by 2018 it increased to over 127 billion dollars. Similarly import dependence on China shows that 23% of Bangladesh's total global imports comes from China, India—15%, Pakistan—24% and Sri Lanka—19%, which were all negligible in the beginning of 1990s.

[41] China's consistent forays into regional initiatives such as the Bangladesh–China–India–Myanmar (BCIM) Forum for Regional Cooperation and the South Asian Association for Regional Cooperation (SAARC) are the third trident bar laced with quite an umpteen number of soft-power tools.

(stabilising periphery). Determinants such as the political system–ideology linkage (*buyiyishixingtai he sheshuizhidulunqingsu*) and super power alliance (*yimeihuaxian, yisuhuaxian*) (Sullivan 2018), which remained the fundamental basis and hallmark of its foreign relations, were increasingly abandoned.

Given the complex influence of China in the quadrangle around India, it would be harrowing for the later to disengage unless there is a transforming enhancement in its comprehensive national power. The gains from these disengagements could be offset by re-induction of countervailing instruments by China through its (India's) neighbouring countries as the borders are porous, open and partially fenced. The fact that federal units/states in India that share the borders extensively with the neighbouring countries have no institutions and required preparedness to deal with these newer designs and indirect game of *weiqi*[42] to penetrate into Indian markets would make the disengagement and decoupling formidably challenging.

Given the accumulated national and global resources China commands and the scale and the nature of its operations in South and South East Asian neighbourhood and also at the global world, India cannot at least for next two decades compete with China on its style, agility and ability to engage bilaterally with these countries. Therefore, new regionalism aided by and integrated with bilateralism (it could not be the other way round) emerges as the only potent instrument for India to both disengage with China at the bilateral and regional levels.

Given the dismal state of regionalism and regional organizations like SAARC, BIMSTEC and BBIN and the role India has played in neglecting and marginalising them, other South Asian countries would be sceptical if India tried to once again enter into the same regionalism process. Therefore, a platform with robust fundamentals of new regionalism has to be floated to rebuild confidence and re-attract the regional partners (Lama 2017). This in a way unequivocally demands that all the border and borderlands interconnections, interactions and infrastructures with the neighbouring countries (Table 8.2) should be refurbished, multiple interactive points need to be built and made more scientifically managed with adequate technological interventions. India has to propagate a conscious mission of inter-dependency in its neighbourhood. There have been remarkable initiatives in the last decade or so in the multi modal borderland connectivity under its Neighbourhood First and Act East policies. All these have to be considered as national interest projects and direct them in fast forward mode so that the lethargy, delay and indifference that plagued India's projects in the neighbourhood are all resolved and consolifdated further. This of course requires a major structural overhauling and institutional reorientation both at the national and state levels.

More than this, it is in the national interest of India that it reconnects with the neighbouring countries including Myanmar and Pakistan more comprehensively using both orthodox machineries and modern instruments like making newer

---

[42] Go or Weiqi, Weichi (simplified Chinese: 围棋; traditional Chinese: 圍棋; pinyin: *wéiqí*) is an abstract strategy board game for two players in which the aim is to surround more territory than the opponent.

https://en.wikipedia.org/wiki/Go_(game).

multi-modal corridors through Pangsau and other passes in Arunachal Pradesh, Mizoram and Nagaland with Myanmar (NITI Aayog 2020; NEDFi 2021) establishment of a power pool for cross border trade in electricity in the North East by pooling power from Bhutan and Nepal (Anbumozhi, Kutani and Lama 2019), by making Bangladesh, Bhutan, Myanmar and Nepal as a part of India's formidable Act East Policy to give them access to South East Asia through India's North East and India-Myanmar-Thailand trilateral highway; rebuilding pre-partition electricity inter-connection between Amritsar and Lahore (FEF 2019; CHAO TRACK 2020) and laying a 44 km land bridge between Dhanushkodi (South-East of Tamil Nadu state) and Thalaimannar (North-West Sri Lanka) (Nexant, USAID 2003).

There have been a large number of studies and techno-economic feasibilities already carried out. In all these critical projects that make South Asia a vibrantly integrated region, India must be the pivot and a full-scale regional player. It must use bilateralism as a potent complement and far-reaching supplement to regionalism and not as a substitute like it has done in the last two decades or so. Strategists and policymakers in Delhi must realize the fact that there can never be any match and alternative to India in its regionalism foray. In other words, no neighbouring countries of India could inject dynamism to South Asia without India playing a Cournot's oligopoly model of leadership.[43] This is going to be one single weapon to steadily disengage with China in various economic and commercial exchanges.

References

Appadorai A, Rajan MS (1985) India's foreign policy and relations. South Asian Publishers, Delhi

Anbumozhi V, Kutani I, Lama MP (2019) Energising connectivity between northeast india and its neighbours. Economic Research Institute for ASEAN and East Asia, Jakarta

Bhattacharjee J (2019) Integrated check-posts on the india-bangladesh border: a field survey and brief analysis. ORF Special Report No. 96, August 2019, Observer Research Foundation. https://www.orfonline.org/research/integrated-check-posts-on-the-india-bangladesh-border-a-field-survey-and-brief-analysis-54559/

Boothalingam R (2020) What futures for India–China economic relations? Occasional Paper, No 53, Institute of Chinese Studies, Delhi

Chand A (1983) Non-aligned states a great leap forward. UDH Publishers, Delhi

CHAO TRACK Policy Brief (2020) India–Pakistan relations: the past decade 2009–2019 Refer to Lama, Mahendra P (2020) India, Pakistan and China: matrices of positive Stakeholding, Inter-dependence and Peace Building, Delhi

CUTS & FICCI (2017) Harnessing the potential for cross-border trade between North East India and its neighbouring countries, Discussion Paper

Das RU (2016) Enhancing India–Myanmar border trade policy and implementation measures. Department of Commerce, Ministry of Commerce and Industry, Government of India, New Delhi

Doval P. Multi-agency probe into Chinese phone makers. Times of India, Delhi, 10 January 2022

ECDC (1983) Economic cooperation among developing countries. ECDC Handbook Documents of the Movement of Non-aligned Countries and Group of 77, Ministry of External Affairs, Government of India, Delhi

[43] https://www.investopedia.com/terms/c/cournot-competition.asp.

FEF (2019) India–Pakistan seed community, Refer to paper by Lama MP, Bengali K, India-Pakistan Cross-Border Electricity Sharing. Fredric Ebert Foundation, Delhi

Jin X. Currency connectivity: assist RMB Internationalisation. New Star Press (year and place of publication not mentioned)

Karackattu JT (2013) India–China economic relations: trends, challenges and policy options. Occasional Paper 6, Institute of Chinese Studies, Delhi

Kuma D, James TC (2021) Pharmaceutical trade: India's growth trajectories. RIS Discussion Paper # 261, Research and Information System for Developing Countries, Delhi

Lama MP (1987) Primary commodities decline in apparent consumption by the developed countries. Research Briefs—RIS digest, Research and Information System for Non-aligned and other Developing Countries, Delhi, January–June 1987

Lama MP (2005) Sikkim-Tibet Trade via Nathu La: a policy study on prospect, opportunities and requisite preparedness. Nathu La Trade Study Group, Government of Sikkim, Sikkim

Lama MP (2017) Renegotiating alternative integration model in SAARC. Int Stud 54(1–4):January–October 2017, 82–105

Lama MP (2021a) Fledgling sub-regionalism in eastern South Asia: reasons for China's shift towards bilateralism in BCIM. Occasional Paper, No 65, Institute of Chinese Studies, January, Delhi

Lama MP (2021b) China's Trishula approach in South Asia: challenges to balancing the end game. In: Ranjan R, Changgang G (eds) China and South Asia: changing regional dynamics, development and power play. Routledge, New York

Liu H. Financing the belt and road: expanded channels for finance and investments. New Star Press (year and place of publication not mentioned)

MEA (1983) Two decades of Non-alignment, documents of the gatherings of the no-aligned countries 1961–1982. Ministry of External Affairs, Government of India, Delhi

Mehta A (1986) Changing alignments in Asia. Banyan, Delhi

Mohanty SK (2014) India–China bilateral trade relationship. Research and Information System for Developing Countries, Delhi

NEDFI (2021) Strategic roadmap for bringing investors from South East Asia (CLMV & Thailand) to North East India: a seed project approach (Principal Author: Mahendra P Lama). North Eastern Development Finance Corporation Ltd (NEDFi), Gauhati

NEXANT/USAID (2003) India–Sri Lanka land bridge project assessment of economic and social impact. Study Team led by Mahendra P Lama consisted of Sirimal Abeyratne. Economics Department, Colombo University, Colombo, Muttukrishna Sarvananthan, Centre for Ethnic Studies, Colombo, John Nigel, Economics Department , Peradeniya University, Kandy, Nawal K Paswan, Centre for Policy Research, New Delhi, Alfred Mariadas, Economics Department, Peradeniya, University, Kandy, CS Sunderasan and Jaya Kumar, Embassy of the USA, Delhi

NITI Aayog (2020) North east region vision 2035, authored by Mahendra P Lama, NITI Aayog, Delhi. http://megplanning.gov.in/circular/3rd%20&%20Final%20Draft%20NER%20Vision%202035.pdf

Pearson LB (1969) A new strategy for global development. https://unesdoc.unesco.org/ark:/48223/pf0000056743

PHDCCI (2018) India–China trade relationship: the trade giant of past, present and future. PHD Chamber of Commerce and Industry, Delhi

Pohit S, Taneja N (2000) India's informal trade with Bangladesh and Nepal: a qualitative assessment. ICRIER, July, Delhi

Raffer K, Singer HW (2001) The economic North-South divide: six decades of unequal development.1835. Edward Elgar

RIS (1987a) UNCTAD VII and the global challenge, Research and Information System for Non-aligned and other Developing Countries, Delhi

RIS (1987b) Raul Prebisch and development strategy, Research and Information System for Non-aligned and other Developing Countries, Delhi

RIS (2011) Expansion of North East India's trade and investment with Bangladesh and Myanmar: an assessment of the opportunities and constraints. Research and Information System, Ministry of Development of North East Region, North East Council

Smith J (2018) Alignment with autonomy. Policy Q & A, National Bureau of Asian Research, US

Sullivan LR (2018) Historical dictionary of Chinese Foreign Affairs. Rowman & Littlefield Publishers

Taneja N (2004) Informal trade in the SAARC region: implications for FTAs author(s), vol 39, no 51. Economic and Political Weekly, December 18–24, 2004, pp 5367–5371

The Brandt Commission (1983) Common crisis: north-south cooperation for world recovery. Pan Books, London

Uberoi P (2014) The BCIM Economic corridor: a leap into the unknown? ICS Working Paper November, Institute of Chinese Studies, New Delhi

Uberoi P (2016) Problems and prospects of the BCIM economic corridor. China Report 52(1):19–44

Yuan J (2016) Sino-Indian economic ties since 1988: progress, problems, and prospects for future development. J Curr Chin Aff 45(3):31–71

Chapter 9
Invoking History and the Way Ahead

Keshav Mishra

As neighbours, India and China are inheritors of age-old and glorious civilisations. Buddhism was the joint spiritual and ethical force in bringing India and China together in ancient times. Indian Buddhist monks actively united the people of these two giant neighbours by fostering cultural ties. The synergy between the cultures and the plight of India and China during the anti-imperialist struggle induced and inspired the nationalists and revolutionaries of India to develop mutual contacts and friendships between the two. Sun Yatsen developed strong links with various Indian nationalists and revolutionaries and, by using his good offices, introduced them to the leading Japanese personages, thus enabling them to carry out their anti-British activities unhindered. During the War of Resistance and Second World War, when China suffered at the hands of the Japanese, the repercussions were also felt in India. Indian National Congress sent a Medical Mission to China in 1938, and Doctor Dwarkanath Kotnis became a martyr. Jawahar Lal Nehru strengthened friendship bonds when he visited China in 1939. Thus, India-China historical interactions have shown how the two civilisations invited each other to learn and grow reciprocally (Deepak 2020).

India and China are the most populous countries in the continent of Asia. Both these countries suffered from imperialist and colonialist aggression and oppression for an extended period in modern times. The people waged great wars of struggle for their freedom and independence before they won their independence and liberation, respectively, in 1947 and 1949. Although both countries initiated the nation-building process generally from the late forties, their development and political system models differed. While India adopted the model of parliamentary democracy, mixed economy, and non-alignment, China, on the other hand, followed the one-party rule of Communism, a state-controlled economy, and joined the Communist camp of the USSR. The different political systems, however, did not come in the

K. Mishra (✉)
Department of History, Faculty of Social Sciences, Banaras Hindu University, Varanasi 221005, India
e-mail: keshav2005@gmail.com

S. Mishra and R. Sheel (eds.), *India-China Dialogues Beyond Borders*,
https://doi.org/10.1007/978-981-99-4326-5_10

way of developing the relationship between these two crucial countries in the era of anti-imperialist and Pan Asiatic sentiment. India and China hoped to reconstruct their respective countries peacefully and develop their friendship as newly independent countries. Only in this way the voice and idea of Asianism could be strengthened.

Prime Minister Jawaharlal Nehru persistently viewed Indian independence and the Chinese Revolution as parallel expressions of resurgent Asian nationalism. He was committed to building a new relationship with China as part of his broader vision of the role of India and China among the comity of nations in the post-colonial world. In this context, there was some response from the Chinese side also. India's efforts for localising the conflict in Korea and advocacy of a seat for the People's Republic in the United Nations were well appreciated by the Chinese leadership. Thus, within two years, the ideas of peaceful coexistence became part of a broader movement for a new kind of international relations. It was in tune with the aspirations of the Afro-Asian states for whom the bipolar conflictual global system was a distinctly negative phenomenon.

The historical journey of these two rich civilisations during the ancient period attests to regular and reciprocal interactions. Even in the modern period, the two countries fought against European colonial power. The architect of independent India's foreign policy Jawaharlal Nehru said, "China was the third great power in tomorrow's world but India was this time to be the fourth." Living in a post-Nehruvian generation, one was used to reading Neville Maxwell's work on *India's China War* (1970). We now have a comprehensive work by Bertil Lintner, which sees *China's India War* as the collision course between India and China on the world's roof.

On numerous occasions and through friendly gestures, both countries have expressed clearly that the problems could be settled through negotiations based on the principles of peaceful coexistence. This principle became the main component of the joint statement issued on 28th June 1954, after the first-ever Summit between Indian Prime Minister Jawaharlal Nehru and Chinese Prime Minister Zhou Enlai in New Delhi.

In April 1955, the Panchsheel, or Five Principles of Peaceful Coexistence, became the basis for the Ten Principles of International Peace and Cooperation enunciated in the Declaration issued at the Bandung Conference of twenty-nine Afro-Asian states. It referred to the five Principles of Peaceful Coexistence, that is, mutual respect for territorial integrity and sovereignty, mutual non-aggression, mutual non-interference in each other's internal affairs, equality and cooperation for mutual benefit, and peaceful coexistence, and symbolised a new approach towards value-based diplomacy between India and China. Both countries viewed Panchsheel as a significant step towards world peace. It was this aspect that Indian Prime Minister Jawahar Lal Nehru emphasised and said: "By this agreement, we ensure to a tremendous extent peace in a certain area of Asia. It would earnestly wish that the area of peace could be spread over the rest of Asia and indeed over the rest of the world" (Verma 1989). The two premiers, Jawaharlal Nehru and Zhou Enlai, exchanged visits which promoted bilateral understanding. The slogan *Hindu-Chini Bhai Bhai* was evoked with enthusiasm by both countries.

Furthermore, the Bandung Conference of 1955 provided the platform for broad-based bilateral friendship in the larger framework of Afro-Asian solidarity. Nehru took upon himself the task of convincing leaders of Afro-Asian countries of China's "honourable credentials." The Chinese Prime Minister approached the Bandung Conference hoping it would provide a political framework for establishing friendly bilateral relations between China and Afro-Asian countries.

In Asia, the Bandung Conference proved to be an important event of the decolonisation era, echoing similar calls for anti-colonialization, furthering peace, and ensuring a role for the decolonised world in global affairs. It attempted to project the united and peace-loving face of the Afro-Asian world. It opened a new chapter of intra Afro-Asian contacts, especially among Asian countries with, more importantly, Communist China and south-east Asian neighbours. The leaders were optimistic that the Conference would produce a broad common approach in matters affecting Asia and Africa and throw its weight on peace. It is a travesty that the peace process became a victim of power politics of strategic self-interest and insecurities.

In this context, Lintner argues that China may have been grossly mistaken in perceiving that Nehru wanted to seize Tibet. The Chinese fear of 'losing' what they have always considered an integral part of their country has been a factor that has shaped relations between India and China for over a century and still does. Moreover, Mao now wanted to become the leader of China and all the revolutionary movements (Lintner 2018).

It may be reiterated here that in International Relations, there is a haste to underplay long-drawn historical connections and overemphasize recent transitions even in phenomena as geo-politically crucial as the nation-states of India and China. In December-January of 1988–89 several magazines and journals flashed pictures of the Indian prime minister Rajiv Gandhi and Deng Xiaoping. It invited scholars' and diplomats' attention to probe how these two modern states, India and China, attempted to normalise relations in the decade of the eighties. It is also known how India reconfigured its ambassadorial ties after 1962 and it was in 1976 when K. R. Narayanan assumed the ambassador's position. During the first non-Congress government of Morarji Desai the then suave external affairs minister Atal Bihari Vajpayee visited Beijing in 1979. In the overall political dimension, the border issue has remained a foremost concern, and forty years have been invested in one or other sort of border resolving mechanism. The border issue, however, is yet to be resolved.

Apart from this historical background in the changing contours of the India-China relationship from 1963 to 1991, almost till the end of the Cold War, a bitter stalemate has remained. Consequently, the intended use of the word rapprochement becomes meaningful. In this context, what China has done in cultivating unique relations with other countries in the South Asian region becomes all the more significant. As John King Fairbank points out, a historical perspective is not a luxury but necessary to understand Chinese leaders' policies and actions. From a historical perspective, one must comprehend China's strategic culture (Ross 2020).

Garver (2015), in his book *Protracted Contest*, highlights the geopolitical clash between India and China's foreign and diplomatic policies. As such, the study analyses the conflictual element of bilateral relations between China and India during the second half of the twentieth century. On the other hand, there is a school of thought in which the adherents are primarily diplomats such as C. V. Ranganathan and Vinod C. Khanna, who, in their *India and China: The Way Ahead after 'Mao's India War'* argue that "India-China relations are not an all or nothing proposition but a mixed bag of issues with varying degrees of solubility" (Ranganathan and Khanna 2000). The point must be noted that there has been a different historical experience in India's dealings with China, which, in considerable measure, is both complex and complicated. Therefore, India must craft its policy towards China in a more realistic but reciprocal framework.

In this context, one must have a realistic view of how Chinese leadership was rattled by India's decision to go for nuclear tests in 1998. From this vantage point, one should remember Jiang Zemin's visit to New Delhi and, later, his visit to Islamabad. In the address to Pakistan's parliament, he discussed putting the Kashmir issue on the back burner in 1996. Later, however, we see that the Chinese again made a turnaround on the Kashmir issue.

The visit of Prime Minister P. V. Narasimha Rao to China in September 1993 was a watershed in strengthening bilateral relations. The most defining feature of the meeting of the two premiers was the conclusion of the "Agreement on the Maintenance of Peace and Tranquillity along the Line of Actual Control in the India China border areas," signed on 7th September 1993. The agreement brings "the two sides to a peaceful resolution of the boundary question through friendly consultations." The year 1996 witnessed the conclusion of the "Agreement on Confidence Building Measures in the military field along the line of actual Control in the India-China border areas" during India's visit of Jiang Zemin. The agreement concluded on 29th November 1996 and comprised twelve articles. The first Article declared that "neither side shall use its military capability against the other side." The Chinese president, Jiang Zemin, termed the agreement a factor that would further enhance peace and security and eventually create a good climate for resolving the boundary questions. Emerging bilateral relations in the first decade of the twenty-first century rested on the bedrock of the agreements concluded in 1993 (Deepak 2005).

It must be noted that India had perception of its role and status in the region and perceived China as an external power in South Asia and believed that facts of geography, culture, and ethnicity reinforced by economic compulsions tied the destiny of the South Asian nations much more with India than with China. In this context, India viewed China's attempts to forge close relations with its South Asian neighbours as hostile acts related to the Cold War period.

Then in the 1980s, there were some significant trends. First, it was in a considerable measure India-centred. Secondly, Chinese South Asian policy was pragmatic and devoid of ideological considerations because, in their political literature, they always talk about revolution and how the masses must be lifted from poverty. Finally, Chinese policy towards the region has a global context. China's regional strategy became a function of its long-term preoccupation with a perceived Soviet threat and relations with the United States, the other superpower.

From 1963 onwards, China's regional strategy was characterised by comprehensive efforts to contain India. At first, China established an extremely close relationship with Pakistan, India's foremost regional adversary. In 1963 Pakistan and China signed a border agreement on the area Pakistan illegally occupied in Kashmir. During the Indo-Pak war of 1965, China adopted a hostile attitude and militarily threatened India. During the Indo-Pak war of 1971, China supported Pakistan and indulged in anti-India propaganda on the Bangladesh issue. China did not recognise Bangladesh and vetoed its entry into the United Nations till Mujibur Rahman died. Secondly, China played an active role in the Himalayan region, providing foreign aid, engaging in strategic road building, and giving political support to the monarchy in its power struggle with Nepal Congress. Finally, by supplying military hardware and armaments to Pakistan, China helped in the arms build-up in the region. China also questioned India's unique relations with Nepal and Bhutan. India perceived China's role in South Asia as a hostile power that determined India's security interests (Mishra 2004).

Until the mid-1980s, Chinese South Asian policy underwent a subtle but significant shift. Now Chinese leaders began to acknowledge India's role as the leading South Asian power and realised that rather than weakening India, Chinese hostility helped to spur India's transformation into a significant conventional military power. Further, Chinese leaders were learning to manage the ambiguous complexities of international relations without making unduly restrictive choices of becoming identified with one side or the other. In this context, Chinese leaders emphasised that the gradual amelioration of tension in India-China relations would not occur at the expense of China's existing relationship in South Asia.

The first part of the work of the special representatives on the boundary issue was completed by signing the agreements on political parameters and guiding principles during the visits. In November 2006, the Indian President paid a visit to China. The two sides released a joint statement outlining a ten-point plan to boost cooperation in all sectors and give the India-China strategic and cooperative relationship more substance during the visit. Later, two more visits by Indian leadership and meetings with Chinese President Hu Jintao were to further the collaborative partnership (*The Hindu* 2020). Despite these agreements, the Doklam incident and stand-off in Ladakh remind us that the bilateral understanding is fragile. The intentions of the People's Republic of China and the People's Liberation Army reinforce each other. This is not for stable and prosperous southern Asia and the Asian continent. Salami Slicing tactics and Wolf Gang diplomacy have recently cast a hostile spell on improving bilateral relations in the Xi Jinping era.

Xi Jinping's Belt and Road initiative and how CPEC cast a hostile spell on India's territorial integrity and state sovereignty needs to be analysed with reference to long-term goals. The Chinese fail to understand the nature of India's democracy and how, as an open society, India debates its own foreign policy and Chinese strategic aspirations. Chinese have their global aspiration similarly. India has its emphasis on multi-alignment. The Chinese leadership is also mindful of the fact of New India.

Nevertheless, even though Wuhan and Chennai reconnect was initiated, the geopolitical, which at one point in time was being critiqued, again emerged with the Doklam and stand-off at Ladakh. History was repeated. Overall, 1962 as an event has left its impact; it is the need of the hour that understanding develops between India and China. For a stable Asia in the twenty-first century, it is crucial that a common understanding develops between India and China. The Border issue has to be resolved peacefully based on the bilateral agreements signed between both sides. Any unilateral steps to change the status quo will cast a damaging spell on overall bilateral relations. The India-China interaction, which is multi-dimensional and multi-layered, has to be nurtured by the leadership and people of both countries. Both civilisational states should show maturity for coexistence in a globalised world. India and China were two pillars of the developing world, and in the twenty-first century, together, they should reinvent a complementary vision for Afro-Asia and the world.

References

70 years of diplomatic relations between China and India [1950–2020]. The Hindu, 31 March 2020, par. 16. http://www.thehindu.com/brandhub/70-years-of-diplomatic-relations-between-china-and-india-1950-2020/article31219737.ece

Deepak BR (2005) India & China, 1904–2004: a century of peace and conflict. Manak Publications, New Delhi

Deepak BR (2020) India and China: beyond the binary of friendship and enmity. Springer, Singapore

Garver JW (2015) Protracted contest: Sino-Indian rivalry in the twentieth century. University of Washington Press, Seattle

Lintner B (2018) China's India war: collision course on the roof of the world. Oxford University Press, New Delhi

Maxwell N (1970) India's China war. Pantheon Books, New Delhi

Mishra K (2004) Rapprochement across the Himalayas: emerging India-China relations in post-Cold War period (1947–2003). Kalpaz Publications, New Delhi

Ranganathan CV, Khanna VC (2000) India and China: the way ahead after "Mao's India War." Har-Anand Publications, New Delhi

Ross C (2020) Competing with China today. Air University (AU), par. 5. http://www.airuniversity.af.edu/JIPA/Display/Article/2458675/competing-with-china-today/

Verma DP (1989) Jawaharlal Nehru: Panchsheel and India's constitutional vision of international order. India Q: J Int Affairs 45(4):301–323. https://doi.org/10.1177/097492848904500401

Chapter 10
India and China in the Pacific Ocean

R. S. Vasan

This paper attempts to see how the concept of Indo-Pacific[1] has evolved over decades and how the present stand-off under the Post-COVID scenario has brought about a new thrust to re-alignments, forging of new strategies affecting both the players, namely, India and China. The major players, whether the USA, Japan, or Australia would also be affected in the unfolding dimensions of global power play. There has been a paradigm change in the way things have developed and galloped post-COVID in terms of how these relations have transformed and how they have metamorphosized. Much speculation was that this happened mainly because of the election year in the USA. (Many policies pursued by Obama may have been temporarily put back on the back banner, like the withdrawal from Indo-Pacific or the TPP[2] (Trans-Pacific Partnership), which has been analysed in terms of its economic impact on the partners), climate change, etc. A lot of these were undone by Trump, but indeed, with the return of Joe Biden, many of these are expected to be reviewed for bringing about a conducive environment for rebalancing of the strained relations. Perhaps the world may witness the emergence of the USA in its old mould when it always interested itself in global affairs and intervened where necessary.

It also attempts to cover a conflict resolution and cooperation dynamics in Indo-Pacific. In this context, analysis of why Deng Xiaoping made this statement on 10 October 1974[3] is of great relevance:

> if one day China should change her colour and turn into a superpower if she too should play the tyrant in the world, and everywhere subject others to her bullying, aggression and

[1] The concept has gained traction after then PM Abe made a reference in 2013 to the confluence of oceans, namely, the Indian Ocean and the Pacific Ocean that would hold the attention of the world for collective peace, prosperity, security, and stability.

[2] Mukhopadhya and Thomassin (2018).

[3] Chansoria (2020).

R. S. Vasan (✉)
Chennai Center for China Studies, Chennai, India
e-mail: directorgeneral.c3s@gmail.com

S. Mishra and R. Sheel (eds.), *India-China Dialogues Beyond Borders*,
https://doi.org/10.1007/978-981-99-4326-5_11

exploitation, the people of the world should identify her as a social-imperialism, expose it, oppose it and work together with the Chinese people to overthrow it.

10.1 Contours of Power Play

How do we define the contours of power play? There are external players of all descriptions both in the Indian Ocean and the Pacific Ocean region. There is a need to know who the major players are, and their strategy and intentions are in the region. Major players in the area of interest are just China and USA with other powers joining one group or another. These are some of the milestones that China has set for itself (to be a major economic power, a military power to challenge the might of USA, a technological power by 2025 and a reasonably prosperous society by 2049[4]).

It has not deviated much from the prescription of bidding for time while building one's strength. A glimpse of it can be seen during the spread of COVID, while there are many theories[5] on the origins traced to the Wuhan lab in the Hubei province of China. The post-COVID predatory tactics and arm twisting for vaccine diplomacy also indicate its long-term aspirations.

So, what are the factors which change the rules of the game the game, whether in the Indian Ocean or in the Pacific region? It has an empowered leader from the communist party. United States of America has tried to drive an origin edge by differentiating between the party and the people. Xi Jinping, who is appointed as the core leader, has the complete command, including the military and the party at his disposal and therefore perhaps able to drive an agenda without internal opposition to realize the Chinese dream. Xi is emphatic about growth with Chinese characteristics.[6] In the military domain, it is about battlespace domination with the restructured command structure, better C4ISR structures using multi-dimensional technology and informatization warfare. This translates to better C4ISR structure, multi-dimensional strategy, and, of course, strategic/military clout to protect the core interest in the Indian Ocean region or in the Pacific. In the South China Sea as clearly brought by the Congressional report,[7] it has been achieved by taking over many of the rocks and reefs that were converted as islands, and they have become military bases. So, one should protect his/her territory not only by reinforcing the first and second line of defence but also by creating an ability to go beyond that. The intentions are to breach those traditional defence lines and move to the Indian Ocean region, which hold the trade and energy routes.

Xi has set targets for the party and military and will ensure that these are achieved in time. As envisioned, by 2025, it is a technology-enabled, moderately prosperous

---

[4] ODI (2021).

[5] Mcdonald (2021).

[6] The idea of Socialism with Chinese characteristics has been propagated by Xi to convey that here is a system that is succeeding.

[7] Congressial Research Service (2021).

community[8]—that is the goal, followed by being the number one, by 2049, the centenary years of the communist party's establishment.

10.2 The Indo-Pacific Arena

Let us look at Indo-Pacific, happening place. One cannot look at Pacific in isolation of Indian Ocean because this is where the confluence of two oceans has been defined as a geographical and geo-strategic construct. The geographic area of Indo-Pacific includes the ASEAN, Australia, Western Pacific, East Coast of Africa, and India as a predominant player because of its geographical position right in the centre of the Indian Ocean region.

Some of the interpretations from the past help to study the present-day scenario. In this context, the study of NSS 2017[9] document, which is available in the open domain, is essential. It emphasizes that nothing much has changed since 2017 in terms of China's aspirations, which needs to be countered in the assessment of the USA by this security document. 'The US Pacific Command[10] covers the Asia Pacific, Southeast Asia, and the South Asian countries of Bangladesh, India, the Maldives, Nepal and Sri Lanka. The idea was mooted by USA Navy secretariat Brathwaite business in the newspaper recently where they are already looking at having another designation for and Indo PACOM fleet, whether it comes from the existing fleet, whether they would redeploy assets or utilize partners is a different issue. However, there is news stating that they are taking it more seriously, complementing it to the NSSC 2017.

India includes the area from the east coast of Africa to the Australian coast end. China rejects the concept; Russia does have reservations about the varied definition of the Indo-Pacific and wonders whether it has military overtones and whether economic engagements are related to this. Countries from South East Asia, South Korea and other players in the Indian Ocean region would like to see how this entire concept unfolds and how India–China would play out this game with the USA taking the lead. Japan and Australia have become active partners. This aspect would be discussed later.

What are the different strokes of the different leaders in finding the common ground for cooperation in areas other than war.

[8] Scobell et al. (2020).

[9] National Security Strategy of the United States of America (2017).

[10] https://www.usa.gov/federal-agencies/u-s-indo-pacific-command Full details of the US Pacific Command are contained in this document, and it is clear that the command would be keeping a close watch on the developments in the Indo-Pacific.

10.3 The Confluence of Two Oceans

The confluence of two oceans[11] is often quoted to say that Japanese Prime Minister Abe talked about the confluence of the two oceans. Traditionally, Admiral Zheng he had forayed into the Indian Ocean region even from the Ming dynasty during the seven voyages[12] undertaken. He did so to establish the authority of the middle kingdom. His troop came here with junkets, and the eunuch admiral went around visiting Sri Lanka, Indian courts and even ports in Africa to say that China continues to be the middle kingdom and the middle kingdom expects recognition from its subjects far and wide! This confluence continues to the present day, i.e., twenty-first century, an Asian century, which is the century of the seas. Here was another statement which said, 'these shared interests give India and the USA a powerful incentive to make sure that the regional architecture for the Asia Pacific is up to answering the questions and delivering results. While addressing the gathering in a huge centenary library in Chennai on 20 July 2011,[13] in Southern India, Hillary Clinton talked about the India–USA shared interests in the Asia Pacific. The concepts of 'strategic economy' and 'inclusiveness' have been core to India's Indo-Pacific policies[14] as proposed by PM Narendra Modi while examining the Indo-Pacific initiative.

The focused areas include creating partnerships among interest rates; enhancing maritime security, sustainably using maritime resources; disaster prevention and management. But as a corollary to this, one can also look at stability, security and growth for all in the region. Maritime neighbourhood first, blue economy initiatives, sustainable development goals. This was highlighted at the EAS summit in 2019, and not much deviation has been from these statements/assertions made by PM Narendra Modi[15] On the contrary, the USA is trying to operationalize some of these concepts by engaging with partners. COVID accelerated the entire process because India was still a hesitant partner or was too worried about annoying China, a big neighbour. But slowly, it has dawned that closing up to China has not helped India in the last seven decades. Therefore, it requires a new way of handling China, a big neighbour.

So, the Indo-Pacific strategy requires more Indian Ocean because of India's position in the centre, just like the Pacific Ocean, which has many areas of interest to India. A lot of China's trade also passes through East Asian countries, but with its active policies, the entire area, whether South China Sea area or the Pacific or the countries located there, including the islands that have engaged separately, is important in Indian initiatives.

When we look at the Indian Ocean and analyse interrelated cogs, the main findings reinforce that its geographical location blesses India with access to the Arabian Sea on one side and the Bay of Bengal on the other side. China also has an entire slew of

---

[11] Mohan (2017), Details of how PM Abe brought out the essence of the confluence of oceans that was central to security stability and prosperity in the Indo Pacific.

[12] Cartwright (2019).

[13] Clinton (2011).

[14] Siddiqui (2019).

[15] Ministry of External Affairs Database (2019).

sea lanes of communication passing across. Therefore, it gives an ability to monitor and even interdict when required for launching pads on both coasts. However, all the countries in the region are also challenged by asymmetric threats such as terror attacks, piracy attacks, poaching, illegal, unregulated, unreported (IUU) fishing[16] as witnessed in the South China Sea and other Exclusive Economic Zones. These factors dictate the way India chooses to respond in the maritime domain. This also has an active component of the government's new initiatives in terms of neighbourhood policies. The developments in the maritime neighbourhood have brought in acute awareness of the need for enhanced maritime domain awareness. The Maritime Domain Awareness (MDA) in the context of India is knowing what is happening in the area right in the search and rescue region, which expands up to nearly 400 nautical miles while the EEZ extends up to 200 nautical miles, the search and rescue region (SAR) expands to 4 million sq. kilometres, which is double that of the search and rescue region. This is an area that is of great importance to India. Traditionally, India has always maintained that it can be a net security provider. But there are question marks on this ability as India or, for that matter, no country on its own has the wherewithal to be a provider. India has all the makings of a maritime nation that can facilitate net security in cooperation with others which is where the USA and other players come in. The Malabar, which is a regular exercise conducted in the Arabian Sea, is an example of collective action. However, for the first time, the Malabar Phase II was conducted in the Bay of Bengal[17] in 2021. The Chinese poaching in the traditional maritime neighbourhood countries has been an issue of concern. India needs to worry about China's engagement in India's backyard, whether it is economical, strategic, or military. The increased activities affect the happenings in the Indian Ocean region and can destabilize existing equations.

In most cases, it has been analysed that India is disadvantaged because economically,[18] India is only 20% of China. So, China is a long way ahead for India, which wants to become a 5 trillion-dollar economy in 2025. India is not even at 3 trillion dollars today, China is already at 14 trillion dollars, and America, by the way, is 20 trillion dollars. So, it is evident that India, which has significant differences with China on its border and other issues of relevance, has to align with other nations and like-minded players. Therefore, India is looking at the Indian Ocean Rim Association, Indian Ocean Naval Symposium and Milan as instruments that can facilitate more profound engagement with the partner nations who are part of these individual organizations.

---

[16] Febrica (2021).

[17] PIB Delhi (2021).

[18] Statisticstimes.com (2021).

10.4 Evolving Dynamics in the Indo-Pacific

One needs to critically examine the emerging nature of power in the Indo-Pacific with China being central to the power equation dynamics in Pacific, and India in the centre of the Indian Ocean region. Also, both Pacific and Indian Oceans are at the centre of geopolitical and economic space by extra-regional powers. So, even USA and China are both extra-regional players in the Indian Ocean region. So, this is where India needs to look at what is changing. In this context, the mention of the Belt and Road Initiative is important. The BRI project[19] was launched in 2013 there have been mixed responses on the success or failure of the project. A trillion-dollar project, it hopes to achieve connectivity, expands China's market share on the one hand, and provides it strategic leverages in the entire region of access, right from Asia, all the way to Africa and even right into Europe. India has chosen to abstain from it. India also kept away[20] from the BRF (**Belt Road Forum**). This is perhaps one major factor that has helped India keep away from China in these crises with the trans—Himalayan aggression. Though the Regional Comprehensive Economy Partnership has come in to being and, the neighbours are still wary of China's economic power, which buys out political leaders and partners.

The USA's redesignation of the Pacific Command as the Indo-Pacific Command indicated the importance of this area. This has also evolved to a QUAD[21] that has been in the making since 2007. Even China, as said by Braithwaite recently, perhaps even the USA, cannot do it alone and requires partners to contain China. So, the QUAD++, the Malabar, and many other initiatives are all related to containing China. India cannot exclude itself from the power game that is going on because it is an active stakeholder, and likewise. At the same time, India is central to the Indian Ocean region; it also needs to acknowledge that ASEAN collectively and individually is also central to the Pacific. Unfortunately, India's engagement with ASEAN as a creative group has mixed results. It has done well with Vietnam, Singapore, and some other members, but collectively, China has been able to get a lot more advantages. Even with the RCEP that has been signed, it appears that ASEAN will continue to do more business with China than with India.

That the pivot to Asia is nothing new. This is an old doctrine that was adopted even in Obama's time. Now it only becomes from Asia-Pacific to Indo-Pacific[22] to serve the interests of the USA and the interests of the democratic countries as it has been showcased. India has witnessed a resolve by PRC for total battlespace domination of China. It has thrown a gauntlet using A2/AD to prevent the carrier patent troops from coming close to India. Moreover, China has created unsinkable carriers in terms of the converted islands, which will allow it to reach out to any aggressor in the Pacific. So, these are the factors driving the QUAD; they are behind the statement

[19] Jacob (2019).

[20] Roy (2019).

[21] Smith (2021).

[22] Heiduk and Wacker (2020).

by Braithwaite[23] Secretary, Navy about forming another fleet just like the seventh fleet in Japan. To have another fleet that will perhaps provide these answers to the growth of China.

10.5 Evolving Nature of Holistic Strategy in the Indo-Pacific

It was Trump who chose to withdraw from the TPP. Some of the salience that will not be abandoned can be seen with Joe Biden coming back or the geopolitical competition between free and repressive visions of world order. Without naming China even once, the Indian Prime Minister Narendra Modi, has indicated on several occasions, has drawn the attention of the world to China's practices, including coercion, penalties, operation, economic assistance, and implied military threats to persuade all the states.

In the case of the Philippines, where a lot of money was poured in, and in Cambodia, Vietnam, everywhere, particularly post-COVID, other weaker economies tried to challenge China, including Australia. They came in with many sanctions—banning of meat export, banning of barley, and many other things. It has many ways to try and control any opposition to its unilateral engagement with other nations on its terms. Coordinating quadrilateral cooperation with Japan, Australia, and India is part of NSS 2017, and one can only thank China for the fact that it is happening. Australia, which kept on requesting inclusion in the Malabar, has finally found the place. And it starts happening for the first time on both sides, not in the Bay of Bengal but also in the Arabian Sea. It shows that it has the potential to operate anywhere, either in the Indian Ocean region or in the Indo-Pacific, to serve the common interests of the players.

10.6 The Strategic Underpinning of Economy and Trade

According to Trump, it was to be pivoted on fair and reciprocal trade and infrastructural investment from the World Bank and the Asian development bank. The importance of the rule of law, individual rights, and freedom of navigation are central to the concept of Free and Open Indo-Pacific (FOIP). The economy and trade would suffer when one nation is seen as misusing the provisions of some of these fair practices. Secretary of State Rex Tillerson,[24] when he came to India some time ago, he had placed heavy emphasis on working closely with India on defence and security across the Indo-Pacific and providing alternatives to the predatory economics of China's Belt and Road Initiative. It is evident that all the nations have not benefitted from the BRI initial investments, and most of them have been dated the deadline. However,

[23] Rej (2020).

[24] Ayres (2017).

it has been done so that it only is a win–win for China and not for others who have accepted investments from China through various instruments. Increased attention to the role of BRICS fund Asia and infrastructural development; as India is drawing from AIIB, this cannot be seen as a contradiction because India is also a partner.

10.7 Power Play Based on Trade and Economy

This is related to the withdrawal of TPP, which created a power vacuum and a trade vacuum, and India has differed from joining RCEP again; there are views in support and in opposition of RCEP, and people are saying that India is going back to protectionism, but we can discuss this later. Fear was that China would use all the liberal policies in RCEP to dump various products in India. Predatory economics in BRI/MSR, chequebook diplomacy leading to debt trap and need for an alternative to BRI, we are looking at AAGC. However, not much has happened at the time; we require the US and some EU members to join the Asia Africa Growth Corridor (AAGC) to create a separate benign instrument to provide attractive terms for developing countries who would like to draw from a separate pool of money for infrastructure. Unless this is activated by pooling resources, AAGC will have limited objectives being served. India is still denied entry into APEC. There are many issues on which China has not necessarily supported India; it has created issues for India, and it is time to explore alternative systems to serve the long interests of India.

10.8 Power Play and Regional Groups

There have been efforts to expand the membership of quad. However, given the changes in the geopolitical scenario, it could also be a counter-quad that is developing because of Turkey, Iran, China, Russia, and Pakistan joining together, which will change the dynamics in the Straits of Hormuz (SOH) the North Arabian Sea. The centrality of ASEAN is important. Therefore, India needs to enhance its engagements by all means, and only then can India hope to enhance its clout in the changing global order.

10.9 Prognosis: Power Play Impact?

There is an ongoing power play that impacts everything, and this is very evident with the possibility of expanding scope of cold war 2.0. Different forms of trade warfare and technology are already taking place in a post-COVID scenario. Furthermore, many nations will be compelled to exercise the hard option. New alignments will be forged. It does not affect China forever because it has a phenomenal amount of buffer in terms of economy and strategic strengths. China has a positive growth in the post-COVID whereas most of the others are struggling with negative growth projections. Players like India and Australia are in the process to overcome 'the hesitations of history' and chart a new course and align without affecting strategic autonomy.

There is a need to revisit the statement that has been included at the beginning of this paper. "If one day china should change her colour and turn into a superpower if she too should play the tyrant in the world, and everywhere subject others to her bullying, aggression and exploitation, the people of the world should identify her as social-imperialism, expose it." Oppose it and work together with the Chinese people to overthrow it—Deng Xiaoping at UNGA 10 October 1974.

It was said that when China was trying to integrate itself with the global economy, the statement was nicely masked to convey that China would be a responsible player. Most of the actions belie the expectation that China would now be a responsible power. Therefore, maybe it is time for the world to come together, expose it, oppose it and work together with the Chinese people to overthrow it.

References

Ayres A (2017) Tillerson on India: partners in a free and Open Indo-Pacific, Council on Foreign Relations Blog, October 18. https://www.cfr.org/blog/tillerson-india-partners-free-and-open-indo-pacific#:~:text=Tillerson%20proposed%20that%20the%20United%20States%20and%20India,,connectivity%20needed%20to%20increase%20trade%20and%20economic%20prosperity. Accessed on 20 Mar 2021

Cai C (2019) The rise of China and international law: taking exceptionalism seriously. Oxford University Press, New York

Cartwright M (2019) The seven voyages of Zheng He, World History Encyclopedia, February 7. http://www.silkroadfoundation.org/artl/hsuantsang.shtml. Accessed on 15 May 2020

Chansoria M (2020) Why did Deng Xiaoping advocate for the 'World to overthrow China' in 1974? Japan Forward, August 4. https://japan-forward.com/why-did-deng-xiaoping-advocate-for-the-world-to-overthrow-china-in-1974/. Accessed on 12 Feb 2022

Christiansen T, Kirchner E, Wissenback (2018) The European Union and China, UK, Macmillan Education

Clinton HR (2011) Remarks on India and the United States: a vision for the 21st Century, US Department of State, July 20. https://2009-2017.state.gov/secretary/20092013clinton/rm/2011/07/168840.htm. Accessed on 20 Jan 2022

Congressial Research Service Database (2021) China primer: South China Sea disputes. https://crsreports.congress.gov/product/pdf/IF/IF10607. Accessed on 20 Jan 2022

Febrica S (2021) Addressing Illegal, Unreported, and Unregulated (IUU) fishing in the South China Sea. https://www.seniafebrica.com/post/addressing-illegal-unreported-and-unregulated-iuu-fishing-in-the-south-china-sea. Accessed on 20 Jan 2022

Heiduk F, Wacker G (2020) From Asia-Pacific to Indo-Pacific: significance, implementation and challenges, SWP, Striftung Wissenchaft und Politik Research Paper 9, Berlin July 2020. http://www.silkroadfoundation.org/artl/hsuantsang.shtml. Accessed on 15 May 2020

Jacob JT (2019) China's belt and road initiative and its implications for India, Henrich Boll Stiftung, Regional Office New Delhi, February 25. https://in.boell.org/en/2019/02/25/chinas-belt-and-road-initiative-and-its-implications-india. Accessed on 25 Jan 2022

McDonald H (2021) Sharri Mrkson's book on Covid's Wuhan lab leak theory raises more questions than it answers. The Guardian, October 8

Ministry of Defence Database (2021) Multilateral Maritime Exercise Malabar 2021-Phase II in Bay of Bengal 12–15 October 21, October 10. https://pib.gov.in/pressreleaseiframepage.aspx?prid=1762720. Accessed on 23 Jan 2021

Ministry of External Affairs Database, November 04, 2019, Prime minister's Speech at the East Asia Summit, 04, November 2019. https://www.mea.gov.in/Speeches-Statements.htm?dtl/32171/Prime_Ministers_Speech_at_the_East_Asia_Summit_04_November_2019. Accessed on 20 Jan 2021

Mohan CR (2017) The confluence of the two sea, Carnegie India, October 26. https://carnegieindia.org/2017/10/26/confluence-of-two-seas-pub-73560. Accessed on 10 Jan 2022

Mukhopadhya K, Thomassin PJ (2018) The impact of Trans-Pacific partnership agreement on the Canadian economy. J Econ Struct 7 Article number 5

National Security Strategy of the United States of America Achieves Database, 2017, Indo Pacfic, p 45. http://nssarchive.us/wp-content/uploads/2020/04/2017.pdf Accessed on 12 Dec 2021

ODI Database (2021) Global China 2049 initiative. https://odi.org/en/about/our-work/global-china-2049-initiative/. Accessed on 12 Feb 2022

Rej A (2020) Us Navy secretary proposes New Indo-Pacific Fleet, The Diplomat, November 18

Roy S (2019) India will not sign off on BRI at Bishek, the India Express, June 14, 2019

Scobell et al (2020) China's grand strategy: trends, trajectories, and long term competition, Santa Monika, Calif, RAND Corporation. https://www.rand.org/pubs/research_reports/RR2798.html. Accessed on 10 Feb 2022

Siddiqui H (2019) Ministry of External Affairs Database: India's concept of Indo-Pacific is Inclusive and across oceans, November 08. https://journalofeconomicstructures.springeropen.com/articles/10.1186/s40008-017-0102-y; https://mea.gov.in/articles-in-indian-media.htm?dtl/32015/Indias_concept_of_IndoPacific_is_inclusive_and_across_oceans; https://mea.gov.in/Speeches-Statements.htm?dtl/32171/Prime_Ministers_Speech_at_the_East_Asia_Summit_04_November_2019. Accessed on 20 Jan 2022

Smith SA (2021) The quad in the Indo-Pacific: what to know, Council on Foreign Relations, May 27. http://www.silkroadfoundation.org/artl/hsuantsang.shtml. Accessed on 15 May 2020

Statistic Times (2021) Comparing China and India by economy, May 16. https://www.cfr.org/blog/tillerson-india-partners-free-and-open-indo-pacific#:~:text=Tillerson%20proposed%20that%20the%20United%20States%20and%20India,,connectivity%20needed%20to%20increase%20trade%20and%20economic%20prosperity. Accessed on 23 Jan 2021

Chapter 11
Growth and Pattern of India–China Trade from 1995 to 2020: A Study

Gadde Omprasad

11.1 Introduction

As both the countries have civilisations that could be traced back to thousands of years, the cultural, religious, social and economic ties between them were connected to the ancient Silk Routes, both south and south-west, linking eastern and north-eastern India with Tibet and Yunan regions of China (Saikia 2020). The earliest mention of the relations between the two countries could be found in the writings of Kautilya of India and Zhang Qian of China (Khwairakpam 2020). As Buddhism entered China from India through, these silk routes, the socio-cultural and religious relations became stronger, with many scholars from China visiting the then-Indian universities (Scott 2016; Sen 2006). This also facilitated mutual sharing of the vast amount of knowledge these two ancient civilisations put up.

During the British rule in India, trade with China was dominated by tea and opium. More than 90% of this trade was dominated by tea (Chung 1973). Relations between the two countries in the first half of the 1950s were cordial. Several mutual high-level visits took place and the signing of The Five Principles of Peaceful Coexistence, also known as Panchsheel in 1954, were momentous (MEA 2022). Soon after, the relations deteriorated with mutual mistrust on political boundary issues, and a Sino-India war broke out in 1962. As a result, political relations, including economic relations were adversely affected till the 1970s. The resumption of bilateral relations took place in the 1980s as the leaders of both countries agreed to expand mutual relations to non-controversial issues, including cooperation in economic and trade sectors. In 1984, both the countries exchanged Most Favoured Nation (MFN) status (MEA 2012). As a result, trade volume increased from less than one hundred crore INR before 1984 to 196.8 crore INR by the beginning of 1989. Though trade volume increased, Indian exports to China were valued at Rs 64 crore, where imports were estimated to be

G. Omprasad (✉)
Centre for South Asian Studies, Jawaharlal Nehru University, New Delhi, India
e-mail: opgadde2@gmail.com

S. Mishra and R. Sheel (eds.), *India-China Dialogues Beyond Borders*,
https://doi.org/10.1007/978-981-99-4326-5_12

Rs 124 crore, indicating a massive balance of trade favouring China (Bhola 1989). In order to increase the trade volume, both countries have negotiated multiple times and signed various treaties. Among these agreements, the 1994 agreement on Double Taxation, the preferential trade agreement in 2003 on the backdrop of the ASEAN meeting in Bangkok, and the Five-Year Development Program for Economic and Trade Cooperation signed in 2014 are significant (PHD Research Bureau 2018). It is imperative to understand the impact of these agreements and the pattern of trade in the post-China's entry into the World Trade Agreement in 2001. It is also necessary to note that by the first half of 2010's China also emerged as the largest manufacturer of goods in the world, surpassing the USA.

11.1.1 Double Taxation Avoidance Agreement, 1994

In 1994, both the countries signed a Double Taxation Avoidance Agreement to encourage private entrepreneurs to increase trading activity and thus to enhance bilateral trade-economic cooperation, including taxation (PHD Research Bureau 2018).

Table 11.1 depicts the India–China trade from 1996 to 2003 after the first Double Taxation Avoidance Agreement. The trade volume increased from US $ 1371.71 million in 1996 to US $ 7008.29 million in 2004 to almost five folds during this period. At the same time, the trade imbalance between the two countries also increased from US $ 142.11 million to US $ 1098 million, recording more than seven times in favour of China. In terms of India's total imports, China accounted for about 1.93% in 1996 and 5.19% in 2004, whereas, in India's total exports, China consumed 1.84% in 1996 and 4.63% in 2004. These figures also indicate that there was a significant increase in trade volume between the two countries in the initial phase of economic engagement. After India's economic liberalisation and a formal agreement to avoid double taxation, the percentage of trade between the two countries in overall trade was less than 6% and well below the significant amount. Although the trade between both the countries did not amount to a significant percentage in terms of their overall exports and imports, the average annual growth rate in this period stood at 28.42%. India's average annual import growth rate accounted for 28.20%, and the export growth rate amounted to 32.61%. The following Fig. 11.1 depicts the same.

During the period, India's imports from China increased from 84 to 95 categories from 1997 to 2003. Though there is an increase in the number of items, only the top 10 items recorded a significant share of more than 75%. Table 11.2 gives the percentage share of the top ten items during this period.

The table also provides a glimpse of India's top 10 items from China from 1996 to 2003. These items constitute more than 75% of the total imports from China. Further, it can also be noted that the items like Organic chemicals, Mineral fuels, Electrical items and nuclear fuels take the major share and occupy more than 50% of the total imports. In the initial stages of the trade from 1996 to 2001, major importing item was Organic chemicals, which accounted for more than 25% but declined to

Table 11.1 India–China trade 1996–2003

(In US $ million)

Year	Imports	Exports	Total trade	Trade balance
1996–1997	756.91	614.8	1371.71	−142.11
1997–1998	1,112.05	717.95	1830	−394.1
1998–1999	1,096.71	427.16	1523.87	−669.55
1999–2000	1,282.89	539.04	1821.93	−743.85
2000–2001	1,502.20	831.3	2333.5	−670.9
2001–2002	2,036.39	951.95	2988.34	−1084.44
2002–2003	2,792.04	1,975.48	4767.52	−816.56
2003–2004	4,053.21	2,955.08	7008.29	−1098.13

Source Based on Author's compilation of the data extracted from, Export Import Data Bank, Department of Commerce, Government of India, https://tradestat.commerce.gov.in/eidb/default.asp

Fig. 11.1 India–China Trade volume growth rate, 1996–2003. *Source* Based on Author's compilation of the data extracted from, Export Import Data Bank, Department of Commerce, Government of India, https://tradestat.commerce.gov.in/eidb/default.asp

less than 17%. One can also observe that after China joined the WTO in 2001, from 2002 onwards, India's major import item from China has been Electrical machinery and equipment, including recorders, Television sets and other-related goods. These goods occupy more than 29% by the end of 2003, indicating the beginning of heavy reliance of India on China over electronic items. At the same time, one also has to note that there has been a rise in manufacturing and exports of high-end electrical and related goods in the post-WTO period. In the post-WTO entry, China's overall exports increased from 2.6 to 7.7% between 2002 and 2007 (Chen 2009). This rise is also because of an increase in Foreign Direct Investments as they recorded a 30% increase within 1 year, from 2001 to 2002 (Fung et al. 2006).

Table 11.2 Percentage share of top 10 import items* from 1996 to 2003

(In %)

1996–1997	1997–1998	1998–1999	1999–2000	2000–2001	2001–2002	2002–2003	2003–2004
Organic chemicals (25.50%)	Organic chemicals (21.63%)	Organic chemicals (21.22%)	Organic chemicals (19.46%)	Mineral fuels, etc. (17.53%)	Organic chemicals (16.85%)	Electric (25.07%)	Electric (29.17%)
Mineral fuels etc. (13.60%)	Mineral fuels etc. (19.17%)	Mineral fuels etc. (12.38%)	Mineral fuels etc. (12.05%)	Organic chemicals (16.59%)	Electric (13.43%)	Organic chemicals (16.78%)	Organic chemicals (15.89%)
Silk (8.04%)	Nuclear reactors etc. (8.14%)	Nuclear reactors etc. (11.31%)	Nuclear reactors etc. (10.71%)	Nuclear reactors etc. (12.56%)	Mineral fuels etc. (12.90%)	Nuclear reactors etc. (10.19%)	Nuclear reactors etc. (12.20%)
Electric (7.51%)	Electric (8.11%)	Electric (10.02%)	Electric (9.40%)	Electric (10.75%)	Nuclear reactors etc. (11.42%)	Mineral fuels etc. (6.27%)	Silk (5.46%)
Nuclear reactors etc. (6.46%)	Chemicals etc. (6.55%)	Chemicals etc. (5.88%)	Silk (7.88%)	Silk (7.54%)	Silk (7.68%)	Silk (5.75%)	Mineral fuels etc. (5.46%)
Chemicals etc. (5.76%)	Silk (5.40%)	Silk (5.72%)	Chemicals etc. (4.36%)	Salt and sulphur etc. (5.49%)	Natural pearls etc. (4.81%)	Natural pearls etc. (4.88%)	Chemicals etc. (2.74%)
Copper and articles thereof (4.11%)	Articles of iron or steel (4.72%)	Project goods, some special uses (4.93%)	Salt and sulphur etc. (2.81%)	Chemicals etc. (3.37%)	Chemicals etc. (3.05%)	Chemicals etc. (2.65%)	Natural pearls etc. (1.69%)
Articles of iron or steel (2.86%)	Copper and articles thereof (2.34%)	Zinc and articles thereof (2.05%)	Sugar and sugar confectionery (2.61%)	Natural pearls etc. (1.80%)	Salt and sulphur etc. (2.98%)	Optical, medical and surgical etc. (1.99%)	Man-made filaments (1.68%)
Project goods, some special uses (2.31%)	Project goods, some special uses (2%)	Iron and steel (1.85%)	Zinc and articles thereof (2.03%)	Zinc and articles thereof (1.55%)	Optical, medical and surgical etc. (2.63%)	Man-made filaments (1.74%)	Fabrics for industrial use etc. (1.63%)

(continued)

Table 11.2 (continued)

(In %)

1996–1997	1997–1998	1998–1999	1999–2000	2000–2001	2001–2002	2002–2003	2003–2004
Salt and sulphur etc. (2.16%)	On and steel (1.92%)	Salt and sulphur etc. (1.71%)	Natural pearls etc. (1.83%)	Optical, medical and surgical etc. (1.35%)	Edible vegetables and certain roots and tubers (1.47%)	Fabrics for industrial use etc. (1.70%)	Optical, medical and surgical etc. (1.58%)
Percentage of top 10 imports in total imports							
78.32	80.01	77.08	73.15	78.53	77.22	77.02	77.51

Source Based on Author's compilation of the data extracted from, Export Import Data Bank, Department of Commerce, Government of India, https://tradestat.commerce.gov.in/eidb/default.asp. * Details of the items are given in the Note section at the end of the paper

Table 11.3 portrays that from 1996 to 2003 organic chemicals, mineral fuels, electrical items and nuclear reactor-related items occupied the share of more than 50% of the total imports. During this period, these electrical and nuclear items have recorded an average growth rate of 20.03, 21.11, 62.42 and 38.72% respectively.

Table 11.4 provides the details of the top 10 export items from India to China from 1996 to 2003. These items occupy a percentage share ranging from 92 to 83% in total exports to China. The average percentage share of these items in the same is about 84% for the period. Further examination of the table indicates that the top four exporting items occupied the share between 55 and 69% during the period. The average percentage share of the top four items was about 63% indicating the importance in overall exports to China.

Further, it can also be noted that there was no consistency in the top four items. The items like Residue and waste from the food industries and prepared animal fodder, which accounted for more than 25% in 1996 and 1997, did not appear in the list of top 10 importing items from 1999 to 2003. At the same time, the percentage share of items like Ore, slag, Ash, Iron and Steel increased their combined share to more than 40% of total items exported to China. It is also to be noted that in the same list, items of industrially manufactured goods were less and insignifact indicating the nature of exports. Thus, it can be argued that one of the main reason for the growing negative trade balance is India's inadequate manufacturing sector output. It is reflected in the table which shows that most of the items exported by India were of raw materials rather than finished goods.

Figure 11.2 gives a glimpse of India's exports to China from 1996 to 2003 in its overall exports. We can observe the growth from 1.84% in 1996 to 4.63% by 2003.

11.1.2 Trade Preferential Agreement 2003

China entered into World Trade Organisation in 2001. The governments of both the countries also took the necessary initiative to turn into dialogue partners in the Association of Southeast Asian Nations (ASEAN). In 2003, Bangkok Agreement was signed between the two countries. Under this agreement, both India and China offered some trade preferences. India provided tariffs for 217 products exported from India (PHD Research Bureau 2018). In 2003, India and China agreed to initiate open border trade via the Silk Route (MEA 2003).

Table 11.5 outlines India–China Trade from 2005 to 2013 after they urned into dialogue partners and extended trade preferences, including opening land border trade through the old Silk Route. Trade volume during this period increased from US $ 7008.29 million in 2004 to the US $ 65,859 million, almost nine folds during this period. At the same time, the trade imbalance between the two countries also rose from US $ 1098 million to the US $ 36,210 million recordings more than three times in favour of China. India's total imports from China more than doubled from 5.19% in 2004 to 11.34% by the end of the 2013–2014 financial year. It is a significant increase, whereas the same trend is on decreasing side on India's share in China's

Table 11.3 Average growth rate of major importing items* (1997–2003)

(In %)

	1997–1998	1998–1999	1999–2000	2000–01	2001–02	2002–03	2003–2004	Average growth
Organic chemicals	24.61	−3.24	7.27	−0.16	37.68	36.49	37.53	20.03
Mineral fuels	107.18	−36.31	13.8	70.35	−0.24	−33.31	26.32	21.11
Electrical items	58.64	36.97	9.74	37.26	69.35	156.06	68.91	62.42
Nuclear fuels	85.09	21.79	10.8	33.89	23.27	22.39	73.78	38.72

Source Based on Author's compilation of the data extracted from, Export Import Data Bank, Department of Commerce, Government of India, https://tradestat.commerce.gov.in/eidb/default.asp. * Details of the items are given in the Note section at the end of the paper

Table 11.4 Percentage share of top 10 exporting items* (1997–2003)

(In %)

1996–1997	1997–1998	1998–1999	1999–2000	2000–2001	2001–2002	2002–2003	2003–2004
Residues etc. (25.18%)	Residues etc. (26.24%)	Ores, slag and ash (26.09%)	Ores, slag and ash (20.23%)	Ores, slag and ash (18.68%)	Ores, slag and ash (27.62%)	Iron and steel (25.43%)	Ores, slag and ash (20.34%)
Ores, slag and ash (19.16%)	Ores, slag and ash (18.29%)	Fish and crustaceans etc. (12.05%)	Fish and crustaceans etc. (16.23%)	Fish and crustaceans etc. (13.93%)	Plastic and articles, thereof (11.95%)	Ores, slag and ash (25.02%)	Iron and steel (20.42%)
Fish and crustaceans etc. (12.02%)	Fish and crustaceans etc. (16%)	Organic chemical (10.99%)	Organic chemicals (12.41%)	Organic chemicals (13%)	Organic chemicals (11.86%)	Organic chemicals (7.87%)	Plastic and articles, thereof (9.03%)
Iron and steel (11.61%)	Cotton (9.30)	Cotton (9.78%)	Cotton (9.78%)	Plastic and articles, thereof (9.74%)	Fish and crustaceans, etc. (8.90%)	Plastic and articles, thereof (7.52%)	Organic chemicals (7.50%)
Cotton (10.87%)	Organic chemicals (5.75%)	Residues etc. (7.67%)	Salt, sulphur etc. (7.02%)	Cotton (8.47%)	Cotton (7.24%)	Fish and crustaceans etc. (5.88%)	Cotton (3.64%)
Organic chemicals (4.81%)	Animal and vegetable fats etc. (4.06%)	Animal and vegetable fats etc. (4.07%)	Animal and vegetable fats etc. (5.92%)	Salt, sulphur etc. (5.77%)	Salt, sulphur etc. (6.07%)	Inorganic chemicals etc. (4.31%)	Inorganic chemicals etc. (3.42%)
Salt, sulphur etc. (3.12%)	Inorganic chemicals etc. (4.02%)	Salt, sulphur etc. (3.82%)	Pharmaceutical products (3.33%)	Iron and steel (3.29%)	Pharmaceutical products (2.27%)	Salt, sulphur etc. (3.49%)	Salt, sulphur etc. (3.05%)
Animal and vegetable fats etc. (2.32%)	Iron and steel (2.12%)	Pharmaceutical products (3.39%)	Plastic and articles, thereof (2.85%)	Pharmaceutical products (2.17%)	Feather articles etc. (2.13%)	Cotton (3.22%)	Fish and crustaceans etc. (2.57%)

(continued)

Table 11.4 (continued)

(In %)

1996–1997	1997–1998	1998–1999	1999–2000	2000–2001	2001–2002	2002–2003	2003–2004
Inorganic chemicals etc. (2.05%)	Pharmaceutical products (1.94%)	Miscellaneous chemical products (2.83%)	Lac, gums etc. (2.63%)	Feather articles etc. (2.14%)	Optical, medical etc. (2.02%)	Pharmaceutical products (1.80%)	Mineral fuels etc. (2.51%)
Pharmaceutical product (1.79%)	Salt, sulphur etc. (1.47%)	Inorganic chemicals etc. (2.43%)	Miscellaneous chemical product (2.09%)	Nuclear reactors-related etc. (2.11%)	Inorganic chemicals etc. (1.95%)	Nuclear reactors-related etc. (1.60%)	Nuclear reactors-related etc. (2.30%)
Percentage of top 10 exports in total exports							
92.93	89.19	83.11	82.50	79.30	82.01	86.14	83.80

Source Based on Author's compilation of the data extracted from, Export Import Data Bank, Department of Commerce, Government of India, https://tradestat.commerce.gov.in/eidb/default.asp. * Details of the items are given in the Note section at the end of the paper

Fig. 11.2 Percentage share of India's exports to China, 1996–2003. *Source* Based on Author's compilation of the data extracted from, Export Import Data Bank, Department of Commerce, Government of India, https://tradestat.commerce.gov.in/eidb/default.asp. * Details of the items are given in the Note section at the end of the paper

overall imports. India accounted for about 6.72% in 2003, which had come down to 4.72% by 2013. These figures also indicate that after China entered into WTO, its percentage of imports from India decreased as China's engagement with other countries increased. During this period, the data indicates that though in 2004 the trade growth rate than the previous year recorded more than 81%, the same trend did not continue in the following years and showed a significant fall to 0.12% by 2013. It even recorded 10% negative growth rate in 2012. Despite this, the average annual growth rate in this period stood at 27.82% lower than the earlier period of 1996–2003–2004, showing not very encouraging trends. The same has been given in Fig. 11.2.

During the period, India's imports from China increased from 95 to 96 categories from 2004 to 2014. Though there is an increase in the number of items, only the top 10 items recorded a significant share of more than 75%. The table below gives the percentage share of the top 10 items during this period. Up to 2005, mineral fuel-related items had a significant share of about 12%, which decreased to less than 0.5% by 2014. At the same time, Electronic items increased its share from 7.51% in 1997 to 27.71% by the year 2014 (Fig. 11.3).

Table 11.6 shows India's top ten goods from China from 2004 to 2014. These top ten goods accounted for more than 75% of the overall imports from China. The Table also depicts that throughout the period, items such as electrical machinery, organic chemicals, nuclear reactors, and boilers accounted for more than 50% of total imports, indicating heavy reliance on China for these items. Electrical-related items accounted for more than 25% of the total imports, followed by Nuclear boiler-related items and Organic chemicals with more than 17 and 10%, respectively (Table 11.7).

Table 11.5 India–China trade 2004–2013

(In US $ Million)

Year	Imports	Exports	Total trade	Trade balance
2004–2005	7,097.98	5,615.88	12,713.86	−1,482.10
2005–2006	10,868.05	6,759.10	17,627.15	−4,108.95
2006–2007	17,475.03	8,321.86	25,796.89	−9,153.17
2007–2008	27,146.41	10,871.34	38,017.75	−16,275.07
2008–2009	32,497.02	9,353.50	41,850.52	−23,143.52
2009–2010	30,824.02	11,617.88	42,441.90	−19,206.14
2010–2011	43,479.76	14,168.86	57,648.62	−29,310.90
2011–2012	55,313.58	18,076.55	73,390.13	−37,237.03
2012–2013	52,248.33	13,534.88	65,783.21	−38,713.45
2013–2014	51,034.62	14,824.36	65,858.98	−36,210.26

Source Based on Author's compilation of the data extracted from, Export Import Data Bank, Department of Commerce, Government of India, https://tradestat.commerce.gov.in/eidb/default.asp

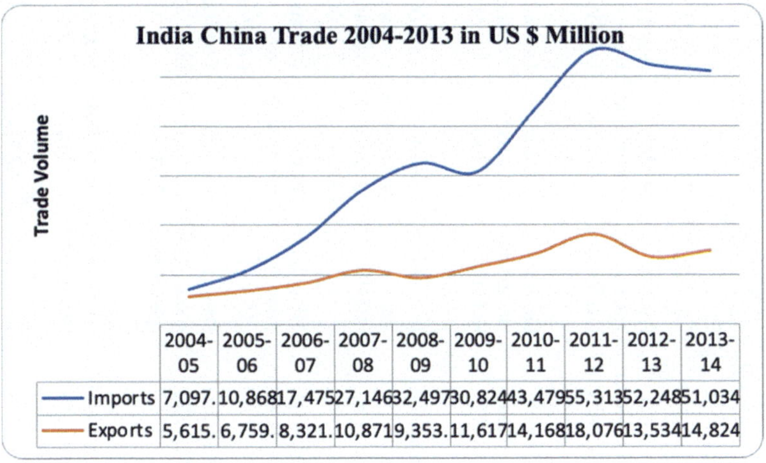

Fig. 11.3 India–China Trade volume growth rate, 2004–2013. *Source* Based on Author's compilation of the data extracted from, Export Import Data Bank, Department of Commerce, Government of India, https://tradestat.commerce.gov.in/eidb/default.asp

In the period 2004–2014, unlike the earlier period, only three items took more than 50% of India's total imports from China. The imports' percentage share of mineral fuel came down significantly, and Electrical items occupied a large part of the share in the imports and grew at the average rate of 29.74%. Similarly, nuclear fuels grew at the rate of 37.02% and organic chemicals at 22.61%.

Table 11.8 imparts the details of the top 10 export items from India to China from 2004 to 2013. These items occupy a percentage share ranging from 90 to 78%

Table 11.6 Percentage share of India's top 10 imports items* from China 2004 to 2014

(In %)

2004–2005	2005–2006	2006–2007	2007–2008	2008–2009	2009–2010	2010–2011	2011–2012	2012–2013	2013–2014	2014–2015
Electric (25.04%)	Electric (25.52%)	Electric (24.30%)	Electric (28.13%)	Electric (30.76%)	Electric (31.36%)	Electric (27.27%)	Electric (25.64%)	Electric (26.77%)	Electric (27.88%)	Electric (27.71%)
Nuclear reactors etc. (14.81%)	Nuclear reactors etc. (19.90%)	Nuclear reactors etc. (18.61%)	Nuclear reactors etc. (17.80%)	Nuclear reactors etc. (16.95%)	Nuclear reactors etc. (20.03%)	Nuclear reactors etc. (17.71%)	Nuclear reactors etc. (18.34%)	Nuclear reactors etc. (19.15%)	Nuclear reactors etc. (18.53%)	Nuclear reactors etc. (16.79%)
Mineral fuels etc. (12.71%)	Organic chemicals (12.06%)	Organic chemicals (9.78%)	Organic chemicals (8.78%)	Organic chemicals (8.68%)	Organic chemicals (9.77%)	Organic chemicals (8.86%)	Project goods, some special uses (9.15%)	Organic chemicals (9.47%)	Organic chemicals (10.57%)	Organic chemicals (10.47%)
Organic chemicals (11.59%)	Mineral fuels etc. (6.63%)	Mineral fuels etc. (7.19%)	Iron and steel (5.37%)	Iron and steel (5.31%)	Project goods, some special uses. (6.84%)	Project goods, some special uses. (7.32%)	Organic chemicals (7.93%)	Project goods, some special uses (7.10%)	Project goods, some special uses (4.17%)	Fertilisers (5.22%)
Silk (4.27%)	Silk (3.54%)	Articles of iron or steel (5.75%)	Mineral fuels etc. (4.77%)	Mineral fuels etc. (3.93%)	Articles of iron or steel (2.78%)	Iron and steel (4.57%)	Fertilisers (4.69%)	Fertilisers (5.74%)	Fertilisers (3.77%)	Iron and steel (4.49%)
Natural cultured pearls etc. (2.18%)	Iron and steel (2.47%)	Iron and steel (4.07%)	Fertilisers (4.37%)	Project goods, some special uses (3.73%)	Iron and steel (2.64%)	Fertilisers (3.49%)	Iron and steel (3.35%)	Iron and steel (2.86%)	Plastic and articles, thereof (2.59%)	Plastic and articles, thereof (2.83%)
Chemicals etc. (2.10%)	Chemicals etc. (1.87%)	Project goods, some special uses (2.87%)	Articles of iron or steel (4.25%)	Articles of iron or steel (3.20%)	Plastic and articles, thereof (1.68%)	Ships etc. (2.79%)	Articles of iron or steel (2.79%)	Articles of iron or steel (2.83%)	Articles of iron or steel (2.39%)	Project goods, some special uses (2.40%)

(continued)

Table 11.6 (continued)

(In %)

2004–2005	2005–2006	2006–2007	2007–2008	2008–2009	2009–2010	2010–2011	2011–2012	2012–2013	2013–2014	2014–2015
Iron and steel (1.77%)	Industrial fabrics etc. (1.80%)	Plastic and articles, thereof (2.19%)	Plastic and articles, thereof (2.31%)	Fertilisers (2.81%)	Vehicles etc. (1.54%)	Articles of iron or steel (2.71%)	Ships etc. (2.49%)	Plastic and articles, thereof (2.17%)	Optical, medical, surgical etc. (2.04%)	Articles of iron or steel (2.30%)
Industrial fabrics etc. (1.59%)	Articles of iron or steel (1.79%)	Silk (1.93%)	Chemicals etc. (1.48%)	Natural cultured pearls etc. (2.56%)	Chemicals etc. (1.47%)	Plastic and articles, thereof (1.97%)	Plastic and articles, thereof (1.91%)	Optical, medical, surgical etc. (1.91%)	Vehicles etc. (1.95%)	Natural cultured pearls etc. (2.04%)
Man-made filaments (1.48%)	Plastic and articles, thereof (1.72%)	Chemicals etc. (1.64%)	Project goods, some special uses (1.47%)	Optical, medical, surgical etc. (1.78%)	Optical, medical, surgical etc. (1.44%)	Vehicles etc. (1.69%)	Vehicles etc. (1.80%)	Vehicles etc. (1.85%)	Iron and steel (1.91%)	Optical, medical, surgical etc. (2.02%)
Percentage of top 10 imports in total imports										
77.56	77.32	78.34	78.74	79.71	79.55	78.38	78.10	79.85	75.80	76.28

Source Based on Author's compilation of the data extracted from, Export Import Data Bank, Department of Commerce, Government of India, https://tradestat.commerce.gov.in/eidb/default.asp. * Details of the items are given in the Note section at the end of the paper

Table 11.7 Average growth rate of major importing items* (2004–2015)

(In %)

	2004–2005	2005–2006	2006–2007	2007–2008	2008–2009	2009–2010	2010–2011	2011–2012	2012–2013	2013–2014	2014–2015	Average growth
Electrical items	50.34	56.04	53.11	79.8	30.91	−3.29	22.66	19.61	−1.4	1.75	17.64	29.74
Nuclear fuels	112.58	105.65	50.43	48.57	14.02	12.06	31.74	31.74	−1.35	−5.51	7.29	37.02
Organic chemicals	27.72	59.3	30.41	39.46	18.35	6.7	13.79	13.79	12.82	9.09	17.25	22.61

Source Based on Author's compilation of the data extracted from, Export Import Data Bank, Department of Commerce, Government of India, https://tradestat.commerce.gov.in/eidb/default.asp. * Details of the items are given in the Note section at the end of the paper

in total exports to China. The average percentage share of these items in the same is about 84.94% for the period. Further examination of the table indicates that the top four exporting items occupied the share between 77 and 55% during the period. The average percentage share of the top four items was about 67% indicating the importance in overall exports to China.

Further, it is also interesting to note that the commodity Ores, Slash and Ash, which accounted for about 20% in 2003, increased its share to more than 50% of India's exports and continued to dominate Indian exports till 2011 with an average share of about 34% during this period. Similarly, commodities like Cotton, which had a share of about 1.56% in 2003 and less than 8% share during 1996–2003, emerged as a top exporting item by the end of 2013 and increased its share to more than 25%. At the same time, it is also noted that this commodity is used as a raw material instead of a final good and heavily depends on agricultural production. Like the earlier period analysis, this period also has seen the dominance of non-industrially manufactured finished goods, highlighting the nature of India's exports.

The Fig. 11.4 shows the share of India's exports to China in its overall exports. In the year 2004, the share of the same was 6.72%, which fell to 4.72% by the end of 2013.

11.1.3 Five-Year Development Programme for Economic and Trade Cooperation, 2014

In 2014, India and China signed Five-Year Development Program for Economic and Trade Cooperation between the two countries in order to lay down a medium-term roadmap for promoting balanced and sustainable development of economic and trade relations between China and India, on the principle of equality and mutual benefit (Ministry of Commerce 2014).

Table 11.9 presents the India–China Trade from 2014 to 2020 in the post-Five-Year Development Program for Economic and Trade Cooperation agreement. The trade volume during this period increased from the US $ 65,859 million to the US $ 86,399.40 million. At the same time, the trade imbalance between the two countries also increased from the US $ 36,210 million to the US $ 44,025 million, recording more than 17% in favour of China. Regarding India's total imports, China recorded a slight increase from 11.34% in 2014 to 16.5% in the 2020–2021 financial year. On the other hand share of China's imports in its overall imports also recorded 7.2% from the earlier 4.72% of 2014. During this period, the data also indicate that the trade growth rate, which fell significantly in 2013 to 0.12% recovered and recorded at 5.53% by the 2020–2021 financial year. The overall average annual growth rate stood at 4.40%, significantly lower than the previous period of 27.82%. Nevertheless, it also has to be observed that during this period, the tensions at Doklam in 2017, border skirmishes at the Ladakh region and India's subsequent crackdown on Chinese Apps took place and further, it has to be looked at in detail (Fig. 11.5).

Table 11.8 Percentage share of top 10 exporting items* (2005–2014)

(In %)

2004–2005	2005–2006	2006–2007	2007–2008	2008–2009	2009–2010	2010–2011	2011–2012	2012–2013	2013–2014
Ores, slad and ash (52.13%)	Ores, slad and ash (51.26%)	Ores, slad and ash (45.90%)	Ores, slad and ash (56.92%)	Ores, slad and ash (51.51%)	Ores, slad and ash (47.94%)	Ores, slad and ash (33.64%)	Ores, slad and ash (25.53%)	Cotton (25.20%)	Cotton (25.86%)
Iron and steel (11.78%)	Cotton (7.62%)	Cotton (9.11%)	Cotton (10.05%)	Pearls, metals etc. (7.91%)	Cotton (10.89%)	Cotton (13.35%)	Cotton (22.24%)	Copper etc. (14.86%)	Copper etc. (12.42%)
Plastic articles etc. (7.11%)	Organic chemicals (6.81%)	Copper etc. (6.43%)	Organic chemicals (5.75%)	Organic chemicals (4.26%)	Copper etc. (4.69%)	Copper etc. (9.64%)	Copper etc. (11.17%)	Ores, slad and ash (14.02%)	Ores, slad and ash (10.59%)
Organic chemicals (6.45%)	Iron and steel (6.28%)	Organic chemicals (6.24%)	Copper etc. (3.69%)	Cotton (4.18%)	Organic chemicals (4.39%)	Mineral fuels etc. (5.82%)	Mineral fuels etc. (6.49%)	Organic chemicals (7.53%)	Mineral fuels etc. (6.90%)
Inorganic chemicals etc. (4.02%)	Inorganic chemicals etc. (4.86%)	Iron and steel (5.75%)	Nuclear reactor-related etc. (2.14%)	Iron and steel (3.86%)	Pearls, metals etc. (3.74%)	Iron and steel (5.28%)	Organic chemicals (4.99%)	Plastic articles etc. (4.65%)	Organic chemicals (6.20%)
Salt, sulphur etc. (2.53%)	Plastic articles etc. (4.05%)	Plastic articles etc. (5.17%)	Plastic articles etc. (2.13%)	Salt, sulphur etc. (2.96%)	Plastic articles etc. (2.69%)	Organic chemicals (4.95%)	Plastic articles etc. (3.41%)	Salt, sulphur etc. (4.49%)	Salt, sulphur etc. (4.57%)
Nuclear reactor-related etc. (1.88%)	Salt, sulphur etc. (2.24%)	Inorganic chemicals etc. (4.24%)	Iron and steel (2.06%)	Miscellaneous goods (2.65%)	Iron and steel (2.64%)	Plastic articles etc. (2.82%)	Iron and steel (3.22%)	Nuclear reactor-related etc. (3.21%)	Plastic articles etc. (3.76%)
Fish and crustaceans etc. (1.79%)	Residues etc. (2.14%)	Salt, sulphur etc. (2.50%)	Salt, sulphur etc. (1.85%)	Nuclear reactor-related etc. (2.46%)	Nuclear reactor-related etc. (2.63%)	Salt, sulphur etc. (2.62%)	Salt, sulphur etc. (2.67%)	Animal and vegetable fats etc. (2.80%)	Nuclear-reactor related etc. (3.26%)

(continued)

Table 11.8 (continued)

(In %)

2004–2005	2005–2006	2006–2007	2007–2008	2008–2009	2009–2010	2010–2011	2011–2012	2012–2013	2013–2014
Cotton (1.56%)	Fish and crustaceans etc. (2.05%)	Nuclear reactor-related etc. (1.88%)	Mineral fuels etc. (1.49%)	Inorganic chemicals etc. (2.27%)	Salt, sulphur etc. (2.38%)	Nuclear-reactor related etc. (2.25%)	Nuclear-reactor related etc. (2.11%)	Mineral fuels etc. (2.41%)	Aircraft parts etc. (2.77%)
Copper etc. (1.17%)	Nuclear reactor related etc. (1.88%)	Mineral fuels etc. (1.31%)	Inorganic chemicals etc. (1.44%)	Residues etc. (1.70%)	Electrical machinery, etc. (2%)	Fish and crustaceans etc. (1.93%)	Animal and vegetable fats etc. (1.91%)	Iron and steel (2.22%)	Iron and steel (2.17%)
Percentage of top 10 exports in total exports									
90.43	89.20	88.52	87.51	83.75	84.00	82.32	83.74	81.39	78.51

Source Based on Author's compilation of the data extracted from, Export Import Data Bank, Department of Commerce, Government of India, https://tradestat.commerce.gov.in/eidb/default.asp. * Details of the items are given in the Note section at the end of the paper

Fig. 11.4 Share of India's exports to, 2004–2013. *Source* Based on Author's compilation of the data extracted from, Export Import Data Bank, Department of Commerce, Government of India, https://tradestat.commerce.gov.in/eidb/default.asp

Table 11.9 India–China trade 2014–2020

(In US $ million)

Year	Imports	Exports	Total trade	Trade balance
2014–2015	60,413.17	11,934.25	72,347.42	−48,478.92
2015–2016	61,707.95	9,011.36	70,719.31	−52,696.59
2016–2017	61,283.03	10,171.89	71,454.92	−51,111.14
2017–2018	76,380.70	13,333.53	89,714.23	−63,047.17
2018–2019	70,319.64	16,752.20	87,071.84	−53,567.44
2019–2020	65,260.75	16,612.75	81,873.50	−48,648.00
2020–2021	65,212.25	21,187.15	86,399.40	−44,025.10

Source Based on Author's compilation of the data extracted from, Export Import Data Bank, Department of Commerce, Government of India, https://tradestat.commerce.gov.in/eidb/default.asp

Though the volume of imports and exports during this period increased, we can also observe significant changes in the percentage of growth and fall in the imports and exports. In the year 2015–2016, though there is an increase of the imports up to 2.14% than the previous year. This trend did not continue, and by the end of 2019, the imports recorded a negative trend of about 7%, showcasing India's decreasing import reliance on China. On the other hand, China is significantly rising in terms of India's exports. The growth of exports to China by the end of 2016 recorded a growth of about 13%, increasing up to 24% by the end of 2020. We can find a reverse trend tilting the trade towards India through the graph.

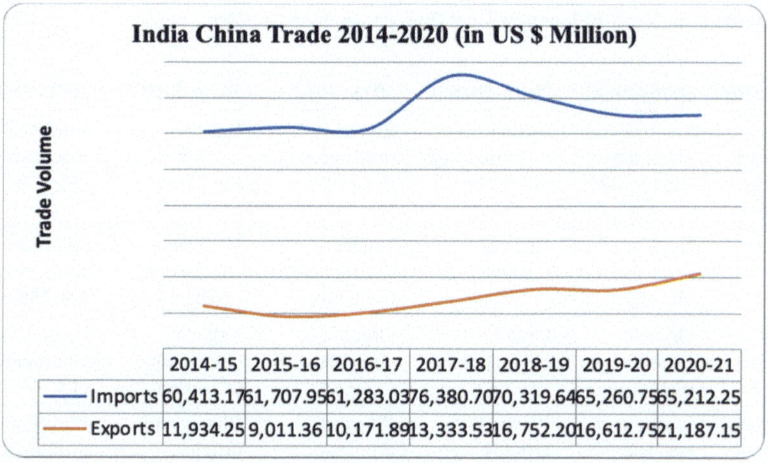

Fig. 11.5 India–China trade volume growth rate, 2014–2020. *Source* Based on Author's compilation of the data extracted from, Export Import Data Bank, Department of Commerce, Government of India, https://tradestat.commerce.gov.in/eidb/default.asp

Table 11.10 provides a glimpse of the share of the top 10 India's imports from China for 2015 to 2020 after the signing of the memorandum of understanding related to the Five-Year Development Program for Economic and Trade Cooperation agreement. During this period, the import of electrical machinery, nuclear reactor-related items and organic chemicals increased compared to an earlier period. The share of imports of electrical machinery increased from 25% to more than 30%; nuclear reactor-related items increased to more than 21% from earlier 17%, and organic chemicals increased to more than 13% from the earlier period of 10% in overall imports. The share of top 10 items that could be found increased to more than 82% from 75% in earlier times (Table 11.11).

It is interesting to note that, unlike the earlier periods, the average growth rate of major import items, i.e. Electrical items, Nuclear fuels and Organic chemicals, was less than 7%, indicating a major shift in domestic import policies. At the same time during this period, total average imports recorded a negative growth rate of below 7%.

The figure above reflects the falling growth rates of top import items for India from China in the three periods, that is, 1996–2003, 2004–2014 and 2015–2020. The electrical items during this period recorded a negative growth rate from 62.42 to 5.12%, nuclear reactor-related items 38.72–5.76% and organic chemicals from 20.03 to 6.88% (Fig. 11.6).

Table 11.12 provides the details of the top 10 export items from India to China for 2014–2020. These items occupy a percentage share ranging from about 75–74% in total exports to China. In the year 2018, the share recorded about 80%. The average percentage share of these items is 76.30% for the period. Further examination of the Table indicates that the top four exporting items occupied the share between 45 and

Table 11.10 India's top 10 import items* from China 2015 to 2020

(In %)

2015–2016	2016–2017	2017–2018	2018–2019	2019–2020	2020–2021
Electric machinery etc. (32.02%)	Electric machinery etc. (35.87%)	Electric machinery etc. (37.54%)	Electric machinery etc. (29.33%)	Electric machinery etc. (29.27%)	Electric machinery etc. (31.17%)
Nuclear reactors etc. (17.10%)	Nuclear reactors etc. (18.15%)	Nuclear reactors etc. (17.73%)	Nuclear reactors etc. (19.03%)	Nuclear reactors etc. (20.41%)	Nuclear reactors etc. (21.45%)
Organic chemicals (9.83%)	Organic chemicals (9.16%)	Organic chemicals (9.28%)	Organic chemicals (12.22%)	Organic chemicals (12.21%)	Organic chemicals (13.76%)
Fertilisers (5.30%)	Plastic and articles, thereof (3.02%)	Plastic and articles, thereof (3.10%)	Plastic and articles, thereof (3.87%)	Plastic and articles, thereof (4.16%)	Plastic and articles, thereof (3.88%)
Iron and steel (3.82%)	Ships etc. (2.37%)	Optical, medical, surgical etc. (2.18%)	Fertilisers (2.92%)	Fertilisers (2.79%)	Optical, medical, surgical etc. (2.66%)
Plastic and articles, thereof (2.74%)	Iron and steel (2.20%)	Iron and steel (2.12%)	Articles of iron or steel (2.47%)	Articles of iron or steel (2.43%)	Fertilisers (2.38%)
Optical, medical, surgical etc. (2.09%)	Optical, medical, surgical etc. (2.15%)	Articles of iron or steel (1.93%)	Optical, medical, surgical etc. (2.26%)	Optical, medical, surgical etc. (2.05%)	Miscellaneous chemical products (2.13%)
Ships etc. (2.05%)	Fertilisers (2.04%)	Vehicles etc. (1.90%)	Vehicles etc. (2.16%)	Vehicles etc. (1.95%)	Vehicles etc. (2.11%)
Articles of iron or steel (1.92%)	Articles of iron or steel (2.01%)	Miscellaneous chemical products (1.77%)	Iron and steel (2.02%)	Miscellaneous chemical products (1.85%)	Articles of iron or steel (2.02%)
Vehicles etc. (1.81%)	Vehicles etc. (1.81%)	Ships etc. (1.58%)	Miscellaneous chemical products (1.84%)	Iron and steel (1.72%)	Iron and steel (1.37%)
Percentage of top 10 imports in total imports					
78.69	78.79	79.13	78.13	78.86	82.93

Source Based on Author's compilation of the data extracted from, Export Import Data Bank, Department of Commerce, Government of India, https://tradestat.commerce.gov.in/eidb/default.asp. * Details of the items are given in the Note section at the end of the paper

Table 11.11 Average growth rate of Major importing items* (2015–2020)

(In %)

	2015–2016	2016–2017	2017–2018	2018–2019	2019–2020	2020–2021	Average growth rate
Electrical items	18.04	11.26	30.43	−28.06	−7.39	6.41	5.12
Nuclear fuels	4.04	5.37	21.75	−1.15	−0.46	4.99	5.76
Organic chemicals	−4.1	−7.45	26.28	21.22	−7.28	12.59	6.88

Source Based on Author's compilation of the data extracted from, Export Import Data Bank, Department of Commerce, Government of India, https://tradestat.commerce.gov.in/eidb/default.asp. * Details of the items are given in the Note section at the end of the paper

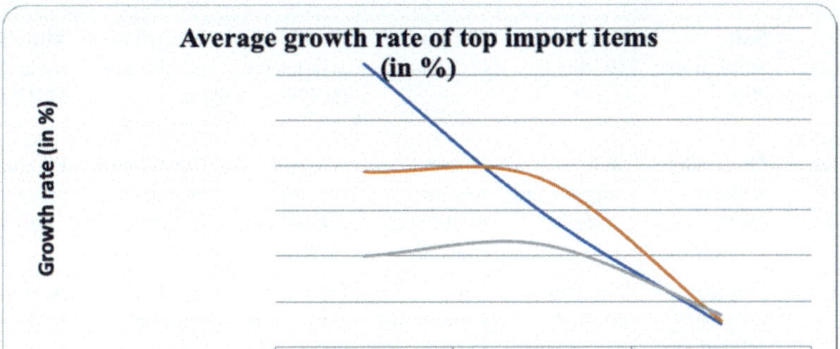

	1996-2003	2004-14	2015-2020
Electrical items	62.42	29.74	5.12
Nuclear fuels	38.72	37.02	5.76
Organic chemicals	20.03	22.61	6.88

Fig. 11.6 Average growth rate of top importing items. *Source* Based on Author's compilation of the data extracted from, Export Import Data Bank, Department of Commerce, Government of India, https://tradestat.commerce.gov.in/eidb/default.asp

55% during the period. The average percentage share of the top four items was about 50.30% indicating the importance in overall exports to China.

Further, it is also interesting to note that Cotton, which accounted for more than 25% in 2013, decreased its share to less than 7%. Similarly, other commodities like Ores, Slash and Ash, which accounted for just 4.29 in 2014, took the top position with 20.68% by the end of 2020. During this period, it must be noted that commodities that could be categorised as raw materials dominated the overall exports to China.

The figure above provides the trend in India's exports to China and depicts the same percentage share in its overall exports. We may observe that the same, which

Table 11.12 Percentage share of top 10 exporting items* (2014–2020)

(In %)

2014–2015	2015–2016	2016–2017	2017–2018	2018–2019	2019–2020	2020–2021
Cotton (19.09%)	Cotton (18.74%)	Ores, slag and ash (16.20%)	Organic chemicals (15.80%)	Organic chemicals (19.40%)	Organic chemicals (16.27%)	Ores, slag and ash (20.68%)
Copper etc. (15.84%)	Copper etc. (12.70%)	Cotton (13.20%)	Copper etc. (11.61%)	Mineral fuels etc. (17.05%)	Ores, slag and ash (14.19%)	Iron and steel (11.86%)
Mineral fuels etc. (10.81%)	Organic chemicals (9.35%)	Organic chemicals (8.67%)	Mineral fuels etc. (11.30%)	Cotton (10.67%)	Mineral fuels etc. (12.81%)	Organic chemicals (11.40%)
Organic chemicals (8.76%)	Mineral fuels etc. (7.12%)	Mineral fuels etc. (7.76%)	Ores, slag and ash (9.45%)	Ores, slag and ash (7.28%)	Fish and crustaceans etc. (8.05%)	Cotton (6.03%)
Salt, sulphur etc. (5.21%)	Salt, sulphur etc. (6%)	Copper etc. (6.90%)	Cotton (7.52%)	Plastic and articles etc. (6.59%)	Electrical machinery etc. (5.19%)	Mineral fuels etc. (4.94%)
Ores, slag and ash (4.29%)	Ores, slag and ash (5.78%)	Salt, sulphur etc. (5.49%)	Nuclear reactor related etc. (5.37%)	Nuclear reactor related etc. (4.96%)	Plastic and articles etc. (5.07%)	Plastic and articles etc. (4.48%)
Nuclear reactor related etc. (4.19%)	Nuclear reactor related etc. (5.13%)	Nuclear reactor related etc. (5.23%)	Salt, sulphur etc. (5.05%)	Fish and crustaceans etc. (4.31%)	Nuclear reactor related etc. (4.84%)	Animal and vegetable oils etc. (4.13%)
Plastic and articles etc. (2.99%)	Plastic and articles etc. (3.42%)	Electrical machinery etc. (3.89%)	Plastic and articles etc. (4.13%)	Salt, sulphur etc. (4.06%)	Cotton (4.68%)	Fish and crustaceans etc. (4.06%)
Electrical machinery etc. (2.35%)	Animal and vegetable oils etc. (3.27%)	Iron and steel (3.39%)	Electrical machinery etc. (3.60%)	Electrical machinery etc. (3.46%)	Salt, sulphur etc. (3.70%)	Copper etc. (3.68%)
Animal and vegetable oils etc. (2.29%)	Electrical machinery etc. (3.16%)	Plastic and articles etc. (2.89%)	Animal and vegetable oils etc. (3.30%)	Animal and vegetable oils etc. (2.36%)	Iron and steel (3.09%)	Nuclear reactor related etc. (3.54%)
Percentage of top 10 exports in total exports						
75.82	74.67	73.63	77.13	80.14	77.89	74.81

Source Based on Author's compilation of the data extracted from, Export Import Data Bank, Department of Commerce, Government of India, https://tradestat.commerce.gov.in/eidb/default.asp. * Details of the items are given in the Note section at the end of the paper

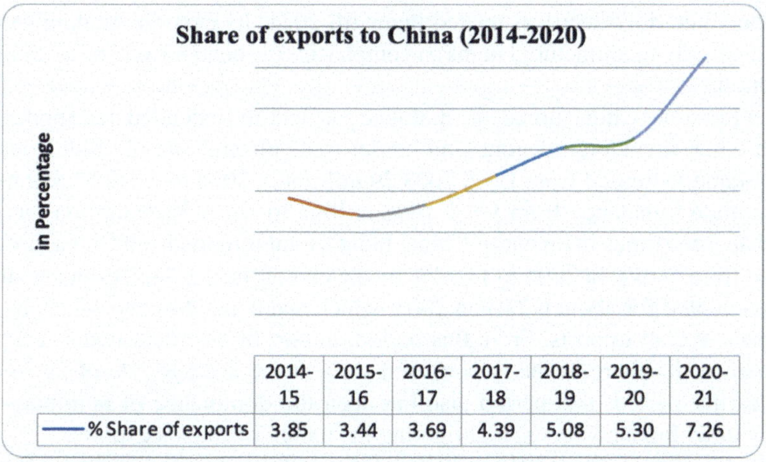

Fig. 11.7 Percentage share of India's exports to China in overall exports. *Source* Based on Author's compilation of the data extracted from, Export Import Data Bank, Department of Commerce, Government of India, https://tradestat.commerce.gov.in/eidb/default.asp

recorded 3.85% in 2014, raised to 7.26 by 2020. Further, the reasons behind the same have to be analysed (Fig. 11.7).

11.2 Major Findings and Conclusion

India–China trade from 1996 to 2003, after the first agreement on Double Taxation Avoidance Agreement increased from US $ 1371.71 to US $ 7008.29 million. The trade imbalance between the two countries also increased from US $ 142.11 million to US $ 1098 million. In terms of India's total imports, China accounted for about 1.93% in 1996 and 5.19% in 2004. In India's total exports, China consumed 1.84% in 1996 and 4.63% in 2004. The percentage of trade between the two countries in overall trade was less than 6% and well below the significant amount. The average annual growth rate in this period stood at 28.42%. India's average annual import growth rate accounted for 28.20%, and the export growth rate amounted to 32.61%. It can also be assumed that in the years following Double Taxation Agreement of 1996 issues such as India's nuclear tests in 1998 and subsequent tensed political relations with China, and its support to Pakistan in 1999 Kargil conflict, have had less impact in the growth of trade volume between the two countries. From 1996 to 2003, organic chemicals, mineral fuels, electrical items and nuclear reactor-related items occupied more than 50% of the total imports. In the list of top 10 exporting items in 1996–2003, the items of industrially manufactured goods were less indicative of the nature of exports. Thus, it can be argued that the main reason for the growing gap between exports and imports is India's inadequate manufacturing sector output. India heavily relied on China for Electrical-related items till 2021. Its exports are dominated by non-industrially manufactured items and emphasise the need for self-reliance in their production.

After India and China turned into dialogue partners and extended trade preferences to each other, including opening land border trade through the old Silk Route, the trade volume increased from US $ 7008.29 million in 2004 to US $ 65,859 million and the trade imbalance from US $ 1098 million to US $ 3620 million recording more than three times in favour of China. India's total imports from China more than doubled from 5.19% in 2004 to 11.34% by the end of the 2013–2014 financial year. India accounted for about 6.72% in 2003, which had come down to 4.72% by 2013 in China's overall imports. From this period, import of electrical items occupied a large part of the share in the imports and grew at the average rate of 29.74%. As in the earlier period, this period also has seen the dominance of non-industrially manufactured finished goods, highlighting the nature of India's exports.

India–China trade from 2014 to 2020 in the post-Five-Year Development Program for Economic and Trade Cooperation agreement rose from US $ 65,859 million to US $ 86,399.40 million. At the same time, the trade imbalance between the two countries also increased from US $ 36,210 million to US $ 44,025 million, recording more than 17% in favour of China. The overall average annual growth rate stood at 4.40, significantly lower than the previous period of 27.82. Nevertheless, it also has to be observed that during this period, the tensions at Doklam in 2017, border skirmishes in the Ladakh region and India's subsequent crackdown on Chinese Apps took place and its further repercussions have to be looked at in detail. One can also observe significant changes in growth and fall in imports and exports. By the end of 2019, the imports recorded a negative trend of about 7% showcasing India's decreasing import reliance on China.

On the other hand, China is significantly rising in terms of India's exports. The growth of exports to China by the end of 2016 recorded a growth of about 13% and increased up to 24% by the end of 2020.

11.2.1 Note

11.2.1.1 Import and Export Items Mentioned in the Tables

Aircraft, Spacecraft and Parts Thereof; Animal or Vegetable Fats and Oils and Their Cleavage Products, Pre-edible Fats, Animal or Vegetable waxes; Edible Vegetables and Certain Roots and Tubers; Electrical Machinery and Equipment and Parts Thereof; Sound Recorders and Reproducers, Television Image and Parts; Fish and Crustaceans, Molluscs and Other Aquatic Invertebrates; Impregnated, Coated, Covered or Laminated Textile Articles of a Kind Suitable for Industrial use; Inorganic Chemicals, Organic or Inorganic compounds of Precious Metals of Rare-Earth Metals or Radi, Elem or Isotopes; Lac, Gums, Resins and Other Vegetable Saps and Extracts; Mineral Fuels, Mineral Oils and Products of Their Distillation, Bituminous,

Substances, Mineral Waxes; Natural or Cultured Pearls, Precious or Semiprecious Stones, Precious Metals, Clad with Precious Metals and Articles Thereof; Imitation Jewelry, Coin; Nuclear Reactors, Boilers, Machinery and Mechanical appliances, Parts Thereof; Optical, Photographic Cinematographic Measuring, Checking, Precision, Medical or Surgical Inst and Apparatus Parts and Accessories Thereof; Prepared Feathers and Down and Articles Made of Feathers or Down, Artificial Flowers, Artificial Human Hair; Residues and Waste from the Food Industries, Prepared Animal fodder; Salt, Sulphur, Earth and Stone, Plastering Materials, Lime and Cement; Ships, Boats and Floating Structures; Vehicles Other than Railway or Tramway Rolling Stock, and Parts and Accessories Thereof; Natural or Cultured Pearls, Precious or Semiprecious Stones, Precious Metals, Clad with Precious Metals and Articles Thereof; Imitation Jewelry, Coin; Nuclear Reactors, Boilers, Machinery and Mechanical Appliances, Parts Thereof; Optical, Photographic Cinematographic Measuring, Checking, Precision, Medical or Surgical Inst and Apparatus Parts and Accessories Thereof; Salt, Sulphur, Earth and Stone, Plastering Materials, Lime and Cement; Ships, Boats and Floating Structures; Vehicles Other than Railway or Tramway Rolling Stock, and Parts and Accessories Thereof.

References

Bhola PL (1989) India's China policy in the 1980s: an assessment. Indian J Asian Affairs 2(1):16–33

Chen C (2009) China's integration with the global economy: WTO accession, foreign direct investment, and international trade. Edward Elgar Pub, Cheltenham

Chung T (1973) The Britain-China-India trade triangle (1771-1840). In: Proceedings of the Indian history congress, vol 34, pp 77–91

Fung H-G, Pei C, Zhang KH (2006) China and the challenge of economic globalization: the impact of WTO membership. M.E. Sharpe, New York

Khwairakpam A (2020) India-China trade in ancient times: Southern Silk Route. https://www.thepeninsula.org.in/2020/07/09/india-china-trade-in-ancient-times-southern-silk-route-2/. Accessed 20 Jan 2022

MEA (2003) Bilateral/multilateral documents: documents signed between India and China during Prime Minister Vajpayee's visit to China. Media Centre (June 23). https://www.mea.gov.in/bilateral-documents.htm?dtl/7692/Documents+signed+between+India+and+China+during+Prime+Minister+Vajpayees+visit+to+China. Accessed 20 Jan 2022

MEA (2012) India-China bilateral relations. https://mea.gov.in/Portal/ForeignRelation/China-January-2012.pdf. Accessed 15 Dec 2021

MEA (2022) http://www.mea.gov.in/Uploads/PublicationDocs/191_panchsheel.pdf. Accessed 10 Jan 2022

Ministry of Commerce (2014) Five-year development program for economic and trade cooperation between the People's Republic of China and the Republic of India. https://commerce.gov.in/wp-content/uploads/2020/05/MOC_636156057952507552_Five_Year_Development_Plan_Commerce_18_9_2014.pdf. Accessed 19 Dec 2021

PHD Research Bureau (2018) India China trade relationship: the trade giants of past, present and future. PHD Chamber of Commerce and Industry, New Delhi

Saikia M (2020) Trade and urbanisation—India's North East in the ancient Silk Route. Int J Hum Soc Sci Invent 9(8):01–05

Scott D (2016) Buddhism in current China-India diplomacy. J Curr Chin Aff 45(3):139–174
Sen T (2006) The travel records of Chinese Pilgrims Faxian, Xuanzang, and Yijing. Educ Asia 11(3):24–33

Part IV
Language, Literature and Culture

Chapter 12
China Through the Eyes of Ba Jin

Devendra Singh Rawat

12.1 Introduction

Writers are a product of their history and culture. Literature is an expression of prevailing society. Therefore, it is essential to view the background and nature of the Chinese society that gave birth to a writer like Ba Jin. A pillar of modern Chinese literature, Ba Jin 巴金*(1904–2005)* is considered a giant of Chinese literature, conscience of intellectuals and a literary witness to century of turmoil.

Ba Jin was the pen name of Li Feigan 李芾甘, who was born into a large feudal family in Chengdu, Sichuan. His father was a county magistrate and his mother a Buddhist. Although, Ba Jin was familiar with the Bible and had briefly considered adopting Buddhism; he became an anarchist in the 1920s and remained faithful to this philosophy until 1949. He regarded Emma Goldman[1] as his 'spiritual mother' but was also greatly influenced by the works of Peter Kropotkin and Leopold Kampf. "An Appeal to the Young" 《告少年》 by Peter Kropotkin and "On the Eve" 《夜未央》 by Leopold Kampf are the two works that profoundly impacted and shaped Ba Jin's ideas. The pen name Ba Jin attests to how enraptured he was by these authors and their works. In Chinese transliteration, Ba 巴 stands for the first syllable of the name Bakunin[2] 巴枯宁, and Jin 金 for the last syllable of the name Kropotkin[3] 克鲁泡特金. But, in his later years, he denied the origin of his pen name. Ba Jin reiterated that he was a product of the May Fourth Movement. His works provide glimpses of his life. He was affectionate towards his family servants as he had grown up with them. He narrates his detestation for being regarded as a young master and desire to

[1] American anarchist and political activist.

[2] A Russian revolutionary and anarchist.

[3] A Russian revolutionary and anarchist.

D. S. Rawat (✉)
Jawaharlal Nehru University, New Delhi, India
e-mail: dsrawat@mail.jnu.ac.in

S. Mishra and R. Sheel (eds.), *India-China Dialogues Beyond Borders*,
https://doi.org/10.1007/978-981-99-4326-5_13

become a man who helped and stood for their rights. The May Fourth Movement was like a spring thunder that awakened him to a brand-new world (Lang 1967, 14–57; Tao 1984, 273–275; Ba 1982c, 436–444; Ba n.d.-a).

Following the defeat of China in the Opium War (1840–42), Sino-Japanese War (1894–95), and after the establishment of the Republic in 1911, Chinese intellectuals felt the need for the introduction of more fundamental changes in the Chinese society. Thus, they called for a critical re-evaluation of China's cultural heritage, recognizing modern society's need for mass literacy and education. For them, the foundation of new order had to be based on western science, democracy, and culture. One of the important innovation in this direction was the introduction of a new literature written in vernacular language (白话) instead of the classical (文言). The new literary movement was supported by most of the younger intellectuals and students. Their new iconoclastic attitude towards China's past was a shattering blow to Confucianism which was the foundation of Chinese Society (McDougall 1971, 1–26).

On 4th of May, 1919, students in Beijing held a mass demonstration against the Versailles Peace Conference on Shandong. The public's anger was at its peak, evoking an immediate national response and pressurizing the Chinese delegation at Versailles to reject the peace treaty. This incident is known as the May Fourth Movement and is regarded by some historians as the first genuine mass movement in modern Chinese history. The May Fourth Movement was a socio-politico-intellectual revolution aimed at achieving national independence and creating a new Chinese culture. The three main achievements of the May Fourth Movements were 'firstly, literary revolution that led to the establishment of the Plain language and the rise of a new literature in Vernacular style, secondly, the influx of diverse foreign ideas and ideologies causing the emergence of two opposing views: the pragmatic, evolutionary method; and the Marxist revolutionary approach. Finally, the intensification of nationalism stimulated the rise of a Young China. However, seen in a historical perspective, the intellectual revolution succeeded primarily in introducing Western thought and destroying Chinese traditionalism' (Hsu 1990, 493–511).

It is also worth mentioning here that the anti-imperialist and anti-feudal spirit of May Fourth Movement opened a new chapter in the history of the Chinese democratic revolution. This movement paved the way for the founding of the Communist Party of China. The course of Chinese history was changed by the October Socialist Revolution and the May Fourth Movement. Jian, Shao and Hua (1981, 140–243) note that prior to the establishment of the People's Republic of China in 1949, China saw a series of civil wars, namely, the First Revolutionary Civil War (1924–1927), the Second Revolutionary Civil War (1927–1937), the War of Resistance against Japan (1937–1945) and the Third Revolutionary Civil War (1945–1949). After 1949, the Anti-Rightist Campaign (1957), the Great Leap Forward (1958) and the Cultural Revolution (1966–1976) had disastrous consequences for the Chinese society as a whole. The death of Mao Zedong in 1976 prompted Chinese leadership to search for a new order. As a consequence, there was a change in the party's principles. Thus, emphasis was put on "Practice is the sole criterion of truth" and "Seek truth from facts" rather than on politics in command. Focus was set on "Four Modernisation" (Modernisation of industry, agriculture, national defence and science and technology) and "Building Socialism with Chinese Characteristics".

In post-Mao China, owing to a serious re-examination of China's history, culture and society there emerged certain genres of literature, namely, the genre of Scar literature 伤痕文学, root searching literature 寻根文学 and the literature of self-reflection 反思文学. It is precisely against this Background the works of Ba Jin can be understood. Ba Jin was witnessed to the new world after the establishment of People's Republic of China in 1949. However, like other writers, he too suffered mental and physical torment during the Cultural Revolution (1966–1976). Ba Jin was rehabilitated in 1977. His post-Mao writings are the reflections of Chinese history and culture especially after 1949.

12.2 China Through the Works of Ba Jin

Ba Jin in an address delivered at the Cultural Lecture Series in Kyoto Japan on 11 April 1980 said:

> Precisely because I'm no good at talking and find myself unable to express my feelings in speech, I turned to writing, using fiction as a means of giving form to my loves and hates: From being a reader of books I became an author. I wrote my first novel, *Destruction*, in France in 1928, and sent it to a friend in China who had it published in the influential *The Short Story Magazine*. This marked my rather effortless entrance on to the literary scene. (Ba 1984a, 126).

Ba Jin's "effortless entrance on to the literary scene" (Ba 1984a, 126) with his first novella *Destruction* 《灭亡》(1929) gave birth to an unforgettable character Du Daxin. Set in Shanghai, the protagonist Du Daxin was a poet who believed that his revolutionary ideas would end injustice and oppression and create an equitable society. Committed to his ideology, despite, suffering from tuberculosis, he finally commits suicide after attempting to assassinate the martial law commander. Nevertheless, a few years later, the movement in Shanghai was led by his friend Li Jingshu (Ba n.d.-b). Destruction depicts the image of China under the rule of Northern Warlord. Through its fictional description of a poor passerby knocked down and killed by a rich man's car, the head of a revolutionary hanged on a pole, the poor having no option but to eat maggots and grass, the sufferings of young people for happy life reflects poverty, misery, oppression and injustice that prevailed during the period.

Critics hold different views about the character of Du Daxin. He has been branded as an anarchist and nihilist. But all of them acknowledge Du Daxin as new kind of hero. He is the prototype of Artzybashev's Shevyrev (Mau-Sang Ng 1981, 67–92). Although Du Daxin's actions can be questioned, his desire and belief for a better world draw sympathy. Ba Jin himself detested Du Daxin's destruction through violence, he could only weep over his death. The novella poses vital questions such as the meaning of love, life and death.

Ba Jin's essay, *A Maidservant*《一个女佣》, reminds one of Du Daxin (*Destruction*). In this essay, a maidservant kills the local tyrant and openly declares that "you with your own eyes, saw me beating him to death, you should catch me and send me to Yamen, I won't run. [self translation]" (Ba 1982a, 429). Ba Jin attests to this being a true story and compares the maidservant to the female heroines in the works of Gorkey (Ba 1982a, 430). The essay through the story of a maidservant shows discontent of the common people towards autocrats. Such was the resentment that the maidservant killed the local tyrant without considering, caring or being afraid of the repercussions. Thus, questioning whether law can be taken into one's hands? Can one subscribe to illegal and violent ways to achieve social justice? Is social justice achievable?

Ba Jin's sympathy for the marginalised and admiration for their hard work, despite, their deplorable condition is reflected in his essay *A Rikshaw Puller*《一个车夫》which narrates the story of a 15-year-old rickshaw puller. "Life, after all, is a mighty furnace. It can temper such a stubborn child. Even the most tragic experience in the world cannot trample him [self-translation]" (Ba 1982b, 435). The 15-year-old with determined eyes wished to kill his father if he chanced to see him. This hatred for his father stemmed from him smoking heroine, driving away his mother, selling his sister, and running away (Ba 1982b, 433). The story highlights social evils like drug addiction, domestic violence and human trafficking among the labouring people.

The Electric Chair《电椅》is the story of the execution of two Italians: Nick, a shoemaker and Barto, a fish pedlar, who were sentenced to death in Massachusetts. Below are the two excerpts from the story:

> 'Dearest brother, pray to our lord! He will surely save your soul', implored his sister, a devout catholic. Her first trip away from, crossing the wide Atlantic alone, she had relied solely on her love and her faith, her love for her brother, her faith in God. She began to sob. She could not speak. For her, only God was the final judge. She could think of nothing to say to her brother other than beg him to pray for the salvation of his soul. (Ba 1984c, 93)

> 'I am an atheist. I do not believe in the existence of God,' he declared, cutting short the priest's sermon. (Ba 1984c, 95)

Nicola Sacco and Bartolomeo Vanzetti were executed on 23 August 1927. There was a worldwide demonstration in their support. It was felt that they were innocent and hadn't received a fair trial. In fact, it was suspected that the verdict was influenced by anti-Italianism, anti-immigrant, and anti-Anarchist bias (Britannica 2020, HISTORY 2021, Mancini 2021). The story clearly reveals that Ba Jin too protested against the execution of two Italians and the impact of Anarchist philosophy on him. It must be reiterated that Ba Jin called Vanzetti "my teacher". However, we may not find certain references to Anarchism in the new edition of Ba Jin" s work. At the same time, BaJin's deep concern about the question of religion and philosophy can be read between the lines in the story.

The General《将军》reflects upon the plight of Russians in China and interrogates the idea of God and faith through the story of Feodor Novikov.

> At first he had no intention of going to the cafe, and said to himself, 'This one time I ought to do what she says.' So he'd sit down properly in a chair, pick up a worn copy of the Bible

> and start reading in the hope of obtaining some consolation. Besides his wife, this Bible was the only thing which had followed him around on all his wandering during the last several decades. He believed in God and knew that whenever his patience came to an end, he could pray to God for salvation (Ba 1984d, 104). But after reading and thinking aloud Novikov felt, 'So what's the use of believing in God?' (Ba 1984d, 105).

With a promotion to the position of lieutenant in St Petersburg, Feodor Novikov's life takes a dramatic turn when he moves to China, making it his home. He lives there with his wife, Anna, in an apartment building run by Chinese people. He spends almost every night in a cafe where he talks to a Chinese waiter who addresses him as "General" and is the only person who respects and believes him in the entire city. Novikov spends all his money on drinking which agitates his wife who desires to return to Russia. Instances in the story also hint at the General's wife, Anna, working as a prostitute in China. References also draw our attention to China as being "good-for-nothing place", "big empty dessert" and "cold". The story concludes with the "General" on his way back home, falling and losing consciousness. When a Chinese man enquires his name, it is incomprehensible as the 'General' replies in Russian. This story too reflects Ba Jin's interest in understanding religion as the protagonist keeps the Bible close to him.

With an unclear description in terms of time and place, *Rain* 《雨》 focuses on the narrator and other characters who are involved in some sort of political activity. These characters are either killed or face a constant threat to their lives. One can sense loneliness, pain, anger, anxiety and anguish throughout the story. The melancholy prevailing in the story is addressed through the lines by Ba Jin (1984b, 123), "how many people have cried since history began? Put all those tears together and you'd have *great long river* [emphasis added]". We may derive various symbolic interpretations of the story but the message is not superimposed. It has been rightly said that:

> Art contains propaganda, assertion and intent if the artist expresses his political views in such a way that they remain distinguishable and separable from the strictly aesthetic factors of his work. In art with an ideological content, on the other hand, the philosophic and corresponding political motifs form an inseparable unity with the work's other component: the universal intent- the ideology- interlocks with the aesthetic structure and is completely integrated into the totality of the artistic creation… (Hauser 1973, 129)

In the preface to *Autumn in Spring* 《春天里的秋天》, Ba Jin declared that "*Autumn in Spring* is not only a sad story but the cry of the whole young generation. I will take up my pen as a weapon and charge for them. To this moribund society, I call out resolutely: 'I accuse!'" (Ba 1988a, 300). The novelette is the tragic love story of Lin Xushu and Zheng Peirong. It deals with the concept of love, importance of youth and questions the traditional concept of marriage (arrange marriage) and the problems arising from such a wedlock (Ba 1988a, 300–348). The discussion of Hollywood actresses Greta Garbo, Norma Shearer, Janet Gaynor and Ramon Novarro (Ba 1988a, 329) reveals that Ba Jin was not only aware but also interested in cinema. This clearly shows how he was deeply interested in the question of women's liberation.

In *The trilogy Love* 《爱情三部曲》, consisting of three novelette's *Fog* 《雾》, *Rain* 《雨》 and *Lightning* 《电》, (Ba 1982e) deals with disease, death, suicide and faith.

Amongst these themes, love plays an integral part in the lives of the protagonists, Zhou Rushui, Chen Chen, Zhang Ruolan, Wu Renmin, Xiong Zhijun, Li Peizhu and Li Jianhong. It confronts the reader with the questions relating to the purpose of human life, marriage, love and family.

The Trilogy Turbulent Stream 《激流三部曲》 consists of *Family* 《家》, *Spring* 《春》 and *Autumn* 《秋》. The Family narrates the story of the Gao family. Set in the Backdrop of the May Fourth Movement, Ba Jin, through the description of three brothers Juexin, Juemin and Juehui exhibits different perspectives on love, life, family and revolution. This new approach with which the brothers are in full agreement was a consequence of the circulation of magazines such as "*New Youth*" and "*Weekly Review*" magazines. Their complex personalities and differing outlooks are reflected through their actions and assessment of each other:

> The younger boys were more radical than Juexin in their approach… Juexin became a man with a split personality. In the old society, in the midst of his old -fashioned family, he was a spineless, supine young Master; in the company of his brothers, he was a youth of the new order. (Ba 1988e, 35–36).

> [Juemin wrote to his brother Juexin] I am doing what no one in our family has ever dared to do before- I'm running out on an arranged marriage. No one cares about my fate, so I h've decided to travel my own road alone. I'm determined to struggle against the old forces to the end. Unless you cancel the match, I w'll never come Back. I'll die first. It's still not too late to save the situation. Remember our brotherly love and do your best to help me. (Ba 1988e, 225).

> [On the contrary, Juehui wrote in his diary that] I have two brothers. One plays mahjong to get on the good side of certain people; the other stays all day at my aunt's house teaching Qin English and doesn't even come home for supper. I must never become like them. (Ba 1988e, 81).

Thus, Ba Jin bestowed his hope on Juehui as in the novel's ending, he wrote:

> A new emotion gradually possessed Juehui. He didn't know whether it was joy or sorrow, but one thing was clear- he was leaving his family. Before him was an endless stretch of water sweeping steadily forward, bearing him to an unfamiliar city. There, all that was new was developing- new activities, new people, new friends. (Ba 1988e, 295).

Describing the death of three female characters Mei, Ruijue and Mingfeng, Ba Jin (1988e, 252–295) dwells upon the theme of people becoming victims of superstition (death of Juexin's wife [Ruijue], prevention from the "curse of the blood-glow"[4] 血光之灾, consulting quacks when medicines fail as was the case of Venerable Master Gao, inviting a witch to "drive out the devils" 捉鬼). Other themes such as hair cut (young girl struggling for a bob-cut) and co-education too reflect Chinese society at that time. We not only find the vivid descriptions of the traditional family life and festivities but also see the picture of youth movement and the events of civil war. *Spring* deals with love and marriage and finally, in the last part of the trilogy, the young generation revolts against the outlook of the older generation of the family and achieves a moral victory (Ba 1982e).

[4] The curse could only be prevented by the departure of the pregnant woman from the compound and the city. It also required her to cross over a bridge (Ba 1988a, b, c, d, e, 265).

Resembling a guidebook for parenting, the *Garden of Repose* 《憩园》 reflects upon questions such as what should be inculcated in children? What are the important things for the development of children that we should keep in mind? How can we live a happy family life? What should be our outlook on life? Ba Jin notes:

> This novel, through the history of a rich mansion, tells the tragic story of two successive owners in the old society…The acquisition of wealth without working for it is the cause of the family's destruction, and provides the context for the degeneracy of the sons and grandsons. A rich parasitic life leads to a youth being drowned, brings about the death in prison through illness of a rich spoilt son of another household, and causes a son to drive away his father and a wife to reject her husband. After the fall of the Yang family, the original owner of the Garden of Repose, the new owners, the Yao family, begin their downward descent. Even the kind- hearted woman who wishes to 'wipe the tears from every eye' will, in the future, suffocate in this mansion, unless she has the courage to break out and escape (Ba 1988d, 177).

Ba jin's *Ward Number Four* 《第四病室》 completed in 1944 resonates the Battle that world is fighting against the COVID-19 pandemic. Locked inside our homes, newspapers covered with reports on the long queues outside the hospitals, crematoriums and burial grounds; the unavailability of hospital beds, and oxygen; rivers with dead floating and pyres burning endlessly. This situation is quite similar to that in Ba Jin's *Ward Number Four,* where war had disrupted life (Ba 1982e; Ba n.d.-d). It has been rightly pointed out that "For Lu Xun, mental disease in China was more crucial than physical disease. However, Ba Jin used both mental and physical diseases to explore humanity in a wartime hospital. Unlike in his early novels in the 1930's, Ba Jin in the 1940's provided readers with a new perspective to explore and understand society" (Kong 2012).

Bitter Cold Nights 《寒夜》 is the story of Wang Wenxuan, who died of tuberculosis, describes the relationship between Wang Wenxuan, his wife Zheng Shusheng and his mother. The plot revolves around the affection of Wang Wenxuan's mother towards her son and her indifferent attitude towards her daughter-in-law. It also describes the discriminatory attitude towards people suffering from tuberculosis in China. Moreover, identity is another theme that is emphasised. Shusheng's letter to Wang Wenxuan reflects the life of a women struggling for her existence:

> Everything I say is true. Please believe me. I feel that there is no happiness in the life we have led, And there can be no happiness in the future. I cannot say it is your fault, nor can I say that I am faultless. We made each other miserable, we made your mother miserable, and she made you and me miserable. I don't understand why this was so. Moreover, we have no way of getting rid of or of lightening this misery. It is no one person's fault. None of us can blame anyone else. But I don't believe it is due to fate. At the very least, these wrongs can be blamed on our circumstances…Moreover, while your mother is alive, there can never be any peace or happiness for us. We must separate. Apart, we can perhaps still remain close friends, but together, we will one day become strangers…But I am thirty- five this year. I can not continue to waste my life. Time for us women is short…I haven't brought the word 'divorce', because according to your mother, we never married. Also, our separation does not require any formalities. I don't ask for alimony from you, nor do I need any written document from you. Even less do I demand to take Xiao Xiao with me. I don't want anything. I only beg you to let me help you get better. From today onwards, I am no longer Mrs. Wang… (Ba 1988b, 428–430).

In this novel, we see the continuities and discontinuities on the theme of family. What is perturbing is that despite economic independence women could not achieve happiness in life. Ba Jin himself wrote: "In the old society, how many people caught tuberculosis and died in pain and misery! How many families lived an inhuman life of poverty and distress, in which there was no assurance that the life which began in the morning would not end by the evening! There were countless people like Wang Wenxuan!" (Ba 1988c, 484).

Among the post-1949 works of Ba Jin, the *Records of Random Thoughts*《随想录》is of significant importance as it provides information about the Chinese history and society. Between 1978 and 1986, Ba Jin wrote 150 essays, which were later published as a five-volume collection titled *Records of Random Thoughts.* This collection is about the mental and physical torment his family and friends suffered during the Cultural Revolution. There are essays about his wife and friends, such as Lao She, Lu Xun and others. Ba Jin strongly believed that a museum of the Cultural Revolution should be established so that another cultural revolution is not allowed to occur in the future (Ba n.d.-c; Castriotta 2000). Ba Jin further makes us ponder over questions related to the definition of literature, its role in society and relationship with politics. Finally leaving us to contemplate the philosophy of life and death.

12.3 Conclusion

Literature is an immensely valuable source for understanding history, culture and society. Creative literature, especially fiction, prose and poetry provide a better understanding of society. Ba Jin's writings are a window to view the twentieth century Chinese society. His works depict the disillusionment, vacillation and *searching*[5] of the young intellectuals who were fighting against the tyranny of the patriarchal family system. The inherent conflicts of life and death, love and revolution, reason, and passion (in their struggle against the old social order) that Ba Jin's protagonists face are a key to understanding the Chinese society as well the kind of society he yearned for. Ba Jin not only focused on themes related to revolution, family but gave equal importance to the plight of the insulted, injured, and oppressed. He wrote that, "...There may be different styles and emphases in my works, but the basic thinking which prompts their creation is the same. Ever since I started writing, I have never stopped attacking my enemies. And who are they? All the outmoded, old ideas, all the absurd systems which have been obstructing the path of social progress and man's development, all the forces which seek to destroy love - these are my enemies...." (Ba 1988b, iii).

Ba Jin's representation of Chinese society in his writings is a reflection of his background and changing circumstances, his journey from anarchism to humanism was

[5] *Searching* implies the quest of the youth for finding answers to the philosophical and spiritual questions of life such as, the meaning of existence, faith, love, marriage, revolution and their goals and ideals.

full of trials and tribulations. However, in a society where people were plagued by poverty, disease, death, war and violence, he gave courage to live, and strength to struggle for building a society in which there doesn't exist exploitation of any kind. He was always concerned with the life, problems, moral difficulties and conflicts of the youth of his time. Ba Jin in his works portrayed the society from the standpoints of his protagonists. The problems of society were clearly described in his writings and he was always searching answers to the questions. Nevertheless, foreign influences on Ba Jin pose a difficulty in understanding him. To mention, in his novel *The Family*, we find the reference to *Treasure Island, Tolstoy's Resurrection, Tales from Shakespeare, Ibsen's A Dolls House* etc. In fact, it is also said that "his early heroes are like Chinese intellectuals in Russian cloaks." (Mau Sang Ng 1981). It must be mentioned here that we do find reference to Gandhi in Ba Jin's *Ward Number Four*《第四病室》. One can only imagine about the conflicting philosophical perspectives that might have troubled Ba Jin in order to find answers to social maladies.

The major works of Ba Jin were written from 1927 to 1946. However, during the cultural revolution (1966–76), he was forced to give up writing. In his post Cultural Revolution writings, *Records of Random Thoughts*, Ba Jin not only critically analysed the past but drew lesson for the future of China calling for the need to establish the museum of the Cultural Revolution. The continuation of Ba Jin's legacy is a testimony to Goethe's lines "The true remains, unlost to after-ages" (Goethe n.d.). After all, "He who strive on and lives to strive/can earn redemption still" (Eagleton 2003, 249).

Appendix

《巴金选集》, 四川人民出版社, 一九八二年, 成都.

唐弢,《中国现代文学简编》, 人民文学出版社, 北京, 一九八四年.
《中国现代散文选》, 人民文学出版社, 一九八二年.

References

Ba Jin (1982a) 一个女佣 [A Maidservant]. In《中国现代散文选》, 第三卷, 人民文学出版社 [Anthology of Modern Chinese Prose, vol 3], 427–431. People's Literature Publishing House

Ba Jin (1982b) 一个车夫 [A Rikshaw Puller]. In《中国现代散文选》, 第三卷, 人民文学出版社 [Anthology of Modern Chinese Prose, vol. 3], 432–435. People's Literature Publishing House

Ba Jin. (1982c) 我的幼年 [My Childhood]. In《中国现代散文选》[Anthology of Modern Chinese Prose, vol 3], 436–444. People's Literature Publishing House

Ba, Jin (1982e) 巴金选集 [Selected Works of Ba Jin, vol 6]. Chengdu: Sichuan Peoples Publishing House

Ba Jin (1984a) My life and literature. Chinese Literature. Spring, pp 126–129

Ba Jin (1984b) Rain. Chinese Literature. Spring, pp 109–125

Ba Jin (1984c) The electric chair. Chinese Literature. Spring, pp 84–98

Ba Jin (1984d) The general. Chinese Literature. Spring, pp 99–108

Ba Jin (1988a) Autumn in Spring. In *Selected Works ofBa Jin, vol.1.* Trans. Shapiro, Sidneyand Wang Mingjie, pp 297–362. Beijing: Foreign Languages Press
Ba Jin (1988b) Bitter cold nights. In Selected Works of Ba Jin, vol 2. Trans. Jock Hoe, pp 209–482. Beijing: Foreign Languages Press
Ba Jin (1988c) On bitter cold nights. In Selected Works of Ba Jin, vol 2. Trans. Jock Hoe, pp 483–500. Beijing: ForeignLanguages Press
Ba Jin (1988d) Preface to the French translation of garden of repose. In Selected Works of Ba Jin, vol 2. Trans. Jock Hoe, pp 177–178. Beijing: Foreign Languages Press
Ba Jin (1988e) The family. In Selected Works of Ba Jin, vol 1. Trans. Shapiro, Sidneyand Wang Mingjie, pp 1–296. Beijing: Foreign Languages Press
Ba Jin (n.d.-a) 巴金《自传》[Autobiography]. http://m.ttd3.cn/book_10941.html. Accessed 12 June 2021
Ba Jin (n.d.-b) 灭亡[Destruction]. https://m.rmxsba.net/56815/. Accessed on 11 June 2021a
Ba Jin (n.d.-c.)《随想录》[Records of Random Thoughts]. http://www.dushu369.com/zhongguomingzhu/HTML/100197.html. Accessed on 18 April 2021
Ba Jin (n.d.-d)《第四病室》[Ward Number Four]. https://www.yeban360.com/book/6368/. Accessed on 15 June 2021b
Castriotta Larissa (2000) Role models in the contemporary Chinese essay: Ba Jin and the post-cultural revolution memorial essays in Suixianglu. Masters Theses 1911 - February 2014. 1383. https://scholarworks.umass.edu/theses/1383. Accessed on 15 April 2021
Eagleton Terry (2003) In Sweet Violence: The Idea of the Tragic. Blackwell Publishers Ltd
Editors of Encyclopaedia (2020) Sacco and Vanzetti. Encyclopedia Britannica. August 24. https://www.britannica.com/biography/Sacco-and-Vanzetti. Accessed on 17 June 2021
Goethe J (n.d.) Faust. Trans. George Madison Priest. https://www.alchemywebsite.com/faust01.html. Accessed on 14 June 2021
Hauser A (1973) Propaganda, ideology and art. In: Mészáros I (ed) Aspects of history and class consciusness. Routledge & Kegan Paul, London, pp 128–151
History.com Editors (2021) The Sacco-Vanzetti case draws national attention. HISTORY. 13 April. https://www.history.com/this-day-in-history/the-sacco-vanzetti-case-draws-national-attention. Accessed on 17 June 2021
Hsu I (1990) The rise of modern China, 4th edn. Oxford University Press, New York, Oxford
Jian Bozan, Xunzheng Shao, Hu Hua (1964) A concise history of China. Beijing: Foreign Language Press
Kong H (2012) Disease and humanity: Ba Jin and His ward four: a wartime novel of China. Front Liter Stud China 6:198–207. https://doi.org/10.3868/s010-001-012-0012-8
Lang Olga (1967) Ba Jin and His writings: Chinese youth between the two revolutions. Harvard University Press
Mancini Mark (2021) 11 things you should know about the Sacco and Vanzetti Case. Metal Floss. 14 April. https://www.mentalfloss.com/article/645425/sacco-and-vanzetti-case-facts. Accessed on 17 June 2021
Ng. Mau Sang (1981) Ba Jin and Russian literature. Chinese Literat Essays, Artic Rev (CLEAR) 3(1):67–92
McDougall Bonnie (1971) The introduction of western literary theories into modern China 1919–1925. Tokyo: The Centre for East Asian Cultural Studies
Tang Tao (1984) 中国现代文学简编 [A short History of Modern Chinese Literature]. Beijing: People's Literature Publishing House

Chapter 13
Metaphorical Discourse, Phraseology, or Study of *Chengyu* in Understanding Chinese Culture and Politics

Hemant Adlakha

At the outset, let me apologize for the heady and boring title of my presentation today. I actually did not mean to use such a title, it just happened. Though I must confess I did conceive the theme for the conference paper in the first place, as it were. As I sat down to write down the abstract and the outline of the paper, I realized my aim was to explore and explain the central position a metaphor or a proverb or an idiom or a *chengyu* occupies in everyday Chinese life and culture. Soon it became clear to me that I can actually do better justice to my presentation, if I simply call it something like **A Word or Two on *Chengyu***.

2020: Year of Rat (Rat is your lot)

H. Adlakha (✉)
Jawaharlal Nehru University, New Delhi, India
e-mail: haidemeng@gmail.com

S. Mishra and R. Sheel (eds.), *India-China Dialogues Beyond Borders*,
https://doi.org/10.1007/978-981-99-4326-5_14

Hand painted Chinese style ink dragon calligraphy Image: pngwing.com

According to **tutorming blog**, "Chengyu, in the Chinese language, can be used to convey standards of beauty, sentiments ranging from impassioned love to raging anger, and various phenomena within the realm of human experiences. And their beauty lies in their simple nature; that is, these four-character entities have the ability to describe the range of human emotions and experiences with incredible depth." Chengyu has impacted Chinese culture for centuries. Pick up any book in Chinese on classical poetry, you will see in it chengyus reign supreme. For a non-native person, even with the knowledge of Mandarin, it will be very challenging to read and understand the four Chinese classics—Journey to the West, the Red Chamber, Water Margin and Three Kingdoms, without familiarity with the Chinese idioms. Many Chinese would tell you, a Chinese drama, a reality television show, or a game show will have the protagonist or individual characters within these programs "often sprouting chengyus like it is very normal."[1]

mǎ	**mǎ**	**hǔ**	**hǔ**
马	马	虎	虎
horse	**horse**	**tiger**	**tiger**

Ma Ma Hu Hu 马马虎虎 Image: chinesewordfun.wordpress.com

According to Jamie Bettles, chengyu not only embodies but is embedded in Chinese culture. Besides, chengyu is used in works of literature to enrich the imagery and conveyance of stylistic expression. Some Chinese families even hang chengyu as works of calligraphy on the walls of their home, shops, and businesses.

[1] Chen (2014).

Some chengyu tales are very popular and are known to everyone in China. For example, the chengyu—a "A Frog in a Well." Let me briefly narrate the tale here:

> There once lived a frog at the bottom of a well. He enjoyed his life in this well very much and felt very powerful as he was the only resident of that well. So one day, this sea turtle passed by the well. Feeling incredibly confident and ready to show off his incredible power, the frog jumps out and says, "Why don't you come here often? Look at how wonderful my abode is. When I'm happy, I can sit on the edges of the well and jump around. When I'm tired, I just go back into the well and go to sleep. I can play with the water and with the mud at the same time."
>
> The sea turtle peered over the walls of the well, and merely saw a hole with water in it. "Have you seen the sea before? The oceans are incredibly big, bigger than this well of yours and deeper than this well of yours. When there are droughts on land, the ocean is still full of water. When there are floods on land, the ocean is still full of water. Living in the sea, not in your well, is the definition of pleasure!"

It is important to note, Chinese idioms or chengyu are fundamentally different from both English phrases and clauses. It is this difference that makes a chengyu a particularly important source of understanding Chinese culture and behavior. Unlike in most languages, the use of a chengyu in Chinese—from everyday conversation to literature to any other formal writing—is quite common and widespread. For example, in the context of social management and political control of society, a frequently cited chengyu in the Chinese political discourse is a set of idioms, first employed by Mao Zedong in the late 1950s. While emphasizing the role of intellectuals in society in general and in the rebuilding of a socialist China in particular, Mao used two idioms or Chinese chengyu, i.e., 走马观花 Zǒumǎ guān huā 下马观话 *Xiàmǎ guān huà* (sohu.com 2021, *In Chinese*). Literally translated, the two chengyu mean "Gazing at flowers while riding a horse" and "Watching flowers after getting down from the horse," respectively. However, the actually nuanced meaning of these two idioms is, "the intellectuals should go down and mix with the masses in order to objectively understand and highlight problems they face, instead of conducting a superficial study based on theory." Just as Professor Wu explains, "An idiom has two aspects. The first aspect concerns semantics. Its meaning comes from the whole unit no matter what the individual constituent may be. The second aspect concerns the structure. None of the constituents of the idioms can be deleted or replaced by another element, nor can one add another element, or change the word or the phrase."

Let me further illustrate the point by citing another chengyu, cited very often in everyday discourse in China but increasingly for wrong reasons. The chengyu, 以德报怨 *Yǐdébàoyuàn*, or "to repay evil with good" in English, is from the Confucian text, The Analects, written or compiled during the Warring States period (475-221 BC). It's a popular Chinese idiom practiced even today, though its meaning has fundamentally changed from its original usage. Nowadays, the idiom is frequently cited meaning practically unattainable moral requirement. But once when Confucius was asked his opinion about the idiom, the sage opposed its usage saying: "If you return good for evil, what do you return for good? One should return injustice with justice, and repay good with good" (Sixth Tone 2021). In other words, this explains what Professor Wu means when he says the Chinese idiom "chengyu" is a set phrase, and in most idioms their meanings are impossible to comprehend unless one knows their *semantic fields or historical sources* (emphasis added). It is precisely this typical Chineseness of "chengyu" that needs to be borne in mind when we outsiders try to decode their exact nuanced meanings. This brings me to turn to the use of chengyu in the Chinese foreign policy discourse.

According to a recent joint study,[2] Chinese media in English, which communicate China's message to the world, abound in native proverbs. With specific focus on the Chinese media coverage of and commentaries on international issues, the study pointed out that Chinese idioms present an effective tool of China's interaction with other countries. "Proverbs convey China's standpoint indirectly but firmly and may be viewed as China's discursive strategy in media-based international discourse," the study observed. In the following part of my presentation, I shall deal with the question of intercultural and international pragmatics of Chinese proverb quotations in Chinese media in English on one hand, and also examine the intricacies and intriguing aspects of frequently used Chinese chengyu in the Chinese language commentaries. The purpose to discuss chengyu used in the Chinese language commentaries is also to reveal misunderstandings or misinterpretations of the chengyu used by the foreign readers or end-users.

Let me illustrate the point by citing a couple of examples of how use of chengyu or idioms—both at the official level by top Chinese leaders and by the commentariat—in the foreign policy discourse has in the recent past either led to different meanings based on different interpretations or misunderstood and therefore ended with wrong conclusions based on complete ignorance and "subjective" approach on the part of the foreign or outside preceptor.

A classic example of course remains the controversial *tao guang yang hui*—a maxim Deng Xiaoping first introduced as the guiding principle for China's foreign policy and China's behavior in the world. The phrase was first heard of in the 1980s and has since remained a sort of Chinese foreign policy "mantra" which all successive CPC leaders have strictly followed until allegedly Xi Jinping became the party general secretary and the state president, respectively. Mostly translated into English as "to keep low profile and bide your time," the maxim dictated by Deng Xiaoping was essentially meant for the Chinese leaders to avoid getting caught into a conflict-like

[2] Olga (2017).

situation with other countries—particularly the United States, for as long as it takes China to develop into a strong and prosperous nation.

However, following China's rise to become the world's second largest economy 10 years ago and the outside world increasingly feeling threatened by "a rising China," the People's Republic of China was being seen as making a lot of noises in the South China Sea, the East China Sea, on the Indian frontier and Hong Kong. Therefore, as David Wolf recently observed in an article in **Peking Review**, it started appearing to the Western China watchers that "China has abandoned the TGYH strategy altogether."[3] Since the phrase has been widely discussed in the foreign policy literature both within China and without, I shall not take up TGYH for a detailed discussion here. And just suffice by saying the entire controversy surrounding the phrase "may seem a petty tempest among the cognoscenti."

My own personal favorite among the chengyu or idioms used in Chinese foreign policy discourse in recent years is an ancient fable called "Master Dongguo, the Old Man and the Wolf" or Dōngguō xiānshēng hé láng in Chinese. Let me briefly narrate the tale:

> Master Dongguo, a pedantic teacher, was always ready to help anyone in distress. One day on a journey through Zhongshan Mountain, he came across a wounded wolf being pursued by the King's hunting party. The wolf glibly and fawningly begged Master Dongguo for help. Dongguo took pity on the wolf and emptied out the sack of books he was carrying and asked the wolf to hide inside the sack. Once the hunting party passed by, Dongguo let the wolf come out. Wolf then suddenly turns to Dongguo "begging" him for one more favour, i.e. to become his feed as the wolf is starving to death. Dongguo starts repenting having saved the wolf. Just at this moment, an old wise man appears on the scene. The old man asked them what was the matter and why the two were quarrelling. Both Dong Both Dongguo and the wolf told their respective versions to the old man. The wise old man then decided that the wolf go back into the bag to prove his version of the story. As soon as the wolf jumped into the sack, the wise old man told Dongguo to tie up the sack and go away.

Master Dongguo and wolf Image: wukong.toutiaio.com

The fairy tale metaphor was employed by several Chinese leftist commentators to fiercely attack the Trump-led US anti-China trade war and direct the angry US and

[3] Wolf (2014).

the world opinion to target China for spreading COVID-19 pandemic. The fairy tale was invoked by China's strategic affairs commentators and particularly the experts on China's relations with the US to warn the Chinese leadership to stop all economic and trade cooperation with America. The argument these commentaries advocated was China had been "rescuing" America financially and economically. Example of 2008 global financial crisis and the huge Chinese buying of the US treasury bonds were cited. Calling America the wolf, these commentators urged the CPC to refuse to cooperate and "rescue" the US in fighting the coronavirus pandemic.[4]

Finally, let me turn to an example explaining how the use of Chinese idioms sometimes can lead to contesting interpretations among different countries and as perceived in different cultural as well as geographical locations. More importantly, even the geopolitics at times plays a determining role in leading to varying interpretations. As the authors of the study cited above have claimed, "Official mass media coverage of international relations is a very delicate field of communication where everything is important. This holds particularly true for the media in a non-native language which target a primarily foreign audience. The appropriateness of quoting a native proverb in such media is a tool of the addresser's pragmatic strategy aimed at bettering interaction for the addresser's benefit."

In 2013, while addressing a gathering of the leaders from the Indian business world in New Delhi, the visiting Chinese Premier Li Keqiang in his address used a Chinese proverb *a distant relative may not be as useful as a near neighbour*. India was a direct addressee of Li Keqiang's speech, and the proverb quotation primarily referred to the shared border of India and China. *The Indian Broadcasting Network* (CNN-IBN) cited the proverb used by Li Keqiang in the context of partnership and cooperation between neighboring India and China: "He [Li Keqiang] also quoted a Chinese proverb—a distant relative may not be useful as a near neighbour—to emphasize on the relations between the two neighbours."

Interestingly, in the United States, the US media and the Obama administration perceived the proverb quoted by Li Keqiang meaning differently. In the United States, judging by the commentaries from the social media devoted to political issues, the effect produced by the proverb was quite different. *A distant relative* was perceived as an unwelcome analogical hint: "And Li topped off the wooing by recalling a Chinese proverb about how a distant relative may not be as useful as a near neighbor, a reminder of the attractions Beijing holds out compared to what Washington is offering."

In a report in the influential newspaper *New York Times*, the proverb was perceived and interpreted differently and the meaning was turned on its head. "In a veiled reference to efforts by the United States to strengthen ties with India, in part to serve as a check on China, Mr. Li said that a country can 'choose its friends but not its neighbors.' 'There is a proverb in Chinese that a distant relative may not be as useful as a near neighbor,' Mr. Li said," the **NYT** reported.[5] Ironically speaking, alarmed by the controversy the proverb invoked differing meanings in both New

[4] Adlakkha (2020).

[5] Gardiner (2013).

Delhi and Washington, the official Chinese media in English on the other hand, in its extensive coverage of Premier Li's India visit, decided to "edit" or "censor" any mention of the proverb. The contextual effect produced by the proverb quotation through international media in English caused misunderstanding, which required some explicit explanations. The social media wrote: "The People's Daily underscored the point by editorializing that the United States should not be jealous of a China-India combination" (Karl 2013), "because the two countries did not want to be America's 'enemy'—they just hoped for cooperation."[6]

To conclude, the difference in the perception of the same proverb quotation by different countries resulted primarily from international relations, both global and bilateral interactions (China–India or China–the USA). Moreover, the other factor which should not be underestimated in proverb quoting is difference in the modes of perception which different cultures display.[7]

The main purpose of this paper was to underline that the study of Chinese proverbs, especially proverbs used in the foreign affairs discourse, though have been studied[8] by scholars engaged in cross-cultural comparison of proverbial images, it is pertinent to also study the proverbs in their intercultural context.[9]

References

Adlakha H (2020) Xi calls-up Trump Amid Rising 'Anti-Americanism' at Home, Experts Warn not to Rescue the 'Wolf'. Indian Def Rev. http://www.indiandefencereview.com/xi-calls-up-trump-amid-rising-anti-americanism-at-home-experts-warn-not-to-rescue-the-wolf/. Accessed 10 Dec 2021

Elliott J (2013) China turns friendly with India but why. Foreign Desk: Blog Indep. http://blogs.independent.co.uk/2013/05/21/china-turns-friendly-with-india-but-why. Accessed 15 Dec 2021

Gardiner H (2013) In New Delhi, Chinese Prime Minister promotes trade ties. New York Times. http://www.nytimes.com/2013/05/22/world/asia/in-new-delhi-chinese-leader-promotes-trade-ties.html. Accessed 15 Dec 2021

https://blog.tutorabcchinese.com/mandarin-chinese-learning-tips/what-is-chengyu. Accessed 29 Dec 2021

Language, Cultural Exchange Warm up China-US Strategic, Economic Dialogue (2009). The Global Times. http://www.globaltimes.cn/content/451813.shtml Accessed 25 Dec 2021

Li L (2000) Intercultural comparison of English and Chinese proverbs (suyu). Lianyungang Tech College J 1:73–76 (in Chinese)

Li K (2013) India, China have far more common interests. Indian Broadcasting Network (CNN-IBN). http://www.ibnlive.com/news/india/china-li-in-mumbai-610557.html. Accessed 20 Dec 2021

Liu J (2013) A comparative study of English and Chinese animal proverbs—from the perspective of metaphors. Theory Pract Lang Stud 3(10):1844–1849

Nettwork (CNN-IBN). http://www.ibnlive.com/news/india/china-li-in-mumbai-610557.html. Accessed 12 Dec 2021

[6] Elliot (2013).

[7] Ibid, Nikolaeva et al. (2017).

[8] Liu (2013)

[9] Nikolaeva et al. (2017).

Nikolaeva V, Olga et al (2017) Chinese proverbs in Chinese media in English. J Intercult Commun (45). http://immi.se/intercultural/nr45/nikolaeva.html Accessed 1 Jan 2021

Sixth Tone (2021) Things confucius never said. https://www.sixthtone.com/news/1008707. Accessed 25 Dec 2021

Sohu.com (2021) "走马观花"不如"下马观花" *"Zǒumǎ guān huā" bùrú "xiàmǎ guān huā"* ("Watching flowers after getting down from the horse" is far more objective than "Gazing at flowers while riding a horse"). https://www.sohu.com/a/500418980_120679710. Accessed 25 Dec 2022

Wolf D (2014) Understanding Tao Guang Yang Hui. Peking Rev. https://pekingreview.com/2014/09/02/understanding-tao-guang-yang-hui/. Accessed 30 Dec 2021

Chapter 14
Making India–China Connections: Tagore and Cheena Bhavan

Avijit Banerjee

China as an ancient civilization had contact with many regions and countries of the world. The cultural relation between India and China can be traced back to more than 2000 years ago. The close contacts between the two countries were extremely fruitful in the dissemination of Indian culture in China. There are numerous references to China in ancient Indian texts like the Mahabharata.[1] Buddhism was a major force in connecting the two countries at that time. When Buddhism declined in India the two became culturally disconnected from each other in many ways.

Political developments in the nineteenth century further prevented close intercourse between the two countries. The old friendship was not resumed until 1924 when the Indian Nobel Laureate Rabindranath Tagore visited China. Clearly, the award of the Nobel Prize to Rabindranath Tagore in 1913 was not only a turning point in the career of the poet, but it was also a reassertion of dignity for both India as well as Asia. Tagore went to China at the invitation of the Lecturer Association of Peiping (earlier name of Peking). During the visit, many Chinese scholars and intellectuals introduced and welcomed Tagore's arrival in various forms. Many of Tagore's works were translated and published during this period.

From April 12 to May 30, 1924, Tagore delivered speeches on Indian culture and civilization in places such as Shanghai, Hangzhou, Nanjing, Jinan, Beijing, Taiyuan and Hankou. People from the political, ideological, literary and artistic circles were very much influenced by Tagore and his ideas, and a large number of news items and comments were published in newspapers and periodicals.[2]

Tagore was a visionary, always forward-looking. During his visit, he sought to promote the cause of China–India understanding, envisioning the essence of India

[1] Agrawal (1964), Pāṇḍey (1960)
[2] Xue (2010).

A. Banerjee (✉)
Cheena Bhavan, Visva-Bharati, Santiniketan, India
e-mail: avijitchinese@gmail.com

S. Mishra and R. Sheel (eds.), *India-China Dialogues Beyond Borders*,
https://doi.org/10.1007/978-981-99-4326-5_15

and China relations to a higher platform of civilizational leadership and fraternal partnership. He emphasized that together they comprised 40% of humanity. He said, "My friends, I have come to ask you to re-open the channel of communion which I hope is still there; for though overgrown with weeds of oblivion its lines can still be traced. I shall consider myself fortunate if, through this visit, China comes nearer to India and India to China—for no political or commercial purpose but for disinterested human love and for nothing else".[3]

Tagore not only wanted India and China to take pride in their rich heritage and draw from their pasts to build their future of friendly contacts, but he was also a forerunner envisioning a globalized world community. His idea of building institutions based on such ideals resulted in successfully founding of the Visva-Bharati University at Santiniketan in 1921. The university was truly international in its philosophy, goals and curriculum. As he said in China in 1924, "Our institution of Visva-Bharati represents this idea of cooperation, of the spiritual unity of man. And I ask you, my brothers and sisters, to take part in building it, you who still have men among you mindful of the bond of love once established between our two peoples of the old". In Tagore's view, the cooperation between Indian and Chinese civilizations was related to the future development of both countries as well as of Asia and the world at large. He thus sought to revive and strengthen historic relationships between the people of both countries. His global vision and sustained endeavour helped establish the Department of Chinese Language and Culture (*Cheena Bhavana*) in 1937, the only one of its kind in India and the subcontinent during that time.

After his successful tour of China, cultural interaction between the two countries gained substantial development both in dimension and depth. A number of people in China related to art and literature gained interest and Beijing University introduced Indian history, philosophy and language in its curriculum. Later, many Chinese scholars and students started visiting India to pursue research here. These scholars included Tan Yun-Shan, Xu Zhimo, Xu Dishan, Xu Beihong, Tao Xingzhi and Zhang Daqia.

On his return from China Tagore started the programme of Chinese studies in Visva Bharti in 1926 with the help of the French scholar Sylvian Levi and a Chinese scholar, Linwo Jiang. When Tan Yun-Shan came to Santiniketan in the year 1928, he worked tirelessly to set up a research programme of Chinese studies. Such efforts crystallized in the Cheena Bhavana in 1937[4] with the following objectives[5]:

i. To conduct research studies in Indian and Chinese learning
ii. To promote the interchange of Indian and Chinese cultures
iii. To cultivate friendship and fraternity between the two nations of India and China
iv. To join and unite the people of India and China
v. To promote jointly, universal peace and harmony of humanity
vi. To help build up "The Great Unity" of the world

[3] Tagore (1924).
[4] Chung et al. (2011).
[5] Yunshan (1957).

Tagore presided over the inaugural ceremony of the establishment of Cheena Bhavana with great joy because his vision of a cultural renewal between the two nations had been translated into reality, and Cheena Bhavana was the living symbol of this reality. Prime Minister Jawaharlal Nehru sent his daughter, Indira, to represent him at the opening ceremony of Cheena Bhavana.[6]

14.1 Cheena Bhavana in the Initial Phase

In its initial phase, Cheena Bhavana offered some certificate and diploma courses. It was primarily a research institution providing facilities for Chinese scholars to study Indian culture, philosophy, regional languages, and for Indian scholars to study Chinese culture and history. Cheena Bhavana also paid special attention to Buddhist studies including the study of Buddhist scriptures and translation work.[7] The institution attracted a good number of students and scholars, particularly from China and various parts of India, and also from almost all Asian countries as well as Africa, Europe, and America.

During this period, the department started the publication of the *Sino-Indian Journal*.[8] Many distinguished personalities and patrons such as Wu Xiaoling, Shi Zhen, Chiang Kai-shek, Soong Mei-Ling, and Zhou Enlai greatly enriched the institution with their donations for financial support. During his stay at Santiniketan, Xu Zhimo (徐志摩) forged a profound friendship with Tagore. Wu Xiaoling, an expert in Chinese classical literature and Sanskrit, came to India in 1942 and joined Cheena Bhavan as a professor. His wife, Shi Zhen, was a Chinese translator and well-versed in Bengali language. In 1942, she enrolled in Rabindra Bhavan as a graduate student and studied the works of Rabindranath Tagore and other Bengali literature. In 1942, Chiang Kai-shek and his wife, Soong Mei-Ling, visited India.

During this visit, they visited Visva-Bharati and donated Rs 50,000 to the university and Rs 30,000 and many rare and precious texts to Cheena Bhavan.

When in 1957, the first Premier of People's Republic of China, Zhou Enlai, visited India, he visited Cheena Bhavan. Here, he presented several books on Chinese literature and donated 60000 rupees for Tagore's memorial. Other notable[9] personalities such as Wu Bei- Hui, Sisir Kumar Ghosh and Chang Renxia were associated with Cheena Bhavan. Their support and contribution in the development of the institution were remarkable.

To be sure, the period between 1937 and 1970 is regarded as the golden period for academic activities in Cheena Bhavana. Various language courses besides Chinese,

---

[6] Tagore (1924).

[7] Tan (1994).

[8] The *Sino-Indian Journal* was edited by Tan Yun-Shan and published by the Sino-Indian Cultural Society in India. The first volume was published in 1947.

[9] Tan (1994).

such as Tibetan and Sanskrit, thrived.[10] Significant publications, lectures and many scholarships provided for students to study and pursue research on China followed the academic ideals of Cheena Bhavana. Buddhism, India–China relations, history of China, Chinese art and comparative studies constituted some of the important research areas. Such studies became the nucleus of China studies research in India.

14.2 Contribution of Some Renowned Scholars of Cheena Bhavana in the India–China Academic and Cultural Interaction

Besides the above, a scholar who made significant contribution to Sino-Indian studies was P. C. Bagchi. He was associated with Cheena Bhavana for 2 years, from 1945 to 1947 as professor and as Director of Research Centre in Visva-Bharati. He was engaged in the study of Buddhism and also went to teach Indology in China. He knew ancient Chinese, Sanskrit, Tibetan, Nepalese and Central Asian languages. He was also the earliest author to write a special historical survey of India-China contacts. The book titled "India and China: A Thousand Years of Cultural Relations" provides information about India and China's ageless affinity. He gave a very scholarly and comprehensive survey of this phase of India–China relations. Bagchi also collected and translated several sections of the Ancient Chinese Annals, which contain references for the history and geography of India during the first few centuries CE. He also translated a Chinese account of India, "the Land of the Sakyas", which Tao-Xuan compiled in the seventh century CE. It is the systematic geography of Central Asia and India compiled from the Buddhist texts and forms an indispensable complement to the famous account of Xuan Zang. Undoubtedly P C Bagchi's contributions lent zeal to understand the legacy of the multifaceted Chinese heritage and its importance to Indian history.

Some of the other renowned scholars associated with Cheena Bhavana were Pandit Vidusekhara Sashtri, P. V. Bapat, V. V. Gokhale, Sujit Kumar Mukhopadhyaya, Santi Bhikksu Sastri, N. Aiyaswami Sastri, and Prahlad Pradhan. Younger scholars included Krishna Kinker Sinha, Amitendranath Tagore, Satiranjan Sen, K. Venkataramanan and V. G. Nair. Translation of a number of *Jataka stories from Chinese Tripitaka* by Amitendranath Tagore, a chapter of the Vinaya of Dharmaguptaka school from its Chinese translation by Prahlad Pardhan,[11] translation of the Chinese version of a Dhyana text attributed to Kumarajiva by Sujit Mukherjea,[12] translation from Chinese of a lost Sanskrit work called Arthavargiya-sutra by P. V.

[10] Yunshan (1957).

[11] He also translated other stories.

[12] Mukherjea also prepared a critical edition of the Vajrasuci with the help of available manuscript materials and its ancient Chinese translation.

Bapat[13] and a comparative study of the different versions of the Sigalovadasuttanta, a Buddhist text, by Rev Pannasiri[14] were some of the notable works.

Pa Chow, a Chinese scholar at Cheena Bhavana, made a comparative study of the existing Sanskrit version of the Avadanasataka and its ancient Chinese translation and collected important materials which shed light on the original version of the text. Krishna Kinkar Sinha, a scholar of Chinese studies, joined Cheena Bhavana in 1942. He learned Chinese Language and studied Chinese Classical texts under Tan Yun-Shan. Sinha was later appointed as the first Indian Professor of Hindi and Indian Culture at the Oriental College in Yunnan, China and became the first Indian professor to teach Hindi in China before India's independence. Sinha also did a number of translation works from Chinese into Hindi such as the translation of "Gandhi and China" by Tan Yun Shan,[15] "San-Min-Chu-I" by Sun Yat Sen,[16] and "China's Destiny" by Marshal Chiang.[17] It may be mentioned that from 1937 till his retirement in 1970 Tan Yun-Shan tirelessly led Cheena Bhavan and in the period the works of above scholars played a remarkable role in highlighting India–China cultural interaction and Buddhism's pivotal role in the history of cultural connectivity of the world.

14.3 India–China Cultural and Educational Exchange with Cheena Bhavana Leading the Way

Since its establishment in 1937, Cheena Bhavana witnessed a significant number of visits by eminent persons besides official and private scholars. Mahatma Gandhi, Sarojini Naidu, Rajendra Prasad, S. Radhakrishnan, Jawaharlal Nehru, Maulana Abdul Kalam Azad visited Cheena Bhavana once or more. Jawaharlal Nehru took a special interest in Cheena Bhavana whenever he visited Santiniketan. The famous Chinese artist Xu Beihong came to Santiniketan in 1939 and was associated with Cheena Bhavana for about a year as Visiting Professor of Chinese Arts. A notable event was the visit of Generalissimo and Madame Chiang Kai-shek in 1941. They visited Cheena Bhavana and made a brief stay in the Uttarayana, Tagore's residence at Santiniketan. The visit of the Premier of China, Zhou Enlai was another event of significance in the history of India-China relations. Zhou Enlai was conferred the Honorary degree of Desikottama by Visva-Bharati in a special convocation on January 30, 1957. While visiting Cheena Bhavana, as already referred to above, he gifted a unique collection of books on modern Chinese literature and history

[13] It corresponds roughly to the Pali Atthakavagga, but there are important differences between the two. Dr Bapat also analysed the Chinese Translation of the Pali-text—the "Samantapasadika", Buddhaghosa's commentary of the Vinaya Pitaka.

[14] Besides the Pali version, there are four different Chinese translations of the text.

[15] Published in Hindi "*Gandhi and Chin*" by "Hindi Journal Vishvavani", in 1948.

[16] Published by "The Sino-Indian Cultural Society", Santiniketan.

[17] Published by "The Sino-Indian Cultural Society", Santiniketan.

and reprints of classics numbering more than ten thousand besides a donation for Tagore's memorial. Prior to this, in 1940, there was the goodwill mission of Dai Jitao, President of the Examination Yuan of the Nationalist government.[18] He wrote an essay in Chinese tracing the historical and cultural amicable relations between India and China and praying for its renewal. This document, engraved on a plaque, was installed on a wall in Cheena Bhavana. The first Chinese Buddhist Mission to India led by Rev. Tai Xu visited Santiniketan and spent a week as a guest in Cheena Bhavana.[19] His prominent disciple, Grand Master Fa-Fang, joined as a Research Fellow in Indian Buddhism in 1942. During his stay at Santiniketan, she studied Pali, Sanskrit and English. In 1945, she went to Ceylon to study further and returned to Santiniketan in 1946 at the invitation of Tan Yun-Shan and became a Lecturer in Chinese Buddhism. Master Fa-Fang contributed immensely to strengthening Sino-Indian cultural exchange. Some of the books that he authored were "Buddhist Outlook on Life", "The Order of a Buddhist" and "Culture of India". Such a contribution spanning over several decades by scholars and statesmen on both sides was significant in the history of India–China relations in modern times.

After the unfortunate India–China border conflict of 1962, there was a bad phase in India–China educational and cultural exchanges, and Cheena Bhavana was also affected by this turn of events. As a result, many activities were stopped or became slow, and even the number of students and scholars joining Cheena Bhavana dropped. After the epoch-making visit of Prime Minister Rajiv Gandhi to China in 1988, there was renewed interest in India-China educational and cultural exchanges. In the 1990s, some of the activities resumed.

14.4 Recent Development in Cheena Bhavana

Scholars who visited Cheena Bhavana in recent years, though for shorter periods, have contributed greatly to re-fostering academic exchange and friendship between India and China. Among them, GengYinzeng, Du Weiming, Zhou Fucheng, Lin Chengjie, Charles Willemen, Dong Youchen and Bai Kaiyuan deserve special mention. Besides them, Wang Lipin and Wu Ou of the Ancient Archives Study Centre of Beijing University came to Cheena Bhavana in January 2009 for 2 months to help catalogue ancient books preserved in the library of Cheena Bhavana.

Cheena Bhavan has also sought academic and cultural cooperation between Viswa Bharti and Chinese universities. In July 2011, Visva-Bharati University, and Yunnan University signed a Memorandum of Understanding. Under this programme, about 500 students from both universities have already visited each other's institute. In November 2014, Xi Jinping conferred upon Cheena Bhavana the "Five Principles of Peaceful Co-Existence Award" for its contribution in upholding the five principles

---

[18] Tan (1994).

[19] Ibid.

of peaceful coexistence, strengthening people to people friendship and promoting world peace and development.

In November 2016, the Cheena Bhavana Library signed the MoA (Memorandum of Agreement) with Shanghai Library. This agreement between the two libraries possesses important significance for India–China educational exchanges. Visva-Bharati University also signed an agreement with Yunnan Minzu University, Kunming, in December 2016, intended to uphold the academic objectives of each institution and promote better understanding between the faculty and students of each institution. In 2017, Cheena Bhavana signed an MoU with Peking University that facilitates five to seven students to pursue a one-semester course in China every year. In addition, regular organization of Teacher's Training Course that draws upon eminent faculties from Beijing University to deliver lectures has provided scope for exchange of knowledge and interaction for Indian teachers and researchers.

14.5 Conclusion

The establishment of Cheena Bhavana is indeed a significant event in the history of India–China educational and cultural exchange. Since its foundation, Cheena Bhavana has provided a stable platform of knowledge building, which in turn has helped strengthen India–China relations in various fields. It has attracted a wide range of scholars and students. As an integral part of Visva-Bharati, Cheena Bhavana is destined to play a significant role in fostering India–China cultural relations and in promoting peace, harmony, mutual friendship and better understanding through regular scholarly exchanges and cultural and educational interactions.

References

2014 Encyclopaedia of India-China Cultural Contacts vol 2. MaXposure Media Group (I) Pvt. Ltd.

Agrawal VS (1964) हर्षचरित: एक सांस्कृतिक अध्ययन. Bihār Rāshṭrabhāshā Parishad. India, p 168

Bagchi, PC (2008) India and China: a thousand years of cultural relations. Munshiram Manoharlal Publishers Pvt. Ltd. (Revised and edited Edition), New Delhi.

Chung T, Amiya D, Bangwei W (2011) Tagore and China. Sage Publishing, India

Marwah R, Swaran S (2021) Revisiting Gandhi: legacies for world peace and national integration. World Scientific Publishing Company

Pāṇḍey VC (1960) Bhāratavarsh kā sāmājik itihās. Hindustānī Akādemī, India, p 9

Ray HP (1992) Indian research programmes on China. China Report (A J East Asian Stud) 28:4. Sage Publications, New Delhi

Sen S (1945) Two medical texts in Chinese translation. Visva-Bharati Annals, I 1945:70–95

Sen T, Tsui B (2020) Beyond Pan-Asiannism: connecting China and India, 1840s to 1960s. OUP India

Sun Y (孙宜学) Eds (2005) Tagore and China (TaigeeryuZhongguo 泰戈尔与中国). Guangxi Normal University Press Guilin (桂林)

Tagore R (1924) Talks in China. Visva Bharati Bookshop

Tagore R (1925) Talks in China: Visva-Bharati Book Shop, Calcutta
Tan C (1994) Indian horizons 43:1–2. Special Issue India and China, Indian Council for Cultural Relations
Visva-Bharati Annals-1945, vol 1, Visva-Bharati Publishing Department, Kolkata pp i-v
Xue K (薛克翘) (2010) 中印文化交流史话 (History of Sino-Indian Cultural Exchange) (in Chinese). 中国国际广播出版社 China International Broadcasting Press
Yin X (尹锡南), Zhang L (张力) (2001) 泰戈尔 1924 年访华在中国知识界的反响 (Tàigē'ěr 1924 niánfǎnghuázàizhōngguózhīshìjiè de fǎnxiǎng, The repercussions of Tagore's visit to China in 1924 in the Chinese intellectual circles), (In Chinese). 四川大学 《南亚研究季刊》, (South Asian Studies Quarterly, Sichuan University.), Sichuan, China
Yunshan T (1957) Twenty years of the Visva-Bharati Cheena Bhavana: 1937–1957. The Sino-Indian Cultural Society of India

Chapter 15
Remembering Ba Jin on His 116th Birth Anniversary

Dayawanti

Ba Jin was born on November 25, 1904, in Chengdu, the capital of Sichuan province, to a family of bureaucratic landlords. His original name was Li Yaotang and his given name was Feigan. When he was born, China was a semi-colonial, semi-feudal country. China was subject to invasion from outside and war from inside. It could be said that it was a time of turmoil and unrest. The political and social situation in which a writer is born and raised plays a very important role in his life. What a writer experiences in his life will have an impact on his writings. Ba Jin was not an exception. He has depicted in his writings whatever he has experienced and witnessed in his life. As in his childhood, Ba Jin was influenced by the real loving human nature of his mother, rikshapullar and servant. He himself had said that my first teacher was my mother. She embodied the word "love" in me. She showed me the warmth of the world: she showed me the happiness of loving and being loved. He himself had said that my first teacher was my mother. She embodied the word "love" in me. She showed me the warmth of the world: she showed me the happiness of loving and being loved (Ba Jin 1996: p 97).

His native place Cheng Du was the center of New Culture Movement in Sichuan. He was 15 when the May Fourth Movement broke out in China. This was the time when foreign ideas entered China. In September 1915, "New Youth", formerly called "Youth Magazine", edited by Chen Duxiu, which was renamed "New Youth" in its second volume and launched in Shanghai, marking the beginning of the New Culture Movement (Huang 1984: p 6) Ba Jin and his brothers enthusiastically read the article about May 4th Movement published in this magazine and was watching the devolvement of the movement with great enthusiasm (Ai 2009: p 7). The articles on Western ideas and opposition to old ideas published in magazine had a deep impact on Ba Jin. He was influenced by the anarchist thinking of Bakunin, Kropotkin, and Emma Goldman. The anarchist thinker Kropotkin's pamphlet "An appeal to the Young", and

Dayawanti (✉)
Jawaharlal Nehru University, New Delhi, India
e-mail: dayawantis@yahoo.com

S. Mishra and R. Sheel (eds.), *India-China Dialogues Beyond Borders*,
https://doi.org/10.1007/978-981-99-4326-5_16

Emma. Goldman's essay on "Anarchism", "Patriotism" and "Marriage and Love" left a deep impact on him. He also referred to Emma Goldman as his "spiritualmother". He himself said that Goldman was once called "my spiritual mother" by me, and that she was the first person who gave me a glimpse of the beauty of Anarchism (Chen 1996: p 211). Although many Western anarchists who believed in anarchism at the time made a deep impression on Chinese intellectuals, the Western anarchist who influenced Ba Jin the most was Kropotkin. After reading Kropotkin's works he understood what justice and humanism are.

"An Appeal to the Young" had influenced Ba Jin. He had said that he got the ideal of love for human being and love for world. He also got the dream of child that a society where everyone enjoys will emerge with the sunrise of tomorrow and all the evil will vanish immediately (Chen 1996: p 213). He himself said that I would like to be a Kropotkinist, which means I believe in the principles of Anarchism as enunciated by him. (Chen 1996: p 209) In his pen name Ba Jin, Jin was derived from the last syllable of famous anarchist Peter Kropotkin's Chinese name (Kelu pao tejin 克鲁泡特金).

He studied at home with his older brother Li Yaomei, his third brother Li Yaolin and his cousins. His elder brother Li Yaomei would bring some new books and newspapers almost every day. They had to discuss every evening the issues published in the magazine such as "New Tide" and "New Youth" (Xu 1996: p 49). Later in his great work "Family" he depicted scenes of discussions between the main characters Juexin, Juemin, Juehui and Qin about articles published in the "New Youth". He grew up seeing the struggles and troubles of his own siblings under the oppression of feudal family values and feudal rituals. He had said, "I can say that I am familiar with the characters and the lives I portray. As I lived in such kind of family till the age of nineteen. Those were the people whom I had seen at that time, and whom I had loved and hated" (Jiang 1996: p 85). He then developed a strong hatred for the big feudal authoritarian family. This also had a certain influence on his later writing. Under the influence of the May Fourth Movement young Ba Jin actively participated in social activities, and step by step came to the forefront of the political struggle against the warlords and the ideological struggle against feudal culture (Ai 2009: p 14). His first novel, "Destruction", also illustrated how the youth of that time were influenced by the May 4th Movement. This was after the May 4th Movement, so as soon as Li Leng arrived in Shanghai, he was influenced by the new tide of thought that was gradually surging. In his letters written to her sister, he often discussed social issues with her, introduced her to new books and newspapers, and later went so far as to pass on his new ideas to her as well (Ba Jin 1989: p 46).

Ba Jin left Chengdu in 1923 to study in Shanghai and Nanjing. In 1928, he wrote his first novel, "Destruction", in France, and published his work in 1929. He has translated "Kropotkin's Ethics" and his other works. He also translated works of Emma Goldman, Berkman and other anarchist's works. Besides Russian anarchist Ba Jin was also deeply influenced by the prominent writer of Russian literature, such as Turgenev, Maxim Gorky, Leo Tolstoy, Vsevolod Mikhailovich Garshin. He had also translated their work into Chinese. While talking about translation of Russian writer Vsevolod Mikhailovich Garshin's short novel "Signal", he said, "Signal" is my first translated work. I like this novel of Garshin. It was selected from the English translation of "Collection of Russian Short Stories" but could not preserve the translation copy of this novel but story remains in my mind for long time. I again translated it in the beginning of 50's with same enthusiasm. I love this novel more than my own works. I found my thought and feeling from this novel. This work is my teacher. All my translated works are my teacher. I translate for the purpose of learning. He further said that translating "Signal" was learning humanism. It can be said that Humanism is the beginning of my writing carrier (Chen 1996: p 362).

From 1928 to 1947, Ba Jin wrote novels. After the founding of the People's Republic of China in 1949, he had written few novels, and he mostly wrote prose.

Most of his works depict stories about the pains, troubles of youths and their sacrifices for the country. He is known as a spokesman for the youth because most of his works depict the stories of the youth. He had a humanitarian and patriotic spirit, which had reflected in his works. He has also depicted in his work the people he knew and met in his life. Ba Jin also depicted the incident of his life in his writings. His works "Destruction", "New Life", "Turbulent Stream", "Family", "Spring", "Autumn", "Love Trilogy", "Fog", "Rain" and "Lightening" depicts young people's rebellion against the old forces, their patriotic spirit of sacrifice for their country and their sacrifice for the pursuit of human equality.

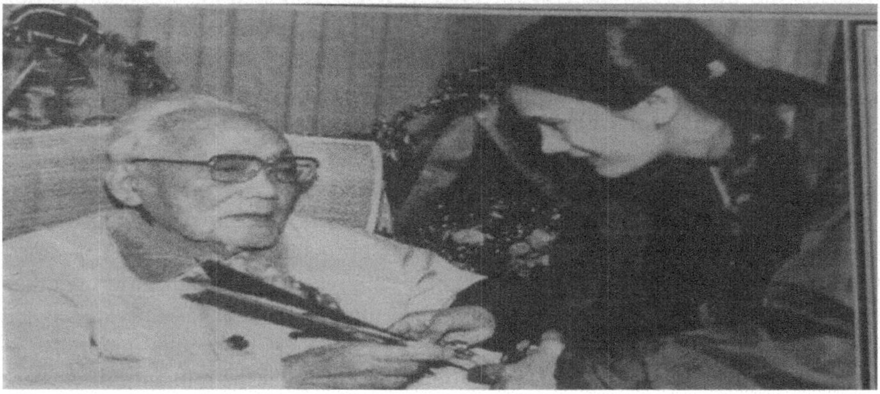

Photo taken by Hu Xiaolan, reporter of Xinmin evening paper, Shanghai. This photo was clicked on 25th November 1997 and published in Xin Min evening paper on 26th November 1997.

Set in Shanghai in 1925 under the rule of the warlord Sun Chuanfang, his work, "Destruction" depicts the story of a revolutionary young man named Du Daxin. The protagonist, Du Daxin, is a believer of "Socialism", and was an "Anarchist" (Huang 1984: p 239). His hatred for the bourgeoisie and love for the workers was obvious. Du Daxin believes that "Human is without sympathy. And it is on the misery of others that he builds his own pleasure". He thought that he could not perish, or at least he could not take his destruction to cause the happiness of these people (Ba Jin 1989: p

135). Du Daxin's revolutionary ideas also influenced the other characters portrayed in the novel, and Zhang Weiqun receives the influence of his ideas. He is a textile worker who is later caught and killed for joining the revolutionary movement, and he dreams of a world "where there is equality, where there is no cause for the oppressed and no distinction between factory owners and workers, where everyone is equal and enjoys the happiness of peace." He does not reveal the names of his fellow revolutionaries who joined the revolution with him. The other two main characters were two siblings, Li Leng and Li Jingshu. Although they belonged to the bourgeoisie, they gave up their rich lives and began to pursue the lives of ordinary people. Li Jingshu falls in love with Du Daxin. Although Du Daxin loves Li Jingshu, but his love for the workers, for the oppressed and love for Zhang Weiqun is even deeper than his love for Li Jingshu. The people he advocated all his life had very finally sacrificed his life for love. His action of killing the commander has the reflection of anarchist way of revolution. He perished by the horrible action of killing the commander, which was a wrong action though. Ba Jin wrote in Destruction that DuDaxin perished in this way, but he did not die in vain. A month or so after his death, a heavy lock was put on the door of the iron shed of the house on Hai Ge Road, where his footsteps were often found. A few years later a general strike was called by textile workers throughout Shanghai, in which the workers took over the factories and forced the factory owners to submit. The leader of this strike was a young woman who was well loved by the workers. She was Li Jingshu (Ba Jin 1989: p 161). Although the whole novel first talks about haters very finally advocated for the love of people.

The story of his work "Family" is woven around the city Chengdu, the city where he was born and raised. Ba Jin in his work "Family" depicts the problem of generation gap. The exploitation of youth because of Confucian rituals forced upon them by their authoritarian parents. How the young under the patriarchy, became victims of feudal rituals and superstition.

Ba Jin has advocated the individual freedom, freedom of love and opposed the hierarchy in his novel, and exposed man-eating Confucian virtue (filial piety), superstition, had been the cause of young individual's oppression and death. How under the influence of May Fourth Movement, Chinese young intellectual has enlightened and condemn the Confucianism for the backwardness of the Chinese and hindrance in the development of China, and the new young people under the influence of western ideas started opposing the old feudal rituals for their rights. How young people came to join the revolutionary movement.

There are so many things that happened in their lives that are depicted in "Family". The character of Gao Juexin reflects his brother. He himself said, "Family" is my own favorite work. I grew up in that kind of family, and I portrayed my grandfather and my elder brother as they were—"an authoritarian parent who had my say" and "a filial son who was submissive". He was going to write a novel for his older brother. What was most obvious to him when he was thinking of characters, his brother's face emerged in his mind. He had mentioned it to his brother. He wrote to his brother, "I am afraid I will put him in the novel, and I have also talked about all the apprehension and difficulties". His reply was unexpected. He encouraged me to write the novel, and he urged me to "use the member of our family as the main characters" (Ba Jin 2006: p 386).

Ba Jin's own life was the same as Gao Juehui's. The three brothers he wrote about, Gao Juexin, Gao Juemin and Gao Juehui, were all brothers in his own family. He also said that we three brothers, like Juexin, Juemin and Juehui, had three different personalities and therefore three different endings (Ba Jin 1996: p 143). The incidents in Juexin's life that are talked about in "Family" are all things that Ba Jin's elder brother experienced in his life. His elder brother like Juexin wanted to go abroad to study; instead, his parents forced him to get married. When Ba Jin talks about his elder brother, he says that he was interested in cultural studies and wanted to study at a famous university in Shanghai or Beijing after graduation; he also wanted to study in Germany in the future. His mind was filled with beautiful fantasies. However, within a few days, his fantasy was very cruelly shattered by his father.

His father had fixed his marriage and asked him to get married (Ba Jin 1996: p 71). When describing the character of Juexin in his work "Family", the same incident is described in his work "Family". He was very interested in chemistry and was planning to continue his studies at a prestigious university in Shanghai or Beijing after graduation, and he also wanted to study in Germany (Ba Jin 2006: p 30). But Juexin's dreams were shattered, just like those of Ba Jin's elder brother. The night Juexin returned with his diploma, his father called him into his room and told him, "Now that you have graduated from high school, I have already fixed your marriage.—you would be getting married within this year" (Ba Jin 2006: p 31).

Although "Family" depicts the traditional family of the old man, Master Gao. There is often conflict in this family because of the difference in thought between the younger and old generation. The elder generation believes in the old feudal rituals and custom, while the younger generation believes in foreign ideas instead. The later generations included Juexin, Juemin, Juehui and several of their paternal cousins and maternal cousins. Juemin and Juehui. Juemin and Juehui had the influence of foreign ideas. They also influenced their sisters. Juehui was active in student activities. Juehui's faith was humanitarianism. He never sat in a sedan chair. When Mrs. Zhang asked the brothers if they came home in a sedan chair, Juehui said promptly, "No, we walked home; we never took a sedan!" "Third brother is always afraid that people would say he was in a sedan, as he was a humanitarian". Juexin explained (Ba Jin 2006: p 7). The young female characters Qin, Mei, Ruijue, and Mingfeng, portrayed in "Family", all have their joys and afflictions. Through them Ba Jin exposes how the status of the women in feudal society was low, and arguably, they did not have any states at all. How they were oppressed in a family dominated by paternalism. One of them, Mingfeng, throws herself into the pool and dies. Master Gao's friend Feng Leshan takes a liking to Mingfeng and wants to marry her as a mistress. Mingfeng kills herself to avoid this marriage. This was her way of rebel. Although Mingfeng opposed the patriarchal system, she lost her life. Mingfeng was nothing more than a maid, how would she openly oppose the orders of Old Master Gao.

Her owner Mrs. Zhou (Juehui's stepmother) also dared not oppose Old Master Gao. Mingfeng begged Zhou, "Madam I am not willing to go I would rather remain maid of this mansion for the rest of my life, serving Madam, serving Miss, serving the young master. — Madam, I only beg you not to send me out, I haven't done enough in this mansion! -I have only been a maid for eight years. Madam, I am still young, please don't send me out. —" (Ba Jin 2006: p 219).

Mingfeng came to beg Zhou with the hope in her heart that Mrs. Zhoushi would save her, but Zhou said instead that she is helpless to help her. She said with a rueful smile, "Firstly I was afraid that you would not be willing to go, frankly speaking, Old Master Feng is too old, and that in terms of age you could be her granddaughter. However, it is the old master's wish and I had to listen to him. But as long as you serve Old Master Feng well there, you won't have a hard time. It's better than marrying a poor man who can't even take care of food and clothing." (Ba Jin 2006: p 219). Mingfeng had no way out, and she committed suicide. This shows that women had no power at all at that time. They had to obey the patriarch. It didn't matter if you were a woman from a wealthy family or a maid, you had no power. In this novel through the character Qin and Qianru, Ba Jin has described the enlighten girl, who has been influenced by the May Fourth Movement.

When Juemin told Qin that they were admitting girls to their school, Qin was very happy. She told her mother about it and told her how she wanted to study in Juemin's school. His mother, Mrs. Zhang, was surprised and angry when she heard about this. She said, "What is the world coming to? It's not enough that there is a girls' school, but now they want to have co-educational school too" (Ba Jin 2006: p 26). No one with old-fashioned ideas could accept co-education. Her friend Xu Qingru was braver than her. At that time, girls were not allowed to cut their hair in Chinese society. Xu Qianru cut her hair to show her rebellion against the old thinking. When she asked Qin to cut her hair, she herself was not sure she had the courage to cut her hair. Qian said, "In your family, only a little poetry, a little drinking, a little card playing, and so on are right; to study in the school is already an exception, and if you want to do something new and cut off your hair like a man, I'm afraid everyone will fight against it. There are many defenders of traditional moral principles in your mansion." (Ba Jin 2006: p 209). She also encouraged Qin, "Yunhua, I believe you are a woman of courage. Don't you remember that you also said that we should fight resolutely, despite everything, to open up a new path for the sisters who come after us?" (Ba Jin 2006: p 211) Qin did not want to the things which will make her mother ashamed. She thought why make her beloved mother angry by asking for the sacrifice of someone she did not know. She didn't want to disappoint her mother. She wasn't awakened until her mother proposed marriage to her. She then decided that she would not sacrifice his love at all.

The Juemin he loved was also strong. When he learned about Feng Leshan's marriage proposal to him, he opposed it. He fled the marriage to resist. He had the support of Juehui. The always compromising Juexin is also unable to convince Juemin. When Master Gao told Juehui to tell him to come back and agree for the marriage, Juehui refused to tell Grandpa where Juemin lived. Then something happened in the Gao family that Grandpa didn't expect. His son Keding had a mistress outside that also a prostitute. Grandpa was angry when he found out about this. This was a degradation of the extended Gao family. He punished Keding for this.

Grandpa's illness is getting worse. The elders of the Gao family proposed to catch ghosts to cure the old grandfather's illness. Juehui opposes this matter. He also criticizes his brother Juexin as well as the elders. He said, "You've studied for more than ten years, but I didn't expect you to be this confused! One is sick, yet you seek wizard to catch a ghost. Even if you have lost your mind, you should not joke with grandpa's life. I saw with my own eyes last night how wizard scared Grandpa. You say your filial sons and grandsons, and you refuse to leave him in peace when he's sick! I saw the ghost-catching trick with my own eyes last night. I said I must see how you plotted to harm him under the guise of catching ghosts, and I did see it. It's not enough that you've been messing around all night. You're going to do it again tonight. Well, I will slap the person who dares to enter my room first. I am not afraid of you!" (Ba Jin 2006: p 319) Juehui's rebellion against the old ideas, the old rituals, the superstitions, and the elders who supported everything grew sharper and sharper.

He saw that the Gao family had sacrificed many people because of these old rituals and old ideas. He didn't want to see anyone being a victim of the old rituals. Although Juemin was successful. But never would have expected that Grandpa's death would make collapsed the Gao family even more. As soon as grandfather died his elders divided his property. He called his brother Coward for always compromising and never opposing his elders. His lack of resistance led to the death of Ruijue. Aunt Chen and the other elders' people told him to leave the house to give birth to the child at another place. There was a superstition that if the dead body of the elder generation was still in the house and someone in the house gives birth to the child, then the light of the blood released by the mother would rush to offend the deceased and much blood would emerge from the deceased's body. The only way to avoid disaster was to move the expecting woman out of the mansion. The only way to avoid disaster was not only to move the mother out of the mansion, as the maternal blood light could return to the mansion, so it was to shift her outside the city. Out of the city would not work either, because the city gates were not strong enough control the maternal blood light either, pregnant woman had to cross the bridge (Ba Jin 2006: p 330). As a result, Ruijue died while giving birth to child. His beloved wife's death made Juexin realize that it was the patriarchal family system, old ritual, and superstition, which causes the death of his wife. It all weighed on his shoulders and held him down for these many years, robbing him of his youth, of his happiness, of the two women he loved most (Ba Jin 2006: p 347).

But it was too late to regret. He had already lost the two women he could have saved. After sister in law's death Juehui began to hate his home even more. She then plans to leave home and go to Shanghai to study. He could no longer stay. Juexin convinces Jue not to leave home, but Juehui is adamant and says to her brother, "No I must go! I am going to go against them and show them what kind of a person I am. I want to be a rebel to the old rituals" (Ba Jin 2006: p 355). Juexin had no choice but to help his brother leave to study in Shanghai.

In conclusion, Ba Jin started writing his novel under the influence of the May Fourth Movement which begins with "Destruction", in which his anarchist ideology has been reflected through the character Du Daxin, who's each action reflects anarchist ideology of individualism. He was a revolutionary, his love for the labor worker and hatred for the ruling class or bourgeois made him to take the extreme step of assassinating commander and sacrificing his life. Du Daxin could not find the right path to indulge in the revolution, through his character, Ba Jin has described the youth of that time who were influenced by the western thoughts and comprehend the problem of society and wanted to save the country. In his work "Family", Ba Jin has exposed his hate for the old family system which practices the filial piety which defends the Confucian virtue of hierarchy. Under the oppression of paternalism young people were either compelled to suicide or they died due to the feudal ritual, and some were compelled to surrender and live miserable life watching their loved one die. As Ba Jin has witnessed all this in his own family. That's why, he was very critical to the old feudal family system. Like other progressive writer Ba Jin was also worried about the future of his country. The reason why most of the characters in Ba Jin's novels are young people because he saw them as the future of China. His masterpiece "Family" and other works influenced the young people of the 30 and 40s. The youth of the time saw their own reactions in his characters; they would see their own lives, their own pains, worries and struggles. His novels mainly portrayed the problem of the society of the time, which can also be described as realistic, but also had romantic elements. His works planted the seeds of patriotism in the hearts of the youth of his time. They were willing to make sacrifices for their country.

Because of his belief in Anarchism, during Culture Revolution (1966–1976). Ba Jin had faced the humiliation and was persecuted as counter revolutionary. His works was called "poisonous grass" and was forced to live in "cow shed". He has written in his book referring to the Culture Revolution that no one wanted to forget the disaster started 20 years ago and no one would like to enter the "cow shed" again (Chen 1996: p 193). After the Culture Revolution, Ba Jin regained his fame and was appointed the Chairman of Chinese *Writers' Association in 1983.* In his later year due to his illness, he was admitted in the East China Hospital (Huádōngyīyuàn) in Shanghai. Our beloved modern literary scholar, novelist and translator died on October 17, 2005, in Shanghai East China Hospital after a long illness. But he will always live in our hearts through his works.

References

Ai, Xiaoming (2009) Young Ba Jin and His Literary Perspective, 1st edn. Fudan University Publication, Shanghai

Ba Jin (2006) Family, 21st reprinting, People's Literature Publishing House, Beijing

Ba Jin (1989) Destruction, New Life, 1st edn. People's Literature Publishing House, Beijing

Ba Jin (1996) Ba Jin Selected Works, Talking About Oneself, Volume 10, Sichuan People's Publishing House

Chen Sihe, Li Cunguang (2014) Legacy of May fourth new literature spirit, 2nd edn. Shanghai San lian Publishing house, Shanghai

Chen Qiongzhi (1996) BaJin's self narration. Unity Press, Beijing

Huang Xiuji (1984) A brief history of modern Chinese literature, 1st edn., China Youth Publishing House

Huang Yue, Song Chang hong (2003) An outline of Chinese literature history in the 20th centaury, 1st edn, Beijing Language University Press
Tan Xingguo (2003) Walk into Ba Jin's World, Sichuan Art Publishing House
Tang Tao (2008) A compendium of the history of Chinese literature (Updated Edition), Fudan University Press
Xu Kailei (1996) The autobiography of Ba Jin, Shanghai Art Publishing House
Zhang Lihui, Li Jin (1986) Research on Ba Jin in Abroad, Hunan Art Publishing House
Zhang Yanqin, Lu Weifen (2001) Research on Chinese Literature in 20th Century, Beijing Publishing House
Zhu Donglin, Zhu Xiaojin, Long Quanming (2007) History of modern Chinese literature 1917–2000 (Vol 1), Beijing University Press
Zhu Donglin, Zhu Xiaojin, Wu Yiqin (2014) History of modern Chinese literature (Vol 1) 3rd edn. Higher Education Press, Beijing

Chapter 16
Staging Tagore's Play in China: Some Reminisces

Mao Shi Chang

Rabindranath Tagore (1861–1941) was awarded the Nobel Prize for Literature in 1913 for his collection of poems, Gitanjali. Tagore was a literary all-rounder. He was a poet, a novelist, dramatist, essayist, musician, painter, director, and actor. He wrote 2933 beautiful poems in 8 volumes, 60 collections and more than 150 short stories, four middle-grade novels, eight full-length novels, 60 plays, 300 essays, 2000 paintings, and was the author of the national anthems of two countries, namely, India and Bangladesh. This multifaceted creativity gives Tagore a unique appeal, both locally and internationally.

Among Tagore's literary works, drama occupies an essential place. His plays are not only numerous and of high quality but also have their characteristic features. According to some critics, he was first a poet, second a dramatist and third a novelist. How many plays did Tagore write? Accounts vary, some putting it at over 40, others at over 20. None of these assumptions, however, is accurate. For one thing, several of Tagore's plays, such as "The Curse at Farewell", "Journey of the Times", and "Karna and Kunti Dialogue", were sung by two or more people in turn. Some have counted them as poems, when in fact they were plays because they were performed as poetic dramas; and, for another, Tagore often adapted his plays. For example, he made "Chitrangada" (i.e., Chitra, which we will discuss shortly) into The Flower Kushion Girl Cabaret a song-dance drama, The Firm Monastery into the Sun Woman, and Chandalika Nrityanatya into Chandalika Nrityanatya song-dance drama. The adapted plays should be counted separately and not as the same play. There are 15 short plays in the Book of Comic Plays, and the Journey of the Ages contains two poetic plays. So, Tagore composed more than 60 plays. The genre included plays, operas, poems, dance dramas, song-dance dramas, symbolic plays, prose plays, burlesques, and sketches. Tagore was a playwright and a director, composer, and actor in the plays he wrote himself, thus making Tagore another theatrical all-rounder.

M. S. Chang (✉)
Lanzhou University, Lanzhou, China
e-mail: ascetics@126.com

S. Mishra and R. Sheel (eds.), *India-China Dialogues Beyond Borders*,
https://doi.org/10.1007/978-981-99-4326-5_17

Of all Tagore's plays, his masterpiece is Chitrangada. The storyline is that by a chance encounter, Chitra, a princess of Manipur, meets one of the five sons of Pandu, Arjuna, who is in self-imposed exile and falls deeply in love with him. She was the only daughter of the king of Manipur, not beautiful, and was raised to be a rugged woman of great strength. Arjuna had no interest in her, saying that he had taken a vow to stay away from women for 12 years and was unworthy to be her husband. Undeterred, Chitra pleaded with Madana, the goddess of love, and Vasanta, the god of spring, to grant her beauty and grace, even for one day. The two gods bestowed upon her a year's worth of beauty. In front of this stunningly beautiful woman, Arjuna succumbed. After this, the duo was immersed in immense happiness. Nevertheless, Chitra was restless in her heart. She spent her days in fear of being abandoned if her former appearance reappeared. In the company of Arjuna, she often compared herself to words that would soon wither; and she found it all the sadder that before a year was up, Arjuna seemed to grow tired of it. Likewise, Arjuna increasingly felt that Chitra was pretentious and unreal. His repeated attempts to find out her true identity, her birth, were rejected by her. As a result, Arjuna also felt pained and unable to guess the secrets of Chitra psyche, as if Chitra were a goddess invisible inside a golden statue. The year was soon coming to an end, and they enjoyed the bliss of their lovemaking to the fullest. At this time, the threat of robbery in the village made people so distraught that they called upon the heroine, the princess Chitra, of great martial prowess and valour, to come to their rescue. As the year ended, on the last night, she disappeared from Arjuna's side. The villagers, in turn, flocked to the triumphant arrival of their heroine. The heroine unveils herself and reveals her original face. Chitra was now in her original image. To her surprise, when Arjuna saw her he did not dislike her, but he felt his life was complete and he had attained supreme happiness. The two of them achieved spiritual fusion, that is, the fusion of souls, and in this fusion, they achieved liberation—the "unity of the Brahman and the Atman".

This play reflects Tagore's view of women and love, which can be summarized as follows: First, love is beautiful, and it is God-given nature for men and women to attract and love each other; secondly, men and women are equal in love; and third, the inner beauty of a woman is true beauty. In Tagore's time, the union of man and woman was a parental command. By reflecting this view through his plays, Tagore boldly challenged the Indian society of his time.

I had the idea of bringing Chitrangada to the Chinese stage when I was a doctoral candidate at Jawaharlal Nehru University in India. Since 2011 marked the 150th anniversary of Tagore's birth, 2012 as the year of Sino-Indian friendship, and 2013 as the 100th anniversary of Tagore's winning the Nobel Prize in Literature, the times seemed conducive. My idea coincided with the idea of Arun Sahu, the Cultural Counsellor of the Indian Embassy. He was in the English Centre of the School of Foreign Languages at Nehru University, and we had a sense of affinity and trust. So, we decided that S. Jaishankar, the Indian Ambassador (who also happens to be an alumna of the School of International Relations of Jawaharlal Nehru University), and Sahu would be the curators on the Indian side and I would be the curator on behalf of the Lanzhou University for the performance of "Chitrangada" in Chinese. The Indian Embassy gave some financial assistance.

The first issue was of the script. The existing Chinese text was Ji Xianlin's translation, which though accurate and elegant, had a short script and could be performed for a maximum of 45 min. One of the characteristics of this script was that there are more static dialogues, which would make the performance seem pedantic. Also, there was the issue of lack of deep knowledge among most Chinese audience about Indian culture. The performance had to have a significant visual and auditory impact for engaging the audience. This required the addition of Indian songs, dances, and music. Further, the script had to be stretched appropriately according to the plots. As Tagore was a poet, poetic language needed to be used as much as possible to be passionate and effective. Also, there had to be some elements of Chinese culture.

Based on these principles, we reworked the script based on the original plots, framework and language. First, we stretched the script appropriately in poetic language, and each line added was repeatedly checked to match the original script. Based on my own understanding of Indian dance in India, I was aware that music and dance were the soul of Indian art. We subsequently added large sections of dance music to each pivotal episode to set the mood. For example, song and dance accompanied the opening scene which had village girls carrying water. This rural scene of song and dance helped immediately transport the audience to the beautiful and mysterious ancient forests of Manipur. In another part where Chitra is transformed into a shy beauty with the help of the gods of love and spring, the nymphs dance for her to cheer her up. Each section of music was carefully selected from Tagore's works set on Indian classical music to enhance the momentum. We changed all static passages to dynamic ones, especially the passionate passages of the hero and heroine, to engage the audience with their words as well as beautiful body movements and expressions. We put the characters' dialogues in poetic words as much as possible to mobilize the audience's emotions. For example, in the first act, when Arjuna turns away, Chitra murmured of the love of her heart as, "O foolish heart, where has your self-importance flown to? If I could give my youth and all my ambitions in exchange for being a heap of dust at his feet, I would feel that it was the most precious of gifts. Good heavens, what has come to add to the confusion at this time? I seem to hear numerous rose buds rustling in my heart, slowly breaking into bloom; countless stars searing in my body; what kind of a strange encounter is this"?

Elements of Chinese culture included the mood from Dream of the Red Mansion and the use of Chinese martial arts. For example, to describe the beauty of Chitra after the transformation, we quoted a poem from the fifth chapter of A Dream of the Red Mansion, in which Jia Baoyu describes the fairy nun in Taixu illusionary realm: "How is her attainment? Spring plum blossoms in snow. How is her purity? Like autumn, the chrysanthemum is covered with frost. How quiet is she? Like pine growing in the empty valley. How is its beauty? Like haze reflecting the clear pond". At the end of the play, when Chitra leads the army and people to fight back the advancing enemy, I added Chinese martial arts to show the strong heroine's spirit of Chitra. Throughout the play, we stuck to one principle: Indian music, dance-songs and dances, completely Indian backdrop, Indian costumes, and Indian choreography. The audience would be bathed in waves of Indian culture.

Tagore's "Chitra" was performed three times in China. On May 7, during Tagore's visit to China in 1924, it was the first time when Chitrangada was performed in English at Beijing Xiehe Chapel to celebrate Tagore's 63rd birthday. Lin Huiyin performed it as Chitra, Zhang Xinhai as Arjuna, Lin Huiyin's father Lin Changmin as Madana, the God of Love, and Xu Zhimo as Vasanta, the God of Spring, with a total of more than 40 guests and hosts as the audience. Due to time constraints, the performance was restricted in character styling, costumes, make-up, music and lighting. Although the performance was a success, the impact was minimal. It was impossible to procure audio and video materials related to the event except for photographs and reports. In December 2007 "Chitrangada" was performed in China for the second time. The teachers and students, particularly students of English Class of the School of Foreign Languages, Lanzhou University, wrote the script in English, directed, and performed in it. I was the chief planner. Indian Embassy in China applied and received the broadcasting rights. The success of this performance not only established an inseparable relationship of the University with "Chitrangada" but also paved the way for its third staging.

The third staging was the first in Chinese language. It was also the largest, the highest quality performance, and the most influential at home and abroad. We invited Professor Chen Ziming of the Central Conservatory of Music as the music consultant, who set the keynote for each play section. Then our music teacher, Ms. Chen Hui, arranged the tunes specifically. We invited Ms. Jin Shanshan, a famous Indian dance artist in China, as dance director. Ms. Jin had studied Indian dance under the older generation of Indian dance artist, Zhang Jun, since she was 6 years old. She studied Hindi at Beijing University, was a senior student of Professor Wang Bangwei of South Asia studies at Beijing University. She went to India and studied Bharat Natyam and Kathak. It may be said that she studied Indian classical dance as avidly and dedication as Xuanzang did for the study of Buddhist scriptures and went to India seven times for that.

With minimal funds in hand, staging the play seemed an uphill task. The above two accomplished artists, however, cooperated without any monetary compensation. Ms Jin came to Lanzhou University and used 3 days to complete the dance rehearsal, working day and night, neglecting food and sleep, laying a solid foundation for our later rehearsals. Ms. Wu Yi, a disciple of Yu Qiu Yu, who graduated from the Shanghai Theatre Academy not long ago, worked on direction of the play. Though not a prominently known director, she proved to be extremely effective. The rest of the sets, props, costumes, and staging were designed by us. The actors were chosen from among students of eight faculties, including School of Arts, and the so-called payment was to drink a bottle of mineral water each time!

On March 24, 2012, "Chitrangada" was staged in Wenxin Hall, Yuzhong Campus, Lanzhou University, with the Indian Ambassador to China and his entourage present to watch the performance. The creativity and enthusiasm of the performers were unanimously praised. The performance had retained the original Indian flavour and intensity. More than 150 media (including online media) participated in Chitrangada's coverage and reproduction, including CCTV foreign language channel, Xinhua News Agency, China News Agency, People's Daily, Guangming Daily and other national media, and the three largest official media in India, Hindustan, Press Trust of India and The Hindu. Two days before President Hu Jintao visited India on March 26 for the BRICS summit, the video of the play was broadcasted on All-India Television. Hong Kong's Wenhui.com and Phoenix.com also reported on it. A network of local media outlets in Gansu formed a three-dimensional platform for the promotion of Chitrangada. There were more than 760 news items reported and reproduced in China, more than 10 TV news items, 21 web videos, and over 10 reports and videos on the website of Lanzhou University alone. The success of the premiere of Chitrangada promoted a positive image of Gansu Province and Lanzhou University as well as became an example of cultural interaction and cross-culturalism.

每日甘肃

新闻中心

16.1 Factors for Success: A Lyrical Script

The Chinese version of Chitrangada performed by Lanzhou University was slightly different from Tagore's original play. The rewritten Chinese version of "Chitrangada" has five acts. Act I Encounter: Chitra, a princess of Manipur kingdom, is brought up as a boy and is brave and good at riding and shooting. One day, she is hunting in the forests in Manipur when she meets Prince Arjuna of Kuru kingdom. Act II: Chitra confesses her love for Arjuna to the God of Love, Madana, and Vasanta, the God of Spring, and feels inferior and embarrassed by her appearance. The two gods graciously grant her a year of beauty and tenderness. Act III Love: The transformed Chitra is flawless and captures the heart of Arjuna, but the beauty of her appearance becomes the love rival of her true self, and she suffers from this conflict at all times. She is flirtatious and sultry when she is with Arjuna, blames herself, and feels guilty when alone. Act IV Bitterness: As the year goes on, Chitra's heart grows more and more anxious about losing Arjuna. Her inconsistent words and actions cause painful melancholy for Arjuna. On the eve of the arrival of one year, the enemy invades the kingdom of Manipur, and Chitra leaves Arjuna to lead the people in a valiant fight against the enemy. Act V Finale: Chitra returns in triumph and reveals her true identity to Arjuna, who is shocked and thrilled. This is the ideal lover of his heart! The two embrace tightly, and love reaches perfection.

Act II of the Chinese version of Chitrangada begins with an intriguing solo by Chitra as well:

Like a vine around a big tree
Hugging the tree tightly
I want you to hold me as usual.
I want you to love me and never leave me.

Like an eagle flying up to the sky,
Two wings are fluttering towards the earth.
I'll pounce on your heart just the same
I want you to love me and never leave me.

Like the sun around the sky and the earth
walking rapidly around and around.
I surround your heart, too.
I want you to love me and never leave me.[1]

The poem is titled "Acacia Mantra" and is taken from the ancient Indian poem "Atharva Veda". The poem uses three remarkable metaphors in three stanzas: my lover is the tree, and I am the vine; my lover is the earth, I am the eagle; my lover is the sky and the earth, and I am the sun. At the end of each stanza, the poem repeats, "I want you to love me and never leave me", because according to an ancient Indian custom, if one chants the mantra repeatedly, the ideal would turn into reality and one's love would be reciprocal. This love mantra expresses a moving emotion that is stronger than lovesickness. The addition of this "Love Mantra" to the Chinese version of Chitrangada does not mean that Chitra is determined to capture the heart of Arjuna, but more to express her desire for a better love. It harmonizes with the poetic style of the play as a whole while not straying from the larger context of Indian culture.

[1] Its Chinese version is poetic:

像藤萝环抱大树,
把大树抱得紧紧,
想你这样抱着我,
要你爱我, 永不离分。
像老鹰向天上飞起,
两翅膀向大地扑腾;
我照样扑向你的心,
要你爱我, 永不离分。
像太阳环绕天和地,
迅速绕着走个不停;
我也环绕你的心, 要你爱我永不离分。

16.2 The Original Indian Flavour

Since it is an Indian play, it has to showcase Indian culture. The sets, music and dance, costumes and props of "Chitrangada" are all very Indian.

Two-stage backdrops were used for the performance of Chitrangada, of which one was of the great forests of Manipur: a large, luxuriant, pristine forest, shaded by trees, with hibiscus, jasmine, purple willow and other flowers blooming everywhere. There is a small stream with flowing water. The sky is blue and white clouds are floating. In the distance are snow-capped mountains with lush trees underneath. Together with the sound effects, crickets chirping, and birds murmuring, it shows the quiet mystery of the deep forests of Manipur, India, which proved to be alluring.

There are also several references to Lord Siva in the play: Siva is so gracious that he promises the royal family of Manipur a male crown prince; Chitra practices rituals in the Siva temple and prays to Lord Siva every day, and so on. The use of the Siva linga as a symbol of male and female passion provided the audience a significant visual impact. This cultural context dramatically enhanced the play's performance.

Music too contributed immensely. The opening music is slow and melodious, and the women carry water jars to fetch water. The music suddenly turns enthusiastic and joyful and the women with water jars on their heads begin to dance to the music. Everyone joins in fully demonstrating the peaceful and happy atmosphere where the villagers live and work. Another example is when Chitra expresses her worship of Arjuna, the sad music moves the heart. This calls of the heart and the out. Similarly, in one scene, Vasanta, the god of spring, sprinkles flowers on Chitra's head, giving her the charm of spring flowers. The joyful Indian music plays simultaneously and Chitra dances and brings forth the beauty of the moment. The love dance between Arjuna and Chitra is accompanied by passionate Indian songs and a shower of flowers. The music changes from soft and soothing to exciting and oscillating as Chitra dances a masked dance, her heart struggling and unable to free itself. The gentle, and poignant music flows gently as Arjuna and Chitra argue, both sad and in pain. The mournful music plays on as Chitra speaks alone of her inner pain, as the snow-capped snow heralds the imminent loss of her spring flower-like beauty. The happy music resumes as the victorious Chitra wins the heart of Arjuna. In the end, the fairies, villagers, Arjuna and Chitra dance in a group to the joyful and bright music, showing the consummation of their love and life. Many such examples could be enumerated.

The most intriguing aspect of the Chinese version of Chitrangada is the use of Indian dances. Bing Xin's "Watching the Dances—Dedicated to Indian Dancer Karama Sisters" vividly portrays one of the varied classical Indian dances, the Bharat Natyam. It features delicately composed dances, splendid costumes, light steps, agile figures, and rich emotions. Bing's essay leaves the reader with a deep impression of Indian dance and its intricacies. She quotes:

Where the hand goes, the gaze follows.
Where the gaze goes, the mind follows.
Where the mind is, the expression accompanies;
where the expression is, the rasa accompanies.[2]

There are six dances in the Chinese version of Chitrangada, mainly, Bharat Natyam, Kathak, Odissi and Manipuri. Regardless of the Indian dance form, the audience is exhorted to read the mood and story through gestures, eyes, facial expressions, body language and musical beats of the dancers. The graceful dance of Chitrangada, the leading actress, was undoubtedly the most compelling. Her entrance in her flamboyant costume became a sight to behold. She danced to the music, with her eyes full of autumn waves, her gestures changing, and her expressions are sometimes happy and sometimes sad. The audience's emotions rose and fell with her dance movements: a happy and excited Chitra after her cocoon transformation into a butterfly; a shy and smiling Chitra when she meets Arjuna again; a smiling Chitra when she falls in love with Arjuna; and a conflicted and sad Chitra when her true self is shaken. The most impressive part of the performance was the dance of love between Arjuna and Chitra in the third act, where heaven and earth, the universe, sorrow and joy, life and death all merge into an unbearable ecstasy. The group dancers finally pull up the veil over their heads, ending with Arjuna picking up Chitra and spinning her around, finally settling on them embracing and kissing each other. The audience also cheered and applauded their reunion. The Indian dance of Chitranganda provided a taste of the long and splendid Indian culture and its arts.

Apart from this, the cast of Chitranganda kept an eye on costume and prop, making for the best choreography effect. The costumes fitted the identity of the characters in the play. Madana, dressed in white with gold trim, wearing a golden headdress and carrying five arrows, is simple and dignified, while the slightly mischievous Vasanta, God of Spring is dressed in green, like a forest spirit. The changes in costume corresponded to the changes in the characters' situations. For example, in the first act, Arjuna is dressed in simple white, the attire of an ascetic, while after falling in love with Chita is dressed in flamboyant colours, a far cry from his former self. In the beginning, Chitra is dressed in a green prince's hunting costume, but after the transformation, Chitra wears a sarong, a tight short dress on top, a long skirt underneath, a belt around her waist, a bright red dress with gold trim, red dots on her eyebrows, a circle of loose diamonds on her eyebrows, and bangles on her hands, making her dance even more graceful and beautiful. The props for the show were all custom-made, and each prop had a design, many of which were referenced from museum exhibits. The design had precise requirements for the size, colour, pattern, and decoration of the props. For example, the bed was required to be decorated with moss and flowers to reflect a strong sense of mythology and the supernatural; the mask, 30 cm long, required a very beautiful Indian woman's face to be drawn on the

[2] Bing Xin's Chinese version is: 手之所至, 目光随之; 目光所至, 心灵随之; 心灵所至, 表情伴之; 表情所至, 拉斯伴之。

left half of the face according to the drawing; the short knife used by Arjuna, 26–30 cm long, required the sheath and handle to be inlaid with precious stones to reflect the richness, and so on. It is these small details that ensured the best performance.

16.3 Recognition of Beauty

In this theatrical style of poetry, music and dance in one, the Chinese version of "Chitrangada" well illustrated Tagore's aesthetic thought—the original truth is beauty, and good virtue is beauty. According to Tagore, perfect perception of the real can bring joy, and perfect perception is the only way to know beauty honestly. This means that truth, goodness, and beauty are in harmony and unity. Recognizing this beauty requires the cooperation of the senses and the help of the mind. It is impossible to attain happiness in attaining beauty without rejecting the false external and seeking the ultimate true face. Its beauty is observed only with the physical eye, in front of us. The walls of what is beautiful and what is not being separated, but if a sense of goodness and virtue is added to the observation, the line between beauty and unbeauty may no longer be so clear. What attracted before may no longer be beautiful, and there may be supreme beauty in those things that are ordinary and simple. In this context, in the Chinese version of Chitrangada, recognizing the beauty of nature is not a difficult task for Arjuna. In the forest of Manipur, he revels in the beauty of spring:

> The tender new leaves have been gathered into a dancing flame.
> The bright red hibiscus flowers converge into a sea of burning blossoms.
> The bird's murmur, and the fragrance is fragrant.[3]

In his eyes, transformed Chitra was flawless, supreme, transcendent, the embodiment of beauty. However, he gradually grew tired of the pleasure that beauty brought, and began to look at it with his heart. More and more, he wanted to know the true self beneath the guise of Chitra's soulful beauty and elegant body. At the same time, having heard of Princess Chitra's bravery and exploits, he becomes increasingly curious about her. His knowledge of beauty gradually deepens, and he restrains his desire for beauty and bends to the acts of Chitra. Chitra, who had given up her true self in favour of beauty to capture the heart of Arjuna, realized that borrowed beauty did not bring her joy; she loathed her empty body, her impoverished soul, and lived in constant remorse and depression, finally returning to that true Chitra at the time of the invasion of a foreign enemy. When Chitra abandons her false self and appears in front of Arjuna as her true self, their love is finally united. Chitra finally realizes the principle that "truth is joy and truth is beauty". The story of Chitra illustrates Tagore's

[3] 嫩绿的新叶已然攒集成朵朵跳荡的火焰,
鲜红的木槿花汇聚成了片片燃烧的花海,
鸟声呢喃, 芬芳馥郁。

aesthetic idea that "to know beauty requires restraint and painstaking search; beauty proclaimed by empty desires is a mirage".

The Chinese version of Chitrangada also has Chinese elements. Chinese audiences will be familiar with the words of Madana, "I have brought the fragrant malt from the realm of the great void".[4] The fifth episode of Dream of the Red Mansions, one of China's Four Great Masterpieces, is Jia Baoyu's journey into the realm of the Great Void. In Dream of the Red Mansions, Taixu Realm is a nebulous place "above the sky of separation and hatred, in the middle of the sea of sorrow",[5] where the immortal nun of the police fantasy is in charge of the love affairs of men and women in the world, much like what we call the God of love today. In Chitrangada, Madana is the lord of love, and under his control, men and women seek love, in chains of pleasure and pain. It can be said that the nun and Madana have the same duties; both were responsible for managing the love affair between men and women. There is also the use of Chinese martial arts. As mentioned earlier, the majestic music in the play interspersed with the sound of clashing swords, with Chinese martial art style, gave a refreshingly Chinese element to the Chinese version of "Chitra". The addition of these Chinese elements brought Chitrangada closer to the Chinese audience. No wonder, the Cultural Counsellor of the Indian Embassy in China said after the performance that Chitrangada was no longer Chitrangada in the traditional sense but reflected a new interpretation encompassing a new spirit in the amalgam of Indian and Chinese culture.

The staging of Chitrangada was a bold attempt on our part. There were many shortcoming: minimal funds affected the design and production of sets, props, staging, costumes and even the choreography. The performance could not be fine-tuned, special singers could not be hired to sing in Hindi. Due to the many valuable experiences, however, efforts to stage Shakuntala of Kalidasa have already commenced. It would require six groups of male and female dancers, 12 in each group, to bring out the classical Indian dances and folk dances to the fullest, to emphasize the characters and the storyline. The costume of the heroine Sakuntala alone has to be changed a dozen times according to the plot. The set has to be transformed a dozen times, and the different staging has to be arranged for each big plot, singing, music and costumes. The actors should be professionals. The aim is to create a Chinese version of the classic nature of Sakuntala.

16.4 Conclusion

The staging of Chitrangada represents successful cultural co-operation between India and Lanzhou University, which has influence round the world. And since then, Centre for India Studies of Lanzhou University has a very friendly relationship with India

[4] 我从太虚幻境给你带来了仙酪。

[5] 离恨天之上，悔恨海之中。

Embassy in China, and we have more and more cultural exchanges. I hope that the slogan *India-China bhai bhai* always echoes in our hearts.

Bibliography

Chinese Embassy Database (2012a) The text of Ambassador's speech during the first ever Tagore's musical drama in Chinese language, Lanzhou. http://eoibeijing.gov.in/eoibejing_listview/OTM4

Chinese Embassy Database (2012b) Indian media reports about the first ever Tagore's musical drama in Chinese language held in Lanzhou University. http://eoibeijing.gov.in/eoibejing_listview/OTM5

Krishnan A (2012) 88 years later Tagore comes to China again. The Hindu, March 24

Lanzhou University Database (2012) 中国学子创排泰戈尔《齐德拉》首演印度大使感动中国武术加入. https://news.lzu.edu.cn/c/201203/4a49801936467a80013648d60d8c0022.html

Patranobis S (2012) Tagore's play Chitrangada staged in Chinese. Hindustan Times, April 10

Part V
Teaching Chinese in India

Chapter 17
Challenges of Teaching Chinese in India

Rathijit Chakraborty

The word 'challenges' should be regarded as a variable term and not a constant one. New challenges keep on changing their dimensions and contexts constantly. Circumstances define the relevance of challenges. This paper strives to explore the imminent problems confronted by concerned teachers, learners, and stakeholders in various aspects of teaching–learning of Chinese language.

17.1 Linguistic Challenges

India is a country of numerous languages spoken by widely diversified communities. Every state has its unique linguistic attributes further branched into distinct dialects in particular pockets. Almost every Indian is a bilingual by birth. An average Indian acquires two to three or more indigenous languages, for social, economic, educational, or religious requirements. We do not have a common dominating language as the Chinese do. In China, the official dialect *Putonghua* or Mandarin is promoted as the medium of instruction across the entire nation. Whereas in India, the official language English is spoken and understood by only a miniscule population (not more than 10%). Imposition of Hindi too did not go down well with the southern states and some regions in the northeast. The absence of a concrete national language policy is an impediment in formulating a foreign language policy. In today's world, denial of English or any foreign language for that matter eventually deprives one of accessing the best of global opportunities.

Acquisition of Chinese as a foreign language normally takes longer as compared to other languages. Indian students are habituated to dealing with alphabetical languages. At the very rudimentary level of learning, they find it hard to imbibe the

R. Chakraborty (✉)
Department of Foreign Languages, Tezpur University, Tezpur, India
e-mail: rc8online@gmail.com

S. Mishra and R. Sheel (eds.), *India-China Dialogues Beyond Borders*,
https://doi.org/10.1007/978-981-99-4326-5_18

components that make Chinese a 'different' (termed 'difficult' otherwise) language, particularly its non-alphabetic and tonal qualities. It appears to them as a weird package of symbolic scripts (logograms) called Chinese characters and numerous homophonous sounds that are each assigned with four to five different tones (pitches or frequencies of sounds). Indians are not completely ignorant of applying intonations in words, phrases, or sentences. However, those are expressions of specific emotions associated with utterances. But in Chinese a specific intonation of a syllable stands for a specific meaning. One needs to memorize or semi-memorize different intonations called tones of Chinese, which are four in the official Mandarin dialect and run up to nine in Cantonese. While some sounds in Chinese are close to English or many of local Indian languages, there are quite a few others that might appear to be absolutely jaw-breakers to the Indian learners. It certainly takes a while with regular practice to master these sounds. Strong Mother Tongue Influence (MTI) with acute local variations is a serious challenge for teaching students from different parts of India, most of whom are educated in vernacular media. They not only find it extremely difficult to deal with nuances of Chinese pronunciations but also falter equally in sounds of English, the conventional medium for learning Chinese or any other foreign language.

In addition, each Chinese script or character is composed of simple to complex strokes, set to be written in a particular sequence or order. Missing or adding one single stroke would either change the meaning of the character or render it wrong. To compound the problems, one finds it even harder to guess a character through its sound with a particular tone assigned, since modern simplified Chinese characters are more pictographic (symbolic) in nature and less related to sounds. Chinese characters are estimated to be over 60,000 in number. One needs to master 3000 to 4000 characters to read a newspaper, and 8000 to 9000 to be a scholar. It is often remarked in jest that one needs three life spans to learn all the Chinese characters—allegorically referring to an impossible task.

17.2 Academic and Pedagogical Challenges

In the present century, teaching and learning of Chinese have gained popularity because of China's global visibility and importance. Mandarin Chinese or Putonghua is taught in almost 200 countries including India. Approximately 100 million learners have been estimated to have enrolled currently for Chinese. And 5 million teachers are required worldwide to train these learners in Chinese. This undoubtedly is the greatest challenge with a massive crisis of qualified Chinese language teachers. This is one key aspect that has upset the plan to promote Chinese language in schools by the Central Board of Secondary Education (CBSE) in India where Chinese is taught in around 20 universities and 8 of these institutions offer full-fledged integrated programs.

In India, the curricula in schools seldom provide scope of developing flair in communicative English. On top of it, opting for Chinese poses a genuine challenge in maintaining an equilibrium between English and the target foreign language, i.e., Chinese. Poor to very poor communicative skills in the second language in India as mentioned earlier act as obstacles in imparting classroom instructions at the basic level of teaching Chinese. Assessing students through classroom interactions and activities and achieving productive outputs prove to be difficult exercises. Traditional method of rote learning that students are accustomed to throughout their school education hampers analytical and critical thinking in the teaching–learning process of Chinese language.

Lack of Chinese textbooks and course books with Indian context further alienates the Indian learners from understanding the target language from Indian perspective. Conventional textbooks that do not relate to Indian society or culture hardly invoke interest among Indian learners. Students find it difficult to identify with the Chinese texts that are compiled majorly to cater to Westerners. A few countries like Japan and Vietnam have already indigenized Chinese textbooks for learning the language easily and comfortably in their native languages. Teaching Chinese through local languages is not possible in India because the set-up is rather complex with hundreds of languages and dialects that do not correspond to each other. We have to accept the fact that in India English cannot be replaced with any local language for teaching and learning Chinese.

The approaches and challenges associated with pedagogical techniques of teaching Chinese to adults are unique and cannot be equated with the techniques of teaching school children. Compiling systematic curricula to meet specific learning objectives and learning outcomes for different levels of teaching–learning Chinese is a great challenge faced by teachers and instructors at the very onset of teaching any program. Training Chinese language teachers in India to be able to utilize existing materials and resources and create new materials for custom-made courses is usually not emphasized as it should be. Local Chinese teachers suffer from their own baggage of educational setting that they are used to. In this process, their teaching method often become repetitive of what they themselves have imbibed as learners. When both course books and teaching methods become redundant, students find it absurd to get involved in the subject. In addition, local teachers following traditional teaching methods face a major problem in creating a Chinese learning environment. Technically speaking, most of the institutes that offer Chinese adhere to teacher-centric pedagogy where the teacher in a traditional book-blackboard-chalk set-up is an authority whom the students are hesitant to interact or to put up a query with. Teaching in such an environment is one-sided, non-creative and unproductive.

With a handful of scholars employed in academics and higher education, serious research in pedagogical methods applicable in teaching Chinese takes a serious setback in promotion of learning Chinese. In fact, only a few of the institutes that offer Chinese as major are able to produce good local teachers. Worse than that, those which support them with consistent professional development are even fewer. Majority of local Chinese instructors are clueless about modern teaching methods like blended or flipped techniques, and unconcerned of student counselling and mentoring, feedbacks from students and stakeholders, etc. With shortage in Chinese language teachers, these issues substantially affect and bring down performances in teaching.

Qualified native Chinese teachers although deputed occasionally to make up for this impediment often fail to discern local hopes and frustrations. This is primarily because they are completely oblivious to the local cultures and ethos. A major cultural gap hinders the teacher-learner bonding making the classroom an unfavourable setting for both. Managing classrooms in India and abroad has been a perpetual challenge for the native Chinese teachers sent outside China as language instructors.

17.3 Technological Challenges

General infrastructural problems like proper utilization of ICT in classrooms and language laboratories, availability of smart classes, affordability of gadgets and devices, network coverage across major areas of India, etc. pose serious challenges to the teaching–learning process of Chinese. Chinese language teachers and instructors, again mostly because they lack professional development, often encounter with major hassles associated with technology, like changeover from the conventional mode to smart classrooms, managing resources available online, integrating ICT content in teaching Chinese, etc. Incompetency in ICT expertise, incapability of optimal utilization of online resources and deficiency in technological know-how among the new generation of native Indian teachers teaching Chinese are practical problems in grooming up students in twenty-first century skills.

Technology is changing rapidly. A drastic transformation from physical to online classes during the COVID-19 pandemic has left teaching of Chinese with the choice of depending only and heavily on technologies linked to conducting virtual classes. Modern gadgets with the latest software applications easily made available to learners who can afford them are slowly replacing the concept of language laboratories that augmented to a considerable extent the teaching of Chinese and other languages. To be able to catch up with the fast-changing technology and simultaneously upgrading individually are suggestive of acute and immediate teaching hazards. These include appropriate utilization of ICT-based technologies in digital learning, e.g., live virtual classrooms, pre-recorded classes, online assessment or evaluation, conducting proctored exams, e-learning, m-learning (using smartphones), online dictionaries, digital flashcards, voice recognition, social media, etc.

Under these circumstances, it is evident that building an inter-dependable teacher-learner relationship of support and empathy is far from feasibility and is ostensibly missing in online teaching. Secondly, drawing and retaining attention of learners who are hooked up with gadgets are routine problems during conducting online classes.

17.4 Socio-economic Challenges

The history of learning Chinese in India is quite old. A formal department for learning the language and culture of China began in the early 30s in Visva-Bharati University at Santiniketan, under the auspices of Gurudev Rabindranath Tagore, to enhance scholarly exchanges, collaborative research, and Indo-China friendship. Initially, the focus was more on culture studies with academic stalwarts contributing outstanding research work from both sides.

In an era where China emerges as the new global superpower, at par with the United States, a worldwide crave for learning Chinese language becomes more obvious. At present, with a surge in the number of aspirants, the focus of study has shifted from long-time research to short-time courses. Takers of these crash courses are more concerned about the applicability of Chinese in a job rather than learning about the Chinese culture. This tendency of learning a language minus the native culture prevents them from understanding the typical qualities of Chinese in their correct frame of references. On an average, a student of Chinese language aims to look for lucrative jobs immediately after completion of an undergraduate course. This phenomenon has given rise to severe shortage of Chinese language teachers and instructors. Post-COVID-19, sluggish employability has slowed down hiring in both public and private sectors. Overpopulated classrooms broadening the gap in teacher-student ratio yields poor academic performance and the graduates are left with very limited options of employment.

Apart from the trend of community hype and related factors, without visible, tangible, and lucrative anticipations, Chinese language usually doesn't appeal to a large number of students, particularly those from semi-rural or rural areas. Metros and industrial cities provide good placement opportunities for regular employments or freelancing compared to rural areas and small towns. Under these circumstances, teachers face challenges to enable students visualize and identify the goals and rewards of learning Chinese.

To reap the benefits of teaching Chinese, creating a steady supply of learners is also a challenge in India. Average annual drop-out of students facing difficulties in learning Chinese at the undergraduate level has a snowball effect towards the end of a 5-year integrated program. Fewer learners lead to fewer people engaging in research and teaching in Chinese.

Students in India come from various socio-economic backgrounds. Some of them also belong to the first-generation learners. If the teacher belongs to a different social and educational setting, it is a tough challenge for him or her to understand the learners' psychology, set clear goals and implement inclusive practices in the classroom. Teachers often tend to be unconcerned about students' hardships in grasping Chinese. Reflecting teaching abilities in the form of intercultural communication is a genuine problem particularly in the Indian context. The social, cultural, and educational conditions of both the teacher and the learner play significant roles in learning a foreign language.

17.5 Challenges in Evaluation

The primary objective of assessment for any program of study is to track the progress of learners, which in turn is necessary for revising and upgrading curriculum and for preparing required teaching materials. This is particular in case of Chinese language and for that matter, all foreign languages that imply the purpose of learning outcome-based curricula. The mode of assessment, however, is quite different from that involved in other streams. In languages, the focus of all assessments is supposed to be on the mastery and competence in that language. In India, and possibly in other parts of the world as well, the COVID-19 pandemic has resulted in a surge of online courses in foreign languages. The future is uncertain and perhaps the current situation that will have a ripple effect for a long time would render it difficult to get back to an entirely regular physical mode of classes. The UGC has probably in this context suggested for a blended mode laying major emphasis on the online classes and evaluation.

While it is needless to mention that teaching Chinese online is a complicated exercise, the entire process of evaluation through various online activities is a challenging task for the teachers. Many students manage to evade or disrupt online exams by arguing on network issues. Since it is not feasible to hold proctored tests for most of the online assessments, many learners fail to realize the solemnity and ethics of hard work. Instead, they indulge in deception by referring to Chinese websites or online translators. This tendency is ruining the learners to a considerable extent. Since many of the Chinese websites display traditional characters, the learners, in this process mess up their writing with both simplified as well as traditional Chinese characters as they fail to distinguish between the two. With disproportionate teacher-student ratios, proper evaluation has become even more unattainable. One great advantage of online evaluation is its cost-effectiveness vis-à-vis the logistics required to arrange physical mode of exams. Simultaneously, it is also fast in delivering feedbacks. However, most institutes in India so far lack smart classrooms associated with suitable learning management systems (LMS) and online assessment tools. Monitoring feedbacks, adopting corrective measures for remedial instructions, re-examining fruitless strategies in teaching, and seeking improved options are time-consuming and have to be carried out beyond normal teaching hours. Mentoring and counselling on correct learning behaviours at regular intervals for tracking progress in different aspects of learning Chinese, particularly the aspects listening, speaking, reading, and writing require both experience and expertise.

17.6 Politico-diplomatic Challenges

The Confucius Institutes (CI), an initiative under China's NOCFL (National Office for Teaching Chinese as a Foreign Language) or *Hanban* was founded early this century with objectives of propagating and popularizing teaching–learning of

Chinese language in countries outside China. Their tie-ups with universities in India including over 50 collaborations with other institutes came under the Indian Government's scanner in 2019. The CIs were viewed with apprehension as they were banned in other countries too.

Border skirmishes and clashes along the LAC have been incessantly marring the relationship and friendly ties between India and China for the last several decades. Lack of proactive confidence-building measures between the two neighbours and a restrained approach have led to mutual distrust and speculations. Recent face-offs in the Doklam and Galwan areas between Indian and Chinese armies spawned an anti-China wave and almost a blanket ban on Chinese apps in India. Chinese language which was earlier included along with other foreign languages to be accommodated in the curricula in schools was dropped. All these factors converge to intensify the scarcity of human resources in teaching–learning of Chinese.

It is relevant to keep in mind that both the era and backdrop in which study of China and the Chinese language were introduced in India for the first time had been entirely different than what they are in the present century with the international mobility of China and its emergence as a major player in global politics. Dynamics have changed and diplomacy seems to be occasionally at stake. Obscure relationship with China diminishes the prospects of the Chinese language.

Bibliography

Chang, Wen-Yu (2019) Building an effective learning environment for chinese language learners. All Grad Plan B Other Rep. 1420. https://digitalcommons.usu.edu/gradreports/1420

Crandall J (2000) Language teacher education. Annu Rev Appl Linguist 20:34–55. https://doi.org/10.1017/S0267190500200032

Delican, Mustafa (2019). The language policy of India

Hui Wen Chua (2015). A review of challenges in learning Chinese characters among non-native learners in Malaysia. Indian J Arts. 5. 93–100. ISBN : 978–0–7923–4931–0

Kissau S, Rodgers M, Haudeck H (2014) Foreign language teaching: an international comparison of teacher beliefs. Res Comp Int Educ 9(2):227–242. https://doi.org/10.2304/rcie.2014.9.2.227

Lam, Sophia (2020) Mapping development and challenges of teaching Mandarin Chinese in England Mandarin as a foreign language, language policy

Li, LI (2020) On three key problems of Chinese language teaching in India—Teachers, teaching materials and teaching methods. Shanghai university of political science and law, Shanghai, In: China 2020 5th International Conference on Social Science and Management (ICSSM 2020) ISBN: 978–1–60595–675–6

Lin, Chin-His, Liu, Haixia, Hu, Ying (2017) Technology and the education of Chinese-language teachers: Where are we now?. Journal of technology and chinese language teaching. 8. 1–15. Literature. Teacher's college, Beihua university, Jilin 132013, China. Adv Soc Sci, Educ HumIties Res. 63. In: International Conference on Advances in Management, Arts and Humanities Science (AMAHS 2016)

Liu S, Wang F (2018) A qualitative study on learning trajectories of non-native Chinese instructors as successful Chinese language learners. Asian J Second Foreign Lang Educ 3:2. https://doi.org/10.1186/s40862-018-0043-5

Lu, Yanbin, Zheng, Ying, Lin, Shihan (2019) Mandarin Chinese teachers across borders: challenges and needs for professional development. Int J Chin Lang Educ

Newell WH (2015) India and the Chinese language problem. Economic and political weekly.1956. 31st month, Issue No. 13 Poole, Frederick J., Teaching Chinese As a Foreign Language: A Foreigner's Perspective. All Grad Plan B Other Rep. 457. https://digitalcommons.usu.edu/gradreports/457

Rizvi F,Bianco J, Wang C, Hay T, Barron R, Khan Atiya (2007) Emerging technologies and the potential and challenges of peer learning of Chinese and english in transnational learning spaces. In: 2018, Conference Proceedings Kochhar SK (2007). Language Problem. Pivotal Issues In Indian Education. Pocket Books. ISBN 978-8128812118

Shuwen, Wang (2014) Multimedia design and application in teaching Chinese language and Singh M, Han J, Ballantyne C (2014) Making Chinese learnable: Research oriented school engaged teacher-researcher Education. Retrieved from http://www.uws.edu.au/__data/assets/pdf_file/0005/555728/4

Sokip Dr (2020) Overcoming the problem of learning foreign language skills in the classroom. Univers J Educ Res. 8. 723–729. https://doi.org/10.13189/ujer.2020.080246

Stern HH (1967) Foreign languages in primary education: The teaching of foreign or second languages to younger children. Oxford U.P, London

Varghese NV (2014) Globalization and Higher Education: Changing Trends in Cross Border Education. 5:7–20

Widdowson HG (1997) Approaches to second language teacher education. Encycl Lang Educ, 4

Xu, Hui (2012). Challenges native chinese teachers face in teaching chinese as a foreign language to Non-Native Chinese students In U.S. Classrooms

Yang, Jia, Yin, Chengxu, Wang, Wei (2018) Flipping the classroom in teaching chinese as a foreign language. Lang Learn & Technol, 22(1) p 16–26

Yao, Tao-Chung, Xiao-Desai, Yang, Magriney, Christopher, Wong, Ka (2011). Teaching Chinese through interactive and collaborative online social networks. J Chin Lang Teach Res US 103–114

Zhang, Dongbo, Zhao, Shouhui, Li, Li (2011). Teachers' perceptions and use of ICT in Chinese language education

Chapter 18
Studying Thy Neighbour: Understanding the Chinese Language Challenge of China Studies in India

Prashant Kaushik

18.1 Introduction

A nation can change its friends but not neighbours. China remains the most significant neighbour for India no matter how we choose to analyse and comprehend. Given the fact that India and China share a long historical civilizational relationship on one hand, and a more contemporary complex relationship marred by several 'Cs', 'Ts' and 'Ps', the need to understand China in India just cannot be overemphasized.[1] This chapter is an attempt to understand the nature of Chinese language challenge facing 'China Studies' in India. Accepting the significance of Chinese language learning for the Indian academia a priori, this chapter attempts to understand, describe and analyse the nature of Chinese language challenge facing the Indian academia. It asks and seeks to answer several relevant questions: What is the Chinese language challenge of China Studies in India? What are its different dimensions? How it hinders the development of China Studies in India? How is China studied in India and vice-versa? How the Chinese language challenge hinders the academic output on China in India?

To do so, first, this chapter provides an overview of the evolution of China Studies in India and locates the problems facing China Studies within the paradigms through which China is mainly studied in India. Second, it elaborates the various dimensions of the Chinese language challenge faced by China Studies in India. Third, it provides

[1] Ye (2013) uses 'four Cs' of competition, cooperation, coordination and conflict to describe the contours of India-China relations. Hu and Jue (2021: 39) describes India-China relations through 'five Ts' of Tibet issue, territory disputes, the third-party factor, trade unbalance and trust deficit. Bajpai (2021) chooses to see the India-China binary through the prism of 'four Ps' of perceptions, perimeters, partnerships and power.

P. Kaushik (✉)
Central University of Gujarat, Gandhinagar, Gujarat, India
e-mail: prashant.kaushik@cug.ac.in

S. Mishra and R. Sheel (eds.), *India-China Dialogues Beyond Borders*,
https://doi.org/10.1007/978-981-99-4326-5_19

an overview of the evolution of India Studies in China to highlight the integration of language learning with the disciplinary knowledge as reflected in the academic output of China's India Studies. Fourth, it winds up the discussion by suggesting several ways of surmounting the Chinese language challenge in India. The conclusion in the end sums-up the need to urgently strengthen Chinese language education in India.

This chapter uses terms like 'Indology', 'India Studies', 'Sinology' and 'China Studies' to understand the Chinese language challenge facing the Indian academia. Although today 'Sinology' and 'China Studies' are sometimes regarded as a single entity, and 'Indology' and 'India Studies' are considered the same in some contexts, their provenance, focus of study and respective methodologies need little explanation here. 'Indology' primarily refers to the study of ancient Indian texts, literature, grammar, culture, religion, mythology, philosophy mainly through the historical–critical methods of philology that was started by the officials of British East India Company during the late eighteenth and early nineteenth century (McGetchin 2009: 27–8. Sengupta 2015). Indology is also being increasingly distinguished between 'traditional Indology', and 'modern Indology', the latter conforming more to the 'Area Studies'. This chapter uses the term 'India Studies' to incorporate both the 'traditional philological Indology' and more 'contemporary Indian Studies' that have evolved post-World War II, particularly with reference to China. 'Sinology'refers to the study of Chinese culture, history, philosophy, classical language and literature undertaken through the methods of philological and textual criticism. Sinology emerged from the tradition of study of the Classics (经) and Dynastic Histories (史) in China involving textual and phonological analysis, and the authentication and compilation of classical texts through careful reading and annotation (Zurndorfer 1995: 4–5). It gained strong roots in Europe through the works of early Christian Jesuits and French sinologists late seventeenth century onwards. Post-World War II study of China also took a turn towards 'Area Studies' underscoring the need to study 'China within a discipline' i.e., first learning Chinese language and then studying China through the methodology of a specific discipline (Zurndorfer 1995: Introduction). This chapter uses the term 'China Studies' as a broader rubric to refer to both the 'Indian Sinology' and India's Chinese Studies founded on Area Studies model.

18.2 China Studies in India

Whenever one talks of understanding China, one of the primary concerns remains that of mastery of Chinese language to read and analyse the primary sources. The lack of rigorous language training of people engaged in 'China Studies' in India or lack of Chinese language competence among India's China experts and research scholars remains a grey area as far as the formation of an independent Indian perspective on China is concerned. This chapter consider this situation as "the Chinese language challenge of 'China Studies' in India". The conspicuous absence and lack of primary Chinese language references in Indian writings on China amply underscores the point that there is an over-dependence of Indian academia on either non-Chinese sources, or limited English writings emanating from China, when it comes to understanding China in an objective manner. However, before delving into the Chinese language challenge, it is pertinent to understand the state of China Studies in India.

Broadly speaking China Studies in India exists in two paradigms. First rooted in traditional Sinology, 'traditional' because it adopted the classical methodology of studying China through its language, literature, and culture, much like the initial European study of China (Sinology) and India (Indology). The 'geo-civilizational' or 'civilizational' paradigm advocated by Tan Chung also falls under this category. The other paradigm is dominated by 'Area Studies' approach, both due to its origins in post- 1962 China-India War period and increasing identification of China as a 'threat' and 'challenge' to India's growth in more recent times.

18.3 Sinological and Civilizational Paradigms

The Sinological and civilizational paradigm of studying China in India are closely related with each other and both inform each other. Sinology focuses on the study of Chinese culture, history, philosophy, classical language and literature. That is, study of China undertaken through the medium of the Chinese language, Chinese concepts, Chinese artefacts and against the background of Chinese cultural sensibilities (Bhattacharjea et al. 1988; Deshingkar 1986). As an independent discipline in its own right Sinology found its beginnings in Europe in the efforts of early Christian Jesuits who went to China starting with Matteo Ricci (1552–1610), the earliest translator of Chinese texts into European languages (Thakur 2020: 516).

The European scholarship played a key role in highlighting the Sino-Indian intellectual engagement in ancient times through many archeological excavations and discoveries in both India and China, and translating the Chinese Buddhist canon. This background of Buddhist exchanges between the two countries and their ancient mutual recognition formed the basis of the first approach to China Studies in India rooted in Sinology, and which also came to be referred to as civilization perspective later (Thakur 2020).

Although sporadic attempts at translating the Chinese classics and teaching Chinese language had begun much earlier in British Bengal with the University of Calcutta starting Chinese language courses in 1918, the establishment of the Cheena Bhavana at Visva-Bharati in 1937 was a watershed moment in the development of Sinology in India. At that time the goal was also to study China within the pan-Asian, anti-colonial context (Sen 2013). The methodology adopted for studying China was of Sinology followed by the well-known centres of Chinese studies in Europe at that time. The major activity centred around textual studies, particularly around those Chinese texts which were no longer available in India in their Sanskrit or Pali versions (Deshingkar 1986). The people who played a key role in establishing and nurturing Cheena Bhavana as the hub of Sinology in India were Rabindranath Tagore (1861–1941), Tan Yunshan (1898–1983) and Prabodh Chandra Bagchi (1898–1956) among others.

Rabindranath Tagore invited Prof. Tan Yunshan to teach at and head the Cheena Bhavana in Visva-Bharati, Santiniketan. Chinese government also donated a great number of books to the Cheena Bhavana and made it one of the most renowned libraries for China Studies in India. Tan Yunshan also initiated and played a vital role in setting up the China-India Society which later became a bridge for academic exchanges and cooperation between the two countries (Liu 2013: 7–8). Visva-Bharati hence invited a great number of renowned Chinese scholars, artists, intellectuals and also trained many young Chinese students in Sanskrit, Bengali, Indian arts aesthetics and so on.

While Tan Yunshan presented the best of China, Visva-Bharati found an amalgamation of the best of India, China and Europe in Prabodh Chandra Bagchi (1895–1956). P. C. Bagchi already had a solid grounding in Sanskrit and Indian history when he started learning Chinese and Tibetan from French Orientalist Sylvain Lévi (1863–1935). Bagchi travelled and worked extensively in Nepal, Indochina, Japan, and went for higher studies to France where he was awarded the degree of Docteur es Letters (State Doctorate) by the Paris University. Bagchi was appointed as the Chair professor of Indian history at the Peking University for two years when the Indian government established this chair at Peking University in 1947.[2] However, his untimely demise in 1956 while he was still serving as the vice-chancellor of Visva-Bharati and the changing trajectory of India-China relations following the disagreements over borders and Tibet also portended an end to Sinology and a sharp turn towards Area Studies in India.

Nonetheless, what started in Cheena Bhavana and what was achieved there lies at the core of the 'civilizational' paradigm of studying China in India, as one of its most famous advocates and son of Tan Yunshan (1898–1983), Tan Chung (1929-) has reiterated time and again, that existing as civilizations China and India historically did not have border disputes, and it is the modern concepts of sovereignty and territorial integrity that ensnarled both China and India. The fact that in the past one thousand years China's population had constituted one-third to one-sixth of the world's population and India's population had sometimes been larger than China's meant that these two countries were most hospitable (Wang 2012: 102). Sharing common origins in the Himalayas, the Ganges and the Indus gave rise to the Indian civilization and the Yellow and the Yangtze to the Chinese civilization, both prospered as agricultural societies for most part of their existence. In the twentieth century the two also shared Asian pride and anti-colonial solidarity. In the long course of history, the civilizational paradigm holds, China's occupation of Tibet, eruption of military hostilities, conflict over border, mutual suspicion and antipathy are relatively recent phenomena which ended up marring the long-standing relationship. Nonetheless, these recent phenomena are germane to the other paradigms through which China is studied in India.

---

[2] *Dr. P.C. Bagchi- Appointment as Professor of History at the National Peking University China.* https://indianculture.gov.in/flipbook/134316 Accessed 23 Oct 2021.

18.4 Area Studies Paradigms: Geopolitics and Geo-economics

The earlier wave of studying China in India through methodologies of Sinology was rooted in the belief of existence of China as another grand fraternal civilization, a co-traveller in the path of 'Pan-Asianism'. This underwent a transformation following the establishment of the People's Republic of China in 1949, its entry into the Korean War (1950–53) and the incorporation of Tibet (1950–51). The Republic of India, and the People's Republic of China emerged on the world scene as quintessential nation-states and started seeing each other as such. Following such developments, the focus shifted more towards studying of China's state policies, particularly politics and foreign policy (Deshingkar 1986: 79). The Indian School of International Studies (ISIS), which later merged with the Jawaharlal Nehru University, New Delhi in June 1970 as School of International Studies (SIS), established in Oct 1955 at the Indian Council of World Affairs, New Delhi came to epitomize the above kind of research.

While the establishment of Cheena Bhavana was a watershed moment in the development of Sinological tradition, the 1962 India-China War proved to be the watershed in the development of study of China within the domain of Area Studies, a framework developed in the United States during World War II to understand 'enemy societies'. To 'know the enemy' became the primary focus of studying China in post-1962 war India. The establishment of the Department of Chinese Studies in 1964 (later renamed the Department of Chinese and Japanese Studies, and today known as the Department of East Asian Studies) in the University of Delhi came to epitomize this new shift. Although the study of China embedded in Area Studies aimed at doing multidimensional studies of China drawing on various social sciences, questions such as How did China's policies, economics, military, society etc. function? How was China likely to develop in future? What were Chinese policies in the international arena? attained more importance than the need to study Chinese philosophy, anthropology, geography, linguistics, history and religion. Since then the growth of China Studies in India has not been organic but has been largely mandated from the top down, with an almost obsessive focus on knowing the enemy (or potential enemy) (Thampi 2021: 27).

> This process of getting to know China from a nation-state and geopolitical perspective was grafted onto the early Tagorean effort to understand China as a civilization with ancient affinities with India, without a serious effort to reconcile these two different perspectives. As a result, there is a certain schizophrenic quality to the field of China studies in India, which is informed by an unresolved and unenlightening controversy over seeing 'China-as-friend' or 'China-as-enemy' (Thampi 2021: 27).

Manifestations of this "unresolved and unenlightening" controversy is amply found in the geo-political and geo-economics paradigms of studying China in India today. The geopolitical paradigm rooted in international relations theory, especially the realism and neo-realism schools, sees China as a large and powerful neighbour and a country directly engaged in reshaping the regional landscape of the sub-continent (Thakur 2020: 535). The logic of balance of power prevails in geopolitics, and the standard tenets of realism such as competition, mutual suspicion, alliance and military build-up determines China Studies in India (Wang 2012: 101).

Yet the almost simultaneous economic growth of China and India also offers a geo-economics paradigm for studying China in India, where the dominant logic is interconnectivity and mutual dependence, which has the potential to turn the zero-sum geopolitical competition into a mutual win–win (Wang 2012: 101). However, even here the idea that dominates is 'whether, when and how, if at all, India will 'catch up' with China' in this competitive economic race (Uberoi 2013: 192).

In an ideal set-up different paradigm would end-up enriching the academic discussion and enhancing the understanding of the subjects under study, but unfortunately that is not exactly happening in the case of China Studies in India, as Prof. Varun Sahni (2009) argues, the area studies programmes in India, of which China Studies is a constituent part, have not achieved their full potential primarily because they suffer from four fundamental fallacies pertaining to their subject matter, disciplinary focus, terms of reference and policy relevance; and nine fatal flaws like the absence of theory, lack of multidisciplinary perspectives, analyses that are based on macro-level research, scarce fieldwork, deficiencies in language skills, lack of quantitative research projects, event-driven research agendas, predominance of secondary sources in research, and taught courses, which are too broad in their formulation and too narrow in their subject matter (Sahni 2009: 50).

It is beyond doubt that mastery of Chinese language, in both its spoken and written forms, and a basic ability to comprehend and translate primary Chinese language sources is fundamental to the creation of any knowledge pertaining to China. It is also beyond any doubt that in the domain of area studies, micro-level studies provide best in-depth knowledge of any area under study, but to carry out that one requires excellent language skills and greater interaction with the common people (Sahni 2009: 50).

However, it is the absence of this prerequisite condition of adequate language skills for carrying out worthwhile study on China that is the point of concern for almost half a century among India's China experts. In fact, the issue of lack of Chinese language training has been a staple in various discussions on studying China, yet it still eludes a viable solution (See Deshingkar 1986; Tan 1986; Thampi 2007; Uberoi 2013; Jacob 2012; Thampi 2021; Chen and Naina 2021). However, before delving into the issue of Chinese language hurdle of China Studies in India, it would be better to first look at the specific problems and challenges facing China Studies in India, language but of course is one of them.

18.5 Problems Facing China Studies in India

First, China Studies in India are marred by issues of content and direction with the same questions, mostly related with foreign policy, being addressed repeatedly or in formulaic fashion over the years lacking in new substantive empirical input (Uberoi 2013: 187). Notwithstanding a growing interest in China's internal dynamics, such research still remains largely derivative depending on non-Chinese secondary sources due to lack of Chinese language skills among Indian researchers (Manoranjan Mohanty in Jacob 2012).

Second, China Studies in India also suffers from the domination of the foreign discourse and models of studying China such as sino-centrism, cultural relativism and modernization theories. Moreover, the number of comparative studies about India and China originating abroad far outnumbers those coming out from India (Manoranjan Mohanty in Jacob 2012).

Third, there is a general lack of financial support from government and the private sector especially for a multidisciplinary approach to the study of China—as opposed to studies related only to either China's strategic and military intentions or its economy, as is usually the case in most Indian think-tanks (Jacob 2012). Lack of access to quality language labs, textbooks, primary research materials, and lack of funds for long-term field work in China have also hemmed in the efforts to enhance the research skills of Indian researchers.

Fourth, the institutionalized silofication of foreign language studies and social sciences/humanities in Indian academic structures and programmes also adversely affects the nurturing of scholars well versed in the disciplinary research methodologies and Chinese language. A curriculum which integrates language study, disciplinary expertise, and imparts analytical tools remains conspicuously absent in India.

Fifth, the number of institutions, both university departments and think tanks, engaged in the study, research and teaching of China in India has been abysmally small, and not at all commensurate with the size of both countries and the importance of China for India. Moreover, the majority is located in Delhi, which hampers the growth of diverse opinions on China (Thampi 2021: 7; Thakur 2020: 534).

The state of China Studies in India also speaks for the overall condition of higher education in India. There are no Indian institutions in the list of the top 100 global universities. To expect China Studies in India to be globally competitive is perhaps expecting too much. However, given the importance of China to the strategic and economic affairs of India, it is imperative that the Indian government devotes sufficient resources to developing the field of China Studies (Sen 2013: 28). The fact that China Studies in India must also learn to raise funds on their own and in such a manner as to preserve their academic independence and integrity also needs to be reiterated in this regard (Jacob 2012). Nevertheless, the lack of Chinese language skills among students of China in India, or what this chapter prefers to call the Chinese language challenge, lies at the core of the inability to break new ground in China Studies in India, and create new analytical models and research methodologies by utilizing primary sources.

18.6 The Chinese Language Challenge of China Studies in India

The building of synergy between language skills and disciplinary research skills has been the core problem of China Studies in India since the very beginning. Scholars with language fluency have mostly specialized in literature and culture, and have lacked background in social science disciplines, while those with solid social science training normally lack language fluency (Sahni 2009: 64).

The Institute of Chinese Studies, New Delhi, has been regularly undertaking assessments and reviews of the development and evolution of China Studies in India for nearly half a century now, and the following words from the latest assessment must be enough to ring the alarm bells:

> *In doing research on China here, one of the biggest hurdles today seems to be, much as it was fifteen years ago, the use of the Chinese language to do research—whether this means using primary and secondary sources in Chinese, or conducting research in the field directly without interpreters. The number of students in India who have learnt some Chinese has gone up significantly, but the number of Indian scholars who utilise Chinese sources in their research remains low. Without this, it hardly needs to be said, very little work that is original, that contributes to the already existing scholarship on China, can be done. Incentives must be put in place to encourage researchers who utilise Chinese seriously in their research.* (Thampi 2021: 24)

However, before delving into the nature and characteristics of this Chinese language challenge it is also important to underscore what does it mean to learn Chinese language well. As Tan (1986) puts it:

> *But what a Chinese language teacher deals with is not merely a language. The Chinese script, for instance, is an ancient phenomenon, with two thousand years of history. We are dealing with a subject which is the embodiment of one of the longest and richest cultures and civilizations of the world. To learn 'bazaar Chinese' might be as easy as learning 'bazaar English'. But to speak Chinese well on all subjects, to read with ease ancient and modern Chinese books, to write seven to ten thousand Chinese characters without stroke and grammatical mistakes, and to translate Chinese literature into fluent English or an Indian language, surely require much greater effort than they do in any other language.* (Tan 1986: 175).

Yet learning is just one side of the coin, and how to teach Chinese language is the other, and as this section will illustrate there are a plethora of issues in teaching of Chinese language as well. Today, Chinese language courses of varying durations are being offered at more than 30 private and public universities all over India (see Table 18.1, it lists the names of institutions which offer Chinese language programmes in India, mentions the courses offered and the faculty strength in respective institutions). Almost all the Chinese language teachers in India employed in government universities have spent time in China learning Chinese language and literature on prestigious government scholarships after graduating from their Indian alma maters. They have learnt Chinese so well that some could also work effortlessly as simultaneous interpreters at high-level conferences. But knowing and learning Chinese well does not automatically translate into teaching it well, since the Chinese

Table 18.1 List of Universities offering Chinese language programmes in India

	Name of the university	Courses offered in Chinese language	Number of Permanent faculty members
1	Aligarh Muslim University	B.A. (H), M.A	1
2	Amity University, Noida (Taiwan Education Centre)	Elective course	Visiting faculty
3	Amity University, Jaipur	Elective course	1
4	Banaras Hindu University	Certificate, Diploma & B.A., M.A., PhD	4
5	Bangalore University	Certificate & Diploma	Visiting faculty
6	Bhimrao Ambedkar Marathwada University	Certificate & Diploma	1
7	Central University of Gujarat	B.A. (H), M.A	4
8	Central University of Jharkhand	Certificate, PG Diploma, 5 years integrated (UG/PG) master's degree	3
9	Department of East Asian Studies, University of Delhi	PG Diploma in Chinese, MA in East Asian Studies	1
10	Doon University	Certificate, B.A. (H), M.A. & 5 Years Integrated B.A., M.A	2
11	IIT Madras (Taiwan Education Centre)	China Studies Centre, PhD programme	Visiting faculty
12	IIT Mumbai (Taiwan Education Centre)	Chinese (Mandarin) Communication Course	Visiting faculty
13	IK Gujral Punjab Technical University	Chinese Language Basic Course	Guest faculty
14	Jadavpur University	Certificate	Guest faculty
15	Jamia Millia Islamia (Taiwan Education Centre)	Certificate & Diploma	1
16	Jawaharlal Nehru University	B.A. (H), M.A., M.Phil., Ph.D	11
17	KR Mangalam University, Gurugram	B.A. (H) Chinese	0
18	Magadh University	Diploma	Guest faculty
19	Mahatma Gandhi Antarrashtriya Hindi VishwaVidyalaya,Wardha	Certificate, Diploma, Advanced Diploma, B.A.& M.Phil	1
20	Manipur University	Certificate	Guest faculty
21	MDU Rohtak	Certificate	Guest faculty

(continued)

Table 18.1 (continued)

	Name of the university	Courses offered in Chinese language	Number of Permanent faculty members
22	Mumbai University (Confucius Institute)	HSK courses and B.A	Guest faculty
23	Nava Nalanda Mahavihara, Nalanda, Bihar	Diploma	Guest faculty
24	OP Jindal Global University, Sonipat (Taiwan Education Centre)	Centre for India-China Studies (CICS) Credit and non-credit elective Mandarin language courses offered to various degree students	Visiting faculty
25	Panjab University	Certificate & Diploma	1
26	Pondicherry University	Students of Pondicherry University have been extended the facility of doing short-term courses in Sichuan University, China	
27	Sanchi University of Buddhist - Indic Studies	Certificate, Diploma & M.A	1
28	Shiv Nadar University	UG electives	Visiting faculty
29	Sikkim University	Certificate Course, BA (Hons), MA and Ph.D	3
30	SRM Institute of Science and Technology (formerly known as SRM University), Chennai, (Taiwan Education Centre)	Certificate	Visiting faculty
31	Tezpur University	Certificate & Elective courses	2
32	The English and Foreign Languages University (EFLU), Hyderabad	Certificate & Diploma, B.A. (H)	2
33	University of Calcutta	Certificate & Diploma	Visiting faculty
34	Various Colleges under University of Delhi	Certificate and Diploma	Taught by guest faculty
35	Vellore Institute of Technology (Confucius Institute)	The Chinese Language Centre (CLC) at VIT. Chinese Training Programs.Beginners and Advanced level courses in Chinese Language	Visiting faculty
36	Visva Bharati Santiniketan	B.A.(H), M.A., M.Phil., Ph.D	6

language programmes in Indian universities does not impart 'teaching skills' per se, and basic pedagogical training regarding how to effectively teach Chinese language is not available in India institutions. Furthermore, there isn't a standard teaching method available to the Chinese language teachers in India as well.[3] Of late some teacher training programs are being offered by China and Taiwan. Cheena Bhavana, Visva-Bharati University Santiniketan also organized one such programme in Feb. 2017, but they are far too less and sporadic. The UGC NET exam in Chinese language falls far short of assessing the teaching skills of a candidate and has actually become a test of assessing rot learning through a set of MCQs.

18.7 Faculty Crunch

Over the past decade or so many new institutions have started Chinese language programmes in addition to the old institutions like Jawaharlal Nehru University, University of Delhi, Visva-Bharati Santiniketan, Banaras Hindu University, Panjab University and Bhimrao Ambedkar Marathwada University. The new institutions are Doon University, Central University of Jharkhand, Central University of Gujarat, Sikkim University, Aligarh Muslim University, Mahatma Gandhi Antarrashtriya Hindi VishwaVidyalaya Wardha (MGAHV), Mumbai University, Sanchi University of Buddhist—Indic Studies, The English and Foreign Languages University (EFLU), Hyderabad, KR Mangalam University, Gurugram, various Taiwan Education Centres and Confucius Institutes most notably at Mumbai University among several others. Among these only Doon University, Central University of Gujarat, Sikkim University, Aligarh Muslim University, and Central University of Jharkhand are offering B.A. and M.A. programmes in Chinese. KR Mangalam University Gurugram and MGAHV Wardha, EFLU Hyderabad have also started offering B.A. Chinese, whereas Mumbai University is offering B.A. for last few years. However, none of these new universities have adequate number of UGC stipulated faculty strength of 4 assistant professors, 2 associate professors, and 1 professor to properly run a department in an efficient manner. Hence, at most of the places permanent faculty is being assisted by guest lecturers to run the programmes. Moreover, all the permanent faculty members at these new institutions are assistant professors with just a handful having completed their Ph.Ds.

Due to the lack of adequate faculty, the quality of teaching tends to suffer. With limited remuneration and no prospects for career advancement the motivation levels of guest faculty members remain low, and they are not inspired enough to put in extra efforts. The few permanent faculty members remain over-burdened most of the times. As a result, even after putting in more than twenty-four hours of teaching per week sometimes a faculty is not able to complete the syllabus in an effective manner.

[3] This is in stark contrast to the teaching of Hindi in China. Today Hindi language courses of various duration are taught in seventeen institutions in China, all of which follows a uniform syllabus. (Information shared by an Indian faculty who teaches Hindi in China).

The issue of resource allocation also gets aggravated due to the absence of senior faculty members in Chinese language departments, mostly in the institutions which have been established in last two decades. Moreover, smaller Chinese language departments are generally subsumed under a bigger department of foreign languages which tend to adversely affect the academic autonomy of Chinese language programmes sometimes.[4]

18.8 Pedagogical Bottlenecks

Being a paratactic language written in characters and different from Indo-European alphabetical language learning Chinese requires greater effort on the part of Indian learners. This 'greater effort' could be best understood in terms of intensive nature of teaching and learning of Chinese language. It is pertinent to note here that intensive teaching or training in Chinese language must involve 15–20 hours of serious classroom teaching per week for not less than 3 years. The classroom teaching should be focused on honing the four core skills: (a) speaking Chinese properly in tones; (b) reading Chinese with proper intonation and prosody; (c) writing Chinese characters stroke-wise neatly; and (d) listening and comprehending the words of native Chinese speakers. The teaching outcome is measured objectively in terms of a students' ability to clear the Chinese Proficiency Test (汉语水平考试) Level 5 or ideally Level 6 after little more effort on completion of under-graduation in Chinese.

Hence, it is noteworthy that the certificate and diploma courses (many times even degree courses, when not taught properly) offered by most of the institutions in India may lack the above-mentioned intensity and are unable to take students very far in their endeavour of learning Chinese. After a certificate or a diploma course, it is a must that the student must persist with further studying Chinese language either in a degree program or an advanced diploma course in India, China or some Chinese speaking region, if they really intend to excel.

18.9 Curriculum Woes

In the realm of Chinese language teaching in India *Elementary Chinese Readers* (*ECR*), first published way back in 1980 and subsequently revised several times, have assumed the status of the most holy book of Chinese teaching–learning. While it remains a very useful textbook, the problem starts when it is used for teaching different courses or skills like spoken/communicative Chinese, listening Chinese, and writing & comprehension. The core competency of the *ECR* remains the lucidity

[4] A separate department of Chinese language does not exist in institutions like AMU, CUJ, Mumbai University, MGAHV Wardha, BRA Marathwada University Aurangabad. The Department of German in Mumbai University offers B.A. in Chinese.

with which it explains basic Chinese grammar to entry level students. For teaching different courses say for listening or spoken Chinese there is a need to use different coursebooks. Instead of being the only textbook, *ECR* could serve as one of the few books.

Another omnipresent practice wherever Chinese is taught is that of giving handouts to students for teaching a variety of courses. However, this practice generally proves inadequate in nurturing desired skills among students as they end up studying a course in a haphazard manner. Here it is important to bear in mind that over the last four decades since the compilation of the *ECR* a revolution has taken place in the field of teaching of Chinese as foreign language in China. "Teaching of Chinese as a Foreign Language" (对外汉语专业) is well-established in China as an independent discipline with numerous institutions offering UG, PG and PhD degrees. The practice of teaching Chinese to foreigners has its own economics and politics in China and beyond. Several series of well-researched and well-structured textbooks and course books have been compiled in China by teams of teachers engaged in teaching of Chinese language to foreigners for last several decades. Such course books can also be utilised in India to ensure desired learning and teaching outcomes. In other words, while it is beyond question that textbooks for teaching Chinese should be developed indigenously in India, keeping in mind the linguistic and pedagogical requirements of Indian students, but in the meantime, one should also keep abreast with latest developments in the same field in China, especially while choosing and selecting the course material for Indian students.

18.10 Chinese Language and Academic Research

Whenever they are confronted with the question why they are studying Chinese, most students tend to reply that they are studying Chinese for earning money. In this monetary reductionism of Chinese language, it becomes tough for China Studies to attract talent. It takes anywhere between 4 and 5 years of serious intensive study for someone to really attain a certain level of Chinese when one reaches the stage of reading and understanding the Chinese journal articles, newspapers, and translating effortlessly between Chinese and some other target language and vice-versa. One rarely find such students in social sciences or other domains who are ready to spend that much of time to study Chinese. In other words, some social science students are keen to learn the Chinese, but they don't have the time required for gaining expertise in it. Simply put, one can read much more of English material (books, articles and so on) than Chinese in a given amount of time. Moreover, financially lucrative options available in the corporate sector and business world act as a pull factor for people with good Chinese skills. So, in the end only a genuine interest in academics, and reasonably strong financial support could sustain a student in the endeavour of mastering Chinese in the long run.

18.11 Chinese Language Challenge of India's Defence Forces

A lot of China-watching in India remains obsessed with "security issues" yet the need and requirement of defence institutions with regards to imparting of Chinese language skills to its officers and personnel is hardly discussed seriously. The School of Foreign Languages, New Delhi under the aegis of the Ministry of Defence, India was among the earliest institutions to start a Chinese language course in 1948.[5] Post 1962, Army Educational Corps (AEC) Training College and Centre, Pachmarhi also started a Chinese language programme in 1963. However, the Indian Army personnel hardly get an opportunity to hone their linguistic skills in a native environment. The level of exposure available to the Chinese language instructors in the army is also very limited.[6] There is an urgent need to scrutinize the syllabus and curriculum of various courses taught in the above institutions given the fact that the Indian defence forces are perennially involved in interacting with their Chinese counterparts. How well they interpret during such interactions is a question worth pondering over which in turn also underscores the need to acknowledge and address the Chinese language challenge faced by the Indian defence forces.

Before discussing the ways to address the Chinese language challenge facing China Studies in India, this chapter seeks to locate it in the broader context of how India is studied in Chinese institutions of higher education.

18.12 India Studies in China

China's interest in studying India have been guided by different factors at different stages in China's history. In ancient times, it started with the study and translation of Buddhist scriptures into Chinese language. Spread of Buddhism in Asia engendered an exchange of ideas, practices and goods unmatched in human history. The

[5] School of Foreign Languages, https://www.ids.nic.in/sfl.php. Accessed on 10 Dec 2020. The SFL conducts the following courses: -

1. Certificate of Proficiency (COP) Courses: COP is a part time course of one year duration for defence personnel posted at Delhi, their dependents and civilians.
2. Advance Diploma of Proficiency (ADOP) Courses: The ADOP is a part time course for one year—only personnel who have cleared COP can appear for the ADOP.
3. Interpreter Ship Courses: The Interpreter ship Course is the Flagship course at the SFL and is a full-time course that ranges from 16 ½ to 23 ½ months duration. This is subscribed by personnel sponsored by the Services.

[6] The author had an opportunity to interact with Indian Army personnel while teaching Chinese language at the National Defence Academy, Khadakwasla.

arrival of Britishers and Opium Wars (1839–1842 and 1856–1860) renewed Chinese interest in India. India became the 'negative example' of a great ancient civilization reduced to a British colony, a fate which China was to avoid at any cost. During the early twentieth century some Chinese intellectuals saw some common traits between India's national movement and China's struggle for overthrowing foreign rule and attaining national unification. Post establishment of the Republic of India in 1947 and the People's Republic of China (PRC) in 1949, the two countries enjoyed robust exchanges till the outbreak of hostilities in 1962. India's nuclear explosion in 1998 and then Indian Defence Minister George Fernandes declaring China as India's 'enemy No 1' further drove China's interest in India at the beginning of the twenty-first century. For Chinese, besides marked by several 'Cs' and 'Ts', the India-China relationship is also a "four-in-one" relationship ('四位一体'), namely, a relationship between neighbouring countries, major powers, developing countries and a relationship playing important role on multilateral forums (Chen 2012: 32). Thus, India remains a key focus of study in China both as an ancient civilization and a modern neighbour.

18.13 Chinese Indology

The interest shown in India by the proponents of both Self-Strengthening Movement (洋务派) and Reform Movement (维新派), revival of Buddhism and the introduction of western knowledge in China during late-Qing period played a significant role in incorporation of India as a subject of study in Chinese universities in the beginning of the twentieth century (Zhang 2017). Peking University took the lead in starting a course on Indian Philosophy in 1916. The course was initially taught by Xu Jishang [许丹(季上)], and 1917 onwards by Liang Shuming (梁漱溟) (Jiang & Yan 2018: 2; Wang 1998: 98). In fact, Peking University emerged as the cradle of Chinese Indology under the able leadership of Cai Yuanpei (蔡元培), who as the president of Peking University was instrumental in introducing the course on Indian Philosophy. Scholars like Hu Shi (胡适) (1891–1962), Chen Yinke (陈寅恪) (1890–1969), Tang Yongtong (汤用彤) (1893–1964), Xu Dishan (许地山) (1894–1941), Xiang Da (向达) (1900–1966) among others helped in laying a solid foundation for Chinese Indology at the Peking University which eventually led to the watershed of establishment of the Department of Oriental Languages and Literature (东方语言文学系) at Peking University in 1946 (Wang 1998: 101). Ji Xianlin (季羡林) (1911–2009), a former student of Chen Yinke and a PhD from Göttingen University with major in Sanskrit, Pali, Tocharian acted as the founding director of the department and was joined by Jin Kemu (金克木) (1912–2000) in 1948 who had studied Sanskrit and Pali in India (Wang 1998: 101). Together they not only developed Peking University into a hub of Chinese Indology but even more importantly trained and nurtured the next generations of China's India scholars.

Since then, the Chinese Indology has broadly progressed along three trajectories: first, the release of new materials, that is the newly discovered manuscripts, mainly

Buddhist manuscripts. The series on "Sanskrit Texts from the Tibet Autonomous Region" (STTAR) jointly published by the China Tibetology Research Center and the Austrian Academy of Sciences and the "Sanskrit Pattra-leaf manuscript and Buddhist Documents Series" of Peking University are illustrative in this regard. Second, the translation and introduction of classical Indian literature in China. Chinese translation of the *Ramayan* and the *Mahabharata* is illustrative in this context (Liu 2015). Third, the historiography of China–India cultural contacts or 'Sino-Indology', a field of study that favours a perspective that looks at India in relation to China in contrast to traditional Indology which considers India a self-contained cultural entity (Jiang and Yan 2018: 4). As will be shown below, the academic output of Chinese Indology has been nothing short of impressive both in terms of quality and quantity.

18.14 Teaching of Indian Languages and India Centres

That the study of Indian languages, both classical like Sanskrit and Pali and modern like Hindi, Urdu, Bengali and so on were considered important to study India in China became evident early on. Ji Xianlin and Jin Kemu established and nurtured the Sanskrit and Pali programmes at Peking University. The first Hindi programme in China was launched in 1942 at the National Institute of Oriental Languages in Yunnan (云南东方语文专科学校) (Yan 2019: 220). It was mainly designed to train wartime language specialists and merged into Peking University in 1949. Peking University began China's first Urdu programme in 1954. Beijing Broadcasting Institute (today's Communication University of China) followed by introducing degree programmes in Tamil, Urdu, Bengali, Hindi and Assamese in the 1960s (Yan 2019: 220). Beginning of such programmes in Indian languages manifested an increased awareness of Indian multilingualism in China which in turn laid a foundation for the development of Indian Studies (涉及印度的研究/印度问题研究) in contemporary China.

Since then, there has been a steady increase in the number of universities offering degree programmes in Indian languages. The number of universities offering undergraduate degree programme in Hindi has soared from three in 2000 to fifteen in 2017 (Jiang and Yan 2018: 7). Peking University opened Bengali courses in 2004. Beijing Foreign Studies University (北京外国语大学) opened Hindi and Urdu majors in 2006 and 2007. Xi'an International Studies University (西安外国语大学) opened the Hindi major in 2006. Yunnan Nationalities University (云南民族大学), Guangdong University of Foreign Studies (广东外语外贸大学), and Shanghai International Studies University (上海外国语大学) opened the Hindi major in 2011 (Yu 2018: 10). Communication University of China (中国传媒大学), Beijing International Studies University (北京第二外国语学院), Tianjin Foreign Studies University (天津外国语大学), Xizang Minzu University (西藏民族大学 (陕西省), Sichuan International Studies University (四川外国语大学), School of International Relations, National University of Defense Technology, PLA (中国人民解放军国防科技大学国际关系学院), PLA University of Foreign Language (解放军外国语学院) and

Yunnan University (云南大学) are some other institutions which offer programmes in Hindi in China.

In terms of research institutions, the Departments of Philosophy, History, the School of International Relations, and the Institute of Asian and African Studies at Peking University; Institute of South Asian Studies, Sichuan University, as well as the Shanghai Academy of Social Sciences, the Yunnan Academy of Social Sciences, Fudan University, Zhejiang University, Hangzhou Buddhist College have scholars engaged in doing research on India.

With an aim to advance region and country specific studies and research, China has also established Centre for India Studies (印度研究中心) in Peking University in 2003, Shenzhen University in 2005, Shanghai International Studies University (上海外国语大学), Lanzhou University (兰州大学) in 2009, Central China Normal University (华中师范大学) in 2018, and Beijing International Studies University (北京第二外国语学院). University-based research centres (e.g., the Centre for South Asian Studies at Peking University) generally have a multidisciplinary/interdisciplinary set-up, whereas non-university-based institutes (e.g., China Institute of Contemporary International Relations) focus more on current affairs and political strategy (Jiang & Yan 2018: 8).

Since the last decade of the twentieth century, the main locations of India-related studies in Chinese academia are the Department of History and School of International Studies of Peking University (北京大学国际关系学院、历史系); China Institutes of Contemporary International Relations (中国现代国际关系研究院); China Institute of International Studies (中国国际问题研究所); Institute of World Economy and Politics, Institute of Asia and Pacific Studies and Research Center for Chinese Borderland History and Geography of the Chinese Academy of Social Sciences (中国社会学院亚洲太平科洋研究所、世界经济与政治研究所、中国边疆史地研究中心); China Institute of International Strategic Studies (中国国际战略研究会); Institute of South Asian Studies of Sichuan University (四川大学南亚研究所); Department of History and Department of International Relations of Yunnan University (云南大学历史系、国际关系系), Shanghai Institute of International Studies (上海国际问题研究所), Institute of Asia and Pacific Studies of Shanghai Academy of Social Sciences (上海社会科学院亚洲太平洋研究所), Department of Foreign Military Studies of Academy of Military Sciences, People's Liberation Army (中国人民解放军军事科学院外国军事研究部), Tibet and South Asia Research Office, Kunming Army Military Academy, People's Liberation Army (中国人民解放军昆明陆军军事学院西藏及南亚研究室), etc. (Chen 2008: 4–5).

More than a dozen scholars work on India studies in the national think tank of China—the Chinese Academy of Social Sciences (CASS). Under CASS, the National Institute of International Strategy (中国社会科学院亚太与全球战略研究院), the Sanskrit Center of Institute of Foreign Literature (梵文研究中心), the Institute of Foreign Literature (外国文学研究所), the Institute of World Religions (世界宗教研究所), the Institute of Philosophy (哲学研究所) are doing research work on India-China relations, Indian history, religion, philosophy, literatures, society, politics, economy, and so on (Liu 2013: 13).

According to Liu Jian (刘建), Director and Researcher of the Cultural Office of the Institute of Asia–Pacific Studies, Chinese Academy of Social Sciences, and Deputy Editor-in-Chief, *South Asian Studies* (《南亚研究》), as of 2013 more than 100 scholars were conducting research on India covering almost all the major areas related to India. This group of scholars are increasingly visible in Chinese academia through their research work, writings and appearances in TV shows and seek to present a comprehensive view of the developments in various areas in India (Liu 2013: 15). Interestingly, there has been popularisation of academic knowledge and the professionalization of popular knowledge with regards to knowledge creation on India in China. Chinese researchers on India have embraced popular mediums like internet and social media to make their ideas more accessible. And there has also been a growth in numbers of non-academic groups, individuals not affiliated with research institutes or universities, self-trained enthusiasts, India-based Chinese workers, travellers and so on who provide popular knowledge about India (Jiang & Yan 2018: 9). It is noteworthy here that the significance attached to India as part of Area Studies in China lies at the core of the above trend.

18.15 India Studies as Area Studies (涉及印度的研究/印度问题研究)

During the 1950s, Indology remained the primary focus of the Chinese academia and a very limited number of Chinese scholars focused on the political and economic developments in India, and China-India bilateral relations (Liu 2013: 9). India Studies under the rubric of Area Studies officially began in China with the establishment of the Institute of South Asian Studies (南亚研究所) jointly by the Chinese Academy of Social Sciences and the Peking University in 1978. Soon after its establishment, the Institute recruited a group of graduate students, and almost all of the topics studied were related to India. These graduate students graduated in the early 1980s, and most of them still work in relevant universities and research institutions, forming the backbone of academic research conducted on India in China. The "*South Asian Studies*" (《南亚研究》) edited and published by the Institute, and the "*South Asian Southeast Asian Review*" (《南亚东南亚评论》) published later, have always been the most important academic publications related to India studies in China. This institute-later renamed the Institute of South Asia and Southeast Asia (南亚东南亚研究所)-was run until 1991, and finally merged into the Institute of Asia and Africa (亚非研究所) and the Department of Oriental Studies (东方学系) at Peking University. Although the Institute of South Asia and Southeast Asia only existed for 14 years, but it was the hub of research on South Asia in China, produced a sizeable academic output, and cultivated the next generation of researchers (Wang 1998: 104).

Owing to India's nuclear experiments and a rising global profile, India Studies in China experienced a multidisciplinary turn through the last decade of the twentieth century under an epistemological urgency felt by Chinese academia to understand

India in a holistic manner holding together India's past with the present. This time period saw Chinese scholars with sound theoretical and methodological training work on India in disciplines such as history, political science, economics etc. (Jiang & Yan 2018: 6).

Today, Chinese academic studies on India can be divided into three categories according to the different research objects: studies on Indian issues, studies on Sino-Indian relations and studies on relations between India and third parties. Since the 1990s, academic monographs on India-related studies produced in China can be divided into three categories. (1) works on China-India relations including the contemporary history of China-India relations, the history of China-India relations before the founding of the PRC, the existing relationship between China and India, the comparative study of contemporary China and India, and the relationship between southwest China and India. (2) Works on the study of Indian issues, including the study of Indian history and national conditions, the study of Indian economic development and economic reform, the study of Indian political, legal and military issues. The study of Indian culture and society, the study of Indian issues most directly related to the study of Sino-Indian relations (such as international relations in South Asia, India's rise and its impact, Indian diplomacy, and exploring the relationship between Indian culture and national defence). (3) Monographs on the study of India's relations with third parties (Chen 2008: 6–14).

In recent years, the National Social Science Fund of China (中国国家社会科学基金) has approved a bunch of projects concerning practical issues (现实问题) and traditional Indology (传统印度学) (Yin 2018: 88). The former includes research on issues such as the Sino-Indian boundary issue, the Belt and Road Initiative involving South Asia, the Indian Ocean region, the Indian think tanks, various dimensions of Sino-Indian relations and so on. The later include study of Sanskrit and Pali Buddhist scriptures, the history of Indian literary theory, "Natyasastra", "Arthashastra", poetry of Kabir, comparison of Chinese and Indian Buddhist literature, Chinese Indology, Indian English literature and so on (Yin 2018: 88). This funding pattern flowing from the top and its institutional operation clearly betrays a focus on both the classical studies and contemporary issues concerning India, and its success can also be gauged from the academic output on India in China.

18.16 Academic Output

Between June 2001 and June 2020, Zhu Xiaolan (朱晓兰) of the National Library of China has published 27 bibliographies of Indology (《中国印度学总书目》) *in South Asian Studies* (《南亚研究》). On the basis of the information available with the author till the year 2013, the bibliography shows that China in the past decades has published 425 books on Indian philosophy and Buddhism, 57 books on Indian social sciences, 154 books on Indian politics, 55 books on Indian military affairs, 88 books on Indian economics, 35 books on Indian culture and education, 46 books on Indian linguistics, 350 books on Indian literature, 33 books on Indian art, 62 books on

Indian history, 78 books on Indian science and technology, medicine, environment, among others. Moreover, about 800 books as well as electron compact discs have been published in Hong Kong and Taiwan (Liu 2013: 13).

Yet another estimate by Prof. Yu Longyu (郁龙余), Director of Centre for Indian Studies, Shenzhen University, shows that nearly 700 Chinese books in the field of broad India studies were published in China between 1925 to 2016. Among them, at least 163 were on Indian literature, 155 on Indian philosophy, 15 on Indian religions, 86 on Indian history, and 44 on Indian languages, and 32 on Indian art, 64 on Indian culture and society, and at least 21 were on the relationship between India and China, India and Central Asian regions or the Western Regions, and the history of transportation. And manifesting the growing interest in India Studies, more than 420 important works, including research papers, translations, and monographs were published on India between 2000 and 2016 (Yu 2018: 11).

It is also noteworthy here that the 'List of Select Works of Chinese Scholars on India' in the Appendix of the *Encyclopedia of India-China Cultural Contacts*, Vol. 2 consists of 623 works, whereas the 'List of Select Works of Indian Scholars on China' only consists of 81 works.[7]

The following search results obtained through CNKI also highlights the academic output related to India in China[8]:

China National Knowledge Infrastructure (CNKI) search results:

Key word	Search categories	Numbers	Url
India	Thesis and dissertation	2451	https://global.cnki.net/kns/brief/default_result.aspx
India	Journal articles	7,336	https://global.cnki.net/kns/brief/default_result.aspx
India	Total Literature	7,867	https://global.cnki.net/kns/brief/default_result.aspx

Overall, when juxtaposed with the output of India Studies in China, China Studies in India seem to be lacking on almost every front. According to Prof. B. R. Deepak (2020) be it research on China or translation of Chinese works in Indian languages, India's performance appears abysmal.

[7] *Encyclopedia of India-China Cultural Contacts*. 2014. Vol. 2, pp. 975–991. http://www.mea.gov.in/images/pdf/India-ChinaEncyclopedia_Vol-2.pdf Accessed 15 July 2021.

[8] A corresponding data could not be collected with regards to India due to the absence of a CNKI like database in India. CNKI lists almost every scholarly publication like journal articles, thesis and dissertations being published in China.

18.17 Solving the Chinese Language Challenge of China Studies in India

Surmounting the Chinese language challenge in India requires a multipronged approach. First, there is a need to train a greater number of students in Chinese language in an intensive result-oriented manner. Given the handful of universities where degree programmes in Chinese are being offered, the total number of students pursuing a degree programme in Chinese language all over India would be around 1000 at best, while there must be several thousand students pursuing some sort of certificate or diploma course in Chinese.

As the way forward, this chapter contends that the students pursuing a degree course in Chinese language provides the best resources who could be trained into disciplinary research by way of first providing them solid grounding in Chinese language through intensive training for three years enabling them to clear Chinese Proficiency Test (HSK) Level 5 at least or ideally Level 6; and then—-presupposing that they would stay to pursue an M. A.—training them in disciplinary knowledge in social sciences, methodological and research tools, and reading and analysis of primary Chinese sources at the post- graduate level, albeit in Chinese language. Obviously, this also requires the Chinese language teachers to put in some extra efforts. The contention is that the Chinese language departments in Indian universities should be imagined as more than just 'foreign language departments' whose purview is limited to language, culture and literature. A robust element of disciplinary studies should also be introduced in them at PG levels to make them multidisciplinary in a true sense. The need for synergy between Chinese language and other disciplines is but obvious since a genuine China expert should have both the linguistic as well as research skills.

At the UG level the learners should be made to inculcate standard Chinese pronunciations, tones, prosody and strokes right from the very beginning through audio-lingual pedagogy which should evolve to a communicative approach of empowering the learners through small conversations, dialogues, presentations and situation-based writing assignments. In fact, a combination of audiolingual, grammar translation and communicative approaches could be utilised without assigning preponderance to one teaching approach in the classroom at the cost of the other. Learners should be empowered through andragogical techniques as they progress to advanced levels. In all this, the choice of the teaching material should be intrinsically linked with the goal of nurturing the four skills of speaking, listening, reading and writing Chinese, and laying a solid foundation of Chinese language on which a learner could very well progress further.

In this context, there are two paths available for teaching Chinese. First is the ideal one which requires 'Indianization' of the content, style, pedagogy, and textbooks. But this is also easier said than done. For instance, it has taken almost four decades, several institutions, and hundreds of teachers and researchers to compile textbooks for teaching Chinese as a foreign language in China. In India, there is sheer absence of such resources, be it funding or manpower. While 'Indianization' is desirable, given the present constraints it is not practical to implement and not expected to succeed. Hence in the meantime, the best possible option is to align the undergraduate teaching of Chinese language in India more closely with the HSK (Chinese Proficiency Test), PRC and Test of Chinese as Foreign Language (TOCFL), Taiwan standards, both of which advocate a graded approach of moving from beginners to advanced, easy to tough standards of learning Chinese in a time bound manner and then evaluating the learners' skills through a comprehensive test of speaking, listening, reading and comprehension abilities.

18.18 Conclusion

It goes without saying that China Studies in India cannot go very far without surmounting the Chinese language challenge. A China expert sans Chinese language remains deprived of the ability to engage and glean through the enormous wealth of primary sources in Chinese language. With such a handicap one can neither contribute original research nor could develop an 'Indian understanding' on China. Hence, there is an urgent need to streamline the teaching of Chinese language in India by recruiting adequate faculty members in institutions of higher learning and updating the pedagogy. The need is also to break the silos in which teaching of disciplines and foreign languages operate in Indian academia to truly nurture multidisciplinary, interdisciplinary and even transdisciplinary studies on China in India. Hope the National Education Policy 2020 will take some concrete steps in this regard.

References

Bajpai K (2021) India versus China: why they are not friends. Juggernaut, India

Bhattacharjea MS, Deshingkar G, et al (1988) Chinese studies in India: perspectives and programmes, a statement prepared by the China study group. China Rep 24(4):473–479

Chen M-M, Naina S (2021). China studies' coming of age story in Taiwan and a few pointers for India. https://www.vifindia.org/article/2021/august/05/china-studies-coming-of-age-story-in-taiwan-and-a-few-pointers-for-india. Accessed 20 Aug 2021

Chen Z (2008) Sino-Indian diplomatic relations after the cold war (1991–2007). World Knowledge Press, Beijing. 陈宗海. 2008.《冷战后中印外交关系研究 (1991–2007) 》, 世界知识出版社, 北京。

Chen Z (2012). The historical trend of 60 years of Sino-Indian relations and current situation—an analysis based on the Firsthand data mainly from Renmin daily. Int Forum 14:32–37. 陈宗海 ("中印关系60年的历史脉络与现实态势 ———以《人民日报》为主要一手资料的立论" 《国际论坛》2012年1月第14卷第1期, 第32–37页。

Deepak BR (2020) Know yourself, know your enemy. The Sunday Guardian. https://www.sundayguardianlive.com/opinion/know-know-enemy. Accessed 28 July 2021

Deshingkar G (1986) Sinology or area studies (Chinese studies in India–1). China Rep 22(1):77–81

Hu S, Jue W (2021) The behavioural logic behind India's tough foreign policy toward China. Contemp Int Relat 7:37–65. http://www.cicir.ac.cn/UpFiles/file/20201103/6373999766705249491072987.pdf. Accessed 20 July 2021

Jacob JT (2012) China studies in India: of caste, class and capital. https://indiandchina.com/2012/10/03/china-studies-in-india-of-caste-class-and-capital/. Accessed 20 July 2021

Jiang J, Yan J (2018) The history of the production of India-related knowledge in post-1950 China. Hist Compass 16:e12448. https://doi.org/10.1111/hic3.12448

Liu J (2013) Indian studies in China: an assessment. https://indiachinainstitute.org/wp-content/uploads/2014/04/Liu-Jian_Submission_2013_Edited.pdf. Accessed 10 July 2021

Liu Z (2015) India studies in China should start from "industry 1.0", 31 May 2015. 刘震, 2015, "中国印度学要从"工业1.0"做起", 2015–05–31, https://cul.qq.com/a/20150531/010537.htm. Accessed 10 July 2021

McGetchin DT (2009) Indology, indomania, and orientalism: ancient India's rebirth in modern Germany. Fairleigh Dickinson University Press, Vancouver

Sahni V (2009) The fallacies and flaws of area studies in India. Int Stud 46(1&2):49–68

Sen T (2013) Is there a need for China studies in India? Econ Polit Weekly 48(29):26–29

Sengupta I (2015) Indology. In: Encyclopedia of early modern history online. https://referenceworks.brillonline.com/entries/encyclopedia-of-early-modern-history-online/*-COM_021345. Accessed 12 Sep 2021

Tan C (1986) Teaching Chinese language in India (Chinese studies in India–2). China Rep 22(2):163–194

Thakur R (2020) Studying China in India: an historical review. MonumentaSerica 68(2):515–545. https://doi.org/10.1080/02549948.2020.1831266

Thampi M (ed) (2007) Review of China studies in India: a colloquium. Delhi, Institute of Chinese Studies, Occasional Studies, No, p 15

Thampi M (2021) Recent initiatives to promote China studies in India: a preliminary report and assessment. Institute of Chinese Studies Occasional Paper No. 66, Delhi. https://www.icsin.org/publications/recent-initiatives-to-promote-china-studies-in-india-a-preliminary-report-and-assessment. Accessed 10 July 2021

Uberoi P (2013) China studies in India-3. China Rep 49(2):185–196

Wang B (1998) Indology at Peking University: a review of eighty years. J Peking Univ (HumIties Soc Sci) general no.186 35(2):98–104. 王邦维 (1998) "北京大学的印度学研究: 八十年的回顾"《北京大学学报(哲学社会科学版)》1998 年第 2 期第 35 卷 (总 186 期), 第98–104页。

Wang VW-C (2012) The rise of China, the rise of India, and the changing geopolitics of Asia: contending perspectives on India–China relations. Politics Faculty Publications and Presentations. 43. Ithaca College Digital Commons @ IC. https://digitalcommons.ithaca.edu/politics_faculty_pubs. Accessed 10 July 2021

Yan J (2019) Beyond the "Bhai-Bhai" Rhetoric: China–India literary relations, 1950–1990. PhD thesis, Centre for Cultural, Literary and Postcolonial Studies, SOAS, University of London

Ye H (2013) Cooperation, coordination, competition and conflict coexist in the 21st century Sino-Indian relations. Natl Human Hist 20:41

Yin X (2018) Reflections on the basic features of China studies in India. South Asian Southeast Asian Stud 2018(2):82–89. 尹锡南 (2018) "印度的中国学研究发展规律及相关问题"《东南亚南亚研究》2018 年第 2 期, 第82–89页。

Yu L (2018) From Buddhist studies, sanskrit studies to indology: a review of chinese indology. J Shenzhen Univ (HumIties Soc Sci) 35(6):5–12. 郁龙余 (2018) "从佛学、梵学到印度学: 中国印度学脉络总述"《深圳大学学报 (人文社会科学版) 》第 35 卷第 6 期 2018 年 11 月, 第5–12页。

Zhang M (2017) @Goodbye to the Buddhist country of the yore: the beginning of modern Chinese Indology. In: Paper presented at the second world conference of indologists, cited in Wu Weilin. 2017. The second world conference of indologists: a summary. Journal of Shenzhen University (Humanities & Social Sciences) Vol. 34 No. 2 Mar. 2017, pp. 158–60. 张忞煜的 (2017)《再见昔日佛国: 中国现代印度学的滥觞 (1840~1916)》第二届世界印度学家大会上的报告,见于吴蔚琳 (2017) "第二届世界印度学家大会会议综述"《深圳大学学报》(人文社会科学版) 第 34 卷第 2 期 2017 年 3 月, 第158–60页

Zurndorfer HT (1995) China bibliography: a research guide to reference works about China past and present. Brill, Leiden

Chapter 19
Culture Specificity in Animal Idioms of Chinese Language and Its Parallels in Hindi

Arpana Raj

19.1 Introduction

Due to the differences in cultural traditions, ecological environments, life habits, historical developments, etc., People all around the world adopted different languages to communicate and express. As animals play a significant role in our lives, animal words eventually took a very important place in almost all languages. Human beings associate their feelings and emotions with several animals according to their unique characteristics, appearances, habits etc. as a result, the names of animals carry explicit cultural connotations. This paper explores idiom sets in the Chinese language where animal words are used.

The paper also studies how there is a similarity while using such expressions in Hindi. However, the similar animal words used in this paper will not necessarily always be an idiom. Some of such animal words in Hindi are proverbs, sayings and other phrases. The paper further focuses on the culture specificity presented in the animal idioms of the Chinese Language and Hindi.

19.2 Animals in Chinese Tradition

Since antiquity, human beings and animals have lived in close proximity in jungles and the lap of nature. Later on, as hunters or farmers, they continued their connection with animals and thus evolved several myths, legends, and folktales related to animals. Varieties of animals and creatures are reflected in myths and folktales. On the other hand, some creatures also get culture-specific meanings through myths,

A. Raj (✉)
Dept. of Far East Languages-Chinese, Central University of Jharkhand, Cheri-Manatu, Ranchi 835222, Jharkhand, India
e-mail: arpana.raj@cuj.ac.in; arpanaindia@yahoo.com

S. Mishra and R. Sheel (eds.), *India-China Dialogues Beyond Borders*,
https://doi.org/10.1007/978-981-99-4326-5_20

legends and folktales. However, other creatures found in Chinese myths—many-headed monsters, dragons, and unicorns—never existed in the real world (Animals in mythology n.d.). Animals have played an important role in human life since ancient times. With time and human development, the Chinese society underwent different phases from primitive, feudal, semi-colonial and semi-feudal to modern society. Also, it brought changes to the relationship between human beings and animals or nature. The core of the human-animal relationship is humans' attitudes towards animals. The linkage between human beings and animals is also reflected in myths, legends, folktales, and even idioms and proverbs.

19.3 Idioms

"An idiom is an expression, word, or phrase that has a figurative meaning that is comprehended in regard to a common use of that expression that is separate from the literal meaning or definition of the words of which it is made (Oxford dictionary 1992)". There are a large number of Chinese idioms (chéngyǔ, 成语) condensed over more than 5000 years of uninterrupted culture and civilization. The Chinese language contains thousands of pithy sayings and idioms that crystallize aspects of Chinese society, politics, art and literature. These idioms, still rolling off the tongues of Chinese people today, spring from the colourful pages of China's long history (Zhang 2000). Most of the Chinese idioms have a historical origin or stories behind them, and these historic events and stories are full of Chinese wisdom and life, which constitute an essential part of Chinese culture.

Most of the Chinese idioms consist of four Chinese characters. As mostly, chengyu are closely linked with various myths, legends, historical facts or stories from which they were originated. The figurative meaning differs typically from the literal meaning or surpasses the sum of literal meanings contained by the four characters.

China and India are Asian civilizations with wide historical, cultural, and geographic variety. Both share geographical and climatic characteristics and similarities in popular domestic and wild animals. Developing countries are centred on agriculture, and animals such as the ox, cow, and horse are comparable in both cultures; hence these animals are frequently employed in common idioms. Both Hindi and Chinese are complex languages with numerous animal idioms. However, the association may have distinct meanings due to the origins of the two languages in different cultural backgrounds, traditional practises, and religious beliefs, which appear in the idiom of animal words in their linguistic system. Chinese and Hindi possess a significant number of animal idioms. Some animal idioms are similar in both languages, having the same associative meanings and expressed by the same animal carriers. However, the exact meaning is sometimes expressed by two different animal carriers in the two languages. For example, the Chinese idioms meaning mighty, fierce and powerful are mostly expressed by using the animal word 'tiger' which is usually expressed by using the animal 'lion' in Hindi idioms. However, all the animal idioms do not necessarily find an equivalent counterpart in the other language. Sometimes, it is also possible that only one language idiom possesses the animal word as a metaphor, and its counterpart in the other language does not carry any animal word in that. Although Chinese and Hindi contain many animal words, the two countries have vastly different cultural backgrounds and ways of thinking. Because of the cultural variances, animal idioms of Chinese and Hindi have diverse figurative meanings. As China is an ancient civilization and possesses rich animal idioms, this paper will deal with the essential culture-specific vehicles in the Chinese language.

19.3.1 Same Animal Vehicles Used in Similar Chinese and Hindi Idioms

The study found that the two neighbours with ancient civilizations share similarities in cultural connotations attached with some animal words and idioms carrying it like frog, parrot, dog, ostrich etc. For example, the Chinese idiom Jǐngdǐzhīwā (井底之蛙, frog at the bottom of the well) also has a frog in the Hindi parallel idiom कुँएकामेंढक (Kuen ka mendhak), गूलरकाकीड़ा (gūlarkākīdā) with the same figurative meaning 'A person with a minimal vision'. The Chinese idiom Yīngwǔxuéshé (鹦鹉学舌, a parrot repeating a person's words) and it's Hindi parallel तोतेकीतरहरटना (tote kitarahraṭna), both carry the same bird reflecting same meaning 'Echo another's words without thinking or understanding'. Similarly, the Chinese idiom with dog, Gǒutuǐzi (狗腿子, dog's legs; dog at the threshold) and its Hindi parallel दहलीजकाकुत्ताहोना (dahlij ka Kuttahona) have the same meaning 'A parasite; hired thug; henchman'. The animal idioms with ostrich also have the same meaning in both the languages, the Chinese idiom Tuóniǎozhèngcè (鸵鸟政策, ostrich policy). The Hindi idiom शुतुरमुर्गहोना (śuturmurghonā, to become an ostrich) have the same figurative meaning showing 'Inability of governments or people to acknowledge that a real problem or danger exists'.

19.3.2 Different Animal Vehicles Expressing Similar Meanings in Chinese and Hindi Idioms

There are also several idioms with animal words found in Chinese and Hindi idioms where different animals are used, reflecting the similar meaning of the idiom. Due to the difference in geographical, cultural and historical connotations of the two countries, the animal vehicles change their associative meanings.

For example, the Chinese idiom with Tiger (hǔ, 虎), Rúhǔtiānyì (如虎添翼, a tiger that has grown wings) means 'strong force being redoubled', and its Hindi counterpart idiom with same meaning शेरबख्तरपहनना (śherbakhtarpahnnā, a lion wearing armour) consists of a lion instead of Tiger.

Chinese idiom, Yǎorúhuánghè (杳如黄鹤, leave like a yellow crane) and the Hindi idiom भीमकेहाथी (bhīmkehāthī, the elephants of 'Bheem') with two different animals have the same figurative meaning 'Leave never to return; be gone forever. Similarly, for expressing the same meaning of 'Reasoning with stubborn people or talking to the wrong audience' cow is used in the Chinese idiom Duìniútánqín (对牛弹琴, play the piano to the cow) gets replaced by buffalo in Hindi idiom expressing the same meaning भैंसकेआगेबीनबजाना (Bhainskeāgebīnbajānām Playing the flute to a buffalo).

The Chinese idiom Māokūlǎoshǔ (猫哭老鼠, Cat weeping over dead mouse) and the Hindi idiom with crocodile मगरमच्छकेआँसू (magarmacchkeānsū) reflect the same meaning of 'Pretence of condolence/superficial grief'.

19.3.3 Language-Specific Idioms with Animal Words

Chinese idioms with animal words.

(1) Chinese idiom: lángbèitáocuàn (狼狈逃窜)

Literal meaning: to flee in utter panic.

Figurative meaning: to flee helter-skelter; to flee hurry-scurry.

Hindi parallel idiom: Chinese idiom: lángbèitáocuàn (जीछोड़करभागना)

(jīchoṛhkarbhāgnā).

Literal meaning: to run for one's life in panic.

Figurative meaning: to flee in panic.

Comparative analysis: Both the idioms mentioned above are used in the negative sense. The animals present in the Chinese idiom láng (狼) is a flesh-eating wild animal, wolf and bèi (狈) is also a wild beast similar to the wolf. Legend has it that bèi (狈) was an animal whose forelegs were so short that it could not move about without crouching atop the wolf (Hanyucidian). Hence the term lángbèi (狼 狈) means to cut a sorry figure of oneself, in a difficult position or a tight corner. Though there is no animal word in the Hindi parallel idiom, it also reflects a similar meaning.

(2) Chinese idiom: hàiqúnzhīmǎ (害群之马)[1]

Literal meaning: evil horse of the herd; a horse that spoils the whole herd.

Figurative meaning: black sheep; rotten apple in the barrel.

Hindi parallel idiom: (i) कढ़ीमेंकंकड़ीहोना (kaṛhīmeṅkaṅkaṛhīhonā), (ii) एकमछलीसारेतालाबकोगंदाकरदेतीहै (ekmachlīsāretālāb ko gandākardetīhai).

Literal meaning: (i) a small stone found in the curry exploits the taste of the whole curry, (ii) one fish can spoil the whole pond.

Figurative meaning: a small defect destroying the whole thing.

Comparative analysis: The above idioms directly reflect the derogatory sense. The evil horse of the herd or a black sheep of the flock is a metaphor for being a pest in society. The idiom manifests a person who brings disgrace or poses a danger to one's group. We do not find such a parallel idiom in Hindi, including horse or any other animal's name. However, the same meaning is reflected by the common occurrence of finding a small stone in any food item, which spoils the taste of the whole food. However, a similar proverb found in Hindi consists of another animal word, 'fish', which means a fish can spoil the whole pond.

(3) Chinese idiom: lángtūnhǔyān (狼吞虎咽)[2]

Literal meaning: to eat like wolves and tigers; to devour like a wolf.

Figurative meaning: devour ravenously; gobble up; wolf down.

Hindi parallel idiom: गपगपखाना (gap gapkhānā).

Literal meaning: to eat very fast.

Figurative meaning: to gulp down the food quickly.

Comparative analysis: The Chinese idiom has the mention of a wolf (láng, 狼) and Tiger (hǔ, 虎) in it, both being ferocious wild beasts. Furthermore, the idiom describes a hungry person eating something so quickly, like a wolf or Tiger swallowing their food in a hurry. The Hindi idiom also means to gulp down the food quickly. It has directly used the verb to eat खाना (khānā) in it and has added the onomatopoeic adverb

---

[1] Xúwúguǐ, Zhuāngzi: "Fūwéitiānxiàzhě, yìxīyǐyìhūmùmǎzhězāi? Yìqùqíhàimǎzhěéryǐyǐ (Xu Wugui, The husband who is the world is also different from the horse herders? It's just the one who harms the horses. Zhuang Zi, 庄子·徐无鬼》: "夫为天下者, 亦奚以异乎牧马者哉?亦去其害马者而已矣") cited in http://baike.baidu.com/view/83065.htm. Accessed on 27 Feb 2019.

[2] Míng·língméngchū, "chūkèpāi'ànjīngqí·liúdōngshānkuājìshùnchéngmén": "Shírénzìláichījiǔ… …xūyúzhījiān, lángsūnhǔyàn, suànláichīgòuyǒuliùqīshíjīnròu (Ming Ling Mengchu's. Amazing at the First Engraving of the Table and Liu Dongshan's Praise of Skills and Shun the City Gate: Ten people come to eat wine in a short while, the wolf swallows the Tiger's throat it is enough to eat 60–70 catties of meat. 明·凌濛初《初刻拍案惊奇·刘东山夸技顺城门》: "十人自来吃酒……须臾之间, 狼飧虎咽, 算来吃够有六七十斤肉), cited in http://baike.baidu.com/view/245515.htm. Accessed on 27 Feb 2019.

गपगप (gap gap) to show the intensity of hunger and act of gulping something very fast. But it does not carry any animal word like the Chinese one.

(4) Chinese idiom: jīngwèitiánhǎi (精卫填海)[3]

Literal meaning: the mythical bird Jingwei tries to fill up the sea with pebbles.

Figurative meaning: dogged determination to achieve one's purpose.

The story associated with this idiom:

Once upon a time, the youngest daughter of Emperor Yan, legendary ruler of ancient China, drowned in the East China Sea and turned into a beautiful bird called 'Jingwei'.

Out of hatred and full of determination, the bird decided to fill up the sea. Every day, it flew to and fro between the mountain and the sea, carrying a twig or a pebble and dropping it into the sea. The idiom "The bird Jingwei is trying to fill the sea" (China's Aesop's Fables). In later generations, people often used this idiom as to metaphor for the arduous and remarkable undertakings undertaken by people with lofty ideals.

Hindi parallel idiom: बूंदबूंदसेघड़ाभरना (būṅdbūṅd se ghaṛhābharnā).

Literal meaning: to fill a pitcher with drops of water.

Figurative meaning: consistent effort brings success.

In Indian culture, these also exist a story with a similar theme in Hindi named प्यासाकौआ (pyāsākauā) [thirsty crow]:

> One hot summer day, a thirsty crow was looking for water. After a long time, she found a pitcher with very little water. The crow could not reach the bottom of the pitcher, so she thought for some ideas. She started picking up the pebbles and dropping them one by one into the pitcher. After her consistent efforts, soon the water level in the pitcher rose high enough for the crow to drink. (Moral stories…, 2017)

Comparative analysis: The Chinese idiom was earlier used having a connotation of deep hatred and determination to take revenge against someone. But later on, the meaning changed into manifesting someone who has a firm determined attitude and does not fear difficulties and thus certainly achieve one's goal. We use it to describe such people present in today's society who are firm and indomitable and do not stop until they reach their goal.

---

[3] Shānhǎijīngjiàozhù: Yándìzhīshàonǚmíngyuēnǚwá. Nǚwáyóuyúdōnghǎi, nìérbùfǎn, gùwèijīngwèi, chángxiánxīshānzhīmùshí, yǐyīnyúdōnghǎi. (Annotation of Shanhaijing《山海经校注》: "炎帝之少女名曰女娃。女娃游于东海, 溺而不返, 故为精卫, 常衔西山之木石, 以堙于东海). 2020 cited in https://www.tspweb.com/key/%E6%BA%BA%E8%80%8C%E4%B8%8D%E8%BF%94%E6%96%AD%E5%8F%A5.html in Enniu.com. Accessed on 27 Nov 2020.

19.3.4 Culture-Specific Animal Idioms

Human beings often associate their feelings and emotions with various animals according to animals' features such as their appearances, habits, and characteristics. The names or images of animals possess specific cultural connotations. Nevertheless, each animal also carries some impressions of its own historical, cultural, and geographical set-up besides these standard features. Every language has its idioms that differ from the other languages, so we must pay attention to the cultural differences and be aware of the cultural connotations associated with the idioms when we do idiom translation from one language to another. Owing to their unique historical experiences, cultural beliefs and geographical conditions, idioms under this section possess some peculiarity. The following section will explore the culture-specific animal idioms found in the Chinese language.

19.3.5 Culture-Specific Animal Idioms in Chinese

Many idioms are related to various animals and their symbolic connotations in the Chinese language. These idioms can be further classified into various groups depending upon the essential traits of the animal. This section will discuss the Chinese animal idioms and their cultural connotations, mainly focusing on the idioms consisting of mythical animals and Chinese idioms animal names related to traditional Chinese customs and beliefs.

(1) Mythical animals and animal idioms (Chinese perspective)

Dragon, Phoenix, Unicorn and Tortoise are the four cardinal animals of Chinese mythology, and these are the mystical figures of ancient Chinese legends. Línfèngguīlóng (麟凤龟龙) (Li Yun n.d.) meaning the unicorn, the phoenix, the Tortoise, and the dragon (formally called the "four spiritually endowed beings") used to illustrate worthy men or men with moral integrity. Since ancient times, there have been several Chinese idioms based on these mythological animals.

Chinese people consider the dragon and phoenix mythical creatures closely associated with Chinese cultural identity. Since primitive society, the dragons were considered the symbol and guardian of certain prehistoric tribes. In ancient China, the dragon was believed as a lucky and mystical creature; people considered it a symbol of power, authority, ability, and good luck (Mythical animal n.d.). As time passed, it became accepted as a cultural and political symbol of China.

According to Tang prose, A mountain becomes famous with a deity on it, does not matter how small a mountain it is; similarly, a river becomes divine with the presence of a dragon in it, does not matter how shallow the river water is. As time passed, different physical attributes got added to it. These include the head of a camel, the antlers of a deer, the eyes of a rabbit, the ears of an ox, the neck of a serpent, the scales of a fish, the mane of a horse, the claws of an eagle, and the palms of a tiger. As noted by Li Shizhen in the Ming Dynasty (1368–1644), in his Compendium of Materia Medica《běncǎogāngmù》(《本草纲目》), the dragon appropriated the distinctive features of many animals to become what it is today (Mythical animals n.d.).

The phoenix has the head of a chicken, the neck of a serpent, the chin of a swallow, the back of a tortoise, and the tail of a fish. Its skin has five colours, and it is over two meters in length. Phoenix is regarded differently at different places and cultural backgrounds with their imaginations.

In Chinese culture, the dragon is considered a powerful celestial creature, roaming high clouds and deep sea, which possesses the command of weather change. The phoenix is regarded as the queen of the birds, with a roaring sound. Chinese people believe that phoenixes always hang around places of treasure. Liu Bang, the first emperor of the Han Dynasty, claimed that his father was a dragon. Moreover, therefore, gradually, the dragon turned out to be a symbol of royal authority and thus started being associated with the emperor.

On the other hand, the phoenix represented the empress. Anything related to the emperor or empress was labelled by dragon and phoenix, respectively. For example, the emperor's countenance was known as lóngyán (龙 颜), his robe as lóngpáo (龙袍), and his descendants as lóngzǐlóngsūn (龙子龙孙). The empress gown was known as fèngyī (凤衣), her crown as fèngguàn (凤冠), her chamber as fènggé (凤阁), and her carriage as fèngniǎn (凤 辇) (Xu Wugui n.d.).

In modern times, dragons and phoenixes carry their association with good luck and auspiciousness. The dragon dance has become a traditional ritual associated with traditional Chinese festival celebrations. Dragon boat races are organized in southern China during the Dragon Boat Festival celebration on the fifth lunar month's fifth day. Several idioms and phrases consist of the dragon and the phoenix, such as Lóngfèngchéngxiáng (龙凤呈祥, the dragon and the phoenix bringing prosperity-extremely good fortune), lóngfēifèngwǔ (龙飞凤舞, flamboyant or bold cursive calligraphy-like dragons flying and phoenixes dancing), lóngxiángfèngzhù (龙翔凤 翥, It is a metaphor for the rushing waterfall), pānlóngfùfèng (攀龙附凤, play up to people of power and influence; put oneself under the patronage of a bigwig), lóngténghǔyuè (龙腾虎跃, dragons rising and tigers leaping—a scene of bustling activity), shēnglónghuóhǔ (生龙活虎 lively dragon and animated Tiger; a metaphor for vigorous and lively, bursting with energy), lóngmǎjīngshén (龙马精神, spirit of a dragon horse-old but still full of vitality), wàngzǐchéng long (望子成龙, hope one's son becomes a dragon- wish to see one's son succeed in life), and fèngmáolínjiǎo (凤毛麟角, as precious and rare as phoenix feather and unicorn horns; rare and precious things or persons). These often refer to a sense of auspiciousness, power, or rarity (Xu Wugui n.d.).

Animals have played an important role in the life and culture of the Chinese people from prehistoric times. When used as symbols, Chinese people do not distinguish between real and mythical animals (Xu Wugui n.d.). China is culturally, ethnically, demographically a diverse country with varied religious beliefs, and Buddhism plays the most important role among all religious beliefs. Chinese culture is one of the rich and ancient cultures of the world, and the ancient Chinese people were deeply linked with mythical creatures. These animals were considered noble, highly privileged, associated with the emperor or high authority, and respected. At the same time, they are pretty rare, precious and auspicious by nature. These mythical creatures occupy an important part of Chinese culture and Chinese peoples' belief systems. These mythological animals and the idioms related to them reflect the cultural specificity of the national culture of China.

As per the Chinese creation myth,

> The mythical empress Nu Wa was considered to create the custodians of the four directions, assigning the Black Tortoise in the North, and giving it control over winter; the Blue Dragon in the east, who was given control over spring; the White Tiger in the West, who was given control over autumn; and the Red Bird in the South, who was given control over summer, with the Gold Dragon, whose special duty was to guard the sun, the moon is protected by the White Deity of the West. The broken pillar of heaven was built up with stones coloured like the five gods (Mackenzie 1986)

As per Chinese traditional culture,

> The four directions, East, West, South, and North, represent the four seasons, spring, autumn, summer, and winter. Including the Centre (Chinese means China) forms the five fundamental points. And the four celestial animals represent these four directions; the dragon denotes the east, the Tiger represents the West, the bird stands for the South, and the Tortoise signifies the North. Each animal also has its specific colour: the dragon is the green of spring, the bird the red of fire, the Tiger of autumn the glittering white of metal (of swords), and the Tortoise black, for night or water. These four celestial animals also represent four divisions of the sky (Walters 1995)

Dragon: Dragon is a mythical animal with a long body, scales, horns, wings and feet, which could walk, fly, swim and gather clouds to pour down rain. In ancient feudal China, the dragon was a symbol of the emperor, and the character was attached with the belongings of the emperor too. And thus, it is still believed as a symbol of strength, prosperity and good fortune in Chinese culture. Chinese people often consider themselves "Descendants of the Dragon" (Lords of the Chinese world 2014).

Phoenix:

> Phoenix is the English translation of the Chinese word Feng Huang, a sacred bird derived from a Chinese mythological story. It contains several miraculous powers, but it differs from the Arabian phoenix and does not carry the tendency of self-immolation. It is generally depicted as a beautiful bird, similar to an ornamental pheasant. The few pictures, artworks found, and their verbal description shows that the phoenix possesses beautiful physical attributes from different animals and birds like swan, unicorn, swallow, chicken, snake, dragon, and Tortoise. Its feathers are of the five magical colours - black, white, red, green and yellow, and it has twelve tail feathers, except in years when there is an extra month, then they have thirteen. It is one of the four symbols of royalty associated with the Chinese empress. In Chinese culture, the Dragon and Phoenix together imply marital bliss. In Chinese cultural symbolism, it has been muddled and combined with the mystic Red Bird (Walters 1995)

Tiger:

> In China, the White Tiger is from the West and is associated with metal. When, therefore, metal is placed in a grave, a ceremonial connection with the tiger god is affected. In Chinese mythologies, the Tiger is a protector, a guardian. To the ancient Chinese people, the Tiger

> was the king of all animals and 'lord of the mountains', and the tiger-jade ornament was specially reserved for commanders of armies (Mackenzie 1986)

The White Tiger is also known as the god of war and slaughter. The white Tiger possesses several divine powers, including the ability to ward off evil, cause calamity, pray for abundance and punish evil, promote goodness, make money and become wealthy, a happily married relationship etc. As per Chinese belief, it is also one of the four spirits transformed from the constellation. The seven western stars or constellations Kui, Lou, Wei, Ang, Bi, Gu, and Shen, made the white tiger shape; it represents the West. Moreover, since the West belongs to the metal element under the five-element theory, which is white, the Tiger is referred to as a white Tiger (Four elephants in ancient China 2007).

Since the origin of white tigers is in Bengal, India and is mainly found in the Indian continent, the White Tiger, a mythological animal in ancient Chinese folktales and Chinese astronomy as mentioned to be coming from the West, must be referring to India.

Tortoise: "The sign of longevity and wisdom is one of the four Celestial beings of Chinese mythology. Chinese people believe that Tortoise's shell represents the Universe's arch." (Walters 1995).

> The Tortoise carried divine qualities in Chinese culture. Tortoiseshell is used to represent static and unchanging qualities. In ancient China, tortoiseshell was used for the divination process too. A gigantic mythical tortoise is supposed to live in the depths of the ocean, and it is believed to possess only one eye located in the middle of its body. It comes to the ocean surface after every three thousand years and turns upside down to see the Sun (Mackenzie 1986)

Dragon is a symbol of imperial power, dignity and divinity and a symbol of good luck, wealth, future and power, a symbol of a flourishing spirit. The expression, lóngfèngchéngxiáng, (龙凤呈祥) reflects the excellent fortune. Dragon and phoenix are important in Chinese traditional culture as auspicious symbols and totems. Some idioms related to phoenix show marital felicity or good fortune. The idiom fènghuángyúfēi (凤凰于飞, a pair of phoenixes flying together) shows the marital felicity, and thus it is a symbol of a happy marriage in Chinese culture.

Both dragons and tigers have impacted Chinese culture significantly. Furthermore, when they come together in idioms, the idioms reflect the powerful, strong, and ferocious nature. The idiom lóngzhēnghǔdòu, (龙争虎斗, fighting between a tiger and a dragon) means a fierce struggle between well-matched opponents or a contest between giants. This idiom describes competitions or very evenly matched challenges, like dragons and tigers fighting each other. Moreover, this phrase clearly shows how the Chinese think of the dragon and Tiger as fighters. Then another Chinese idiom, lóngténghǔyuè, (龙腾虎跃), which means dragons are rising and tigers leaping, is used as a metaphor for a scene of bustling activity. Similarly, the idiom lóngyínhǔxiào, (龙吟虎 啸, dragons singing and tigers roaring) referring to resonant sound is used for the howling of the wind or the roaring of waves, etc.

When dragon and phoenix come together in Chinese idioms, it simply reflects excellence and brilliance. Like, lóngjūfèngchú, (龙驹凤雏, dragon colt or young phoenix) expresses a brilliant young man and lónggānfèngdǎn, (龙肝凤胆, dragon liver, phoenix bladder) means rare delicacies in Chinese culture. Similar to this idiom, phoenix and unicorn come together to symbolize the rarity of rarities in the idiom fèngmáolínjiǎo, (凤毛麟角, phoenix feathers and unicorn horns). The phoenix and unicorn are among the rare and precious mystical animals and birds of Chinese historical culture, and therefore, their feathers and horns become much rare and precious. Thus, even today, this idiom is used to show a unique and valuable object in Chinese society.

(2) Animal idioms related to Chinese customs and beliefs

Apart from mythical creatures such as the dragon and phoenix, Chinese people also value other animals that are considered to help them get happiness and auspiciousness in their lives. Chinese folklores and idioms based on that effectively represent traditional Chinese belief system. Following is an example of the famous Chinese folklore associated with today's modern Chinese society and the Chinese festival of lovers, highlighting the significance of animals in Chinese customs and beliefs.

According to Chinese folklore of NiúLáng (牛郎, Cowherd) and Zhi Nü (织女, Weaver maid), the main character of the story, the orphan and poor Cowherd is helped by an animal, the celestial cow, throughout his life. Moreover, when the Queen Mother separated the Cowherd and Weaver girl by drawing milky way between them, it was again another animal, magpies, xǐquè (喜 鹊, which in Chinese means joyful bird), helped the couple to reunite. As believed, the love of the separated couple touched the magpies, so tens of thousands of magpies came to build a bridge for the Cowherd and Weaver maid to meet each other. Finally, the Queen Mother, wángmǔniángniáng (王母娘娘) was also moved and allowed them to meet once a year on the seventh day of the seventh lunar month (Shi 2003). Chinese people believe that on the seventh day of the seventh lunar month the Cowherd Niu Lang (牛郎) and his lover, the weaver girl Zhi Nu (织女), come on the bridge made by magpies for their once annual meeting. As a result, the idiom quèqiáoxiānghuì, (鹊桥相会, meeting at the magpies' bridge) was created to mean the reunion of a couple or lovers after a long separation. Another idiom with this bird, Xǐquèdēngzhī, (喜 鹊登枝, magpie settles on the bough) is a metaphor of good omen or a harbinger of good news. Sparrows also enjoy a similarly favourable status in Chinese culture. If sparrows make nest on the roof of a Chinese family's house, the hosts will never disturb them because it is believed that it will bring luck to the family.

In Chinese, the word for fortune, fú (福) is a homophone for the word for bat fú (蝠). Likewise, deer lù (鹿) is a homophone of lù (禄), which means something like official rank and salary. As per traditional Chinese customs and beliefs, the crane was assumed to be divine and symbolized longevity. According to the Chinese cultural belief, 'tortoise' carries two meanings. One means longevity; the other implies 'foolish people'. The significance of Tortoise being one of the four mythical animals of China is already discussed in the previous section, as the línfèngguīlóng (麟凤龟龙, unicorn, phoenix, turtle, and dragon-the four spiritually endowed beings in Chinese legend) represents good fortune, honour, and long life. However, another idiom, suōtóuwūguī (缩头乌龟, a turtle that pulls its head in), means a coward.

19.3.6 Inter Complementarities Observed in Mythical Animals or Birds, Especially in Dragon, Phoenix and Unicorn

Following examples of Chinese idioms show the inter complementary association of the mythical animals and birds which are already discussed in the previous section of the paper:) fènghuángyúfēi (凤凰于飞, a pair of phoenixes flying together-Martial felicity), fèngmáolínjiǎo (凤毛麟角, rare and precious things or persons; as precious and rare as phoenix feather and unicorn horns), lóngfēifèngwǔ 龙飞凤舞, flamboyant or bold cursive calligraphy), lóngfèngchéngxiáng (龙凤呈祥, reflects the excellent good fortune), lónggānfēngdǎn (龙肝凤胆, dragon liver, phoenix bladder-rare delicacies), lóngjūfèngchú, (龙驹凤雏, brilliant young man) etc. When dragon and phoenix come together in the idioms, they simply reflect good fortune, excellence and brilliancy.

Inter complementarities observed in idioms related to dragon and Tiger:

lónghǔjīngshén (龙虎精神, dragon and tiger spirit),lóngpánhǔjù (龙蟠虎踞, dragon coiling and Tiger crouching—forbidding strategic point),lóngtánhǔxué (龙潭虎穴, dangerous spot as a dragon's pool and Tiger's den—a danger spot), lóngténghǔyuè (龙腾虎 神, dragon soaring and Tiger leaping), lóngxiānghǔbù (龙 蟠虎步, walk like a dragon and pace like a tiger; martial gait), lóngyínhǔxiào (龙吟虎 穴, dragons singing and tigers roaring), lóngzhēnghǔdòu (龙争虎斗, the dragon wars, the tiger battles; a fierce battle between giants), shēnglónghuóhǔ (生龙活虎, lively dragon and animated Tiger), wòhǔcáng long (卧虎藏龙, hidden dragon, crouching Tiger), lóngxínghǔbù (龙行虎步, dragon-like prancing and tiger-like pacing—majestic gait; imposing air; full of power and grandeur) etc. When the dragon comes together with Tiger or other powerful animals in the idioms, it doubles its strength and might.

19.3.7 Different Animal Words, Similar Cultural Connotations in Chinese and Hindi

The people of Chinese and Indian society with different language communities, due to their different historical and social experiences and customs, look at things differently. At the same time, different animal words carriers might also generate the same cultural associations in Chinese and Indian cultures as the Chinese people believe that the Tiger is the king of beasts, which is the symbol of power and bravery. On the contrary, Indians think the lion is the king of beasts. Even though these animal words are different, they have similar connotations in their respective cultures.

(1) शेर (śer) and 虎 (hu) [lion and tiger]

Compared to the lion, the Tiger bears more significance in Chinese culture. With the word Wáng (王) on its forehead, Tiger has long been considered the king of all beasts since ancient times in China. Thus Tiger became the symbol of power and authority. The tiger-shaped copper talisman as imperial authorization for generals for troop movement was called hǔfú (虎符). The Chinese character for tiger hǔ, 虎 is an ideograph with an image of a tiger in a squatting posture. In Chinese, Tiger equals to brevity and ferocity, such phrases as shēnglónghuóhǔ (生龙活虎, doughty as a dragon and lively as a tiger-full of vim and vigour), wòhǔcáng long (卧虎藏龙, hidden dragon, crouching Tiger-talented individuals in hiding) etc.) are used to eulogize people. Furthermore, because of its courage and strength, the Tiger is often found in male names such as 大虎, 金彪, etc. And in some countryside, there remains the custom of dressing the newborn baby in tiger-shaped shoes and a hat in the hope that he or she would grow up healthy. In Hindi idioms and Indian culture, a lion occupies a similar place as a tiger in the Chinese language and culture. For example, the idioms शेर/सिंहहोना (śer/siṅhhonā), शेरसेपंजालेना (śer se paṅjālenā), शेरकेदाँतगिनना (śerkedaṁtginnā), शेरकीखालमेंगधा (śerkīkhālmeṅgadhā) all illustrate the strength, power, superior quality and danger factor attached to the animal. Nowadays, lions that have lost the mien of "the king of the beast" can be found everywhere in zoos. Nonetheless, it is still one of the strongest animals of the animal kingdom. In ancient days, lions were rarely found in China. During the Tang dynasty, lions were considered to have come to China from the West (what is west here, is not clear) and were seen as stronger and more terrible than tigers. Therefore, Chinese people acknowledged lions by their majestic look and extraordinary manner. Otherwise, lions were recognized as the symbol of India and Buddhism with their symbolic religious connection. The Chinese metaphor 'the roar of lions' means "Buddha preaching the sermon to entire worldly creatures". Lord Buddha is considered as the magnificent lion among human beings (Song Wei 2004).

From the above-discussed examples of Chinese idioms, it is observed that animals play a prominent and diverse role in the religion, history, culture, folklore, language, and literature of various cultures. Chinese animal idioms also form an essential element of their respective folk literature. Besides being invaluable embellishments for languages, these are also storehouses of information and knowledge about the respective cultures, lives, practical wisdom, thinking, and beliefs.

19.4 Conclusion

As we know, language is a cultural carrier. Culture-loaded vocabulary plays a vital role in a language. Different social backgrounds and cultures significantly affect the cultural connotations of vocabulary. Connotative meaning is subject to different cultures and experiences. It may vary according to culture, historical period, and the individual's experience, thus indeterminate and open-ended. We observe a widespread use of two different animals' names in a single idiom in Chinese idioms. Sometimes, the two different animals used together are similar in meaning that complement each other and thus emphasize its meaning. However, in some other idioms, two animals of different qualities are used together, antithetical. The Chinese are excellent philosophers and observers. As such, they understand the deeper meanings of animals and utilize the characteristics of each creature to represent traits they wish to call upon in their own lives. Chinese animal symbols serve as reminders, charms, omens, and sentiments.

As human beings live on the same planet, there must be some similarities in human cognition of the world. However, because of the differences in the environment, lifestyle, values, beliefs, history, the detailed understanding of the world would be different from age to age and from society to society. Their cultural background influences the formation of idioms in any language. Translators need to know the exact meaning and cultural connotations of the source and target languages' idioms and the characteristics of the idioms of both languages. Translating something is not just about translating a language. Instead, it also means translating the culture into another language. Therefore, the cultural connotation of words varies according to the cultural content, tradition, psychology, etc. Chinese and Hindi may have unique cultural connotations about the same animals due to different cultural backgrounds. Chinese and Hindi idioms come from different cultures, including specific ideologies and philosophies. Through the comparative study of various animal idioms, it is revealed that cultures significantly affect languages. Knowing the similarities and differences will help us in inter-cultural communication and help in the translation of cultural texts.

References

A Comparative Analysis of Chinese and Thai Animal Idioms, cited in http://www.56ggmm.com/a/gxlw/yylw/yyxlw/2010/0918/641.html. Accessed on 21 Oct 2018

Animals in Mythology, cited in http://www.mythencyclopedia.com/Am-Ar/Animals-in-Mythology.html. Accessed on 09 Sept 2018

Buy Your Favorite Chinese or Japanese Proverb on a Wall Scroll, Oriental outpost. http://www.orientaloutpost.com/ancient_chinese_proverbs_and_philosophy_phrases.php#roar%20lioness. Accessed on 29 July 2018

Chengyu yuZhongguoWenhua (4) (Idioms and Chinese Culture (4)), cited in http://tieba.baidu.com/f?kz=296612915. Accessed on 23 Oct 2018

China's Aesop's Fables- Stories of Chinese Idioms (1), cited in http://www.chinadetail.com/Culture/LanguagesChinasAesopsFables1.php. Accessed on 12 Sept 2018

English Idioms and cross-cultural translation strategies, cited in http://eng.hi138.com/?i50777. Accessed on 11 Sept 2018

Four Elephants (2007) Ancient China: the origin of Qinglong, White Tiger, Suzaku, and Xuanwu, cited in http://news.sohu.com/20070109/n247501148.shtml. Accessed on 26th Nov 2021

Francis HT, Thomas EJ (eds) (2014) Jataka tales. Cambridge University Press. http://www.archive.org/stream/jatakatales00fran#page/154/mode/2up. Accessed on 22 Sept 2018

Gregor RS (1997) The Oxford Hindi–English dictionary. Oxford University Press, USA (ENGLISH)

Hanyucidian, lángbèitáocuàn (Chinese dictionary). https://cd.hwxnet.com/view/applimiogcbmknnk.html. Accessed on 27 Feb 2019

Hinkhoj Hindi ShabdKhoj (शब्दखोज)—Hindi English translation and word meanings. http://dict.hinkhoj.com/

http://www.baidu.com/

Idiom Stories, cited in http://sina.echineselearning.com/english/contents/idiom-stories/jdzw.html. Accessed on 21 Oct 2018

Indian Hindi proverbs and sayings. http://www.scribd.com/doc/3190917/indian-hindi-proverbs-and-sayings. Accessed on 17 July 2018

Jin D (1998) Yindiyu-Hanyu Chengyu Cidian (Dictionary of Hindi-Chinese Idioms. Commercial Press, Beijing (CHINESE)

Kaleidoscope of culture, mythical animals. http://education.imextrade.ru/review/kaleidoscope-of-culture/mythical-animals/?lang=en. Accessed on 08 Oct 2018

Kapoor B (2007) Hindi Muhavre our LokoktiKosh (A Dictionary of Hindi Idioms and Proverbs). Lokbharti Prakashan, Allahabad (HINDI)

Li Y (2003) YinghanDongwuci de WenhuaNeihanBijiao Ji Fanyi (Cultural Connotation and Translation of English and Chinese Animal Words). J Cent S Univ (Soc Sci) 9(5). Wenzhou, Zhejiang

Lǐ Y (2018) Lǐjì: Línfènggυīlóng, wèizhīsìlíng (The Lin Feng, Turtle and Dragon are called the Four Spirits). Book of Rites (《礼记·礼运》: "麟凤龟龙, 谓之四灵") cited in http://zhidao.baidu.com/question/27979133.html. Accessed on 09 July 2018

Line Dictionary, Chinese-English. http://www.nciku.com/

Lords of the Chinese world: the dragon and phoenix (2014), cited in http://en.chinaculture.org/chineseway/2014-07/31/content_553822.htm. Accessed on 19 Oct 2018

Mackenzie DA (1986) China and Japan myths and legends. Bracken Books

Mackenzie in the four Gods, cited in https://www.angelfire.com/anime2/firestorm/four_gods.html. Accessed on 16 Sept 2018

Míng·língméngchū, "chūkèpāi'ànjīngqí·liúdōngshānkuājìshùnchéngmén"(Ming Ling Mengchu's. Amazing at the First Engraving of the Table and Liu Dongshan's Praise of Skills and Shun the City Gate. 明·凌濛初《初刻拍案惊奇·刘东山夸技顺城门》), cited in http://baike.baidu.com/view/245515.htm. Accessed on 27 Feb 2019

Moral stories, narratives, anecdotes, prophet stories, short stories and more (2017), cited in http://www.ezsoftech.com/stories/mis18.asp. Accessed on 12 Mar 2019

Mythical-animals, cited in http://education.imextrade.ru/review/kaleidoscope-of-culture/mythical-animals/?lang=en. Accessed on 08 Oct 2018

New Century Chinese-English Dictionary (2002) Learner's Publishing, Foreign Language Teaching and Research Press, Beijing (CHINESE)

On Idioms and Their Translation from Chinese into English, cited in http://www.qqcate.cn/english-essay-traslation/On-Idioms-and-Their-Translation-from-Chinese-into-English/. Accessed on 11 Sept 2018

Ren F (2003) Metaphorical meanings of Hindi and Chinese animal words and their translation. J PLA Univ Foreign Lang 26(1). Luoyang

Saraswat M (2007) The World of Idioms and Phrases (Eng.-Hindi). Upkar Prakashan, Agra (ENGLISH)

Shānhǎijīngjiàozhù. (Annotation of Shanhaijing《山海经校注》) (2020), cited in https://www.tspweb.com/key/%E6%BA%BA%E8%80%8C%E4%B8%8D%E8%BF%94%E6%96%AD%E5%8F%A5.html in Enniu.com. Accessed on 27 Nov 2020

Sharma GS (2009) VishvaMuhavaraShabdkosh (World Idioms Dictionary). Vishv Vijay Pte. Ltd., New Delhi (HINDI)

Shi L (2003) The Cowherd and the Weaver Girl, cited in http://en.chinaculture.org/focus/focus/2010qixi/2010-08/16/content_391106.htm. Accessed on 4 July 2018

Singh VN (2003) Look-MuhawraKosh (Dictionary of Proverbs and Idioms). Delhi: Granthlok (HINDI)

Song W (2004) Traditional Chinese culture and animal, written for International Animal Law Conference. Animal Legal and Historical Web Center, San Diego

The four Gods, cited in https://www.angelfire.com/anime2/firestorm/four_gods.html. Accessed on 16 Sept 2018

The Oxford Companion to the English Language (1992a) 495–496, cited in http://en.wikipedia.org/wiki/Idiom. Accessed on 3 July 2018

The Oxford Companion to the English Language (1992b) 495–496, cited in http://en.wikipedia.org/wiki/Idiom. Accessed on 3 July 2018

Tiwari B (1993) What Hindi MuhavraKosh (Comprehensive Dictionary of Hindi Idioms). Sahitya Sahkar, Delhi (HINDI)

Traditional Festival, Qixi Festival Legend. http://www.ebeijing.gov.cn/feature_2/Traditional_Fesitival/Qixi_Festival/Legend_QX/t1021736.htm. Accessed on 4 July 2018

Von Krenner WG, Jeremiah K (2016) Creatures real and imaginary in Chinese and Japanese art: an identification guide. McFarland

Walters D (1995) Chinese mythology: an encyclopaedia of myth and legend. Diamond Books

Walters, in The four Gods, cited in https://www.angelfire.com/anime2/firestorm/four_gods.html. Accessed on 16 Sept 2018

Wángzhènyà. Yǔyányǔwénhuà [M]. Běijīng: Gāoděngjiàoyùchūbǎnshè. Dìèrbǎn. 2002, 6, cited in dòngwùcízàihànyīngwénhuàzhōng de yùyìjíqífānyì, shīxiǎoqīn, (Wang Zhenya. Language and Culture [M]. Beijing: Higher Education Press. Second Edition. 2002, 6, cited in The metaphorical meaning of animal words in Chinese and English culture and its translation, Shi Xiaoqin; 王振亚. 语言与文化 [M].北京: 高等教育出版社.第二版. 2002, 6, cited in 动物词在汉英文化中的喻义及其翻译, 施小钦), http://www.studa.net/Translates/080520/15062391.html. Accessed on 6 July 2018

Wu J, Press BFLT (2002) Xin ShijiHan-Ying Cidian (New Century Chinese-English Dictionary). Learners Publishing and Foreign Language Teaching and Research Press, Beijing

Xin Ying-Han Cidian (Shiji ban) [New English-Chinese Dictionary (Century edition)]. 2002. Shanghai: Shanghai Translation Press (CHINESE)

Xúwúguǐ Z (2019) "Fūwéitiānxiàzhě, yìxīyǐyìhūmùmǎzhězāi? Yìqùqíhàimǎzhěéryǐyǐ (Xu Wugui, The husband who is the world is also different from the horse herders? It's just the one who harms the horses. Zhuang Zi, 庄子·徐无鬼》: "夫为天下者, 亦奚以异乎牧马者哉?亦去其害马者而已矣") cited in http://baike.baidu.com/view/83065.htm. Accessed on 27 Feb 2019

Zhang C (2000) Chinese idioms and their stories. Foreign Languages Press, Beijing

Part VI
Poster Presentations

Chapter 20
India China Relations Under the Reign of Harshvardhan and Taizong

Rakesh Kumar Mishra

20.1 Introduction

Harshavardhan was born in 590 AD. He was one of the most famous and influential kings in Indian history. He established a mighty dynasty in Northern India named Vardhan dynasty[1] and reigned for more than forty years (Zhang 2015). He paid very much attention for establishing contacts with foreign countries during his period, especially with Tang China, which emperor Taizong ruled. Tang Taizong was the second emperor of the Tang dynasty. He reigned China for more than twenty years (626 AD to 649 AD). After fighting many battles, he centralized his power and ascended the throne in 626 AD. Under his reign, the glory of Tang China was at its peak in terms of literature, peace and prosperity. It is also considered a golden period in developing the relationship between India and China.

From 641 to 648 AD, around six diplomatic missions were exchanged between India and Tang China. Harshavardhan sent three diplomatic missions to Tang China, and in return, Taizong sent three diplomatic missions to India. These missions are recorded mainly in Old *History of the Tang Dynasty* (旧唐书 jiu tang shu),[2] *New History of Tang Dynasty* (新唐书 xin tang shu),[3] Xuanzang's travelogue *Great Tang*

[1] The Vardana dynasty, also known as the Pushyabhuti dynasty, ruled parts of northern India in the sixth and seventh centuries.

[2] "Old History of the Tang Dynasty" is China's first classic historiography of the Tang Dynasty, with 200 chapters in total, which is one of the twenty-four histories, it is originally compiled during the Five Dynasties and Ten Kingdoms period of China.

[3] "New History of Tang Dynasty" is an official history book covering the Tang Dynasty, with ten volumes and 225 chapters.

R. K. Mishra (✉)
Banaras Hidnu University, Varanasi, India
e-mail: mrakesh216@gmail.com

S. Mishra and R. Sheel (eds.), *India-China Dialogues Beyond Borders*,
https://doi.org/10.1007/978-981-99-4326-5_21

Records on the Western Region (大唐西域记 da Tang xi yu Ji)[4] etc. In the following paragraphs, I attempt to study the exchanges in different fields during these two great kings.

20.2 India and China Interaction in the Seventh Century AD, During the Reign of Harshavardhan and Taizong

During the seventh century, when the Tang dynasty was flourishing under the leadership of emperor Taizong in China, India was thriving under the reign of the great King Harshavardhan.

The Tang dynasty of China is often called China's "golden period" in terms of literature, foreign policy and cultural exchanges with neighbouring countries. It was when Tang China established religious, educational, cultural and trade connections with western regions[5]; it was also a time of incredible literary works, painting and ceramic arts. Tang dynasty of China witnessed many finest poets like Li Bai, Du Fu, Wang Wei, Bai Juyi, Cui Hao, etc.

During the seventh century, in the Tang period, literature greatly impacted India-China cultural exchanges. Poetry in Tang Dynasty was the most developed. Interestingly we find references of Tang poets having contacts with monks from India. They often wrote poems mentioning people from India, for example, Li Bai's *Seng Jia Ge* (僧 伽歌).[6] (Xue 2010).

During Taizong's reign, China made a special effort to contact the outside world. The Hu people from the western regions came to China for business, settled there, and even started working in the imperial court. Moreover, the emissaries from the Tang Dynasty were constantly sent to the Western Regions. In this regard, we also see Buddhism as an important factor behind communication and exchanges of knowledge between the Tang people and South Asian countries. Buddhist monks frequently travel as a part of the dharma-seeking movement. With this, communication between governments also reached a new stage. The opening of the Ancient Tang and Tibetan roads widened the cultural exchanges between China and India. The exchanges during this time were more profound than before and reflected the integration of many cultures. Tang and Kannuaj (mainly during the reign of Harshavardhan) thus are known as cosmopolitan societies.

---

[4] Great Tang Records on the Western Region is narrative of Xuanzang's journey from Chang 'an to the Western Regions.

[5] The Western region or Xiyu (西域) is a historical name specified in Chinese records in ancient times that referred to regions to the west of China.

[6]《真僧法号号僧 伽，有时与我论三车。问言诵咒几千遍，口道恒河沙复沙。此僧本住南天竺，为法头陀来此国。戒得长天秋月明，心如世上青莲色。》True monk, whose Buddhist name is Sangha, and he once explained to me the so-called three vehicles. Reciting sutras and mantras thousands of times, it is said that it will never be exhausted, just like the sand in the Ganges River. This monk originally lived in Nantianzhu (Southern India) and came to this country as Buddhist monk. Abstain from long days, autumn and moonlight, and hearts like the green lotus in the world.

Harshavardhan ascended the throne in 606 AD. Within five to six years, he united his kingdom in Northern India. He was very popular for his religious broadmindedness, good administrative system, and diplomatic relations with the other countries. Harshavardhan especially maintained diplomatic relations with China. He sent many envoys to China during his rule, which played a vital role in developing India-China cultural exchanges.

Buddhist missionaries, ambassadors, and merchants also played a significant role in developing these interaction and contacts. Indian traders went to many countries in search of new business opportunities. Ancient universities in India, on the other hand has also been of utmost importance in cultural and scholarly exchanges. They attracted many scholars and students from foreign countries. Scholars from abroad often visited Nalanda University, especially the library of Nalanda University, searching for knowledge and original Buddhist texts. Renowned Chinese traveller Xuanzang described in detail all the universities of India in which he went, stayed, or studied. For example, he specifically mentioned two of these universities—Nalanda University in the east and Vallabhi University[7] in the west. Another university that he mentioned in his travelogue was The Vikramashila. It was situated on the eastern banks of the Ganges (Xue 2010).

About the reign of Harshavardhan, after the Gupta Empire, the Pushyabhuti dynasty of Thaneshwar came into power. It was a significant dynasty of Northern India and was also known as the Vardhan dynasty in Indian history. Harshavardhan was one of the most influential rulers (though the last ruler) of this dynasty. Harshavardhan was born in 590 AD and ascended the throne at the age of 16 in 606 AD. His reign (606AD to 647AD) was the peak of the Vardhan dynasty in terms of prosperity, power, literature, the spread of Buddhism and diplomatic ties with the foreign countries, especially with Tang China. We see this period as one of the most favourable periods in history regarding India-China interactions. Anarchy spread again in North India after his death and Kannauj was captured by a ruler named Arjuna.

Harshavardhan has gained an endless reputation for his peaceful governance of the country. He tirelessly maintained his empire. He travelled to the different parts of his empire to personally look into the affairs of state (Mazumdar 1927). His administration was feudal and decentralized. The land was granted to the priest for special service and was also granted to the officers. As far as Harsha's revenue is concerned, it was divided into four parts; one part for the expenditure of the king, second part for the scholars, third part for officials and fourth part for the religious purpose. Law and order under his reign was not maintained very well (Sharma 1977).

Banabhatta's *Harshacharita*[8] tells us many important aspects of Harshavardhan's reign. He was a great Sanskrit poet and writer in Harsha's court. He has mentioned

[7] Valabhi University was an important centre of Buddhism learning and championed the cause of Hinayana Buddhism.

[8] Harshacharita is a Sanskrit text composed by Banabhatta. In this the biography of the Indian emperor Harshavardhana is described.

the life of Harshavardhan in detail and talked about Harshavardhan's most exemplary administrative system along with his achievements in his book. Apart from the *Harshacharita*, Xuanzang, who visited India during Harsha's reign and studied at Nalanda University for more than six years, wrote about Harshavardhan's life. He had also mentioned a few of Harsha's achievements, such as establishing the Buddhist Mathas and Viharas, organizing Buddhist religious works, etc., in his travelogue *Great Tang Records on the Western Regions*.

About Taizong, he was the second ruler of Tang dynasty. Emperor Gaozu was the first emperor of the Tang Empire. Taizong preceded him. Taizong since the very beginning had a vision of an advanced society. He ruled China for more than 20 years in his reign; he worked so much in this direction that the capital Chang'an became a truly cosmopolitan city. It is said that all the major Asian roads during those days, led to Chang'an. Emperor Taizong developed diplomatic ties and trade relationships with Asia and beyond. Since second century BC, Chinese envoys travelled across the Indian Ocean to India. But it was during the Tang Dynasty that China found a strong maritime presence in the Persian Gulf and the Red Sea, into Persia, Arabia, Egypt, and Somalia. On the other hand, thousands of foreigners came to China, lived in many cities, and established trade and business ties with China.

The administrative system in China during Taizong's reign was excellent (Lily 2009). To restore the land captured by wars, he implemented a benevolent rule of distributing those lands among the farmers and then levying taxes. To avoid conflicts with the surrounding territories, he also adopted a conciliatory foreign policy in his early reign. During this time, the Tang dynasty also laid the foundation for close contact with its powerful state in the western regions (Lily 2009).

Taizong's achievements towards developing Buddhism in China and establishing contact with western reigns are extraordinarily notable. In his period, he sent many envoys to western regions. His objectives of sending these envoys were to search for the original Buddhist Sutras, establish relationships with western region countries, and search for the longevity drug. Taizong personally sent three missions to India. The first mission, he sent under the leadership of Liang Huaijing in 642 AD. In 643 AD, he sent his second mission to India, led by Li Yibiao and Wang Xuance. He sent the third mission to India in 647 AD, which was led by Wang Xuance. Among these, Xuanzang and Wang Xuance were the most prominent personalities. In the following paragraph, I discuss the visit of Xuanzang and Wang Xuance, as their visit played a significant role in strengthening the India-China cultural contacts.

Xuanzang, a very famous Chinese Buddhist monk and traveller visited India searching for original Buddhist scriptures during this time. He is famous for his seventeen years of journey in India. Xuanzang had a profound influence on the spread of Buddhism in China and played a significant role in convincing Harshavardhan to establish diplomatic ties with Tang China (Sen 2001, 2003). Xuanzang travelled to many parts in India. Here, he visited sacred places and conducted a deeper study of Buddhist scriptures. He came to India around 225 years after Faxian.[9] He travelled

[9] Faxian (法显) also known as Fa-Hien, was a famous Chinese Buddhist monk, who travelled by foot to India in fourth century CE.

to Gandhara, Kashmir, Punjab, Kapilvastu, Banaras, Gaya, and Kushinagar, but he spent maximum time during his India visit in Kannauj, the capital of Harsha's empire. At the invitation of King Harshavardhan, he lived in Kannauj for more than eight years, approximately from 635 to 643 AD. He also studied at Nalanda University for six years. He started his return journey to China from the capital itself. It is believed that Xuanzang took more than 150 Buddha's relics, statues made of gold, silver, and sandal, and manuscripts of 657 books from India with him. In 645 AD, he returned to Chang'an and was warmly welcomed by Emperor Taizong. He was designated to live in Chang'an to translate those Buddhist scriptures. Xuanzang built a five-story pagoda in Chang'an City to store the scriptures brought from India. That is today known as Giant Wild Goose Pagoda. From here on, Xuanzang spent the rest of his life in translation. This led China to become an important centre of Buddhist learning outside India or South Asia, from which Buddhist teachings have spread to Korea, Japan and other neighbouring countries (Sen 2006). He is the most important among the Chinese travellers who visited South Asia searching for Buddhist Sutra; therefore, he is called the 'Prince of Travelers' (Bagchi 1944).

In The *Great Tang Records on the Western Regions*, Xuanzang described the history, geography, religion, folklore, language, and script of more than138 countries. His records are a precious treasure to study the history and society of ancient Central Asia and South Asia. Ji Xianlin, a well-known historian and Chinese Indologist, comprehensively evaluates Xuanzang's achievements. He said, "Xuanzang was a well-known eminent monk in the Tang Dynasty, a Buddhist idealist theorist, a traveller who is not afraid of hardships, an excellent translator, a typical example of giving up one's life and seeking the Buddhist Sutra, and the embodiment of India-China friendship." ("大唐西域记校注" Dàtángxīyùjìjiàozhù) Xuanzang is always remembered for the extensive yet careful Chinese translations of Indian Buddhist texts and the recovery of lost Indian Buddhist texts and historical details with the help of the Chinese translations he made.

Wang Xuance was an official and diplomat of the Tang Dynasty; he travelled to India three times. Some scholars even believe that he travelled to India four times (Xue 2010). As per Zhang's writings about Wang Xuance, he travelled to India three times, including two times during the Taizong period and one during the Gaozong period (Zhang 2015). Wang Xuance's envoys were very notable in the promotion of India China relations. His records about India are quite comprehensive, it includes religion, geography, politics and law, art, folk customs and many other aspects. Wang Xuance came to India for the first time as a deputy envoy with Li Yibiao in 643 AD-644 AD. It was just a return visit sent by Taizong to India after Harshavardhan's second envoys to Tang China (Xue 2010). The second time he was sent by Taizong as ahead of his third mission to India, it was a return visit of Harsha's third mission in the first half of 647 AD. The Tang mission arrived in India at the time of Harsha's death. Harsha's minister Aluonashun (阿罗那顺) (Arjuna?)[10] usurped his throne,

[10] Different scholars have different narratives about Aluonashun. For example, Zhang Yuan in his article "Harṣa and China: The Six Diplomatic Missions in the Early 7th Century" refers him as ArunaĞa and Arunaśa. Tansen sen in his book "Buddhism, Diplomacy, and Trade: The Realignment

and there was turmoil in the entire country under his rule (Zhang 2015; Sen 2003; Xue 2010; Mazumdar 1927).

During the Xian Qing period[11] (656 AD–660 AD), Wang Xuance visited India the third time. He visited various Buddhist places in India. The purpose of his third and Tang dynasty's fourth mission to India was to carry a monastic robe on behalf of Emperor Gaozong to present at the Mahabodhi Monastery. The head of the Mahabodhi Temple held a Great Dharma meeting for the Chinese Embassy and presented various gifts to Wang Xuance, including pearls, ivory, Buddha's relics, statues and various images of Buddha (Sen 2003). Wang Xuance made noteworthy observations on India, Nepal and other neighbouring countries of China. After returning to China, he wrote a book titled *"中天竺国行记" (Journey to Middle India)* (Xue 2010).

According to the *Old History of the Tang Dynasty*, the *New History of Tang Dynasty*, Xuanzang's travelogue *Great Tang Records on the Western Regions*, and many other rare Chinese inscriptions, there were altogether six diplomatic missions were exchanged between India and China during the reign of Harshavardhan and Taizong (641 AD–648 AD). These six missions have different objectives and significance. In the following paragraphs, I will try to study these exchanges.

During Harshavardhan' reign, India established diplomatic relationships with many foreign countries. In this context, Devahuti states trade and cultural contacts with China (Tang court), Persia, Arabs, Central Asia, South-East Asia and Ceylon (present-day Sri Lanka) (Devahuti 1970). In New History of Tang Dynasty, it is mentioned that Harshavardhan sent envoys to China to present credentials after his first meeting with Xuanzang around the end of 640 AD or the beginning of 641 AD. Harshavardhan sent a letter to the Chinese emperor Taizong, which might be an introductory letter indicating his interest in opening diplomatic relations with Tang China. Tang emperor responded by sending a messenger Liang Huaijing (梁怀璥) in 643 AD. Liang Huaijing carried a letter from Taizong and handed it over to Harshavardhan.

According to both the Old History of the Tang Dynasty and the New History of Tang Dynasty, when the first mission came to India from China, Harshavardhan was surprised. He asked the people, "Have envoys from Mahacina (Peoples of Western regions called China' Mahacina') ever come to our country? before?" People answered, "Never." Harshavardhan bowed with great respect and accepted the credentials (*Old History of the Tang* Dynasty vol. 198: 5307), (*New History of Tang Dynasty* vol. 221A:6237–6238).

Harshavardhan was very happy to see Taizong's diplomatic interest in India. Harshavardhan greeted them with great enthusiasm. He accepted the credentials send by Taizong to him with great respect Taizong's envoys were very much impressed by his gestures. When they narrated this to Taizong upon their return, he was equally impressed. He consequently promoted official communication between India and China. Harshavardhan again sent an envoy to escort the Chinese envoy. With this

of Sino-Indian Relations, 600–1400" also translated Aluonashun as Arunasa. R.C Mazumdar in his book "Outline of Indian History and Civilisation" refers him as Arjuna and Arunasva.

[11] Xianqing was the year title of Emperor Gaozong of tang dynasty.

envoy of Harshavardhan, formal diplomatic ties were established between Kannauj and the Tang court (Sen 2001).

The second mission between Harshavardhan and Taizong was quite significant (642 AD–643 AD) in the development of cultural exchanges between the two kingdoms. Harshavardhan sent his representatives (second mission) to China with Liang Huaijing in 642 AD (Zhang 2015). His representative (in 642 AD) carried fire pearls, turmeric, a Bodhi tree (sample), various sutras and treasures as a gift to the Tang emperor. This is regarded as one of the very important missions of Harshavardhan. In *Harṣa and China: The Six Diplomatic Missions in the Early 7th Century*, Zhang Yuan states that Taizong was very happy to see Harsha's representatives. This mission prompted Taizong to promote the India-China interaction to a new level. After this, Taizong decided to send envoys to visit India formally. In 643 AD, Taizong again sent his representatives to India led by Li Yibiao and Wang Xuance.

The second Tang mission was sent to India to escort Harṣhavardhan's envoys. These envoys was directed to visit sacred Buddhist sites in India and to learn sugar-making skills. Sugarcane has been produced in India and people here have been using sugarcane since ancient days. This was first introduced to China through Buddhist scriptures. Information on India's sugarcane juice production spread in China during the Jin Dynasty and the Southern and Northern Dynasties, mainly through Buddhist scriptures translated since the Jin Dynasty, such as The Law of the Maha Sangha, The Law of Five Points, and The Law of Four Points, (Xue 2010).

As noted above, the Buddhist scriptures had carried the technique of making sugar to China; in this regard, Buddhist monks played a significant role. These monks were involved in the propagation of Buddhism and the fetching of sugar making information to Tang China. So, their role is not limited to the diplomatic contacts between India and China. These monks played an important role in spreading the information on sugar making technology to China from India (Sen 2001, Xue 2010). During this period, apart from the sugar making technique, the knowledge of the astronomical calendars was also introduced to China from India through the translation of several Buddhist doctrines. It had a significant impact on the development of the Chinese astronomical calendar (Xue 2010). At that time, Buddhist monks from China and India carried many Sanskrit texts on astronomical calendars to China from India, which can be seen in their translations of those Sanskrit texts. For example, Xuanzang translated "Ju She Lun"; Yijing translated "Su Yao Jing" and others. Among these translations, "Su Yao Jing" is quite important. In "Su Yao Jing" astronomical knowledge is explained in detail, for example, information about twenty-seven Nakshatras (宿Sù), seven days of the week (七曜 Qīyào) and twelve zodiacs (十二宫 Shí'èrgōng) etc. These materials were very important for studying the astronomical calendar in ancient China (Xue 2010).

Li Yibiao, the Tang ambassador who headed the second Taizong's mission to Kannauj in 643 AD, mentioned another Indian king of Kamarupa[12] he had met in India in a report to Taizong when he returned to China. The King of Kamarupa

[12] Kamarupa was one of the ancient South Asian states in the Indian subcontinent. Its capital was Guwahati in present day Assam.

requested Li Yibiao for the Sanskrit Version of Laozi's (Lao Tzu) Dao De Jing or Tao Te Ching (道德经).[13] Emperor Taizong asked the Daoist priest and Xuanzang to translate the Dao De Jing into Sanskrit in response to his request. However, it is unclear whether the Sanskrit version of the Dao De Jing had arrived in India (Zhang 2015; Sen 2001).

The second Tang mission to India played a significant role in religious exchanges between India and China. These envoys aimed to visit sacred Buddhist sites in India. This envoy and leader Li Yibiao and Wang Xuance visited the Buddha's footprint stone in Asoka's Vihara in Magadha. There they found a large rock, from which they carved a portion to carry back to China. These envoys also arrived at the city of Rajagṛha, where they visited the Gardhrakuta Mountain (耆闍崛山), where Buddha attained his Nirvaṇa more than a thousand years ago. The Grdhrakuta Mountain in Rajagṛha is well-known because Lord Buddha once trod on this mountain and preached here. These places are marked by Stupa inscriptions that represent Buddha's life period of birth, enlightenment, preaching and death.

During the visit to Rajgrarha, these envoys engraved some inscriptions on the Grdhrakuta Mountain (Zhang 2015; Sen 2003). They engraved some formulaic words that mainly talk about the achievements of the Tang Empire, their splendid culture, foreign and domestic policy, the geography of the country, their people, and most significantly, the importance of Daoism and Confucianism in China. This was the very first time that any Chinese inscriptions were engraved on the Grdhrakuta Mountain in India; however, these original inscriptions do not exist anymore on the Grdhrakuta Mountain.

Taizong's second mission to India has also played a pivotal role in establishing the monument in the Mahabodhi Monastery of Magadha. They set up this monument under the Bodhi tree where Lord Buddha got enlightenment thousands of years ago, and they had also engraved some inscriptions here. This was the first time that the Chinese envoys set up a monument in the Mahabodhi Monastery of Magadha.

After Taizong's second mission to India, Harshavardhan sent his third mission to China in the first half of 647 AD. This third mission was to promote inter-cultural communications between India and China. According to the Old History of the Tang Dynasty and New History of Tang Dynasty records, the envoys of Harshavardhan's third mission carried many precious things, such as fire pearls, tulips, and the samplings of the Bodhi tree as a tribute to the Tang emperor. It is interesting to note that Taizong was very much curious about the Longevity drug, which he learnt that it's a life-prolonging drug and that it's produced in India. It was a time when he was not keeping well, and he wanted a quick treatment for his failing health. Thus, he sent a mission to India in 647 under Wang Xuance's leadership to find and bring this drug (Sen 2001).

Wang Xuance arrived in India for this mission with many precious gifts for the Indian King. Aluonashun attacked the Chinese mission and robbed the precious gifts they carried. Wang Xuance, his vice Ambassador Jiang Shiren with his few

[13] Dao De Jing is a philosophical work written by Laozi (Lao Tzu) in the Spring and Autumn Period. It is an important source of Taoist philosophy.

companions, somehow managed to escape Tibet. They took military help from the King of Tibet and Nepal, re-entered in India, and attacked the capital city. Wang Xuance then defeated the Indian King Aluonashun (Bagchi 2011). The story of borrowing troops from Tibet and Nepal to defeat Aluonashun is widespread in China. It was considered the most splendid achievement in Wang Xuance's life.

Wang Xuance returned to Chang'an in 648 AD. He brought the longevity drugs and an expert physician (who could manufacture the longevity drug) (Brahman doctors). This was part of Taizong's mission to bring this drug from India. Unfortunately, this was of no help. This longevity drug and the expert Brahman doctors could not save Taizong. Taizong died in 649 AD, at the mere age of 52.

20.3 Conclusion

The reign of Harshavardhan and Taizong can be marked as an essential milestone of India–China relations during the seventh century AD. There were altogether six missions exchanged between Harsha and Taizong. Harsha sent three missions to China, and Taizong also sent three to India. These official or government visits of both the countries started with the non-government visit of Master Xuanzang. He somehow managed to convince Harshavardhan to establish diplomatic relations with Tang China. Each mission between the two countries has its aims and objectives. The first mission was a kind of self-introductory mission to each other. The main aim of the second Tang's mission to India was to visit sacred Buddhist sites in India and fetch the sugar-making skills. The third mission focused on the search for longevity drugs and promoting intercultural communications between India and China. One can conclude that the period of 7 years, from 641 to 648 AD, was a golden period in India-China relations, especially in the developments of scholarly and cultural exchanges between these two ancient civilizations. Whereas Knowledge and exchanges of astronomical calendar knowledge and Sugar making techniques introduced to China from India through Buddhist scriptures, papermaking techniques and sericulture reached from China to India became popular during this period. In this view, the paper concludes that the periods discussed in this paper were crucial and significant in India China relationship and paved way for further interactions and exchanges.

References

Bagchi PC (1944) India and China: a thousand years of cultural relations. Hind Kitabs Limited, Bombay, pp 1–120

Bagchi PC (2011) India and China: interactions through Buddhism and diplomacy: a collection of essays. In: Bangwei W, Sen T (eds). Anthem Press

Devahuti D (1970) Harsha: a political study. Oxford University Press, Ely House, London

Goyal S (2006) Recent historiography of the age of Harsa, annals of the Bhandarkar oriental research institute, 1991–1992, vol 72/73, no 1/4, Amrtamahotsava (1917–1992) Volume (1991–1992), 331–361

Lily HWA (2009) Tang Taizong 唐太宗TángTàizōng, 597–649 Second emperor of the Tang dynasty. Berkshire Publishing Group LLC

Mazumdar RC (1927) Outline of ancient Indian history and civilisation, Calcutta

Panikar KM (1922, Sri Harsha of Kanauj: A monograph on the history of India in the first half of the 7th century AD, Bombay: D.B. Taraporevala Sons & Co

Sen T (2001) In search of longevity and good karma Chinese diplomatic missions to middle India in the seventh century. J World Hist 1–28

Sen T (2003) Buddhism, diplomacy, and trade: the realignment of Sino-Indian Relations, 600–1400, 15–54. Association for Asian Studies & University of Hawaii Press, Honolulu

Sen T, winter (2006) The travel records of Chinese Pilgrims Faxian, Xuanzang, and Yijing, Education About Asia, vol 11, no 3

Sen T (2018) India, China, and the world: a connected history, 29–110. Oxford University Press

Sharma, Ram, Shankar (1977) Ancient India, 154. National Council of Educational Research and Training, New Delhi

Tatz M, summer (1978) T'ang dynasty influences on the early spread of Buddhism in Tibet. Tibet J 3(2):3–32

Zhang Y (2015) Harṣa and China: the six diplomatic missions in the early 7th century. Delhi Univ J Hum Soc Sci 1–24

季羡林 (Ji Xianlin) (1990) 佛教与中印文化交流,江西人民出版社

薛克翘(Xue Keqiao) (2010) 中印文化交流史话, 45–88, 中国国际广播出版社

Chapter 21
Xuan Zang's Pilgrimage to the Western Heaven: India

Saumya Pandey

21.1 Buddhism in China and Xuan Zang's Journey

The earliest arrival of Buddhism in China can be traced back to when the Han dynasty in China was on the verge of its decline. The unrest due to corruption, the clash between empires and peasant uprisings in the country were high. People were unable to find the answers in the already present philosophies of Taoism and Confucianism. It was a time of heavy disturbance and agitation in China, and people searched for some guidance through religion and philosophy. This made the path easy for Buddhism to find a place in China. Buddhism is the only foreign religion in China to be accepted by the people so as their own.

Along with the exotic merchandise that came through the silk route, Buddhism reached China from India. China had become a cruel and brutal place in the times of the fall of the Han dynasty, and the Buddhist doctrines suggested the idea of non-violence, seeking nirvana and peace. This would have appealed well to the people of China. Thus, Buddhism started being accepted as an alternative to Taoism and Confucianism by the people of China. The first Buddhist text known to have been translated is 'sutra in forty-two sections' in the Eastern Han. Monasteries and Buddhist temples started being built, and the religion also found a place in the royal families. Since the religion reached China through trade, it is evident that it was initially accessible only to the riches and elite sections of the society. In China, the first Buddhist temple is the "white horse temple" in Luoyang, Henan (Jain and Chakravarty 2010: 387). It was built in 68 A.D. by Emperor Ming in the Eastern Han dynasty.

Buddhist texts also started being translated either by Indians, who were not proficient in Chinese, or by Chinese who were not good with Sanskrit. This made the translations vague and not true to their original texts. Many similarities can be found

S. Pandey (✉)
Jawaharlal Nehru University, New Delhi, India
e-mail: saumyap299@gmail.com

S. Mishra and R. Sheel (eds.), *India-China Dialogues Beyond Borders*,
https://doi.org/10.1007/978-981-99-4326-5_22

in Taoism and translated Buddhist texts. The translators could not find the exact vocabulary to express what the Buddhist texts said and used familiar terms from Taoism to express the same. This also made the translated texts appear less foreign to the people and contributed to the spread of Buddhism. The religion continued to spread throughout China among all classes. China saw the peak of Buddhism in the late fifth century and early sixth century. During that time, China saw a rapid growth in Buddhist temples and monasteries. Buddhism started being practised frequently, in at least the elite upper class of the society and eventually spread through all sections of the Chinese society.

This was the time of Xuan Zang. He was born in a scholar family in Henan and was converted to a Buddhist monk at a very young age. Xuan Zang was an ardent scholar and started studying Buddhism intensely. He found that the available texts were incomplete to answer his queries, which confused him badly. He tried looking for the answers, but any monk or the texts could not answer his questions because of the restricted content. Although many monasteries and Buddhist temples were already set up in China by that time, this obstacle in his path of deeply learning Buddhism proved to be highly unsettling for him. Though incomplete and confusing, the available texts were enough to spark a fire of curiosity and unrest in Xuan Zang for a complete and deep study of Buddhism (Chandra and Banarjee 2008: 198). He was so attracted to study Buddhism that he started looking for a better understanding of Buddhist philosophy.

Xuan Zang decided to go to India, the birthplace of Buddhism. He realized that only going to the origin of Buddhism could quench his thirst. But unfortunately, international travel was forbidden by the then emperor of China, Tai Zong. This was because King Tai Zong had recently forcefully occupied the throne, and there was large-scale civil unrest in the country. Therefore, anyone was not allowed to travel outside the country. It was not easy to cross the international borders and reach India, and Xuan Zang knew all about the challenges.

21.2 The Journey

Having not got permission from the king, Xuan Zang secretly started his journey in 627 A.D. from Chang'an. He travelled over land through the route, which is now known as the silk route (Chandra and Banarjee 2008: 276). After losing his companions, Xuan Zang travelled at night without any guide (Hui-li and Beal 2012: 11). Facing many difficulties, he reached the westernmost frontiers of China in the Gansu province but fell in great trouble. The Chinese army caught him in an attempt to cross the borders at one of the final outposts. They found that he was travelling without a permit, they wanted to send him back to the Chinese court. Xuan Zang, who was as determined as a stone, refused to go back, saying he could offer his life but will not step back. Miraculous enough, the army chief was a Buddhist and allowed Xuan Zang to cross the border when he learned about Xuan Zang's intentions and determination (Huili 1995: 21). Xuan Zang was cautious enough in the later outposts and somehow avoided being caught, but could not find much food and water and was left weak and pale by the time he reached Turfan. Reaching Turfan proved to be fatal for Xuan Zang. He stayed in Turfan and preached Buddhism for about a month before the king, Qu Wentai, invited him. The king was fascinated by the monk's knowledge of the Buddhist texts, and soon Xuan Zang realized that the king did not want Xuan Zang to leave. It was very difficult to leave the place, and he was finally able to resume his journey only after a hunger strike and a promise to stay in Turfan for three years upon his return.

Xuan Zang reached India travelling through Samarkand, Balkh, Bamyan, Kapisi, Adinapur, Gandhar, and Peshawar. He covered over 16,000 km on foot, crossing the highest mountain ranges in Asia, Tianshan, Hindukush, Pamir, Karakoram and Himalayas (Chandra and Banarjee 2008: 143). In his way, he came across numerous Buddhist monks and texts and monasteries. Grasping all that he could, he reached Taxila, a Buddhist kingdom.[1] Then, to find more than 5,000 monks in about 100 monasteries. He went to Kashmir in 631 A.D. and met some learned monks, stayed with them for months and studied. He wrote some of the earliest writings about king Kanishka's kingdom and later visited Lahore, Jalandhar (Punjab) and Mathura. He spotted the presence of more than 2,000 monks of both branches, Mahayana and Hinayana, in Mathura, despite it being a Hindu-dominated city. Eventually, he reached Kannuaj, King Harsha's capital and encountered 10,000 monks in 100 monasteries of both branches. Xuan Zang was fascinated by the king's knowledge and scholarship. Xuan Zang was highly respected in King Harsha's region. Here, he also got opportunities to get involved in numerous public discussions. He spent some time studying the content available here and carried on his journey crossing Ayodhya, Sravasti, Kausambi and reaching Lumbini. After this, he visited some major Buddhist sites, which are very well known today. He visited Kushinagar, buddha's death place; Sarnath, where Buddha gave his very first sermon and found more than 1,500 monasteries there. He crossed Varanasi, Vaishali, Patliputra and Bodhgaya, finally reaching a major site, Nalanda (Hui-li and Beal 2012: 90).

21.3 Xuan Zang in Nalanda

Nalanda was a huge Buddhist university at that time in the present Indian state of Bihar and hence, one of the major destinations for Xuan Zang. He accompanied thousands of monks who were already present at the university and studied not only Buddhism but Sanskrit, grammar, logic and Yogacara school of Buddhism. He spent about two years in Nalanda. This is where he met, Silabhadra, the abbot of the Nalanda University (Hui-li and Beal 2012: 91). It is said that Silabhadra was once quite ill and he wanted to die. He dreamt of Buddha saying that a monk from the west

[1] Taxila or Takshashila flourished as an important educational hub for Buddhist philosophies. Although Xuan Zang described that the region was in ruins when he reached there, still he found many functional monasteries there.

is soon to visit him to study Buddhism. Silabhadra was instructed to keep teaching and his body would heal, and he was told to take great care that the monk from the west was well facilitated with whatever he needed. This would help in the spread of the holy religion and teachings of Buddha. Silabhadra was overwhelmed as he welcomed Xuan Zang and religiously followed what he was instructed in his dream. Silabhadra was trained by the founders of Mahayana Buddhism, so he was the most abled man to help out Xuan Zang with his overall goals. Thus, Xuan Zang meeting Silabhadra is a major event in the life of Xuan Zang.

After Nalanda, Xuan Zang continued his journey along both the coasts of India, exploring the east and, later on, south India. He must have developed a good appetite for knowledge at Nalanda, which made him travel further. He visited Amravati and Nagarjunkonda, the birthplaces of Nagarjuna and Dharmapala, two major Buddhist philosophers. He eventually reached another major destination of his journey, Kanchipuram. The port city was the capital of the Pallava kingdom and a central hub of Buddhism. His travels through south India are less detailed than the northern destinations. Xuan Zang also wanted to visit the island with the sacred tooth relic of Buddha, Simhala (Sri Lanka). But, when he learned about the king's death, famine and civil war that was going on in Simhala, he had to change his mind. Although Xuan Zang did not visit Simhala, he wrote a detailed account based on what he heard about the place. This account to date helps to find important historical accounts about Sri Lanka, about which no such historical details are to be found.

After spending more than seventeen years on a journey, Xuan Zang decided to return to China via Kashgar, Khotan and Dunhuang. King Harsha well felicitated his return with a military escort, elephants, silver and gold for the travel expenses, and other gifts (Hui-li and Beal 2012: 153). King Harsha tried his best to ensure complete security and comfort in the return journey of the saint. Xuan Zang finally arrived in Chang'an in 645 A.D. When Xuan Zang returned in 644 A.D., the honour and respect he was provided by king Tai Zong were immeasurable. This compelled China to think about India, the birthplace of Buddha, as a holy land, where there is justice and happiness, value for education and respect for the learned. Xuan Zang immortalized India as the Western Heaven.

21.4 The Study

Xuan Zang's travel was not an ordinary pilgrimage meant only to visit holy sites. When talking about Xuan Zang, the discourse cannot be completed without discussing the major branches of Buddhism and other philosophies he explored. He wanted to grasp the depth of these philosophies, which is why we talk about him today.

Before starting his journey, he had already mastered Mahayana, Mahaparinirvanasutra and all other locally available texts (Chandra and Banarjee 2008: 278).

Yogacara[2] was one of the main interests of Xuan Zang that made him come to India (Chandra and Banarjee 2008: 275). This eventually came to be true when he reached the Nalanda University. There could not have been a better teacher than Silabhadra,[3] the chief of Nalanda University himself instructing Xuan Zang. He noted that there were around 8,500 students with more than 1,500 teachers then in the university, and it was rich with a wide range of disciplines with the best education of the time. Xuan Zang also received an Indian name in the Nalanda University, Mokshadeva.[4]

Xuan Zang started his studies under Silabhadra in 636 A.D. and studied in detail the Yogacara lineage of the Mahayana doctrine. Apart from these Buddhist doctrines, he studied many more disciplines including Nyaya, Shabdavidya, Hetu-vidya, Sanskrit grammar, exegesis of Mahayana texts like Mahayana-sutralamkara and Madhyamika doctrines etc. The Madhyamika doctrine goes mid-way between Realism of school of Sravastivada, and Idealism of Yogacara School. Xuan Zang worked to combine both these doctrines in a more comprehensive Mahayanism and wrote his synthesis in treatise "Hui ZongLun[5]" with the permission of his mentors.

Xuan Zang believed that it was important to learn about Buddhism and other disciplines for a comparative and comprehensive approach. Thus, he learned in detail about Hinduism and Jainism as well. He became a critic of two philosophical systems of Hinduism that opposed Buddhism, "Samkhya and Vaiseshika". "He also critiqued atheistic monism" of Jains.

Towards the last days of Xuan Zang in India, he gained huge fame in the eyes of the king of Assam and great king Harsha, who was regarded as a Buddhist saint on the throne. They were both too amazed by the ardent pilgrim. King Harsha was quite excited to arrange a great debate in Kannauj in 643 A.D. to showcase his (Xuan Zang's) knowledge. This debate was attended by kings of 18 vassal kingdoms, 3,000 Buddhist monks and 2,000 Hindus and Jains. Xuan Zang successfully debated Mahayana Buddhism's superiority over Hinduism and Jainism. This made Xuan Zang earn a great name and fame for himself.

---

[2] Yogarara/Yogachara of the mind-only/doctrine of consciousness school of Buddhism is one of the two major schools of Indian Mahayana Buddhism. According to Yogacara, also called Vijananavda, only vijnana or consciousness is real and everything else that appears to be external are only states of consciousness.

[3] Silabhadra was a Buddhist monk and the abbot of the Nalanda University. He was an expert of the Yogacara school of Buddhism, and he personally mentored Xuan Zang.

[4] Xuan Zang was given an Indian name "Mokshadeva" by his teacher, Silabhadra at the Nalanda University.

[5] HuizongLun (會宗論/*Hui-tsüng-lun* or *On the Harmony of the schools*) is a 3000-stanza treatise written by Xuan Zang in Nalanda. Xuan Zang combined Madhyamika and Yogacara schools of Buddhism in a more comprehensive Mahayana Buddhism and also expressed his personal views and derivations in this book.

21.5 Xuan Zang's Return and Its Impact in China

Many Rulers, monks, students and teachers, and common people bid goodbye to Xuan Zang as he started his return journey (Hui-li and Beal 2012: 153). Thankfully his return journey was more accessible and safer than the former.

In 644 A.D. Xuan Zang arrived in Khotan. Emperor Tai Zong was the king of the then Tang dynasty in China. Xuan Zang sent a report to the emperor talking about his 16-year pilgrimage and his visit to India's Buddhist sites and universities and other countries as well (Sen 2001: 10). He mentioned that he was returning with many Buddhist texts and relics. The emperor was delighted enough to issue an imperial decree and arrange a grand welcome for the master (Chandra and Banarjee 2008: 199). Xuan Zang arrived in Chang'an of China in 645 A.D. He came back with a total of 657 texts, over 150 relics and around 520 scrolls of Buddhist sutras (Chandra and Banarjee 2008: 199). A major part of this was Mahayanism texts with 224 Mahayanism Sutras and 192 Mahayanism Sastras. He started a translation workshop for translating the texts and sutras he had brought back in the Hung-fu monastery (Hui-li and Beal 2012: 183). The emperor appointed many scholars from China and India skilled in Chinese, and the Sanskrit language assisted Xuan Zang. He later moved to Ci'en (大慈恩寺), and then to Ximing monastery. He shifted to Yu'hua palace in 657 A.D. and turned it into a monastery (Chandra and Banarjee 2008: 199). Along with translations, Xuan Zang trained many disciples, teaching them Buddhist doctrines and popularising theory based on his Buddhist studies.

Xuan Zang focused on translating Yogacara-Bhumi texts in the initial six years. He spent later ten years translating Abhidharma-Kosa Sastras. In the last four years, he focused on translating Mahaprajna-Paramita Sutras. Many texts translated by Xuan Zang have their original texts in Sanskrit missing. In 659 A.D., Xuan Zang's disciple Kuiji insisted he translates Vasabandhu's "Triṃśikā-vijñaptimātratā", thirty verses on conscious-only. Xuan Zang blended ten commentaries on this by Vasabandhu into a single text, namely **WeishiLun.**[6] The main idea of this text is that the whole world is a mere representation of the mind only. This, later on, became the root text for Chinese and Japanese Yogacara doctrine.

One of the most important pieces by Xuan Zang is the Da Tang Xi You Ji 大唐西游记 (Great Tang Dynasty's Records of the Western Regions), the travel account of Xuan Zang which he dictated to be written. This contains a detailed account of his pilgrimage to India and other countries. This included major information about geography, society, religion and culture, rulers etc. This travelogue is the only evidence for many historical accounts in the present day. Xuan Zang's Da Tang Xi You Ji later led to the writing of Wu Chengen's Journey to the West, which is the Chinese equivalent to Ramayana in India. Journey to the west is almost Da Tang Xi You Ji, rewritten as fiction. A traveller is shown travelling to the west with an extraordinary companion, a monkey. This monkey depicts humankind helping the traveller to an unknown land. Again, this famous book has the contributions of Xuan Zang in its roots.

[6] Also called *ChéngWéishìLùn* (成唯識論).

Xuan Zang also translated some Chinese texts and sent them back to India. This included the translation of Laozi's "Dao De Jing" into Sanskrit in 647 A.D. (Sen 2001: 14). This could be a part of the diplomatic relations that were established because of Xuan Zang between the Chinese court and King Harsha.

Xuan Zang spent 20 years translating the texts until his demise. He had completed the translation of 74 texts written in 1,335 volumes and was given the Master of Tripitaka Dharma title at the age of 65. In 664 A.D. Xuan Zang died in Chang'an 長安市. The Tang court called an off for all audiences for three days after the death of Xuan Zang. He was buried in the capital of Tang court. Later in 669 A.D., his remains were shifted to the north of the Fan-Chuen valley, and a tower was constructed to give befitting honour to the monk (Hui-li and Beal 2012: 185). Later, the tower was destroyed, and his remains were shifted many times due to wars. Finally, after many negotiations, it was decided that Xuan Zang's remains would be divided into five parts, one would be in Japan and the rest in different museums and monasteries of China.

21.6 Impact on Chinese Buddhism

Though Xuan Zang was interested in studying the Yogacara school of Buddhism, he also studied the Abhidharma and Madhyamika literature. Thus, he knew well about these too and could do a comparative study or merge the literature. In total, his interest in these literatures was aimed only towards the best understanding of Buddhism.

After returning to China, Xuan Zang and his disciple Kuiji established 'Faxiang', the Chinese school of Buddhism. This is based on the Indian school of Yogacara by Asanga and Vasubandhu. The core text of the Chinese school of Yogacara was 'WeishiLun' by Xuan Zang. Two significant books for this school include 'Fa Yuan Yi Lin Zhang' and 'Cheng WeishiLun Shu Ji' by Kuiji (Chandra and Banarjee 2008: 281). Kuiji has systemized his master's ideas in these two books. This school strongly argues that the external world does not exist and is the product of our consciousness only. This school is also called idealistic or 'Weishi' for its belief that only ideation exists.

This idealistic school was called "Faxiang" in China and "Hosso" in Japan (Chandra and Banarjee 2008: 281). Faxiang translates to the compilation of many dharmas in Sanskrit. Justifying its name, the Faxiang School has five categories of dharmas. The school flourished in the presence of Xuan Zang and Kuiji. Kuiji is remembered as the first patriarch of this school. But since the detailed philosophy of the mind, consciousness and senses were very new in China. The school declined soon after Xuan Zang and Kuiji. Its doctrines are continued to be read in other successful schools.

21.7 Conclusion

Xuan Zang is not just a traveller or pilgrim who came to India. He was neither a mere monk who studied the intricacies of Buddhist classics in India. His contributions are not limited to 74 translated texts from India, nor the foundations of the Faxiang school in China, which led to Hosso school in Japan, which later found its way to Korea. To note, Hosso's school of Buddhism continues until today. He was the saint whose journey led to the first diplomatic relations between the Tang court and King Harsha. After returning to China, Xuan Zang sent back Chinese texts translated into Sanskrit. This could be thought of as the first diplomatic transaction between India and China (Sen 2001: 11). The classics carried by Xuan Zang to China have changed their forms significantly, but the influence caused cannot be ignored.

The Himalayas serve as natural borders between India and China. In such a case, the transfer of culture and religion from India to China, which already had many successful ideologies, is excellent. Interculturalism and cross border interaction were given historical perspectives.

Xuan Zang's accounts of the journey, Da Tang Xi You Ji, are critical documents from historical records. Had Xuan Zang not travelled to India and not recorded the Da Tang Xi You Ji, there would have been an unrepairable void in India's history and other countries. There are numerous monuments with Xuan Zang inscribed on them, which give us the hint of the grandeur of his travel. We would have known lesser about how many subjects were taught or how many students and teachers were present, or how far reached the fame of India's Nalanda University. The detailed accounts of the kingdoms of Kanauji and Kanchipuram would have been missing. It provides the archaeologists and historians with a great deal of vital information that lacks alternate evidence. We would be devoid of many important aspects of India's history if this Chinese traveller were a little less determined (Chandra and Banarjee 2008: 230).

Xuan Zang came here just because he wanted to enlighten himself and take back something for the people in China to learn. He, of course, was very successful in accomplishing that, but little did he think about making a mark in history and contributing to the generations in the centuries to come. He was rightly called the "Jewel of the empire" by emperor Tai Zong.

References

Chandra L, Banarjee R (2008) Xuan Zang and the Silk Route. Indira Gandhi National Centre for Arts, Munshiram Manoharlal Publishers Pvt. Ltd., New Delhi

Hui-li, Beal S (2012) The life of Hiuen-Tsiang. Rupa Publications India, New Delhi

Jain A, Chakravarty R (2015) Indian-style Buddhist temple in Luoyang, China, Material Religion. J Object Art Belief 6(issue 3):387–390

Li HJ (1995) A biography of the Tripiṭaka master of the great Ci'en Monastery of the great Tang dynasty. Numata Centre for Buddhist Translation and Research
Sen T (2001) In search of longevity and good karma: Chinese diplomatic missions to middle India in the seventh century. J World Hist Univ Hawaii Press 12(1):1–28

The manufacturer's authorised representative in the EU is Springer Nature Customer Service Centre GmbH, Europaplatz 3, 69115 Heidelberg, Germany. If you have any concerns regarding our products, please contact ProductSafety@springernature.com

Printed and bound by CPI Group (UK) Ltd, Croydon, CR0 4YY
01/10/2026
02225892-0006